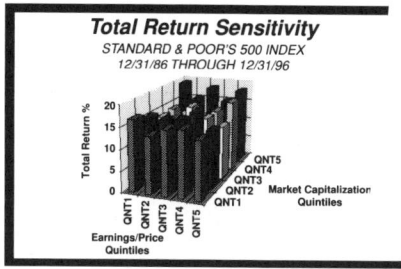

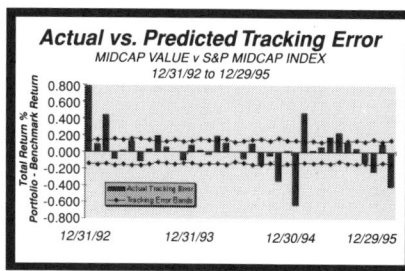

Atlas' powerful risk models allow the manager to identify structural bets and explicitly control the resulting return variance of the portfolio relative to the benchmark over time.

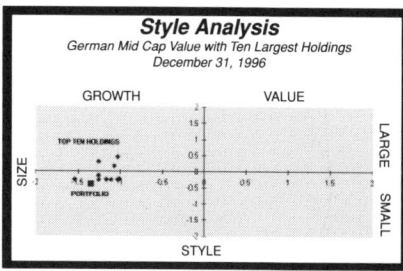

Wilshire's new global style analysis allows managers to monitor the impact of individual stocks on the total portfolio style orientation.

W I L S H I R E

Now in Windows™ 95 and NT

For more information please contact:

Santa Monica
T 310.451.3051
F 310.458.0520

www@wilshire.com
e-mail: quantum@ wilshire.com

or leave a voice message at:
310.319.2501

London
T 44.171.814.7355
F 44.171.814.6611

©1997 Wilshire Associates Incorporated. All rights reserved.

The Handbook of Equity Style Management
Second Edition

Edited by

T. Daniel Coggin, Ph.D.
Director of Research
Gerber/Taylor Associates

Frank J. Fabozzi, Ph.D., CFA
Adjunct Professor of Finance
School of Management
Yale University
and
Editor
Journal of Portfolio Management

Robert D. Arnott
President and Chief Executive Officer
First Quadrant, L.P.

Published by Frank J. Fabozzi Associates

 © 1997 By Frank J. Fabozzi Associates
New Hope, Pennsylvania

ALL RIGHTS RESERVED. No part of this publication may be reproduced, stored in a retrieval system, or transmitted, in any form or by any means, electronic, mechanical, photocopying, recording, or otherwise without the prior written permission of the publisher and the copyright holder.

This publication is designed to provide accurate and authoritative information in regard to the subject matter covered. It is sold with the understanding that the publisher is not engaged in rendering legal, accounting, or other professional services.

ISBN: 1-883249-18-X

Printed in the United States of America

T. Daniel Coggin

*To my mother and
the memory of my father and brother*

Frank J. Fabozzi

*To Francesco,
Brianne, and Charlie*

Robert D. Arnott

*To my children,
Robin Lindsay and Sydney Allison*

About the Editors

T. Daniel Coggin is Director of Research for Gerber/Taylor Associates, an investment consulting firm based in Memphis, Tennessee. Dr. Coggin has 18 years of experience in investment management and consulting. Before joining Gerber/Taylor Associates, he was Director of Research for the Virginia Retirement System and a Visiting Professor of Applied Finance at the University of North Carolina at Charlotte. Dr. Coggin has authored and coauthored a number or articles and book chapters on quantitative investment management, and serves on the editorial boards of several journals including the *Journal of Portfolio Management* and the *Review of Quantitative Finance and Accounting*. He has a Ph.D. in political economy from Michigan State University.

Frank J. Fabozzi is an Adjunct Professor of Finance at Yale University's School of Management and the editor of the *Journal of Portfolio Management*. From 1986 to 1992, he was a full-time professor of finance at MIT's Sloan School of Management. He is on the board of directors of the BlackRock complex of closed-end funds and the board of directors of the family of open-end funds sponsored by The Guradian Life. Dr. Fabozzi is a Chartered Financial Analyst and Certified Public Accountant who has authored and edited numerous books on investment management. He has a Ph.D. in economics from The City University of New York.

Robert D. Arnott is President and Chief Executive Officer of First Quadrant. He has authored more than 40 articles and has won the AIMR Graham & Dodd Scroll four times. The award is given for the best published articles on investment theory. Mr. Arnott is a member of the Editorial Board of the *Journal of Portfolio Management* and *Investing*, the Chairman's Advisory Council of the Chicago Board Options Exchange, and the Product Advisory Board of the Chicago Mercantile Exchange and the Toronto Stock Exchange. He is the coeditor of *Active Asset Allocation*. Prior to joining First Quadrant, he held positions at Salomon Brothers and TSA Capital Management. He graduated from the University of California in 1977 with highest honors in economics, applied mathematics, and computer science.

Table of Contents

About the Editors iv
Preface vii
Overview of the Book viii
Contributing Authors ix

1. **Equity Style: What It Is and Why It Matters** 1
   Jon A. Christopherson and C. Nola Williams

2. **Understanding the Differences and Similarities of Equity Style Indexes** 21
   Melissa R. Brown and Claudia E. Mott

3. **Return-Based Style Analysis** 55
   Steve Hardy

4. **Fundamental Factors in Equity Style Classification** 73
   David R. Borger

5. **Style Return Differentials: Illusions, Risk Premiums, or Investment Opportunities** 93
   Richard Roll

6. **Style Betas: An Approach to Measuring Style at the Security Level** 121
   Keith Quinton

7. **Value-Based Equity Strategies** 133
   Gary G. Schlarbaum

8. **Investment Styles, Stock Market Cycles, Investor Expectations, and Portfolio Performance** 151
   W. Scott Bauman and Robert E. Miller

9. **Analyzing the Performance of Equity Managers: A Note on Value versus Growth** 167
   T. Daniel Coggin and Charles Trzcinka

10. **The Effects of Imprecision and Bias on the Abilities of Growth and Value Managers to Out-Perform their Respective Benchmarks** 171
    Robert A. Haugen

11. **The Many Sides of Equity Style: Quantitative Management of Core, Value, and Growth Portfolios** 179
    David J. Leinweber, Robert D. Arnott, and Christopher G. Luck

12. **Structuring Returns from Global Market Neutral Strategies** 209
    David J. Leinweber, Christopher G. Luck, and Peter Swank

13. **Comparing International Style Indexes: Independence International Associates versus Parametric Portfolio Associates** 221
    David A. Umstead

14. **The Role of Completion Funds in Equity Style Management** 229
    Christopher J. Campisano and Maarten Nederlof

15. **Equity Style Benchmarks for Fund Analysis** 239
    Mary Ida Compton

16. **Style Management: The Greatest Opportunity in Investments** 251
    Garry M. Allen

17. **The Persistence of Equity Style Performance: Evidence from Mutual Fund Data** 257
    Ronald N. Kahn and Andrew Rudd

18. **Global Performance Evaluation and Equity Style: Introducing Portfolio Opportunity Distributions** 269
    Ron Surz

19. **Value and Growth Index Derivatives** 279
    Joanne M. Hill and Maria E. Tsu

20. **Is Equity Style Management Worth the Effort?: Some Critical Issues for Plan Sponsors** 301
    Charles Trzcinka

Index 313

Preface

Equity style analysis has now solidified its hold on a position of intense interest and activity in the world of domestic and international investment management. As this interest and activity have grown, there have been a number of changes and additions to the concepts and tools used to define and analyze equity style since the first edition of *The Handbook of Equity Style Management* was published two years ago. The response to the first edition was very positive. In addition, we are proud to note that the first edition has been translated into Japanese by the Nomura Research Institute. We were therefore convinced that we should consider a second edition, in which we allow our current contributors and new contributors to incorporate the new events in this rapidly evolving field.

In this edition, we have tried to preserve the quality and focus of the first edition, while broadening our coverage of the topic. The original authors were given an opportunity to expand and update their chapters, and some important new chapters have been added. Specifically, we have gone from 13 chapters in the first edition to 20 chapters here. We are again fortunate to have convinced the best people working in this area to contribute to our book. Rob Arnott, President of First Quadrant, has joined us as a coeditor. Rob brings another perspective which we feel has enhanced the scope and quality of the second edition. The second edition will be translated into Korean by the Daishin Economic Research Institute.

One clarifying comment is in order. While the concept of "equity style" has been around for decades, it is still a relatively new area of focused inquiry. The Frank Russell Company and Wilshire Associates first introduced equity style indexes in 1986, followed by S&P/BARRA in 1992. As a result, some basic terminology has yet to be finalized. Hence the reader will see in this book minor variations in basic terms used by different authors. For example, one author will use the term "completion fund," while another will substitute "completeness fund." Don't let this trouble you. It is merely a typical symptom of a rapidly evolving field.

Overview of the Book

Rather than repetitively noting that a chapter is carried over from the first edition, we will use an asterisk (*) to identify such chapters. Chapter 1* by Christopherson and Williams sets the stage by defining equity style management and explaining why it matters to investors. Chapter 2* by Brown and Mott provides an exhaustive overview of the major equity style indexes currently in use. The two major approaches to equity style analysis are return-based and portfolio-based. Chapter 3* by Hardy describes the use of return-based style analysis, while Chapter 4 by Borger discusses the portfolio-based approach.

Chapter 5* by Roll shows that the three major equity style descriptors (size, earnings/price and book/market) have different risk profiles, and that the CAPM and APT risk/return models cannot fully explain the differential performance among equity styles. Chapter 6* by Quinton presents the notion of growth-value betas as a means of clarifying differential equity performance on the growth-value dimension. Chapter 7 by Schlarbaum shows how a value-based investment strategy can lead to higher returns. Chapter 8 by Bauman and Miller presents research indicating that stock market cycles and analysts forecasts can influence the differential return between value and growth styles. Chapter 9 by Coggin and Trzcinka present research showing that it is harder for value managers than for growth managers to beat their respective benchmark portfolios. Chapter 10 by Haugen offers an explanation for this result. Chapter 11 by Leinweber, Arnott, and Luck discusses the methodologies and techniques used in the style management of institutional equity portfolios.

Chapter 12 by Leinweber, Luck, and Swank discusses the relationship between equity style and global market neutral investment strategies. Chapter 13 by Umstead provides a comparison of two popular international equity style index providers, International Investment Associates and Parametric Portfolio Associates. Chapter 14* by Campisano and Nederlof describes and discusses the role of completion funds in the equity style management of pension funds. Chapter 15* by Compton gives an overview of the use of equity style management from the plan sponsor perspective. Chapter 16* by Allen argues that equity style management is one of the most important recent developments for plan sponsors, consultants, and investment advisors.

Chapter 17 by Kahn and Rudd present new evidence that past returns are not a good predictor of future returns for equity style managers. Chapter 18 by Surz offers a new tool for global equity style performance measurement, the portfolio opportunity distribution universes. Chapter 19 by Hill and Tsu describe and discuss value and growth index derivatives. Chapter 20* by Trzcinka discusses equity style management from the perspective of academic finance.

Contributing Authors

Garry M. Allen, CFA	Virtus Capital Management, Inc.
Robert D. Arnott	First Quadrant, L.P.
W. Scott Bauman, DBA, CFA	Northern Illinois University
David R. Borger, CFA	Wilshire Asset Management
Melissa R. Brown	Prudential Securities Inc.
Christopher J. Campisano, CFA	Xerox Corporation
Jon A. Christopherson, Ph.D.	Frank Russell Company
T. Daniel Coggin, Ph.D.	Gerber/Taylor Associates
Mary Ida Compton	Alan D. Biller & Associates
Steve Hardy	Zephyr Associates, Inc.
Robert A. Haugen, Ph.D.	University of California — Irvine
Joanne M. Hill, Ph.D.	Goldman, Sachs & Co.
Ronald N. Kahn, Ph.D.	BARRA, Inc.
David J. Leinweber, Ph.D.	First Quadrant, L.P.
Christopher G. Luck	First Quadrant, L.P.
Robert E. Miller, Ph.D.	Northern Illinois University
Claudia E. Mott	Prudential Securities Inc.
Maarten Nederlof	Capital Market Risk Advisors, Inc.
Keith Quinton, CFA	Putnam Investments
Richard Roll, Ph.D.	University of California, Los Angeles
	Roll and Ross Asset Management Corporation
Andrew Rudd, Ph.D.	BARRA, Inc.
Gary G. Schlarbaum	Miller, Anderson & Sherrerd, LLP
Ron Surz	Roxbury Capital Management
Peter Swank, Ph.D.	First Quadrant, L.P.
Charles Trzcinka, Ph.D.	State University of New York at Buffalo
Maria E. Tsu	Goldman, Sachs & Co.
David A. Umstead, Ph.D., CFA	Independence International Associates, Inc. A Subsidiary of Independence Investment Associates, Inc.
C. Nola Williams	Frank Russell Company

Chapter 1

Equity Style: What It Is and Why It Matters

Jon A. Christopherson, Ph.D.
Senior Research Analyst
Frank Russell Company

C. Nola Williams, CFA
Senior Investment Strategist
Frank Russell Company

INTRODUCTION

Today the concept of equity styles permeates the way investors think about the U.S. equity market and investment managers. What was once an arcane idea promoted by consultants and embraced only by their large corporate clients has spread so that the popular press promotes it to the small investor. The public at large now has access to the same measurement tools as the large investor and, like the large client, is able to invest in style index mutual funds as an alternative to active management. Further, the concept of equity investment style has resulted in a veritable explosion of indexes designed to measure different segments of the equity market. No longer can a manager count on being successful by beating the broad market averages; the manager is highly likely to be held accountable for exceeding the appropriate style proxy.

This introductory chapter covers a broad range of topics concerning equity styles, from basic style definitions to potential applications of style analysis. Our intent is to define the term "style," provide some historical perspective, discuss style-related tools, and apply the concept to asset deployment. Our contention is that equity styles exist and that style matters.

DEFINING EQUITY STYLE

The notion of differing equity styles began in the 1970s as members of the investment industry began more actively gathering and analyzing data on market averages and investment managers (the advent of computerization doubtless did much to facilitate this effort). Although style descriptions weren't as well defined as they are today, analysts noted clusters of portfolios with similar characteristics and performance patterns. Groups of managers shared certain ideas about the best way to approach investing. The data were a manifestation of philosophical views about key determinants of stock price movements.

To see this point, consider two investors who are evaluating the same statistic from two opposing perspectives. They assess a stock's prospects using a ratio commonly applied in the industry, the price/earnings ratio. The "growth" investor is primarily concerned with the *earnings* component of the ratio. If the investor believes the company will deliver a particular future growth rate, and if the price/earnings ratio remains constant, then the stock price will have to increase as earnings materialize, and the investor will be rewarded. The key risks for the growth investor are that the future growth does not occur as expected and that the P/E multiple declines for some unanticipated reason.

The "value" investor, on the other hand, is concerned primarily with the *price* component of the ratio and cares much less, if at all, about the future earnings growth of the company. For this stock to be of interest, the value investor must deem the P/E ratio "cheap" by some comparison. The value investor's assumption is that the ratio is too low (perhaps due to an overly pessimistic assessment of the company's future) and that the P/E multiple will revert to normal or market levels when others realize that prospects are not as bad as thought. If so, the stock price will rise. In this analysis, the investor is relying on movement in price, rather than earnings, to be the reward. The investor anticipates that the price/earnings multiple will rise, with little or no increase in the earnings portion of the ratio. The value investor's primary risk is that the stock's cheapness is misread, and that the market's concerns about the company are indeed correct.

These two investors may assess the same stock at different points in its price and earnings pattern and from the opposing perspectives as shown in Exhibit 1. Often the value investor is the earlier buyer of a stock. If investor predictions are right, the price increases. This may or may not be accompanied by earnings increases, although that is not the investor's primary motivation to buy the stock. As the price increases, the value investor becomes uncomfortable with what seem to be expensive multiple levels and sells.

By now the growth investor has noticed the improving fundamentals of the company, which prompt interest in its future growth potential. The growth investor will purchase the same stock the value investor viewed as too expensive, and retain it for as long as the growth pattern emerges as anticipated.

Both investors are following logical courses, and empirical evidence can be found to support the profitability of both approaches. Their views of what is important to investing are diametrically opposed, however; and at the same time they reach opposite conclusions about the same stock. They buy and sell the same stock at different points along the price and earnings curves, both of which offer investment potential so long as the stock follows its typical pattern.

Exhibit 1: Change in Price Versus Earnings

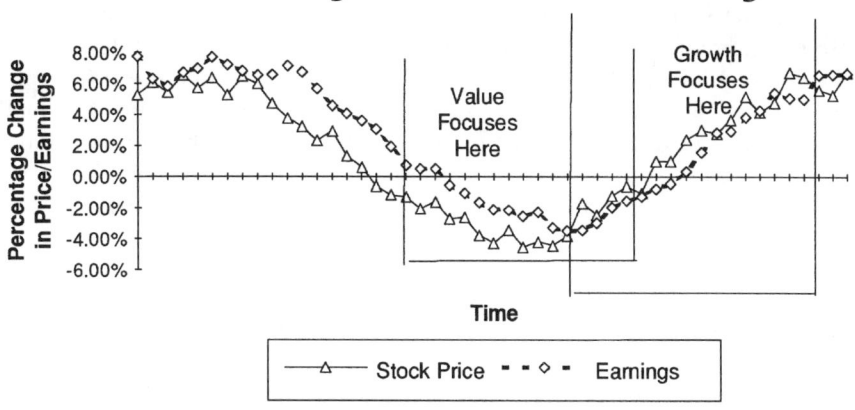

Note, however, in Exhibit 1 that there is a period of overlap when both the value and the growth investor may hold the same stock. An analysis of industry group performance also shows that stock groups often migrate from one group of investors to the other as equities experience a full business cycle.

To constitute a style, these investment philosophies must be held in common by a group of investors. While exact implementation of the shared philosophy may differ, the group agrees upon the factors that determine stock prices. If a philosophy is unique to a single manager, it is more appropriately called an investment "insight" that belongs to that firm alone. Such a firm would not rely on a certain factor, like growth or value, to add alpha and would have a set of portfolio characteristics different from a style group.

TYPES OF EQUITY STYLES

While industry terminology for U.S. equity styles varies somewhat, the style descriptions developed by the consulting firm, Frank Russell Company, typify those used today. Russell identifies four broad style categories:

- Value.
- Growth.
- Market-oriented.
- Small-capitalization.

Exhibit 2 depicts how these styles relate to different segments of the equity market.

Value

While value managers differ in how they define "value," they consider the stock's current price as critical. Some organizations focus on companies with low absolute or relative P/E ratios (price in the numerator), while others stress issues with above-market yields (price in the denominator). Additional valuation measures these investors often consider are price-to-book value and price/sales ratios. A stock whose price has declined because of adverse investor sentiment (i.e., price behavior) may also attract some of these managers. Their portfolios frequently have historical growth and profitability characteristics well below market averages, contrasting sharply with the characteristics of growth managers.

The value style can be viewed as consisting of three substyles:

- Low P/E.
- Contrarian.
- Yield.

Low P/E managers focus on companies selling at low prices relative to current, normalized, or discounted future earnings. These companies typically fall into defensive, cyclical, or out-of-favor industries.

Contrarian managers emphasize companies selling at low valuations relative to their tangible book value. They often favor depressed cyclicals or firms with virtually no current earnings or dividend yield. Contrarian investors purchase stocks in hope that a cyclical rebound or company-specific earnings turnaround will result in substantial price appreciation. The quality of companies owned is frequently below average, largely because corporate earnings are depressed and financial leverage is relatively high.

Yield managers are the most conservative value managers, focusing on companies with above-average yields that are able to maintain or increase their dividend payments.

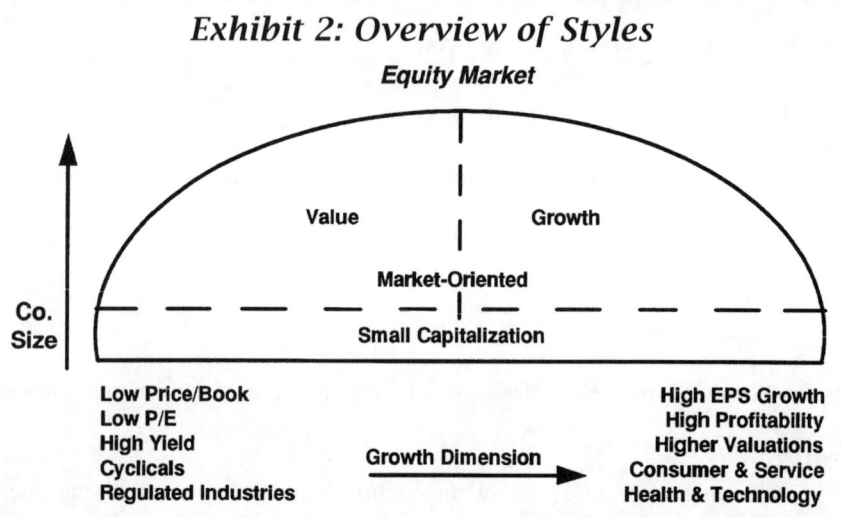

Exhibit 2: Overview of Styles

Growth

Growth managers attempt to identify companies with above-average growth prospects. They frequently pay above-market multiples for the superior growth rate/profitability they anticipate. Other typical characteristics of growth managers include selection of higher-quality companies; an emphasis on consumer, service, health care, and technology stocks; and lighter weightings in deep cyclicals and defensive stocks. Regardless of the source of expected future growth or the level of the current multiple, growth not reflected in the current price is the key focus.

There tends to be two substyles of growth managers:

- Consistent growth.
- Earnings momentum.

Consistent growth managers emphasize high-quality, consistently growing companies. Because such businesses have very predictable earnings and extensive records of superior profitability, valuation multiples are frequently well above the market. These managers typically underweight cyclicals, as they tend to purchase market leaders in consumer-oriented industries.

Earnings momentum managers, by contrast, prefer companies with more volatile, above-average growth. They attempt to purchase companies in anticipation of earnings acceleration. They are usually willing to purchase companies in any economic sector, as long as the equities offer the best potential earnings growth.

Market-Oriented

Market-oriented managers do not have a strong or persistent preference for the types of stocks emphasized in either value or growth portfolios; consequently, their portfolio characteristics are closer to market averages over a business cycle. A wide variety of managers with different philosophies fall into this category. Some may find a more "pure" growth or value orientation overly restrictive, and prefer selecting stocks wherever they might fall on the growth/value spectrum; others may purchase securities embodying both growth and value characteristics; or some wish to control nonmarket risk by reducing growth or value biases from their portfolio structures.

The managers in this group tend to follow four substyles:

- Value bias.
- Growth bias.
- Market-normal.
- Growth at a price.

Value-biased managers or *growth-biased* managers have portfolios with a tilt toward either value or growth. The tilts are not sufficiently distinct to put them in either the value or growth styles.

Many *market-normal* managers construct portfolios with growth and valuation characteristics that are similar to the broad market over time. Also included are those willing to make meaningful bets in growth or value stocks across time, but with no continued preference toward either.

Growth at a price managers seek companies with above-average growth prospects selling at moderate valuation multiples. Unlike managers in other market-oriented substyles, growth at a price managers generally do not offer wide diversification in portfolio structure or capitalization breadth.

Small-Capitalization

The major distinguishing feature of small-capitalization managers is a focus on small companies. Many investors are drawn to this market segment because they find more opportunities to add value through research, since the companies are less widely followed by institutional investors.

Typical characteristics of small-capitalization portfolios include below-market dividend yields, above-market betas, high residual risk relative to broad market indexes, and a thin following by Wall Street analysts. Just as in the large- and medium-capitalization segments of the market, managers in the small-cap arena focus on different stock characteristics. As a result, the substyles within small-cap closely resemble the broad categories of large-cap styles:

- Value.
- Growth.
- Market-oriented.

Small-cap *value* managers seek underresearched small companies that sell at low valuations relative to assets, earnings, or revenues. They correspond to large-cap value managers.

Small-cap *growth* managers focus on less seasoned companies with above-average growth prospects. They primarily invest in the technology, health care, and consumer sectors, and their portfolios exhibit high growth and valuation characteristics.

Small-cap *market-oriented* managers focus on small companies that, over time, exhibit growth and value characteristics similar to the broad small-cap marketplace.

EVIDENCE OF STYLES

Portfolio Characteristics

Different management styles produce different portfolio characteristics and performance patterns. Exhibit 3 gives a profile of fundamental data for representative value, growth, market-oriented, and small cap managers. Also shown for comparison is the Russell 3000® Index, a broad market benchmark. Note that all statistics shown are dollar weighted, so that they accurately reflect where the managers are investing their funds.

Capitalization Distribution The capitalization categories presented are determined by the rank ordering of companies within the Russell 3000 Index by market value, rather than by arbitrary capitalization cutoffs. The "large" category refers to the 50 largest companies in the market, the "medium/large" to companies 51 to 200, and so on. The Russell 3000 Index covers over 97% of the entire equity market.

Exhibit 3: Comparison of Equity Manager Style Characteristics as of December 31, 1993

Characteristic	Value	Growth	Market-Oriented	Small Cap	Russell 3000® Index
Capitalization Distribution					
% Large (Top 50 stocks)	16.2	30.9	26.6	0.0	34.4
% Medium/Large (51 to 200)	25.4	25.0	38.9	1.4	26.3
% Medium (201 to 500)	22.9	37.3	21.0	3.7	19.3
% Medium/Small (501 to 1,000)	24.3	5.9	11.0	33.6	11.2
% Small (1,000+)	11.2	0.9	2.5	61.4	8.8
Valuation Characteristics					
P/E on Normalized EPS	12.9	22.8	17.3	28.6	18.1
Price/Book	1.43	5.32	2.54	3.44	2.60
Dividend Yield	2.70	0.62	2.09	0.35	2.51
Growth Characteristics					
Long-Term Forecast I/B/E/S Growth	9.8	20.6	12.9	19.3	11.9
Return on Equity	12.7	25.5	17.2	12.7	16.3
Earnings Variability	88.8	62.4	56.5	84.5	48.5
Economic Sectors					
% Technology	6.2	25.8	13.7	18.3	11.6
% Health Care	8.2	9.8	6.1	11.2	8.8
% Consumer Discretionary	7.2	29.2	19.9	23.4	14.2
% Consumer Staples	3.5	0.0	7.3	0.0	9.0
% Integrated Oils	4.9	0.0	6.5	1.0	5.3
% Other Energy	6.2	3.6	3.8	2.7	2.7
% Materials and Processing	21.8	6.5	7.6	4.7	8.3
% Producer Durables	2.3	0.0	6.1	9.9	4.2
% Autos and Transportation	1.5	3.4	3.5	4.4	5.8
% Financial Services	29.6	15.6	18.7	16.1	14.8
% Utilities	7.5	6.1	6.7	6.4	14.8
% Sector Deviation	24	25	12	19	0

As expected, the large-cap managers have the vast majority of their funds invested in the top 1,000 stocks in the market, which account for over 90% of the equity market's capitalization. The small-cap manager, by contrast, has the bulk of its money invested in the bottom 2,000 stocks in the market, which account for only 9% of the broad market.

Valuation Characteristics Styles divide on valuation characteristics as expected according to our descriptions of investment philosophy. The value manager demonstrates below-market P/E and price-to-book ratios, and an above-market yield. The growth manager's characteristics are the opposite of those in the market. The market-oriented manager is close to market levels on these ratios. The small-cap manager shown here happens to have a growth substyle, so its valuation ratios are above-market; as discussed earlier, there is a full range of equity substyles in small-cap, so these characteristics are not necessarily representative of all small-cap managers.

Growth Characteristics Earnings growth characteristics (here noted as those forecasted by institutional investment analysts and historical return on equity) conform to expectations, given the differing investment philosophies. The earnings variability statistic refers to the historical behavior of quarterly earnings relative to long-term trend-line growth; the higher the number, the greater the cyclicality of earnings. We noted earlier that the value manager tends to have higher earnings variability relative to other large-cap managers, and that is evident here. This usually occurs because of the value manager's greater willingness to purchase companies with cyclical earnings. The small-cap manager also has a higher earnings variability number, but in this case it is due to the less seasoned nature of the companies held, rather than due to ownership of cyclicals.

Economic Sectors Economic sector exposure supports the other statistics shown in Exhibit 3 and confirms our sense of manager style. The value manager is overweighted relative to the Russell 3000 Index in financial services (typically a lower-multiple sector) and materials and processing, which in this case includes many manufacturing companies. The growth manager is overweighted in two traditional growth sectors, technology and consumer discretionary. The market-oriented manager has spread its bets the most among the sectors, as indicated by the sector deviation score. This score measures in aggregate the difference between the manager's overall sector allocations and those for the Russell 3000 Index; the higher the number, the more the manager's economic sector exposure differs from the market. Interestingly, the small-cap manager's bets relative to the broad market are smaller than those for all but the market-oriented manager. Often small-cap manager sector bets are larger since a small stock universe has different industry composition from a large-cap universe.

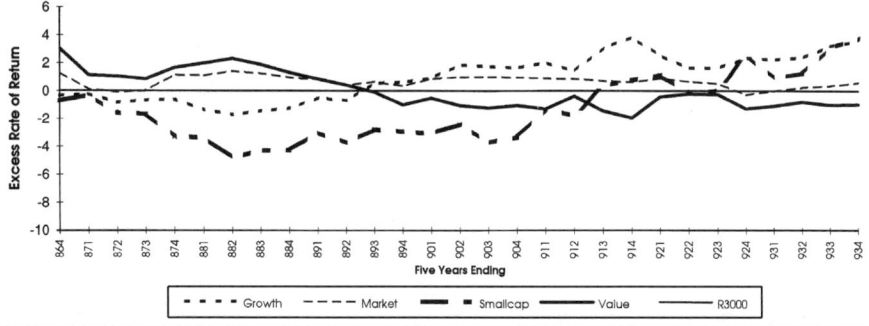

Exhibit 4: Five-Year Rolling Excess Returns Growth/Market-Oriented/Small-Cap, and Value Accounts Universe Means Versus Russell 3000 Index Periods Through December 31, 1993

Performance Patterns

Differing portfolio characteristics result in different performance patterns, particularly over short time horizons. Exhibit 4 shows performance for manager universes for the four different styles. In this example, we have plotted excess returns net of the Russell 3000 Index for rolling five-year periods that shift quarterly; the Russell 3000 Index is represented by the horizontal line.

Note the rotation of style performance over time, and the difference that style can make in shorter-term results. Growth lagged large-cap styles throughout much of the 1980s, but became the most dominant style in 1989, 1990, and 1991, ebbing somewhat thereafter. Value managers behaved in an inverse fashion from growth managers. Throughout all periods, the market-oriented group tracked market returns most closely, which would be expected, given their tighter factor bets relative to the market. The most prominent cycle is that of the small-cap style, which lagged significantly relative to large-cap styles in the 1980s, outperforming only recently.

HISTORICAL PERSPECTIVE ON STYLES

Interestingly, while the style definitions we describe are commonly used today, they have changed fairly significantly over the years. Exhibit 5 shows the growth and percentage of change in manager style universes over a fourteen-year period.

- In the 1970s (not shown in this exhibit), the vast majority of large-cap institutional managers used a growth investment approach; value managers were far fewer in number, and the term was much less frequently used. Value became more universally recognized as a style as more investors embraced it during the 1980s. Exhibit 5 shows the large increase in the number of value and price bias investors during that decade.

Exhibit 5: Growth in U.S. Equity Manager Style Membership

Style/Substyle	1980	1988	1990	1993	% Change 1980 to 1993
Growth	45	61	48	53	18
Market-Oriented					
Earnings Bias	13	16	15	18	38
Market Normal and Growth at a Price	58	50	51	42	−28
Price Bias	5	17	17	18	260
Value	18	58	70	67	272
Small-Cap	NA	48	70	99	NA
Growth + Earnings Bias	58	77	63	71	22
Value + Price Bias	23	75	87	85	270

- Small-cap investing did not emerge as a separate style until the early to mid-1980s; instead, a more nebulous notion of style prevailed that was more aggressive in its use of high-growth and smaller-cap stocks. The idea that small-cap investing could encompass a full spectrum of investment styles did not fully emerge until a few years ago, and in fact, many investors still equate small-cap with high-growth investing. Exhibit 5 shows the large increase in small-cap managers in the early 1990s.

More recently, a new "style" has emerged in the marketplace called "mid-cap" investing. The argument for this style is that medium-cap stocks have different performance patterns from their large- and small-cap counterparts.

While statistical analysis supports the case for medium-cap stocks as a differentiated segment of the *market*, it is debatable whether it is an actual investment *style* according to the criteria set forth in this chapter. Recall we have said: (1) managers adopt a style because they have a guiding philosophical belief that it will add value, and (2) many investors need to share a belief in order for adherence to it to constitute a style. Finally, a style should result in a clustering of factor tilts or portfolio characteristics among portfolios that share that style.

The mid-cap example is the first time that a style concept may have been introduced *before* broad adoption among investment managers. The differing behavior of medium-cap stocks in the equity market was noted in research and press articles, yet few investment managers had produced portfolios with a mid-cap profile. While they have typically owned a broad array of medium-cap securities (and many certainly have a medium-cap bias relative to cap-weighted benchmarks), managers had not adopted this concept separately as an investment philosophy.

A simple screen for mid-cap portfolios (defined as 70% exposure or more to stocks in the Russell Midcap Index) resulted in only 28 managers when this style started appearing in the press. This contrasted with 89 small-cap managers and 183 large-cap managers.

Whether mid-cap investing is truly a style or not, history and its appearance demonstrate that style concepts evolve over time, and undergo refinement in the process.

CAPM, FACTOR MODELS, AND STYLE INDEXES

One might sensibly ask how styles and style indexes behave in light of capital asset pricing model (CAPM) theory and the assumption of efficient markets. If the equity market is efficient, then all stocks are correctly priced, given all available information. By extension, any choice of a market subset will yield a market return subject to variation due to sample size and the random character of specific risk. Yet this is true only if the CAPM determines the prices of assets, that is, if all stocks are driven by the same single factor, the market. As a consequence, all stocks will move up or down depending on their beta, and all other return will be specific return.

In such a world, no stock characteristic would lead to differential return. The implication of the one-factor CAPM is that stocks are not differentially sensitive to changes in interest rates or industrial production or any other economic variable. It is just this limitation of the CAPM that lead Barr Rosenberg and associates to develop their fundamental factor model and Stephen Ross to develop the APT factor model. Multifactor models recognize stock differential sensitivity to forces that can change stock prices above and beyond the effect of the market.

A few points follow from this discussion. If styles exist, then certain other things must also exist. First, the returns to style portfolios and style indexes must be significantly different for the market. Second, the style portfolios and index style returns must be significantly different from each other. Third, style portfolios and style indexes should have on average different factor exposure patterns from the market as a whole and from each other.

The existence of universes of managers created according to style characteristics suggest that it is possible to create indexes based on the types of stocks the managers typically select. The virtues of an index are that (1) it is unbiased and not subject to the vagaries or fads of managers implicit in universes, and (2) it offers a passive alternative to purchasing managers when active management is not perceived as productive.

Chapter 2 will review the growing number of indexes that have been created over the years since Russell first introduced its indexes in 1988-1989. The variety and diversity of style index definitions are covered there, and we do not review all style indexes here. We do use the Russell 1000 Growth and Value Indexes to demonstrate the presence of style cycles that are somewhat independent from manager portfolios.

Briefly, the Russell Growth and Value indexes are created by rank ordering all stocks in the Russell 1000 by price/book. The capitalization-weighted median is computed. All stocks above the median breakpoint have greater weights in the Russell 1000 Growth Index, and all stock below the median have greater weights in the Russell 1000 Value Index. The choice of price/book is the result of extensive research.[1] While it is a simple rule, it is not simplistic and is supported by subsequent academic research.[2]

The returns of these indexes begin in 1979. As shown in Exhibit 6, the spread in quarterly returns between the Russell 1000 Growth and Value indexes and the spread between the Russell 1000 and 2000 is often different from zero. Over the period, large-cap stocks outperformed small-cap stocks much of the time. The same can be said for value stocks, which outperformed growth stocks about twice as often.

Exhibit 7 shows the cumulative return differences from 1979 through first quarter 1994. Returns will look different depending on the beginning date, but over this period the advantage of value over growth has been about 2%. At the end of the fourth quarter of 1991, however, the cumulative return differential since first quarter 1979 was essentially zero. From second quarter 1989 through fourth quarter 1991, growth recovered all the return differential it had lost from 1983 through 1989.

This raises the issue of whether we can expect any one style to underperform consistently for a long period of time. If one believes that value outperforms growth in the long run (as has been suggested by Fama and French and others), then the recovery of growth is an anomaly. If, on the other hand, one believes in efficient markets, then no market segment such as growth should be consistently underpriced. Hence, we would expect to see the type of recovery seen in the 1989 to 1991 period to happen again. Being able to time when growth becomes undervalued provides an obvious investment opportunity.[3] In any case, the index returns demonstrate that the style segments of the market behave differently from the market as a whole and do so consistently.

Style indexes are useful for performance evaluation of individual managers and combined manager mixes. In this sense, they can be used as normal portfolios.[4] If the style indexes accurately measure manager style, we would expect that the mean returns of universes of managers would behave more like the style indexes than broad market measures.

---

[1] For a discussion of the research paths explored see Kelly Haughton and Jon A. Christopherson, "Equity Style Indexes: Tools for Better Performance Evaluation and Plan Management," *Russell White Paper* (Frank Russell Company, Tacoma, WA 1989). Stocks above the third quartile of P/E are 100% in the Growth index and 0% in the Value index while stocks below the first quartile of P/B are 100% in the Value index and 0% in the Growth index. Stocks between the first and third quartiles are in both indexes to some degree. Stock at the median P/B are 50% in both indexes.

[2] Eugene F. Fama and Kenneth R. French. 1993. "Common Risk Factors in the Returns on Stocks and Bonds, " *Journal of Financial Economics* (February 1993), pp. 3-56.

[3] For a discussion of the valuation compressions between growth and value stocks that suggested in 1989 that growth was undervalued, see Jon A. Christopherson, Natalie LaBerge, and Dennis Trittin, "Has Growth Become Value?" *Russell Research Commentary* (Frank Russell Co.: Tacoma, WA, September 1989).

[4] For a discussion of Normal portfolio construction and the role of style indexes in providing more precise manager benchmarks than broad market benchmarks, see Jon A. Christopherson, "Normal Portfolios and Their Construction" in Portfolio and Investment Management, Frank Fabozzi (ed.) (Probus Publishing: Chicago, 1989), pp. 381-397.

Exhibit 6: Growth/Value and Large-Cap/Small-Cap Return Spreads

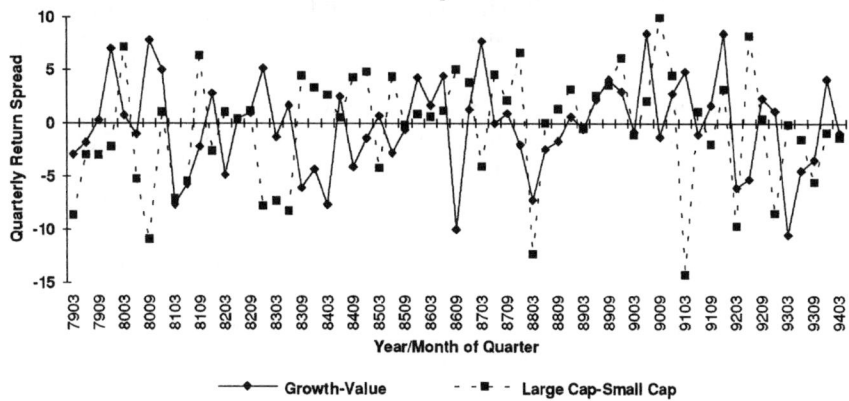

Exhibit 7: Cumulative Growth/Value and Large-Cap/Small-Cap Returns

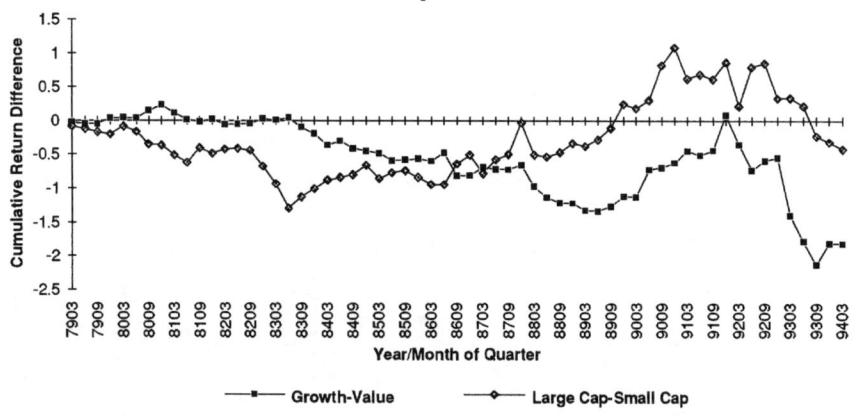

Exhibit 8 shows the regression statistics of the means of Russell Style Universe returns against the appropriate Russell style indexes. A benchmark that matches the universe of stocks from which the managers choose (i.e., its normal portfolio) will have a beta close to 1.0 (risk that is the same), an alpha close to zero (no abnormal excess return), and an R^2 close to 1.0 (a tight fit in return space).

For each style universe except market-oriented, the Russell style index has a beta closer to 1.0 than the alternative broad market benchmarks, the Russell 3000 and the S&P500.[5] The alphas of the style indexes are also closer to zero, except for market-oriented. For the market-oriented managers, the Russell 3000

---

[5] While recognizing that the S&P 500 has serious drawbacks as a broad market benchmark because of its sector biases and capitalization biases, we include it in these analyses because of its familiarity.

and 1000 are all alternative broad market measures. The market-oriented betas are all less than 1.0, which is due to cash holdings.

We conclude from Exhibit 8 that using style indexes allows us to separate out style effects from manager universe group behavior, manager skill, and manager risk. Knowing the riskiness of small-capitalization versus the market as a whole, we can manage the plan to take this into account.

Style indexes by their nature also provide a passive alternative when hiring one or more active managers is problematical. Small pension plans may not have sufficient funds to hire a diversified set of active small-cap managers to manage their plan. Rather than hire one manager with a style bias, they may wish to simplify management and hire a passive fund manager or manage the money in-house. Alternatively, some large funds have so much money that to place all their funds they would have to hire an extremely large group of managers. Rather than deal with the headaches of managing all these managers, they often choose to index part of their money.

STYLE MANAGEMENT: PRACTICAL APPLICATIONS

Performance Measurement

It should be apparent that taking style into account can make a difference in evaluating manager results. Look at Manager X's performance compared to a broad market index like the S&P 500:

Exhibit 8: Benchmark Comparisons
Manager Universe Means versus Style Indexes
10 Years Ending December 31, 1993

	Beta	Quarterly Alpha	Annualized Standard Error	R^2
Growth:				
Versus Russell 1000® Growth Index	0.992	0.368	3.210	0.970
Versus S&P 500	1.136	−0.043	5.208	0.922
Market-Oriented:				
Versus Russell 1000® Index	0.962	0.158	1.308	0.993
Versus Russell 3000® Index	0.945	0.256	1.178	0.994
Versus S&P 500	0.975	0.113	1.982	0.984
Value:				
Versus Russell 1000® Value Index	0.969	−0.110	2.474	0.970
Versus S&P 500	0.882	0.145	3.690	0.934
Small Capitalization:				
Versus Russell 2500™ Index	1.033	0.249	3.586	0.971
Versus Russell 2000® Index	0.924	0.769	4.462	0.955
Versus S&P 500	1.211	−0.418	8.958	0.819

	Annual Periods (%)					Annualized Periods Ending December 31, 1990		
	1986	1987	1988	1989	1990	3 Years	4 Years	5 years
Manager X	11.2	1.4	24.6	16.4	−11.5	8.7	6.8	7.6
S&P 500	18.2	5.2	16.5	31.4	−3.2	14.0	11.7	13.0

Given only this information, one would conclude that Manager X had not performed well. Yet when the manager's performance is compared to an appropriate benchmark (verified first by an analysis that the portfolio has small-capitalization characteristics), the conclusion regarding results changes markedly:

	Annual Periods (%)					Annualized Periods Ending December 31, 1990		
	1986	1987	1988	1989	1990	3 Years	4 Years	5 years
Manager X	11.2	1.4	24.6	16.4	−11.5	8.7	6.8	7.6
Russell 2000®	5.7	−8.8	24.9	16.2	−19.5	5.3	1.6	2.4

Applying a benchmark that more closely embodies the stock universe in which the manager invests yields more information about manager skill.

One might ask (and many do) why comparisons that take investment style into account should be of such importance. The thinking is if investors cannot hire managers to outperform the broad market, then what is the point?

Over the very long term, managers should be able to beat the market regardless of style biases, or else they are not earning their fees. But in defining "long term," it is necessary to go beyond the typical five-year time horizon many investors choose. Style cycles can last, and have lasted, that long and longer.

One of the longest style cycles in recent years was the underperformance of small-capitalization stocks in the 1980s, which was shown in Exhibit 4. Small stocks grossly underperformed their large-cap counterparts for the better part of seven years, beginning in 1984 and ending in 1990 (there was one short-lived period of outperformance in 1988, but this quickly reversed). Managers who invested in that sector of the market were clearly underperforming the market consistently.

In a much broader context, the cycle of underperformance in the 1980s is not unheard of. While this period is certainly at the higher end of the range for small-stock underperformance cycles, similarly long cycles have occurred before.

Exhibits 9 and 10 show long-term data for the Ibbotson-Sinquefield Small Stock Index versus the S&P 500 from 1926 to 1993. These data demonstrate how much longer-term one needs to think in evaluating performance.

Unfortunately, the normal temptation is to use shorter time horizons. Also, it is unusual to find managers with 20-year track records where style effects would diminish in importance. This is why style analysis is so important. If investors select managers on the basis of historical performance versus a broad market benchmark, they may unknowingly hire a manager at a peak in performance that may be due solely to a style cycle. Conversely, they will be sorely tempted to fire a manager who has experienced underperformance solely because the manager's style category has lagged. These decisions can translate into a "buy high/sell low" pattern, which can be extremely damaging to performance. Of course, this analysis assumes that the managers being evaluated perform the way they do solely for style reasons and that other factors are not also at work.

Achieving Target Equity Returns

The ramifications of style analysis go beyond merely selecting individual managers. Style orientation can play a critical role in the performance of an entire equity plan.

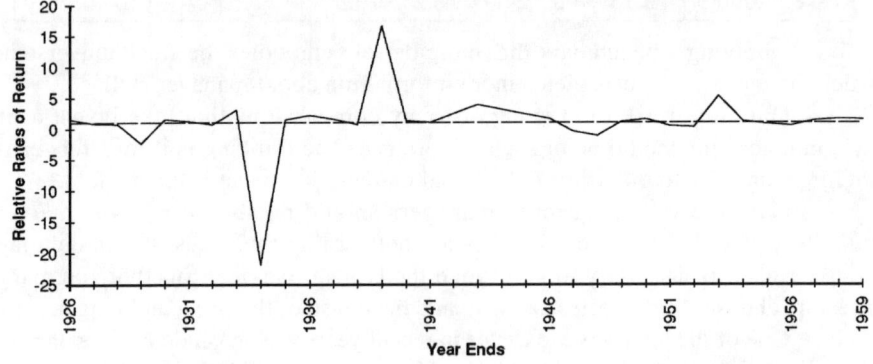

Exhibit 9: Performance of Small Stocks versus Large Stocks
Ibbotson and Sinquefield Index Relative to the S&P Index
Annual Rates of Return from 1926 to 1959

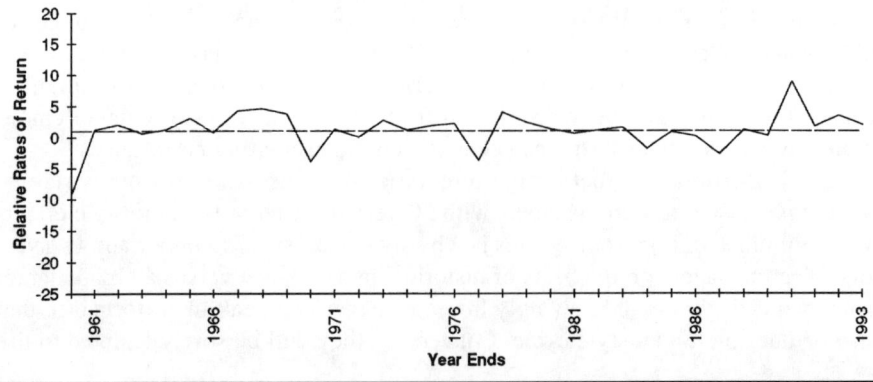

Exhibit 10: Performance of Small Stocks versus Large Stocks
Ibbotson and Sinquefield Index Relative to the S&P Index
Annual Rates of Return from 1960 to 1993

The first step in constructing a coherent equity strategy is to determine not only the investor's goals, but, more importantly, how the investor defines risk. While this sounds like an obvious statement, this step is often overlooked. Most investors prefer to think of themselves as having long-term investment horizons and a fairly high tolerance for risk. But not many have examined equity performance patterns in detail and considered what their response would be to potentially long periods of underperformance due to style biases. As we noted above, style cycles may not fit the general notion that "long-term" is five years.

Risk is often also misdiagnosed. In the investment industry, risk is still often referred to as volatility of total return (i.e., standard deviation), when the investor really may be most concerned with a result that falls short of the overall equity market return (i.e., downside semivariance and/or probability of shortfall). Increasingly, the alternative investment is some passive instrument, so investor focus is appropriately on how an equity plan performs versus an index. For volatility reduction, the investor looks to other asset classes, with allocations according to long-term goals. Thus, investors may not rely on individual equity managers as the primary source of risk reduction, but instead, to deliver a better than equity market return.

Once an investor's risk tolerance has been defined, the second step is to diagnose the aggregate equity investments already held for potential structural biases versus the overall market. This step is important in determining whether there are *unintended* biases in overall structure. For example, an investor may have unknowingly built in a bias toward a certain capitalization segment of the market or a tilt toward growth or value. This may be particularly true if current manager selection has been made primarily on the basis of short-term historical performance without regard to style. Such a structure will subject the entire plan to underperformance from *unintended* style bets. An appropriate discussion for the investor in this case is whether these biases are appropriate for the risk tolerance level, and whether they should be modified.

Note these biases are separate from *intended* bets taken because of a conviction that they will pay off or a belief that the investor has hired the best possible managers regardless of style. But in either of these cases, presumably the investor knows the consequences of these choices and will not be alarmed at short-term underperformance because of this style structure.

Assuming investors have no preconceived ideas about style structure and are concerned with shorter-term risk, they can construct a style-neutral portfolio from managers with offsetting biases. The goal then becomes to produce outperformance from stock selection, rather than relying on a style bias to win over time. Style analysis plays a critical role in forming an accurate sense of manager portfolio structures and whether they indeed have diversifying performance patterns.

Regardless of the type of equity strategy selected, style analysis delivers, at a minimum, a key benefit in enhancing investor understanding of their investments. This should lead to better implementation of any change to an overall equity portfolio, as the reasons for the change and its potential performance impact will be better understood.

BEYOND STYLE DIVERSIFICATION

A style-diversified approach is best for investors who have no special insights into the equity markets, have multiple parties to whom they must explain performance results, have shorter time horizons, or have low risk tolerance. The style-diversified choice does not answer the question of whether one style is "best." All styles have their proponents, as anyone who has met investment managers will testify. But should any one style consistently perform better than the others over time?

The answer is "maybe." There are many studies that support the concept of value investing, and a recent article in particular provides some support for this approach.[6] Presented with such evidence, one feels compelled to consider it as "proof" that value and/or small cap must be the best style. Whenever one is confronted with such data, however, several issues need to be settled in order to structure an equity strategy around it.

- What sort of portfolios result from the criteria used to define "value"? How would the investor involved react to their structure? If the style definition used results in concentrated economic sector exposure (e.g., a heavy tilt toward value sectors like financials or utilities), would the investor feel comfortable holding that portfolio through potentially significant short-term performance volatility?
- Does the performance derive from the factor being studied? Or are there other effects that need to be "disentangled" in order to determine that value is really what is driving the study results? Could some other effect be a factor?
- How many investors employ the approach today compared to the time the study was performed? The number of value investors has increased dramatically over the last decade, for instance, which may have increased efficiency in that market segment, making it more difficult to find mispriced assets. A similar trend has begun to emerge in the small-cap sector, although indications are that there is still far less institutional research available in that arena.
- Finally, why should history necessarily repeat itself? What is the relevance of the test period to the current market? While this type of analysis poses some risk of rationalizing whether markets are truly "different this time," some attention to the economic and market backdrop of the historical analysis is appropriate. Otherwise, there is a risk for assuming parallels exist where there are none.

---

[6] Fama and French, "Common Risk Factors in the Returns on Stocks and Bonds," op. cit.

Beyond obtaining the highest absolute return, risk adjustment can also influence the answer for investors for whom risk reduction is important. Over its history, the Russell 1000® Value Index has outperformed the other style indexes. Perhaps more importantly, it has superior risk characteristics relative to the other indexes. To those concerned with volatility of absolute returns (rather than performance deviations from the broad market), this risk adjustment is worth something. Even if value had underperformed the other styles, to some degree an investor might be willing to give up superior performance for a superior risk position.

In summary, even though there are no clear answers to the question of which style is best, the numbers alone point toward value as the superior style. These numbers, however, beg a host of qualitative considerations.

SUMMARY

In this chapter we have defined certain styles of equity investment. We have shown that portfolios based on style concepts have different equity characterisitcs from each other and from the market. Style portfolios also behave differently from each other and from the overall market. These consistent differences in performance have implications for equity plan structures. Failure to pay attention to the equity style of a manager can lead the investor to take unintended factor bets and lead to unnecessary plan risk. Styles exist and style matters.

Chapter 2

Understanding the Differences and Similarities of Equity Style Indexes

Melissa R. Brown, CFA
First Vice President
Director of Quantitative Research
Prudential Securities Inc.

Claudia E. Mott
First Vice President
Director of Small-Cap Research
Prudential Securities Inc.

INTRODUCTION

Over the past few years, the need to measure the performance of equity investment styles (such as growth and value) has preoccupied many plan sponsors and consultants (who are creating more and more indexes to track these styles). At the same time, fund managers have had to keep pace with these new benchmarks. It has become increasingly important to understand the characteristics of the various equity style benchmarks commonly used, especially since the style characteristics differ not only from growth to value, but also among indexes that are presumably benchmarks for the same style.

For investment managers being measured against a style benchmark, it is critical to know the characteristics of that index. If a portfolio's sector or size dis-

---

The authors gratefully acknowledge the help of Eddie Cheung, Dan Coker, Kevin Condon, Steven DeSanctis, Michele Eschert, Susan Levine, Rita Quadrino, Karen Shao, and Tara Stergis.

tribution is very different from the benchmark against which it is being measured, performance may be better or worse than the index largely because of those differences, rather than because of the manager's capability. A value manager, for instance, may be compared against a value index that is very heavily weighted in financial services and utility stocks. If those stocks have done well during the time period in which the manager is being measured, and the portfolio is underweighted relative to the style index (but perhaps not relative to the "market"), the shortfall may be attributable not to poor stock selection but rather to the manager's relative weighting decision. Most managers are reluctant to position portfolios with weightings that are as extreme as in many of the indexes.

Fund sponsors using style indexes either to judge outside managers or to make asset allocation decisions need to be aware of these characteristics as well. To be able to judge outside managers fairly, plan sponsors should know the biases of the respective style indexes and how their managers' portfolios deviate. This knowledge should lead to the choice of the most appropriate style benchmark for the manager. Thus, subsequent performance reviews need not dwell on benchmark misfit, but on stock selection success or failure.

Making asset allocation decisions on the basis of historical performance patterns of styles also assumes a knowledge and understanding of the various benchmarks. Different construction practices yield different characteristics. Hence what looks like a performance shift from growth to value may turn out to be a surge in performance by the interest rate-sensitive stocks. An asset allocation program built on incorrect assumptions may cause the plan to fall short of its investment targets.

In this chapter, we describe many of the style benchmarks developed to measure the performance of growth and value across the large-, mid-, and small-cap equity classes. We start with a simple explanation of the construction methodologies and then compare the resulting indexes. Our comparisons examine the indexes from two angles — how indexes differ across a single style, and how the two styles themselves differ.

DATA

In all our discussions of size, we depend on similar sets of exhibits. Because exhibits are not referenced specifically, we describe their contents here. The characteristics described are as of June 28, 1996. The appendix to this chapter describes the methodology used to calculate fundamental characteristics.

Descriptive Characteristics
Separate exhibits for each size category describe the number of companies, rebalancing frequency, exchange distribution, average size, and largest and smallest holdings.

Size Distribution
Understanding how diverse or concentrated an index is can aid in understanding performance. In addition, the performance of smaller stocks can differ dramati-

cally from that of larger issue. Size distribution exhibits divide the companies into size categories by percentage of market capitalization. We take this approach because mean and median market-cap statistics do not enable a thorough understanding of the size distribution of companies within the indexes. Different index providers use different sources to calculate shares outstanding. In addition, some (such as Frank Russell) use shares floating rather than shares outstanding to determine a stock's weighting. If a provider supplies shares, market value, or weight, we use that number to calculate the weighting wherever we're looking at a weighted number. For the size distribution tables, we use the company's total market value (price times shares outstanding according to FactSet) to assign a company to a size category; for the cap-weighted table, we use the provider-based weights. We feel this gives a better representation of the range of companies within each index and allows a company to appear in the same size category no matter what index we're examining.

Macroeconomic Sector Distribution
Differences in performance are frequently attributable to an index's macroeconomic sector weightings. These exhibits break down the indexes into 13 sectors according to percentage of market capitalization.

Fundamental Characteristics
We calculate weighted-average values for trailing price/earnings ratio (both with and without negative earnings), forecast P/E using I/B/E/S, price-to-book, price-to-sales, debt-to-capital, and P/E to growth ratios, historical 5-year earnings and sales growth, return on equity, return on assets, and average daily volume. We also include the average yield and the percentage of stocks that are dividend-paying.

Performance Statistics
We look at the annual returns of the indexes from 1979 (when many indexes' data begins) through 1995, and provide annualized averages for the entire period (if available) and the standard deviation of the returns.

DEFINING THE MAJOR STYLE INDEXES

We have included indexes from four of the major services that provide widely-used style indexes divided into size categories. Standard & Poor's (in conjunction with BARRA) publishes large-cap growth and value indexes based on the S&P Composite, Mid-Cap 400, and Small-Cap 600 indexes. Frank Russell produces three sets of large-cap style indexes (based on the Russell 1000, Russell 3000, and Russell Top 200), mid-cap, and small-cap (using both the Russell 2000 and Russell 2500 indexes). Wilshire Associates and Prudential Securities divide their style worlds into three size categories: large-, mid-, and small-cap.

There are two schools of thought in the creation of these benchmarks: to sort by price/book, or to screen based on a set of criteria. S&P and Russell use the price/book sort method, while Wilshire and PSI use screening criteria to generate their portfolios. The method of construction, as well as the universe of companies from which the index is formed, can lead to substantial differences in the style index characteristics.

Although the indexes are constructed using different methodologies and universes, indexes of the same style tend to move in the same direction. The relative performance is generally very similar for the various pairs of indexes as well (see Exhibits 1-3, 9-11, and 17-19).

It is worth mentioning some of the issues related to the different construction methodologies.

The Value of Book Equity

The simplest and most popular method of discriminating between value and growth stocks is to divide stocks into two mutually exclusive portfolios based on price-to-book equity ratios. Recent deterioration of book equity as a result of the vagaries of accrual accounting, FAS (Financial Accounting Statement) 106 and 109, other accounting changes, and corporate restructurings calls into question the viability of this number as a way to distinguish between styles. Index providers try to place all companies on a comparable basis using various amortization methods to spread out some of the charges.

Mutual Exclusivity

The indexes that rely on sorting a universe by price-to-book ratio require that every company from the main universe fall into one or the other style index. The argument can be made that some companies probably don't belong in either index. In addition, value is often in the eyes of the beholder, so some companies may fit both styles.

Lack of Diversification

Some of the standard style indexes tend to be overwhelmed by one or two sectors. Many current value indexes, for example, tend to overweight financial services and utility sectors to a degree that is unacceptable to most managers. The three sections that detail the style indexes by economic sector will discuss this further.

DESCRIPTION OF THE INDEXES

The Prudential Securities Large-Cap Growth and Value Indexes are selected by screening stocks in the top 15 percentiles of market capitalization in the Compustat universe (excluding REITs, ADRs, and Limited Partnerships) for companies with growth or value characteristics. Mid-cap encompasses percentiles 8 through 25, and the small-cap style indexes include the 20th through 45th percentiles.

- Growth stocks have historical sales growth greater than 10%, rank in the top half of their size universe on the I/B/E/S forecast growth rate, and have low dividend payouts and debt-to-capital ratios.
- Value stocks rank in the bottom 50% of the universe on the basis of a normalized P/E (where the average of the five-year peak earnings and the current year forecast according to I/B/E/S is used for earnings). Additionally, companies that are dividend-paying must have sustainable dividend rates; that is, they have covered their four-quarter dividend for the past three years.

Russell Growth and Value Indexes are available for all three of Russell's large-cap benchmarks, the Top 200, the 1000, and the 3000; the mid-cap style indexes are based on the Russell Midcap, and for small cap based on the Russell 2000 and Russell 2500. The methodology is the same for all size categories. Each company's book/price ratio is calculated by adjusting the book value to amortize the FAS 106 write-offs. The corresponding rank is combined with a rank based on the I/B/E/S long-term growth rate, and a composite rank is calculated. This rank is used to compute the probability that a stock is either growth or value. About 30% of the stocks in the large-cap Russell style indexes appear in both the growth and value indexes, in different proportions based on the probability calculated; the sum of the shares in each index is the total number of shares floating. The remaining 70% of the companies are in one style index only.

The following should be noted regarding the Russell universes. The Russell 3000 Index includes 3,000 large U.S. companies, which together represent 98% of the U.S. equity market by market capitalization. Only common stocks of U.S. companies are included in the index; in the case of multiple classes of stock, generally only one is allowed. Combined, the style indexes are all-inclusive and mutually exclusive. The Russell 2000 represents the bottom two-thirds of the largest 3,000 publicly traded companies domiciled in the United States. The 1000 are the 1000 largest stocks, the 2500 is the 3000 less the 500 largest names (not the S&P 500), the Top 200 are the biggest 200 and the midcap are the next 800, so that the Top 200 plus the Mid Cap make up the Russell 1000.

The *S&P/BARRA Growth and Value Indexes* are constructed by sorting the S&P 500 companies based on their price-to-book ratios, with the low price-to-book companies constituting the value index and high price-to-book making up the growth index. Each S&P 500 company is included in either the growth or the value index, and the two indexes are constructed so that they each have approximately the same market value at the semiannual rebalancing. When new companies are added to the S&P Composite index, they are placed into the appropriate style index based on the price-to-book cutoff. Companies in the growth index tend to be bigger, so it includes roughly 40% of the S&P 500 companies. The same methodology is used on the S&P MidCap and SmallCap indexes.

The *S&P 500* (also known as the S&P Composite) is constructed so that, in aggregate, it represents a broad distribution by industry group comparable to that of stocks traded on the New York Stock Exchange. Decisions about stocks to be included and deleted are made by the S&P Index Committee. The S&P Mid-Cap 400 index includes companies chosen by committee at Standard & Poor's for their size and industry characteristics. The *S&P SmallCap 600* was introduced in October 1994 and includes companies chosen based on their size, industry, and liquidity characteristics. None of the companies in the SmallCap or MidCap indexes overlap with each other or those in the S&P Composite. Some companies in the S&P MidCap, however, are larger than those in the S&P Composite, and some in the SmallCap are bigger than those in the MidCap, which is a function of the normal drift that takes place in any index as some companies' stock prices appreciate and others depreciate.

Wilshire chooses the stocks for the *Wilshire Growth Indexes and the Wilshire Value Indexes* by using a set of criteria to eliminate names from its (large-cap) Top 750, Mid Cap 750, and (small-cap) Next 1750 indexes. Elimination criteria for the Growth index include history of less than five years, high dividend payout, low growth, low price-to-book, and low ROE. Companies with high relative P/E, low relative dividend yield, and high relative price-to-book are eliminated from the Value index.

The *Wilshire Top 750* index represents the largest 750 companies in the Wilshire 5000, which in turn consists of all securities traded in the United States for which price data are available. The *Wilshire 5000* actually includes far more than 5,000 companies — over 7,000 as of mid-year 1996. The *Wilshire Next 1750* is derived by taking the next 1,750 stocks (after the top 750) from the top half of the Wilshire 5000. The *Wilshire Mid Cap*, which is quite a bit smaller than either Russell's or Standard & Poor's mid-cap index, uses the smallest 250 names in the Top 750 and the largest 500 names in the Next 1750.

THE LARGE-CAP STYLE BENCHMARKS

Style indexes for large-cap stocks have been around longer than the mid- and small-cap categories, but they were created much more recently than most of the other major benchmarks. The Wilshire and Russell indexes have been around for since 1986, while S&P, jointly with BARRA, released its large-cap indexes in 1992. Prudential Securities (PSI) released its own versions of style indexes in 1993 to address some problems it saw in some of the other style indexes. Exhibits 1-8 display the price performance, descriptive characteristics, and size and sector distributions of large-cap growth and value indexes. Although not available for use then, most indexes are cast back to the late 1970s.

Growth Indexes are Not Created Equal

The 12 large-cap growth indexes covered in our analysis show a variety of differences that result from not only the construction method, but also the selection universe. These characteristics and the resulting differences can change a lot over time as well, usually owing to the rebalancing of the underlying indexes. Currently, the Russell Top 200 and S&P/BARRA indexes (which are selected from the index with the fewest stocks) have the heaviest large-company profile, with weighted average capitalizations of $51.7 billion and $46.8 billion, respectively.

The PSI growth index has the smallest size profile, with a weighted average market cap of $14.3 billion and only 38.3% of the capitalization in the largest-company size category. Much of this difference is attributable to the placement of one stock — General Electric, which fell into growth in all of the growth indexes detailed below except PSI

The macroeconomic sector distribution points out a number of variations across the six growth indexes as well. Technology figures prominently in the PSI Large Growth index, with 30.8% of the capitalization, whereas the sector makes up only 14.5% of the weight in the S&P/BARRA Growth Index. Consumer staples, however, comprises 23.5% of the S&P/BARRA index; the weighting falls to 18.5% for the Russell 1000 and just 9.9% for PSI. Other sectors in which the weights vary widely include consumer services, financial services, and health care.

In most cases, the fundamental characteristics of the growth indexes are comparable, but the construction methodology and selection universe do lead to some differences. The PSI and Russell 3000 growth indexes have the highest I/B/E/S forecast long-term and next-year growth rate and the highest P/Es based on this year's earnings, although PSI has much higher historical sales and earnings growth rates. Return on equity and return on assets are much higher for the Wilshire index than for the others.

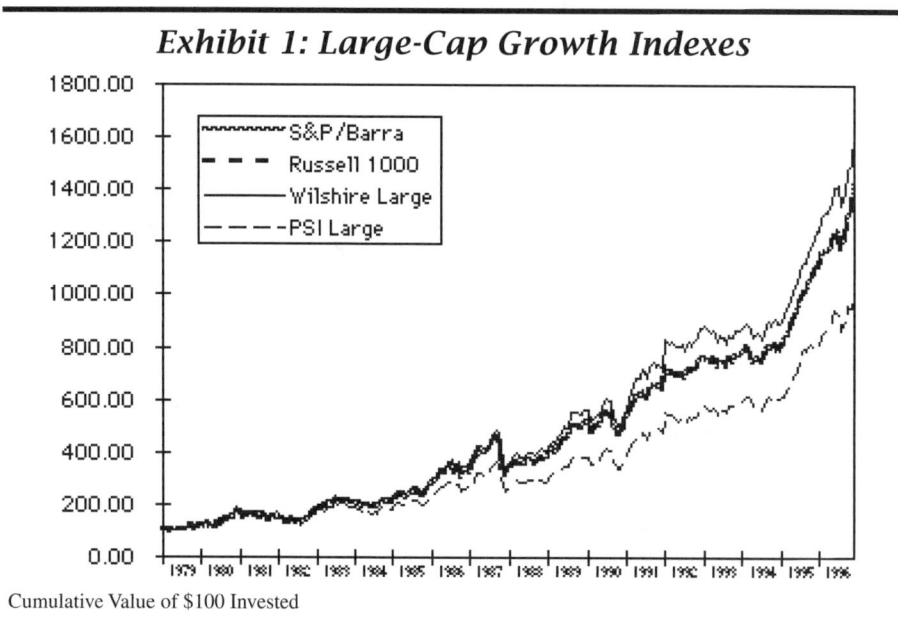

Exhibit 1: Large-Cap Growth Indexes

Cumulative Value of $100 Invested

Exhibit 2: Large-Cap Value Indexes

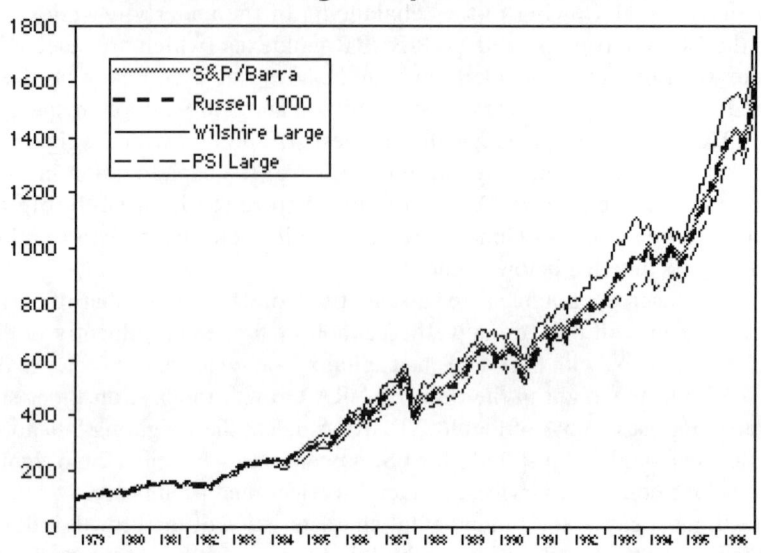

Cumulative Value of $100 Invested

Legend: S&P/Barra, Russell 1000, Wilshire Large, PSI Large

Exhibit 3: Large-Cap Growth Relative to Value

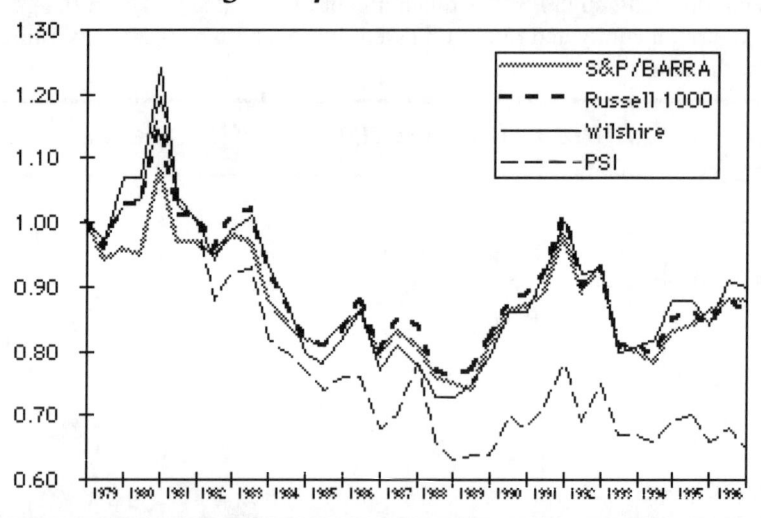

Legend: S&P/BARRA, Russell 1000, Wilshire, PSI

Yield is another distinguishing feature of the indexes. In both the S&P and Russell Top 200 indexes, about 82% of the companies pay a dividend. Recall that these indexes are built from the overall universes with the fewest companies and are heavily focused on the biggest of the big-cap names, most of which pay a dividend.

Value Should be Looked at Closely

The value indexes also show a wide variation in size characteristics. General Electric is the biggest company in the PSI index (it is also the biggest company traded in the U.S., beating out the next-biggest, Coca-Cola, by about $20 billion), whereas Exxon dominates the Russell and S&P indexes with at least a 3.5% weighting. For the Wilshire large value index, however, the biggest holding is IBM (ranked 13th in size for the overall Wilshire universe) which is less than half the capitalization of GE. The Russell Top 200 Value index, with 143 names, has the largest weighted-average, mean, and median market caps, because it is not "weighted down" by smaller companies. The Wilshire large value index, in contrast, has the smallest weighted average market cap despite having only 149 companies, with many of the very largest stocks excluded based on Wilshire's screens. The concentration of companies in the various size categories is a bit more homogeneous in the value indexes. All have at least 75.0% of the capitalization of the index in names over $3.0 billion in size. The value indexes have at a minimum 95.0% of the companies listed on the NYSE as well.

From a sector perspective, large-cap value is heavily concentrated in financial services, utilities, and energy, and the index construction process determines which takes on the biggest proportion. By requiring companies to pay a dividend, Wilshire has the heaviest utility weighting at 31.0%, while S&P/BARRA, which has no such restriction, has the lightest at 11.3%. Financial services ranges from 28.1% to 23.0%, suggesting that, regardless of definition, value means financials. The energy weighting varies from over 20.0% for S&P/BARRA, to the 7.5% for Wilshire. It remains one of the three heaviest sectors in all of the other indexes, however. These large differences obviously highlight the importance of knowing your index.

The fundamentals of the value indexes point up the differences that a definition can create. The heavy utility weighting in the Wilshire index influences many of the valuation parameters, causing the lowest P/E and price-to-book values, along with the highest yield. The largest companies and their weightings can also make a big difference. For example, having General Electric at almost 5%, PSI's ROE is 16.4% and its ROA 5.3%, much higher than in all of the other value indexes. In the other indexes, ROA ranges from 4.0% to 4.5%, whereas the return on equity has a much higher range of values, 11.9% (Russell 3000) to 15.4% (Wilshire).

Growth Differs from Value in Many Ways

The value indexes tend to be much more heavily weighted in financials, utilities, and energy (although the weightings vary dramatically based on how the indexes are constructed and from which universe), where dividend yields tend to be higher and P/Es and price-to-book ratios are lower. Consumer cyclicals also figure more heavily in value than in growth. Value tends to have a much lower weighting than growth in consumer staples, consumer services, health care, and technology, where P/Es tend to be higher.

Exhibit 4: Descriptive Characteristics of Large-Cap Style Benchmarks

	Large-Cap Growth						Large-Cap Value					
	PSI	Russell Top 200	Russell 1000	Russell 3000	S&P/BARRA	Wilshire	PSI	Russell Top 200	Russell 1000	Russell 3000	S&P/BARRA	Wilshire
Number of Companies	419	122	646	1,960	159	206	478	143	651	1,874	341	149
First Full Year of Return	1976	1986	1979	1986	1977	1978	1976	1986	1979	1986	1977	1978
Index Rebalancing	Semi-Annually	Annually	Annually	Annually	Semiannually/As Needed	Quarterly	Semi-Annually	Annually	Annually	Annually	Semiannually/As Needed	Quarterly
Weighting Method	Market Cap	Float*	Float*	Float*	Market Cap	Market Cap	Market Cap	Float*	Float*	Float*	Market Cap	Market Cap
Returns Calculation	With Income	Principal & w/Income	Principal & w/Income	Principal & w/Income	With Income	With Income	With Income	Principal & w/Income	Principal & w/Income	Principal & w/Income	With Income	With Income
Exchange Distribution												
Nasdaq	26.2%	12.4%	17.7%	22.6%	10.8%	16.1%	3.7%	0.9%	4.1%	7.1%	3.2%	2.5%
NYSE	71.8	87.3	81.7	76.4	89.2	83.4	96.0	98.7	95.2	92.0	95.8	97.2
ASE	2.0	0.3	0.6	1.0	0.0	0.5	0.3	0.4	0.7	0.9	1.0	0.3
Total Capitalization	$2.1T	$2.8T	$4.0T	$4.6T	$2.6T	$2.1T	$3.1T	$2.6T	$3.9T	$4.4T	$2.5T	$1.1T
Average Size												
Wtd. Mean	$26.9B	$51.7B	$37.4B	$33.6B	$46.8B	$45.5B	$29.2B	$30.8B	$21.9B	$19.6B	$22.5B	$18.2B
Mean	5.1B	22.7B	6.2B	2.3B	16.1B	10.2B	6.4B	18.3B	6.0B	2.4B	7.3B	7.2B
Median	2.2B	14.4B	2.3B	518.8M	7.1B	4.2B	2.6B	11.4B	2.5B	567.9M	4.2B	4.0B
Size Range												
Largest	$122.5B	$144.0B	$144.0B	$144.0B	$144.0B	$144.0B	$144.0B	$144.0B	$144.0B	$144.0B	$144.0B	$144.0B
Smallest	1.0B	1.9B	571.2M	80.7M	453.0M	1.4B	1.0B	1.9B	642.7M	80.7M	312.2M	1.4B
Concentration												
Largest 10	29.0%	38.9%	27.5%	24.6%	33.1%	39.0%	22.6%	25.7%	17.3%	15.5%	21.1%	33.2%
Largest 50	56.3	81.6	57.6	51.6	76.2	73.8	51.6	67.1	45.2	40.4	51.7	71.0
Largest 100	69.2	98.5	70.1	62.8	92.7	87.2	67.0	91.4	61.5	55.0	70.0	90.3

* See section on index construction.
Note: Data are as of June 28, 1996.

Source: Prudential Securities Inc.

Exhibit 5: Size Distribution of Large-Cap Style Benchmarks

	Large-Cap Growth						Large-Cap Value					
	PSI	Russell Top 200	Russell 1000	Russell 3000	S&P/BARRA	Wilshire	PSI	Russell Top 200	Russell 1000	Russell 3000	S&P/BARRA	Wilshire
$20.0B & Over	39.8	72.7	51.3	46.0	66.4	58.1	41.4	53.4	36.1	32.3	36.8	37.2
$10.0B–$20.0B	10.6	16.6	11.7	10.5	16.2	12.7	17.4	29.1	19.6	17.5	21.5	16.7
$5.0B–$10.0B	15.1	10.6	13.1	11.7	11.3	12.2	17.5	17.3	18.5	16.5	22.3	23.5
$1.0B–$5.0B	34.5	—	23.1	21.0	6.0	17.0	23.8	0.3	25.5	23.2	18.6	22.6
$500M–$1B	—	—	0.7	5.3	0.1	—	—	—	0.2	5.2	0.6	—
$250M–$500M	—	—	—	3.8	—	—	—	—	—	3.6	0.1	—
Less than $250M	—	—	—	1.7	—	—	—	—	—	1.6	—	—

Note: Data are as of June 28, 1996.
Source: Prudential Securities Inc.

Exhibit 6: Macroeconomic Sector Distribution of Large-Cap Style Benchmarks

	Large-Cap Growth						Large-Cap Value					
	PSI	Russell Top 200	Russell 1000	Russell 3000	S&P/BARRA	Wilshire	PSI	Russell Top 200	Russell 1000	Russell 3000	S&P/BARRA	Wilshire
Basic Industry	5.9	2.7	5.6	5.8	6.4	4.7	10.6	9.0	11.0	11.4	10.8	9.6
Business Services	5.3	6.1	6.5	6.7	7.8	6.5	1.2	4.1	3.8	3.8	1.7	0.8
Capital Spending	1.3	7.7	6.3	6.2	7.1	8.6	7.7	3.7	4.1	4.2	3.9	1.0
Conglomerates	0.1	0.9	0.8	0.7	1.6	0.1	1.6	1.7	1.1	1.1	0.6	0.6
Consumer Cyclical	1.1	—	0.7	1.0	0.3	1.4	4.8	5.6	5.1	5.1	6.	11.0
Consumer Services	21.4	12.8	14.5	14.6	12.2	14.4	3.3	3.1	4.8	5.5	6.6	3.5
Consumer Staples	9.9	23.6	18.4	16.7	23.5	17.3	8.3	4.1	3.5	3.6	1.5	0.7
Energy	2.5	0.7	2.1	2.2	1.1	0.5	11.5	16.0	13.9	13.0	19.3	7.5
Financial Services	7.1	3.7	4.3	4.3	3.6	8.2	24.6	25.8	25.8	25.7	23.0	28.1
Health Care	13.8	21.3	18.4	18.6	17.2	15.1	7.9	3.5	3.0	3.0	3.7	—
Technology	30.8	19.5	21.1	21.6	14.5	23.2	5.6	8.0	7.0	6.8	11.5	6.1
Utilities	0.7	1.1	1.2	1.2	4.7	0.1	13.0	15.5	16.5	15.6	11.3	31.0
REITs	—	—	0.1	0.4	—	—	—	—	0.3	1.3	—	—

Note: Data are as of June 28, 1996.
Source: Prudential Securities Inc.

Exhibit 7: Fundamental Characteristics of Large-Cap Style Benchmarks

	Large-Cap Growth						Large-Cap Value					
		Russell						Russell				
	PSI	Top 200	1000	3000	S&P/BARRA	Wilshire	PSI	Top 200	1000	3000	S&P/BARRA	Wilshire
LTM P/E	26.9	26.5	27.2	28.3	25.3	23.9	14.5	15.4	15.4	15.6	15.7	12.7
LTM P/E – W/O Neg Ear	27.9	25.9	26.3	26.5	25.3	25.3	15.9	17.1	16.6	16.7	17.3	13.8
P/E – I/B/E/S FY1 Foreca	23.2	21.9	22.0	21.9	21.3	21.5	14.2	13.9	14.1	14.1	14.6	12.4
P/E – I/B/E/S FY2 Foreca	19.4	18.7	18.5	18.4	18.3	18.4	12.8	12.7	12.7	12.7	13.0	11.4
Price to Book	4.4	5.2	5.0	4.9	5.2	4.7	3.1	2.9	2.6	2.6	2.3	2.2
Price to Sales	2.8	2.8	2.6	2.6	2.6	2.6	1.5	1.4	1.3	1.3	1.2	1.2
Yield												
% of Companies	44.9	82.0	56.0	35.2	81.8	72.8	89.1	93.0	82.9	68.9	87.1	100.0
Weighted	0.6	1.5	1.3	1.2	1.7	1.2	2.9	3.0	2.9	2.9	2.7	3.9
Debt to Capital	29.1	39.3	38.0	36.8	41.7	34.9	51.9	53.2	52.1	51.3	47.1	56.9
P/E to Growth	1.3	1.3	1.3	1.3	1.3	1.2	1.6	1.6	1.7	1.7	1.6	2.0
Long-term Forecast Gro	19.8	15.8	17.	17.7	14.7	15.9	10.0	9.3	9.4	9.6	10.0	7.5
Historical 5-year EPS Gr	20.1	13.8	14.5	14.6	11.4	17.4	7.6	7.4	6.4	6.4	7.4	5.1
Historical 5-year Sales Gr	17.6	11.6	12.2	12.2	10.4	14.0	4.6	3.7	4.0	4.2	4.5	3.7
Return on Equity	23.4	25.9	23.7	22.8	25.2	25.0	19.7	17.9	16.4	15.8	15.2	16.7
Return on Assets	10.8	10.3	9.8	9.6	10.0	10.9	5.8	4.5	4.3	4.3	4.3	4.0
Average Daily Trading Vol	1,961	2,427	1,904	1,726	2,055	2,223	1,031	1,183	909	822	1,049	1,020

Source: Prudential Securities Inc.

Note: Data are as of June 28, 1996.

Exhibit 8: Performance Statistics — Annual Returns of Large-Cap Style Benchmarks
(Percent Returns)

	Wilshire Indexes						S&P/BARRA Indexes					
	Annual Returns			5-Year Rolling Returns			Annual Returns			5-Year Rolling Returns		
	Growth	Value	Value/Growth Relative	Growth	Value	Value/Growth Relative	Growth	Value	Value/Growth Relative	Growth	Value	Value/Growth Relative
1979	29.5	20.7	-6.8				15.7	21.1	4.7			
1980	41.1	21.9	-13.6				39.4	23.6	-11.3			
1981	-10.9	10.5	24.0				-9.8	0.0	10.9			
1982	14.5	15.9	1.2				22.0	21.0	-0.8			
1983	17.4	25.4	6.8	17.0	18.8	1.5	16.2	28.9	10.9	15.6	18.5	2.5
1984	3.0	19.1	15.7	11.7	18.4	6.0	2.3	10.5	8.0	12.8	16.3	3.2
1985	32.9	30.2	-2.1	10.4	20.0	8.7	33.3	29.7	-2.7	11.8	17.5	5.1
1986	15.5	22.2	5.9	16.3	22.5	5.3	14.5	21.7	6.3	17.2	22.2	4.2
1987	4.7	4.7	0.0	14.2	20.0	5.1	6.5	3.7	-2.6	14.1	18.4	3.8
1988	15.4	22.8	6.4	13.8	19.5	5.0	11.9	21.7	8.7	13.2	17.1	3.4
1989	35.2	25.1	-7.4	20.2	20.7	0.4	36.4	26.1	-7.5	19.9	20.2	0.2
1990	0.3	-7.6	-7.9	13.6	12.7	-0.8	0.2	-6.8	-7.0	13.3	12.5	-0.7
1991	46.6	25.6	-14.3	19.2	13.3	-4.9	38.4	22.6	-11.4	17.7	12.7	-4.2
1992	5.9	14.4	8.0	19.5	15.3	-3.4	5.2	10.6	5.1	17.4	14.1	-2.7
1993	-0.5	13.5	14.1	15.9	13.5	-2.1	1.5	18.5	16.7	15.1	13.5	-1.3
1994	3.0	-4.3	-7.1	9.8	7.6	-2.0	3.0	-0.6	-3.5	8.8	8.3	-0.5
1995	37.9	43.5	4.1	17.0	17.5	0.4	39.8	35.4	-3.1	16.3	16.7	0.3
1979-1995												
Compound Return	16.0	17.2	1.1				15.3	16.3	0.9			
Arithmetic Average	17.2	17.9	1.6				16.3	16.9	1.2			
Std. Deviation	16.6	12.0	10.3				15.5	11.6	8.1			

Exhibit 8 (Continued)

	PSI Indexes						Russell 1000 Indexes					
	Annual Returns			5-Year Rolling Returns			Annual Returns			5-Year Rolling Returns		
	Growth	Value	Value/Growth Relative	Growth	Value	Value/Growth Relative	Growth	Value	Value/Growth Relative	Growth	Value	Value/Growth Relative
1979	23.7	20.0	-3.0				23.9	20.6	-19.3			
1980	44.6	24.1	-14.1				39.6	24.4	-28.4			
1981	-16.0	1.1	20.4				-11.3	1.3	12.8			
1982	10.0	19.8	8.9				20.5	20.0	-17.0			
1983	13.7	26.4	11.1	13.4	17.9	3.9	16.0	28.3	-13.8	16.5	18.5	1.8
1984	-1.2	5.6	6.9	8.5	14.9	6.0	-1.0	10.1	1.0	11.4	16.4	4.5
1985	28.6	30.1	1.2	5.9	16.0	9.5	32.9	31.5	-24.7	10.3	17.7	6.7
1986	7.7	21.0	12.4	11.3	20.3	8.0	15.4	20.0	-13.3	16.2	21.7	4.8
1987	5.7	2.2	-3.3	10.5	16.5	5.5	5.3	0.5	-5.0	13.1	17.5	3.9
1988	9.3	20.7	10.5	9.6	15.5	5.4	11.3	23.2	-7.5	12.2	16.5	3.9
1989	29.6	27.7	-1.5	15.7	19.9	3.7	35.9	25.2	-25.2	19.5	19.6	0.0
1990	-0.9	-5.5	-4.6	9.8	12.5	2.4	-0.3	-8.1	2.4	12.9	11.3	-1.4
1991	44.8	25.9	-13.1	16.5	13.4	-2.7	41.2	24.6	-29.2	17.5	12.2	-4.6
1992	4.3	8.7	4.2	16.2	14.8	-1.2	5.0	13.8	-4.3	17.5	15.0	-2.1
1993	3.4	14.4	10.6	14.9	13.6	-1.2	2.9	18.1	-1.9	15.6	14.0	-1.4
1994	2.5	0.5	-1.9	9.7	8.3	-1.3	2.7	-2.0	-2.8	9.3	8.6	-0.7
1995	33.7	39.8	4.5	16.4	17.1	0.6	37.2	38.3	-27.2	16.5	17.8	1.1
1979-1995												
Compound Return	13.1	16.0	2.5				15.2	16.4	1.0			
Arithmetic Average	14.3	16.6	2.9				16.3	17.0	-12.0			
Std. Deviation	16.6	12.2	8.9				15.9	12.4	12.2			

Value has Outperformed Growth over Time

Since 1979 (the year when many of the major indexes begin) value has done much better, on average, than growth, with a lower standard deviation of annual returns. The difference between value and growth returns is most pronounced in the PSI indexes, in which value outperformed growth by 2.5%, on average. The relative return for the other index families is about 1%. There can be substantial differences in returns each year, between growth and value and within each style category. In 1982, for example, the PSI large-cap growth index gained 10% and the S&P/BARRA large-cap growth index rose 22% (keep in mind these indexes purportedly measure the same thing). That same year, the PSI, Russell, and S&P large value indexes all gained around 20%, but the Wilshire large value index was up 15.9%. The spread between best and worst index has been as high as 13.8 percentage points for the growth category (in 1979) and 13.5 percentage points for value (in 1984). When a longer time frame is measured, however, the differences get smaller. For five-year rolling compounded returns, the highest spread was 1988-1992's 2.1 percentage points for growth (PSI was the lowest and Wilshire the highest) and 3.0 percentage points for 1984-1988 in value (Russell had the lowest and Wilshire the highest). Still, for a manager being compared against a benchmark, these return differences can mean losing or keeping a customer.

Most years seem to be dominated by one style or the other. Most recently, 1991 has been dubbed a growth year, while 1992 and 1993 were value years. In 1994, growth was slightly in favor again, but in 1995 the returns were substantially equal for Russell, Wilshire and PSI experienced fairly strong value bias, and S&P's growth index dominated its value index. (Exhibits 1, 2, and 3 present the historical returns on a cumulative and relative basis for the eight indexes.)

One of the most noticeable differences between growth and value indexes is their sector exposures. The growth indexes have over 30% of their weighting in consumer services and consumer staples, while the value indexes tend to fall below 10% in those groups. Among other sector differences are heavier technology and health care weightings for growth and the overabundance of financial, utility, and energy issues for value.

The size of the selection universe and the weighting scheme can also make a difference. In years in which smaller stock fare better than larger ones, the indexes that start with a bigger universe, and therefore have smaller average market capitalizations tend to do better. In addition, value indexes generally have a smaller profile, whereas the growth indexes tend to include more large names (because value indexes generally contain "cheaper" stocks), which is borne out in the larger weighted-average capitalization figures and the greater percentage of the index in names over $10.0 billion in market cap.

Value stocks tend to have lower P/E, price-to-book, and price-to-sales ratios, and lower growth rates as well. Dividend yields for value stocks are higher, as is the percentage of companies that are dividend-paying. Stocks in the growth portfolios tend to be traded more actively; i.e., the weighted-average daily trading volume is substantially higher than it is for of value.

THE MID-CAP STYLE BENCHMARKS

The notion of mid-cap investing existed only in the minds of a few prior to S&P's launch of its index in May 1991. Wilshire was first out of the box with its screen-based portfolios in late 1991, and the PSI style indexes were developed in mid-1993. S&P/BARRA launched its price-to-book sort-based indexes on the S&P MidCap 400 in April 1994. Rounding out the field, Frank Russell Company offered its style indexes in June 1994. Exhibits 9-16 cover the details regarding the three mid-cap indexes for which data are available.

Mid-Cap Growth Shows Sizable Variations

The size profile is one of the more striking differences of the three mid-cap growth indexes. This is one of the major starting points in the choice of style benchmark — choose one that is invested in companies similar in size to the managed portfolio. As a result of the very different selection universes, the weighted-average market value ranges from $3.3 billion for Russell to $1.4 billion for PSI. The mid-cap indexes all have their heaviest concentration in companies from $1.0 to $5.0 billion in capitalization. Russell has 19.1% of its weight in companies between $5.0 and $10.0 billion while S&P has a 10.3% weighting. Yet, PSI and Wilshire have no names over $5.0 billion but significantly more weight in the $500 million to $1.0 billion size category.

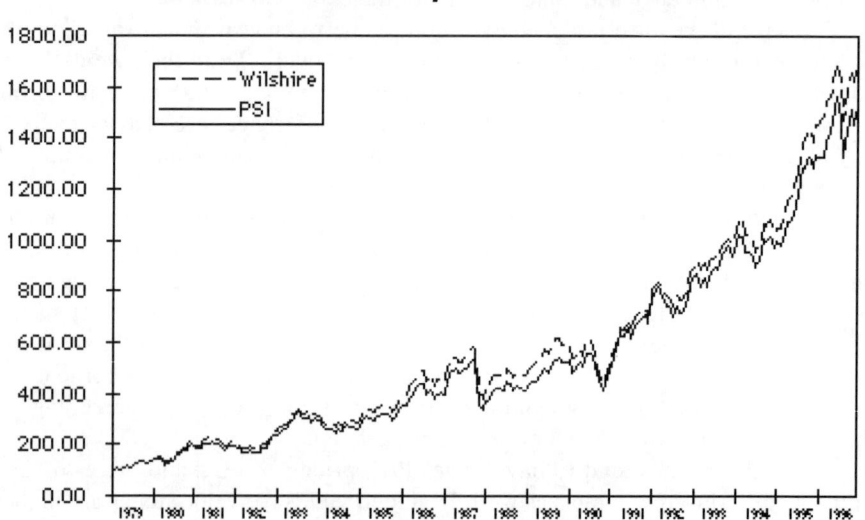

Exhibit 9: Mid-Cap Growth Indexes

Cumulative value of $100 invested.

Chapter 2　37

Exhibit 10: Mid-Cap Value Indexes

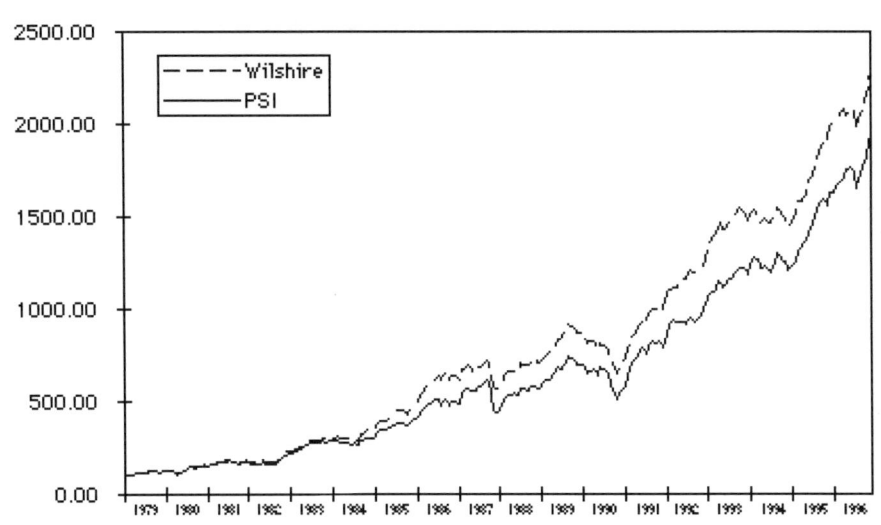

Cumulative value of $100 invested.

Exhibit 11: Mid-Cap Growth Relative to Value

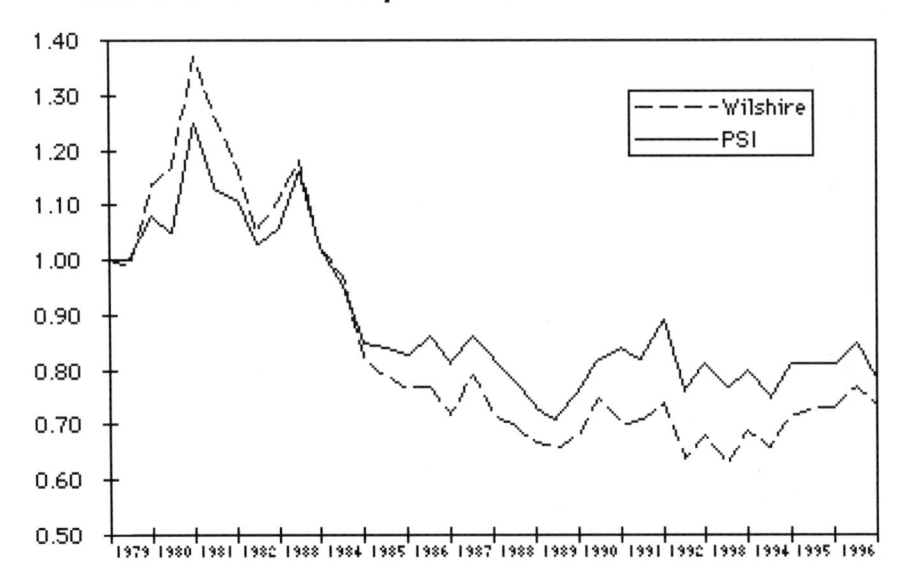

Exhibit 12: Descriptive Characteristics of Mid-Cap Style Benchmarks

	Mid-Cap Growth				Mid-Cap Value			
	PSI	Russell	S&P/BARRA	Wilshire	PSI	Russell	S&P/BARRA	Wilshire
Number of Companies	519	524	147	148	439	508	253	92
First Full Year of Return	1976	1986	1992	1978	1976	1986	1992	1978
Index Rebalancing	Semiannually	Annually	Semiannually/ As Needed	Quarterly	Semiannually	Annually	Semiannually/ As Needed	Quarterly
Weighting Method	Market Cap	Float*	Market Cap	Market Cap	Market Cap	Float*	Market Cap	Market Cap
Returns Calculation	With Income	Principal & With Income	Principal & With Income	With Income	With Income	Principal & With Income	Principal & With Income	With Income
Exchange Distribution								
Nasdaq	50.2%	30.5%	37.8%	37.8%	19.4%	10.7%	16.5%	15.9%
NYSE	46.4	68.2	60.8	59.4	79.4	87.9	81.7	84.1
ASE	3.4	1.4	1.4	2.9	1.2	1.4	1.8	0.0
Total Capitalization	$558.8B	$1.3T	$302.6B	$195.0B	$528.0B	$1.3T	$314.4B	$136.7B
Average Size								
Wtd. Mean	$1.4B	$3.3B	$3.0B	$1.5B	$1.5B	$3.5B	$1.8B	$1.7B
Mean	1.1B	2.4B	2.1B	1.3B	1.2B	2.5B	1.2B	1.5B
Median	897.7M	1.9B	1.8B	1.2B	1.1B	2.0B	1.0B	1.3B
Size Range								
Largest	$2.7B	$6.9B	$7.5B	$2.5B	$2.7B	$24.0B	$4.3B	$2.7B
Smallest	465.0M	660.3M	166.5M	478.8M	464.6M	660.3M	187.0M	706.6M
Concentration								
Largest 10	4.6%	7.1%	18.4%	11.8%	4.9%	6.8%	11.5%	18.1%
Largest 50	20.3	28.5	58.7	50.2	21.9	28.5	41.8	71.0
Largest 100	36.5	47.5	86.9	80.2	39.6	46.9	66.0	100.0

* See section on index construction.
Note: Data are as of June 28, 1996.

Source: Prudential Securities Inc.

Exhibit 13: Size Distribution of Mid-Cap Style Benchmarks (Market-Cap-Weighted)

	Small-Cap Growth				Small-Cap Value			
	PSI	Russell	S&P/BARRA	Wilshire	PSI	Russell	S&P/BARRA	Wilshire
$10.0B & Over	—	—	—	—	—	0.6	—	—
$5.0B-$10.0B	—	19.1	10.3	—	—	21.1	—	—
$1.0B-$5.0B	64.0	78.6	82.0	76.2	73.2	77.6	76.4	82.9
$500M-$1.0B	32.9	2.3	7.2	23.5	25.2	0.7	18.0	17.1
$250M-$500M	3.1	—	0.3	0.3	1.6	—	5.0	—
$100M-$250M	—	—	0.1	—	—	—	0.6	—
Less than $100M	—	—	—	—	—	—	—	—

Note: Data are as of June 28, 1996.

Source: Prudential Securities Inc.

Exhibit 14: Macroeconomic Sector Breakdown of Mid-Cap Style (Market-Cap-Weighted)

	Small-Cap Growth				Small-Cap Value			
	PSI	Russell	S&P/BARRA	Wilshire	PSI	Russell	S&P/BARRA	Wilshire
Basic Industry	6.7	12.8	9.4	11.5	20.1	15.1	14.2	12.9
Business Services	8.4	7.5	10.9	4.9	1.9	3.3	3.9	3.2
Capital Spending	1.6	3.0	2.9	4.2	4.0	4.8	4.4	1.5
Conglomerates	0.5	0.6	0.4	0.4	0.4	—	0.1	—
Consumer Cyclical	2.7	2.4	4.0	6.0	4.7	4.0	0.9	4.3
Consumer Services	20.1	18.4	17.3	18.8	6.5	8.5	7.7	8.4
Consumer Staples	0.8	6.0	2.2	1.4	3.2	2.3	6.4	2.9
Energy	5.2	5.5	5.4	2.6	6.0	9.7	7.5	4.9
Financial Services	4.9	5.8	6.7	7.4	28.3	25.9	17.9	24.6
Health Care	19.0	11.6	13.1	12.6	3.0	2.1	6.3	0.6
Technology	27.6	25.0	25.5	29.1	9.4	4.8	6.7	3.2
Utilities	2.5	1.3	2.3	1.1	12.6	18.7	23.9	33.5
REITs	—	0.3	—	—	—	0.8	—	—

Note: Data are as of June 28, 1996.

Source: Prudential Securities Inc.

The stock exchange distribution has a bias toward NYSE issues in three of the four indexes, with over 60.0% weightings for the S&P/BARRA, and Russell, 59.4% for Wilshire, but only a 46.4% weighting for PSI. This weighting is quite a bit different from the large-cap growth indexes where the NYSE dominates. Nasdaq picks up a bit of weight when moving into the mid-cap universe from the large caps. PSI's growth index is 50.2% Nasdaq issues, while the other index's weightings top 30.0%.

Sector weightings have become more homogenous over time. Technology ranks as the heaviest sector in all four universes with Wilshire having the greatest weight at 29.1% and Russell the lowest at 25.0%. Consumer services has the second biggest representation across all the indexes, while health care ranks third in all but Russell.

Exhibit 15: Fundamental Characteristics of Mid-Cap Style Benchmarks

	Small-Cap Growth				Small-Cap Value			
	PSI	Russell	S&P/BARRA	Wilshire	PSI	Russell	S&P/BARRA	Wilshire
LTM P/E	31.0	29.2	31.2	22.0	13.1	15.4	16.1	12.7
LTM P/E – W/O Neg Ear	28.1	27.4	28.3	25.9	14.0	15.6	17.1	13.4
P/E – I/B/E/S FY2 Foreca	18.0	18.0	17.3	16.9	11.2	12.8	13.4	11.6
Price to Book	4.2	4.4	4.5	4.2	2.1	2.1	2.0	1.7
Price to Sales	2.5	2.3	2.6	2.5	1.2	1.3	1.3	1.1
Yield								
% of Companies	24.1	50.0	49.7	45.9	76.1	80.1	77.9	100.0
Weighted	0.2	0.7	0.6	0.6	2.4	2.8	2.6	4.1
Debt to Capital	28.2	35.0	31.6	27.2	49.8	49.9	44.3	49.8
P/E to Growth	1.7	1.3	.1	1.0	1.6	1.9	1.9	2.7
Long-term Forecast Gro	23.2	20.3	21.0	19.4	10.8	9.8	10.6	7.5
Historical 5-year EPS Gr	23.9	17.3	20.8	25.6	7.3	4.3	5.9	5.4
Historical 5-year Sales Gr	19.9	14.2	17.6	17.6	5.8	4.6	8.0	3.6
Return on Equity	16.1	18.2	18.5	20.7	14.8	13.2	12.9	14.1
Return on Assets	8.2	8.7	9.6	10.7	5.1	4.0	4.5	4.4
Average Daily Trading Vol	392	653	713	387	221	345	193	152

Note: Data are as of June 28, 1996.
Source: Prudential Securities Inc.

Although the valuation criteria (P/E, price-to-book, and price-to-sales) for the growth indexes are comparable, there are some differences in fundamentals worth mentioning. The more industrial orientation of the Russell index creates a higher debt-to-capital ratio as these companies tend to have more leverage than health care and technology names. Additionally, this index has a much higher percentage of companies that are dividend paying and has a higher yield as well. The net result of the growth-oriented screens are higher historical growth rates for the PSI and Wilshire indexes.

Mid-Cap Value Shows More Consistency

The mid-cap value indexes show a bit more consistency between them in terms of exchange distribution. The lion's share of the companies trade on the NYSE, but the percentages range from 79.4% for PSI to 87.9% for Russell. Nasdaq has the remainder of the companies, with the AMEX accounting for less than 2.0% (actually 0% in the case of the Wilshire Value index). The impact of different selection universes does show up in the capitalization characteristics. At the low end, PSI has a weighted average market cap of $1.5 billion, while Russell is at the other end of the spectrum with a $3.5 billion weighted average.

In terms of size distribution, all of the mid-cap value indexes have their heaviest representation in names between $1.0 billion and $5.0 billion in market cap. However, while PSI has over 20.0% in names under $1.0 billion, Russell has as much in names over $5.0 billion.

Chapter 2   41

Exhibit 16: Annual Returns of Mid-Cap Style Benchmarks
(Percent Returns)

	Wilshire Indexes						S&P/BARRA					
	Annual Returns			5-Year Rolling Returns			Annual Returns			5-Year Rolling Returns		
	Growth	Value	Value/Growth Relative	Growth	Value	Value/Growth Relative	Growth	Value	Value/Growth Relative	Growth	Value	Value/Growth Relative
1979	43.8	25.7	-12.6									
1980	43.6	20.1	-16.4									
1981	0.8	17.7	16.8									
1982	23.2	30.5	5.9									
1983	22.0	32.7	8.8	25.6	25.2	-0.3						
1984	-4.6	18.3	24.0	15.7	23.7	6.9						
1985	30.2	38.7	6.5	13.5	27.3	12.2						
1986	14.8	23.2	7.3	16.5	28.5	10.3						
1987	-5.4	-5.9	-0.5	10.5	20.3	8.9						
1988	15.1	23.0	6.9	9.2	18.5	8.5						
1989	22.0	21.5	-0.4	14.7	19.2	3.9						
1990	-12.9	-16.4	-4.0	5.8	7.7	1.7						
1991	55.4	48.5	-4.4	12.4	11.8	-0.6						
1992	12.3	22.6	9.2	16.4	17.9	1.3	6.9	16.0	8.5			
1993	15.8	12.8	-2.6	16.5	15.8	-0.6	13.7	13.4	-0.2			
1994	0.9	-2.7	-3.6	12.2	10.8	-1.2	-7.0	-0.6	6.9			
1995	39.0	37.2	-1.3	23.2	22.3	-0.7	27.3	37.0	7.7			
	10.2	3.8										
1979-1995												
Compound Return		19.3	1.9				2.2	3.5	1.3			
Arithmetic Average	208.1	20.4	2.3				10.2	16.5	5.7			
Std. Deviation	15.7	16.0	9.7				12.4	13.5	3.5			

42 Understanding the Differences and Similarities of Equity Style Indexes

Exhibit 16 (Continued)

	PSI Indexes						Russell 1000 Indexes						
	Annual Returns			5-Year Rolling Returns			Annual Returns			5-Year Rolling Returns			
	Growth	Value	Value/Growth Relative	Growth	Value	Value/Growth Relative	Growth	Value	Value/Growth Relative	Growth	Value	Value/Growth Relative
1979	39.4	28.6	-7.7									
1980	39.3	21.1	-13.1									
1981	-0.7	11.7	12.5									
1982	22.0	27.3	4.3									
1983	26.1	31.5	4.3	24.3	23.8	-0.4						
1984	-9.3	8.0	19.1	14.1	19.6	4.8						
1985	30.6	34.7	3.1	12.6	22.2	8.5						
1986	12.1	14.6	2.2	15.4	22.8	6.4	17.6	17.9	-14.9			
1987	-4.9	-5.6	-0.7	9.8	15.7	5.4	2.8	-2.2	-2.7			
1988	13.5	26.7	11.6	7.5	14.8	6.8	12.9	24.6	-11.4			
1989	24.7	20.5	-3.4	14.5	17.3	2.5	31.5	22.7	-23.9			
1990	-7.3	-16.6	-10.0	6.9	6.6	-0.3	-5.1	-16.1	5.4	16.3	11.6	-4.0
1991	56.4	47.2	-5.9	14.3	12.1	-1.9	47.0	37.9	-32.0	17.3	14.5	-2.1
1992	11.7	23.0	10.1	18.0	18.2	0.1	8.7	15.6	-10.1	17.3	14.8	-2.1
1993	14.8	16.6	1.6	18.3	16.2	-1.8	11.2	15.6	-10.1	10.5	9.8	-0.7
1994	0.7	-0.4	-1.1	13.4	11.9	-1.3	-2.2	-2.1	2.2	18.4	20.7	1.9
1995	32.8	32.8	0.0	21.8	22.8	0.8	34.0	34.9	-25.4			
1979-1995							10.4	7.6				
Compound Return	16.4	17.8	1.3				8.4	8.2	-0.3			
Arithmetic Average	17.8	18.9	1.6				15.8	15.5	-12.1			
Std. Deviation	18.1	15.5	8.2				16.0	16.4	11.6			

The greatest discrepancies in sector weightings are in the utilities and basic industry areas. Wilshire's yield requirement generates a 33.5% weighting for the utility sector, and the S&P 400 MidCap index's heavy exposure to utilities relative to other mid-cap indexes causes these issues to fall into its value index giving it a 23.9% exposure. PSI has the smallest utility weighting at 12.6%. PSI also has the heaviest weighting in basic industry (20.1%) because the normalized P/E screen is specifically designed to allow cyclical companies to remain in value regardless of the stage of the business cycle. Wilshire shows the lightest weighting in this sector at 12.9%.

The price-to-book based universes show higher valuations on just about every measure when compared to those created by screens. Because no companies are excluded from the price/book based style indexes, they are apt to contain stocks with higher valuations when the market is moving strongly and these names hover around the breakpoint, whereas PSI and Wilshire's screens would find some of these names too expensive causing them to fall into the orphan universes rather that either growth or value. From a valuation perspective, the S&P/BARRA index has the highest P/E ratios of the three value indexes on both a trailing and a forecast basis. Wilshire, with its yield requirement, has 100% dividend-payers and the highest yield of the four indexes at 4.1%. In terms of fundamentals, there is little difference in either the debt/capital, historical growth rates or the return on equity/asset values.

What Distinguishes Mid-Cap Growth from Mid-Cap Value?

Mid-cap value is dominated by NYSE companies, with as much as 87.9% trading on this exchange. In mid-cap growth, Nasdaq takes on a bigger role, accounting for 52.2% of the PSI portfolio at the high end and a more modest 30.5% of the Russell universe.

In three of the four indexes, value includes more large issues than growth. This shows up in the capitalization characteristics and in the size distribution as well. The mean market value for the Wilshire mid-cap value index is $1.7 billion, compared to $1.5 billion for the growth index. Additionally, 82.9% of its value index is made up of companies over $1.0 billion in size, compared to 76.2% for growth.

Over the past ten years, as well as the longer term, mid-cap value has beaten mid-cap growth in two of three indexes with enough return history. On a ten-year annualized basis, value is up 14.4%, according to PSI, compared to 14.1% for growth. This can at least in part be explained by the economic environment of generally falling interest rates between 1984 and 1993. The heavy utility and financial weighting in value makes it more interest sensitive and likely to benefit more than growth from declining interest rates. The long-term relative performance could reverse during a period when interest rates climb steadily. Additionally, growth tends to be more volatile, as indicated by greater standard deviation and higher beta. Of course there are times when growth shines, most recently in 1991 when two of the growth indexes available were up over 55.0%.

There is no overlap in the sectors with the heaviest representation in the growth and value universes. Technology, consumer services, and health care are tops in the growth indexes with a combined weighting that ranges from 55.0% in the Russell growth index to 66.7% in the PSI portfolio. Value, on the other hand, is dominated by utilities, financial services, and basic industry. At its most extreme, these groups account for 71.0% of the Wilshire value universe and comprise 56.0% of the S&P index at the low end. Growth and value investors will find no more than 20.0% of the other's top three sectors in their style-appropriate benchmark.

Fundamentally, the value portfolios have lower valuation figures on P/E (trailing or forward), price-to-book, and price-to-sales. Naturally, the growth portfolios have substantially higher historical sales and earnings growth rates and higher ROE and ROA as well. Typically, growth stocks have little debt and finance their expansion through equity offerings and internally-generated growth. This is evident in the much lower debt-to-capital ratios for the growth portfolios. The mid-cap value indexes, like their large-cap counterparts, have many more dividend-paying companies and higher yields than their small-cap counterparts. Growth stocks have substantially higher average daily trading volumes.

THE SMALL-CAP STYLE BENCHMARKS

For a number of years, Wilshire Asset Management was the sole purveyor of growth and value style indexes for the small-cap sector of the market. In mid-1993, both Frank Russell (with style portfolios based on the Russell 2000) and Prudential Securities developed benchmarks. S&P launched their own small-cap index in October 1994 and in conjunction with BARRA started style benchmarks in October of 1996. Exhibits 17-24 describe the characteristics of the small-cap style indexes.

How Do the Growth Portfolios Compare with One Another?

As time passes and the market appreciates, the methodology for creating benchmark universes is having its impact on size characteristics. PSI's methodology of using the 20th to 45th percentiles has kept it in stocks smaller than any of the other indexes. The weighted-average market cap for the PSI Small growth index is $337 million while the S&P/BARRA index has an $821 million weighted average cap. The size distribution also shows the drift of a successful market. Previously, most of the companies in these benchmarks fell well below the $1.0 billion range, but now 29.4% of the S&P/BARRA and 26.8% of the Wilshire indexes are in names between $1.0 billion and $5.0 billion in size.

Exhibit 17: Small-Cap Growth Indexes

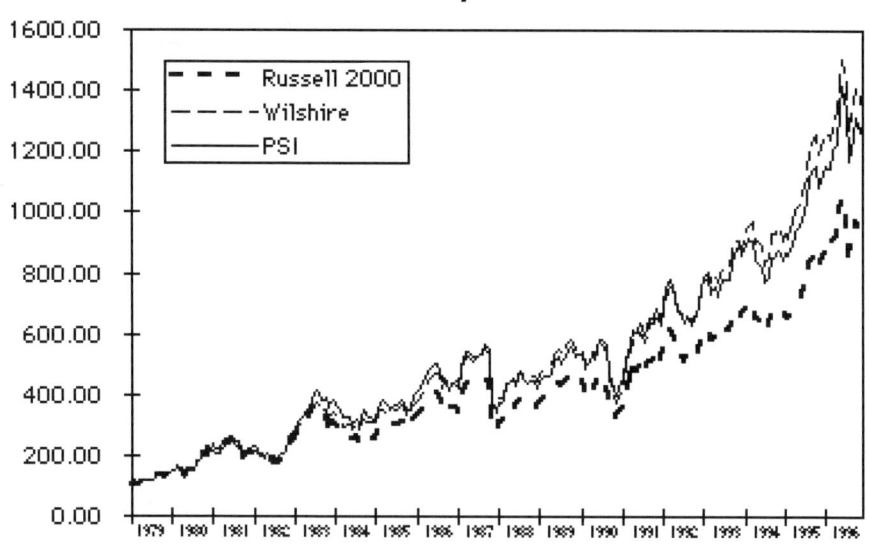

Cumulative value of $100 invested.

Exhibit 18: Small-Cap Value Indexes

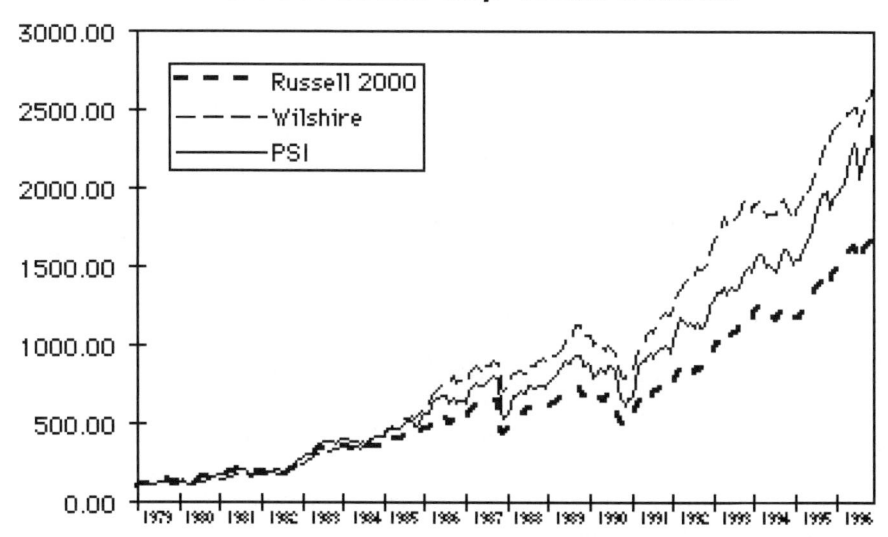

Cumulative value of $100 invested.

Nasdaq is an ever greater percentage of the small-cap growth indexes than in either the large-cap or mid-cap size segments. This exchange's weighting ranges from a low of 45.9% (Wilshire) to 75.6% (PSI).

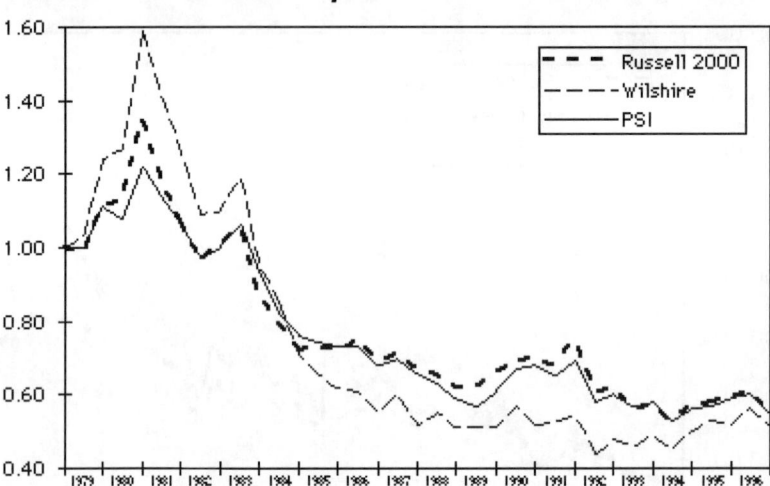

Exhibit 19: Small-Cap Growth Relative to Value

[Line chart showing Russell 2000, Wilshire, and PSI indexes from 1979 to 1996, with values ranging from 0.40 to 1.60]

The screening methodology, with its emphasis on growth rates, tends to weight the indexes more heavily in sectors with high growth (such as technology). PSI is 31.0% technology and Wilshire has a 32.5% representation in the group, while Russell has a 26.3% weighting and S&P/BARRA a 25.4% weighting. Health care shows a distinct difference among the four growth indexes. This sector constitutes over 19.0% of the Russell Growth index, but is only 9.9% of Wilshire's. Consumer services also has a double-digit weighting in all four of the benchmarks.

Fundamentally, a few differences stand out among the small-cap growth indexes. The valuations are all comparable, whether one looks at P/E, price-to-book or price-to-sales, and all have debt-to-capital ratios of over 20.0%. Although the forecast growth rates are fairly consistent across the four indexes, the historical growth rates vary sizably. The S&P/BARRA index has historical EPS growth of 24.1%, while the PSI index's is the lowest at 16.0%. Sales growth for all four indexes is lower than EPS growth, but shows the same wide range, from 18.3% for S&P/BARRA to 12.7% for PSI.

The Value Indexes Have their Differences

In three of the four benchmarks, better than 60% of the stocks in the value style portfolios trade on the NYSE (PSI has a 51.5% weighting). As with the small-cap growth portfolios, the different selection universes create widely differing market cap characteristics. PSI has the lowest weighted average at $347 million while Wilshire has the highest value at $723 million. The largest company in the Russell and S&P portfolios is $1.6 billion in market value, yet PSI's is a much smaller $575 million. The size distribution of the value portfolios shows just as wide a variation. Russell and Wilshire have their heaviest weighting in the $500 million to $1.0 billion range, but the greatest representation for S&P/BARRA and PSI can be found in the $250 million to $500 million category.

Exhibit 20: Descriptive Characteristics of Small-Cap Style Benchmarks

	Small-Cap Growth					Small-Cap Value				
	PSI	Russell 2000	Russell 2500	S&P/BARRA	Wilshire	PSI	Russell 2000	Russell 2500	S&P/BARRA	Wilshire
Number of Companies	811	1,314	1,644	221	255	501	1,314	1,541	379	184
First Full Year of Return	1976	1979	1986	1994	1978	1976	1979	1986	1994	1978
Index Rebalancing	Semi-Annually	Annually	Annually	As Needed	Quarterly	Semi-Annually	Annually	Annually	As Needed	Quarterly
Weighting Method	Market Cap	Float*	Float*	Market Cap	Market Cap	Market Cap	Float*	Float*	Market Cap	Market Cap
Returns Calculation	With Income	Principal & w/Income	Principal & w/Income	Principal & w/Income	With Income	With Income	Principal & w/Income	Principal & w/Income	Principal & w/Income	With Income
Exchange Distribution										
Nasdaq	75.6%	64.9%	51.7%	53.6%	45.9%	45.2%	32.8%	22.5%	36.8%	33.5%
NYSE	20.5	30.7	45.5	43.4	49.6	51.5	64.9	75.4	61.1	66.2
ASE	4.0	4.4	2.8	2.9	4.5	3.2	2.3	2.1	2.1	0.3
Total Capitalization	$230.1B	$520.6B	$1.0T	$127.4B	$161.3B	$144.6B	$504.9B	$1.0T	$131.1B	$107.4B
Average Size										
Wtd. Mean	$337.2M	$507.7M	$1.1B	$821.3M	$772.M	$347.1M	$546.0M	$1.1B	$524.7M	$723.3M
Mean	283.8M	396.2M	621.0M	576.6M	632.5M	288.6M	412.8M	652.8M	346.0M	583.7M
Median	256.7M	328.9M	407.2M	517.8M	570.0M	256.7M	342.4M	427.9M	290.6M	502.0M
Size Range										
Largest	$575.1M	$1.5B	$2.7B	$2.5B	$1.5B	$575.2M	$1.6B	$2.7B	$1.6B	$1.4B
Smallest	122.6M	80.7M	80.7M	56.2M	193.4M	122.6M	80.7M	80.7M	45.0M	246.1M
Concentration										
Largest 10	2.5%	3.1%	3.8%	13.3%	8.3%	3.9%	3.1%	3.6%	9.8%	11.8%
Largest 50	11.8	12.6	15.4	44.0	34.6	18.4	13.8	15.7	31.7	45.8
Largest 100	22.4	22.5	27.0	69.0	58.7	34.3	24.6	27.2	51.2	73.0

* See section on index construction.

Note: Data are as of June 28, 1996.

Source: Prudential Securities Inc.

Exhibit 21: Size Distribution of Small-Cap Style Benchmarks (Percentage of Market Cap)

	Small-Cap Growth					Small-Cap Value				
	PSI	Russell 2000	Russell 2500	S&P/ BARRA	Wilshire	PSI	Russell 2000	Russell 2500	S&P/ BARRA	Wilshire
$10.0B & Over	—	—	—	—	—	—	—	—	—	—
$5.0B-$10.0B	—	—	—	—	—	—	—	—	—	—
$1.0B-$5.0B	—	2.8	48.0	29.4	26.8	—	3.9	51.9	9.8	23.5
$500M-$1.0B	15.1	44.3	25.4	45.3	49.5	16.7	46.9	23.9	33.4	46.2
$250M-$500M	54.3	36.3	18.2	20.8	23.2	53.0	34.0	16.7	36.9	30.0
$100M-$250M	30.7	16.6	8.3	4.0	0.6	30.3	15.1	7.4	18.2	0.2
Less than $100M	—	0.1	0.1	0.4	—	—	0.2	0.1	1.7	—

Note: Data are as of June 28, 1996.
Source: Prudential Securities, Inc.

Exhibit 22: Macroeconomic Sector Breakdown of Small-Cap Style Benchmarks

	Small-Cap Growth					Small-Cap Value				
	PSI	Russell 2000	Russell 2500	S&P/ BARRA	Wilshire	PSI	Russell 2000	Russell 2500	S&P/ BARRA	Wilshire
Basic Industry	8.0	7.1	9.2	10.0	10.9	16.6	14.7	15.3	14.4	11.7
Business Services	6.8	8.3	7.4	9.0	5.5	2.4	3.7	2.6	1.6	3.5
Capital Spending	4.3	4.9	3.9	4.4	5.9	6.9	5.0	4.9	3.8	4.1
Conglomerates	—	0.1	0.5	—	0.5	0.2	0.5	0.3	0.8	—
Consumer Cyclical	2.7	3.2	2.8	3.6	5.0	8.0	4.7	4.1	6.0	2.9
Consumer Services	15.2	15.4	18.2	13.2	14.7	17.2	11.2	10.2	17.9	6.1
Consumer Staples	2.0	2.5	2.1	3.5	1.9	2.5	3.9	2.8	1.7	6.3
Energy	4.0	3.3	4.8	5.5	5.6	2.6	5.8	7.9	7.8	5.5
Financial Services	5.8	5.0	4.4	4.0	7.3	20.0	24.4	24.6	27.5	35.3
Health Care	19.1	19.7	19.3	20.3	9.9	4.6	3.0	3.2	4.8	1.4
Technology	31.0	26.3	24.8	25.4	32.5	14.5	5.0	5.9	8.1	0.6
Utilities	1.0	1.1	0.9	1.0	0.3	4.4	7.6	11.9	6.0	22.0
REITs	—	2.8	1.8	—	—	—	10.5	6.2	—	0.6

Data are as of June 28, 1996.
Source: Prudential Securities Inc.

Sector distribution points up the major deviation in the style portfolios. The low P/E, high-yield screen of Wilshire generates very heavy weightings in the financial services and utilities sectors. As of mid-year 1996, the Wilshire value portfolio had 35.3% in financial services and 22.0% in utilities, or 57.3% of the portfolio. Russell, S&P/BARRA, and PSI also show a heavy financial concentration at 24.4%, 27.5%, and 20.0% respectively, but the utilities weighting for all three is under 8.0%. As a result of its concentration in two sectors, Wilshire has almost no weight in technology at 0.6%, compared with 14.5% for PSI, 8.1% for S&P/BARRA, and 5.0% for Russell. The Russell value portfolio stands apart from the others in its exposure to REITs. Frank Russell is the only index purveyor that includes REITs in its selection universe and the value portfolio has a 10.5% weighting in the sector.

Exhibit 23: Fundamental Characteristics of Small-Cap Style Benchmarks

	Small-Cap Growth					Small-Cap Value				
		Russell		S&P/			Russell		S&P/	
	PSI	2000	2500	BARRA	Wilshire	PSI	2000	2500	BARRA	Wilshire
LTM P/E	39.6	43.5	35.6	36.4	20.5	16.0	17.6	16.2	18.0	13.1
LTM P/E – W/O Neg Ear	27.7	28.0	27.8	28.2	26.0	15.1	17.5	16.5	17.9	13.9
P/E – I/B/E/S FY2 Foreca	17.2	17.4	17.4	18.0	17.0	11.0	11.9	12.1	12.1	11.7
Price to Book	3.9	4.3	4.3	4.3	3.7	2.0	1.8	1.9	1.8	1.7
Price to Sales	2.4	2.5	2.4	2.5	2.1	1.0	1.4	1.3	1.2	1.2
Yield										
% of Companies	15.3	25.0	28.3	28.7	31.1	52.1	61.5	64.2	58.4	98.9
Weighted	0.2	0.4	0.5	0.4	0.3	1.4	2.5	2.7	1.6	3.8
Debt to Capital	22.7	26.5	31.0	28.0	26.7	40.4	43.9	46.4	38.9	44.4
P/E to Growth	0.9	1.2	1.1	1.1	0.9	1.0	1.4	1.7	1.2	2.0
Long-term Forecast Gro	25.5	23.4	22.1	21.0	20.7	13.9	11.5	10.5	13.5	8.3
Historical 5-year EPS Gr	16.0	17.0	20.0	24.1	19.4	7.3	6.0	5.2	13.2	5.0
Historical 5-year Sales Gr	12.7	12.9	14.5	18.3	16.2	7.5	7.2	6.1	9.4	4.6
Return on Equity	13.0	13.9	15.2	15.6	19.6	12.7	10.5	11.8	11.0	13.0
Return on Assets	6.9	7.3	7.5	8.5	10.2	5.3	3.7	3.9	3.8	3.8
Average Daily Trading Vol	166	189	305	239	253	117	91	156	116	63

Data are as of June 28, 1996.

Source: Prudential Securities Inc.

Wilshire's yield requirement shows up in the 98.9% dividend-paying companies compared about 60% for Russell and S&P/BARRA. In addition, the yield is more than twice as high as two of the other portfolios at 3.6%. The S&P/BARRA and Russell indexes, which are developed with a price/book sort have higher P/E valuations across the board. Presumably, the low P/E screens used by PSI and Wilshire eliminate some of the higher valuation companies that might find their way into the other portfolios at the very high end of their break points. Although the historical growth rates aren't consistent across the four portfolios — the S&P/BARRA historical EPS growth is 13.2% compared to 5.0% for Wilshire — the ROE and ROA are much closer. The values for these fundamental characteristics range from 11.0% to 13.0% for ROE and 3.8% to 5.3% for ROE.

There are Few Similarities Between Small-Cap Growth and Value

In the small-caps, the growth portfolios have a higher percentage of companies that trade on Nasdaq, while value portfolios are more heavily weighted with NYSE issues. In the case of sectors, the small-cap growth portfolios have heavy weightings in consumer services, health care, and technology, with negligible weights in utilities. The value portfolios are dominated by financial services, utilities, and consumer services issues, with very low health care weightings.

Exhibit 24: Annual Returns of Small-Cap Style Benchmarks
(Percent Returns)

	PSI Indexes						Russell 2000 Indexes						
	Annual Returns			5-Year Rolling Returns			Annual Returns			5-Year Rolling Returns			
	Growth	Value	Value/Growth Relative	Growth	Value	Value/Growth Relative	Growth	Value	Value/Growth Relative	Growth	Value	Value/Growth Relative
1979	49.1	34.6	−9.7									
1980	43.0	29.5	−9.4									
1981	2.1	17.9	15.5									
1982	30.3	37.9	5.8									
1983	30.0	40.0	7.7	29.8	31.7	1.5						
1984	−13.0	6.3	22.2	16.6	25.7	7.8						
1985	28.9	34.1	4.0	14.2	26.5	10.8						
1986	3.3	11.6	8.0	14.4	25.2	9.4						
1987	−11.7	−9.9	2.0	5.9	14.9	8.6	−15.8	2.3	21.5			
1988	17.4	32.2	12.6	3.7	13.6	9.6	31.0	31.1	0.1			
1989	21.1	16.3	−4.0	10.8	15.7	4.4	3.6	7.4	3.7			
1990	−14.3	−22.3	−9.3	2.1	3.7	1.6	−10.5	−7.1	3.8			
1991	54.1	51.0	−2.0	10.6	10.2	−0.4	20.4	29.5	7.6			
1992	9.7	25.6	14.5	15.5	17.8	1.9	20.2	12.4	−6.5	0.5	6.0	5.5
1993	14.4	18.2	3.3	15.0	15.2	0.2	−17.4	−21.8	−5.3	4.3	11.6	7.1
1994	−2.6	1.4	4.1	10.1	12.0	1.8	51.2	41.7	−6.3	11.9	13.7	1.6
1995	33.0	27.4	−4.2	20.2	23.7	2.9	7.8	29.1	19.8	2.1	2.6	0.5
		13.5					13.4	23.8	9.2	10.1	8.4	−1.5
							−2.4	−1.6	0.8	14.3	15.8	1.3
							31.0	25.8	−4.0	12.9	14.8	1.6
										8.3	11.7	3.2
										18.8	22.9	3.5
1979–1995												
Compound Return	15.5	19.2	3.2				6.4	8.9	2.3			
Arithmetic Average	17.3	20.7	3.6				11.0	14.4	ERR			
Std. Deviation	20.9	18.3	9.1				20.1	18.1	ERR			

Exhibit 24 (Continued)

		Wilshire Indexes				
	Annual Returns			5-Year Rolling Returns		
	Growth	Value	Value/Growth Relative	Growth	Value	Value/Growth Relative
1979	51.8	22.8	−19.1			
1980	52.8	18.6	−22.4			
1981	−1.2	25.0	26.6			
1982	19.2	35.9	14.0			
1983	22.6	42.3	16.1	27.3	28.6	1.0
1984	−9.0	22.1	34.2	14.9	28.5	11.8
1985	26.5	43.9	13.8	10.7	33.5	20.7
1986	10.1	23.5	12.1	13.1	33.2	17.8
1987	−8.6	−3.1	6.1	7.2	24.5	16.1
1988	19.3	22.4	2.6	6.7	20.8	13.3
1989	18.9	18.1	−0.7	12.5	20.0	6.6
1990	−19.0	−19.4	−0.5	2.9	6.9	3.8
1991	56.8	49.0	−5.0	2.9	6.9	3.8
1992	13.2	29.2	14.2	15.3	17.5	1.9
1993	18.0	14.1	−3.3	15.1	15.9	0.7
1994	0.5	−2.0	−2.5	11.3	1.7	0.4
1995	35.2	29.8	−4.0	23.3	22.8	−0.4
1979-1995						
Compound Return	16.1	20.6	3.9			
Arithmetic Average	18.0	21.9	4.8			
Std. Deviation	21.4	17.1	14.2			

The past ten years have been kinder to value than to growth in all of the small-cap style universes. The value indexes' annualized average returns range from 12.3% to 14.6%, while the growth indexes have returned between 10.1% and 12.6%. Taking an even longer look back in time we can see a similar performance spread between the two styles. While the betas of the value indexes are quite a bit lower than those of growth, it is interesting to note that standard deviations of return have been more comparable. Whereas some years are particularly good for value (1981, 1984, 1992, for example), there have been few years in which a provider's small-growth index has handily beaten the small-value index — 1979, 1980, and 1991 for instance.

The polarization of sector exposures exists in the small-cap style universes as it does in the mid-cap indexes, but is less extreme. Technology and health care rank in the top three sectors in all four small-cap growth indexes, while financial services is clearly one of the significant sectors in value. But, unlike the mid-cap indexes, consumer services can be found with as heavy a weighting in a growth index as it has in a value index. Technology, health care, and consumer services have a combined weighting which ranges from 57.1% in Wilshire to 65.3% of PSI, while financial services and basic industry comprise as little as 13.2% of the growth benchmarks. However, these three sectors range from 41.0% of the PSI value index to 69.0% of the Wilshire index. On the other hand, investors will find weightings in technology, health care, and consumer services that range from Wilshire's low of 8.1% to PSI's high of 36.3%.

From a valuation point of view, the small-cap growth indexes trade at higher multiples than the value indexes. In fact, the price-to-book ratios for growth are almost twice those of value. Where value stands out is in higher debt-to-capital ratios, dividend yields, and number of dividend-payers. Of little surprise is the fact that the historical and projected growth rates for the small-cap growth indexes are much higher than those of value. Historical growth rates show dramatic differences. For instance, the Wilshire value index's historical earnings growth rate is 5.0%, compared to 19.4% for its growth index. Small-cap value also has lower ROEs and ROAs.

CONCLUSION

The concept termed "equity style" has now become widely accepted in investment management. This chapter has provided a unified treatment of the major equity style indexes, emphasizing their differences and similarities. The clear message here is that, while there are important similarities, there are also important differences from one index to another. Those differences can have a significant impact on investment management and research.

APPENDIX: METHODOLOGY USED TO CALCULATE FUNDAMENTAL CHARACTERISTICS

The calculation of fundamental characteristics for a benchmark can be an onerous task. Many methodologies can be employed and many different measures calculated. Suppliers constantly try to provide the most accurate and representative calculations.

One of the main problems in calculating benchmark fundamentals has to do with exclusion of outliers. Outliers are numbers that are so different from the rest of the numbers that they have a distorting effect on measures of central tendency. The meaningfulness of such excessively high or low numbers is questionable. In addition, outliers are often extreme because calculation of that particular ratio is considered inappropriate because of a particular circumstance, occurrence, or accounting peculiarity. For example, many people exclude all negative earnings in the calculation of P/E or exclude heavily leveraged financial companies when calculating debt-to-capital.

We chose to use the same interquartile range methodology adopted by the Frank Russell Company in excluding outliers. The advantages of this methodology are that:

1. It does not automatically assume data at the top and bottom of the distribution are outliers.
2. It can be applied consistently as a quantitative method for all fundamental characteristics.

Calculating the Critical Points

The upper and lower critical points — that is, the highest and lowest value to be included in the calculation are calculated for a global universe of stocks that includes both small — and large-cap stocks. The Frank Russell Company uses the Russell 3000 as its universe, while we use the combined PSI small-cap and large-cap universes.

The Interquartile Range

The interquartile range, or IQR, is calculated by subtracting the value of the fundamental characteristic of the company at the 75th percentile from the value of the fundamental characteristic of the company at the 25th percentile.

The Critical Values We multiply the IQR by three, then add it to the value of the 75th percentile and subtract it from the value of the 25th percentile to form the critical values. All values higher than the upper critical value and lower than the bottom critical value are excluded as outliers.

Notes On Fundamental Data Fundamental data are taken from Compustat, I/B/E/S, or Value Line via Factset as of December 31, 1993. We use latest 12-month earnings for LTM P/E and I/B/E/S fiscal-year 1 estimates for forecast EPS. For P/E to growth, we use P/E with forecast EPS and I/B/E/S long-term growth estimates. Return-on-equity and return-on-assets are for the last 12 months. Debt to capital uses long-term debt, and the average daily volume is for the 40 days prior to June 28, 1996.

Averages We recommend the harmonic average for ratios of "something" per "something else." A harmonic average is also best for ratios for which a low number is considered good but a negative number is considered bad or not meaningful (for example, P/E, P/E to growth, and price-to-book). Our harmonic average is a weighted harmonic average.

Chapter 3

Return-Based Style Analysis

Steve Hardy
President
Zephyr Associates, Inc.

THE THEORY

William F. Sharpe, a 1990 Nobel Prize winner in economic science, developed the theory of return-based style analysis.[1] This theory asserts that a manager's investment style, both past and present, can be determined by comparing the manager's returns to the returns of a number of selected indexes. The beauty of the theory is its simplicity, speed, and accuracy. There is no need to look at the individual holdings in a manager's portfolio to determine investment style; information can be obtained simply by analyzing the manager's monthly or quarterly returns.

An example of the theory in its simplest form will probably be helpful. Assume you are given a manager's quarterly returns from January 1, 1983 to March 31, 1994. Your job is to determine what kind of investment manager generated these returns. At this point, you don't know whether this is a stock, bond, or real estate manager, or whether the manager is dealing with international or domestic securities. In fact, you know absolutely nothing about the "mystery manager."

The only other information you have at your disposal is returns for a number of generic indexes that measure various asset classes. These indexes include the Morgan Stanley EAFE Index, the Lehman Brothers Government and Corporate Bond Index, the S&P 500 Index, and four Russell Style Indexes (the

---

[1] William F. Sharpe, "Determining a Fund's Effective Asset Mix," *Investment Management Review* (November/December 1988), pp. 59-69.

All of the computations and graphs in this chapter were generated by the Zephyr Associates, Inc. Style Advisor software program.

Russell 1000 Large Growth, the Russell 1000 Large Value, the Russell 2000 Small Growth, and the Russell 2000 Small Value).

First, you compare the pattern of the manager's returns to the pattern of the Lehman Corporate Bond Index. To compare these returns statistically, you calculate the R^2, which is the squared correlation between the manager and the index. You notice first that the R^2 of the manager's returns to the bond index is a very low 3.9%. You repeat the calculation with the other asset class indexes, and find R^2s with EAFE, 19.9%, and S&P 500, 82.6%. With an R^2 of 82.6% for the S&P 500, it should be obvious that the manager is a domestic equity manager.

You next want to know what particular investment style the manager follows. Although there are many different ideas of what constitutes style, you limit consideration of domestic equity styles to two general categories — value versus growth, and small versus large. You define four investment styles: large-capitalization value, large-capitalization growth, small-capitalization value, and small-capitalization growth. To represent these styles, you can use Russell's Style Indexes.

You can now compare the manager's returns to the returns of the four Russell Style Indexes in the same way you compared them to asset class returns. The resulting R^2s are as follows:

Style Index	R^2 to Manager (%)
Large Growth	82.4
Large Value	78.2
Small Growth	91.7
Small Value	84.4

You can now see that the manager tracks the Russell Small Cap Growth Index most closely, with a 91.7% R^2. It is safe to say that the manager is a small-cap growth domestic equity manager.

When we talk about looking at a manager's pattern of returns, we don't necessarily mean performance in terms of the manager's total returns compared to the total returns of the index. Managers may wonder, "If I'm a growth manager, and growth underperformed value during a given period, but I did well during that period, then would I be mistaken for a value manager?" The answer to that question is *no*.

It makes no difference how well a manager performs over a particular period, since it is the month-to-month, or quarter-to-quarter pattern of those returns that identifies the manager's style. It is this pattern that Professor Sharpe refers to as a "manager's tracks in the sand."

To demonstrate that performance in terms of annualized returns has nothing to do with the R^2, Exhibit 1 plots returns for the mystery manager and the four Russell Style Indexes. Exhibit 2 compares annualized returns for each index along with the respective R^2s to the mystery manager. It is important to note that the index with the highest R^2, Small Growth, is the index that is the farthest from the mystery manager in terms of the annualized returns for this period.

Exhibit 1: Performance of Mystery Manager versus Russell Style Indexes In-Sample Simulation

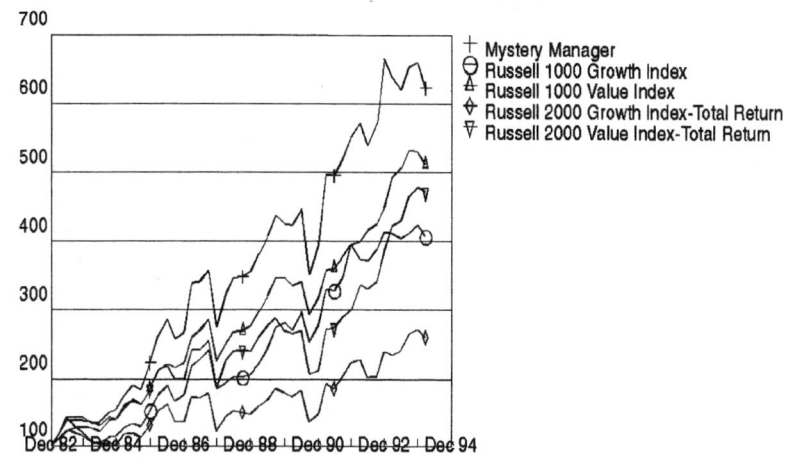

Legend:
+ Mystery Manager
○ Russell 1000 Growth Index
△ Russell 1000 Value Index
◇ Russell 2000 Growth Index-Total Return
▽ Russell 2000 Value Index-Total Return

Exhibit 2: Return Comparison

Index/Manager	R^2 (%)	Annualized Returns (%)
Mystery Manager	100.00	17.67
Large Growth	82.40	13.31
Large Value	78.20	15.65
Small Growth	91.70	8.86
Small Value	84.04	14.78

Very few managers can be classified as pure small-cap growth, large-cap value, and so on. Rather, managers tend to be shades of styles. To determine what shades of the four styles a manager may be, we apply a more sophisticated procedure. Using a quadratic optimizer, we find what *combination* of style indexes gives us the highest tracking or R^2 to the manager's returns.

When we do this with the mystery manager, we find the optimum combination of style indexes to be 19.5% Large Growth, 26.8% Small Value, 53.6% Small Growth, and nothing in Large Value. This combination of Russell Style Indexes has an R^2 of 94.8% to the manager's returns. The higher we can get the R^2, the more information we can get about the manager's style. The information we can't get (the difference between 100% and 94.8%) can best be attributed to the manager's stock selection.

Exhibit 3 is a style chart we have developed that allows us to represent a manager's style graphically. The style chart measures value-to-growth on the horizontal axis and size on the vertical axis. The four corners are represented by the four Russell Style Indexes. The upper left-hand corner is the Large Value Index;

the upper right-hand corner is the Large Growth Index; the lower right-hand corner is the Small Growth Index; and the lower left-hand corner is the Small Value Index. These reference points allow us to determine a manager's style by seeing where the manager's style point falls on the chart. The mystery manager's style point falls in the small-cap growth quadrant.

So far, we have taken 11 years of quarterly returns to calculate one style point for the entire period. Next, we would like to know how consistent this manager's style has been, and how much it has changed over this period of time. To do this, we will look at a series of style points generated over a number of rolling 12-quarter periods (if we were using monthly data, we would use a series of rolling 36-month periods).

We calculate our first style point by calculating the R^2 on the first 12 quarters of data. We then move that 12-quarter window each quarter, thereby calculating one style point for each of these periods until we have calculated the most recent style point, which would be based on the most recent 12 quarters of data. This generates 34 style points on the manager style chart (see Exhibit 4). Each style point is represented by a cross. The crosses get larger in size as time passes. So, the smaller crosses represent the manager's earlier style, and the larger crosses represent the more recent style.

In this example, we can see that the mystery manager's earliest style was large growth. The style then began to move to small-/medium-cap value and, more recently (over the past four to five years), the style has consistently remained small-cap growth. This analysis took only a few seconds on a 486 laptop computer. Imagine how much time it would take if we were to analyze the holdings in each of these portfolios for each of these 34 quarters!

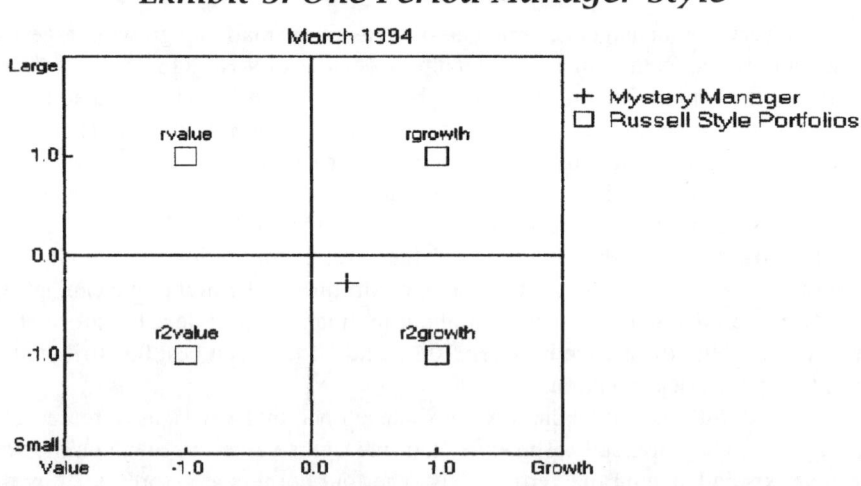

Exhibit 3: One-Period Manager Style

March 1994

Exhibit 4: Multi-Period Manager Style
December 1985 - March 1994

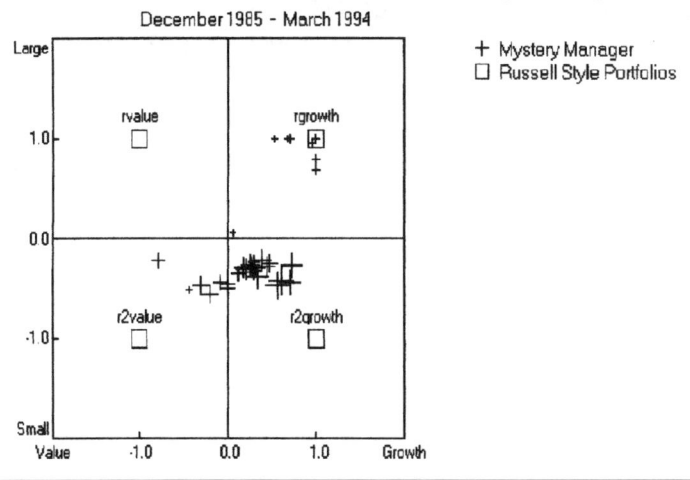

USING STYLE INDEXES TO BUILD CUSTOMIZED BENCHMARKS

I have explained how we can identify a manager's style in terms of percentages of style indexes. We can also use those same indexes and percentages to construct a customized benchmark. If we want to construct one benchmark for the manager over the entire time frame, that benchmark would be 19% Large Growth, 27% Small Value, and 54% Small Growth. We can build such a composite style benchmark using the Russell indexes. Exhibit 5 shows the performance of such a benchmark compared to the manager's actual returns. For comparison's sake, we also include the returns for the S&P 500 Total Return Index.

There are several problems with this benchmark. First of all, it does not in any way reflect how the manager's style has changed over time. If the manager today is much larger or has changed investment philosophies, or if there has been a turnover in portfolio managers, that manager's style may be much different today from ten years ago. In this case, building a benchmark for today that includes ten-year-old data doesn't make sense. On the other hand, if we simply look at what the manager has done over the last six months or the year, we may be looking at too short a period of time to determine style accurately. We believe that the most reasonable window to use when building a manager's benchmark is about three years, so with this in mind I use a 12-quarter window to build a benchmark for the mystery manager.

There is one other problem with a static ten-year benchmark: It is created after the fact. A benchmark, by definition, should be specified in advance of the period in which it is to be used to judge the manager's performance. To accomplish this, we build our benchmark "out-of-sample" by taking the first 12 quarters of returns to determine what the benchmark will be for the next, or the 13th quarter. This is done at the beginning of the 13th quarter and not at the end. In this way, we are determining the benchmark in advance and predicting what the manager's style will be on the basis of the past three years. Our out-of-sample benchmark has the following characteristics:

1. The benchmark is dynamic in that it will always represent the manager's style over the past 12 quarters.
2. The benchmark is specified in advance by being "out-of-sample."
3. The benchmark is investable, since one could invest in passive portfolios designed to replicate the Russell Style Indexes.

Exhibit 6 compares the performance of the out-of-sample benchmark (dashed line) to the actual performance of the mystery manager (line with crosses). The shaded area at the bottom of the graph is the cumulative excess return that the manager has achieved over and above the style benchmark. I believe this represents the manager's skill primarily in stock selection within his or her particular style.

One doesn't hire an active manager and pay active management fees for "market-like" returns, because the same results can be achieved for much less money through an index fund. Similarly, one does not hire an active manager to deliver "style index-like" returns, as those too can be realized through investing in passive portfolios designed to replicate style indexes. We do, however, hire active managers and pay active management fees for a manager's skill in stock selection. This skill is seen in a manager's ability to select stocks that provide above-average performance within a particular style. It is this excess return over the style benchmark that warrants active management fees. This excess return can be measured only by developing proper style benchmarks. This important fact is revolutionizing the investment management profession.

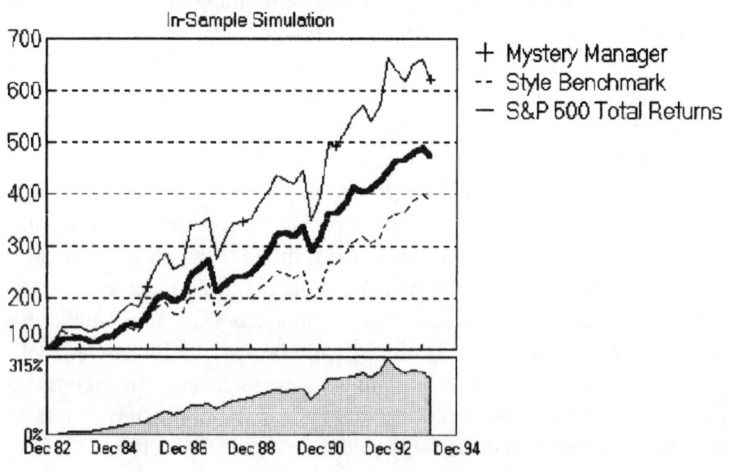

Exhibit 5: In-Sample Performance/ Cumulative Excess Return

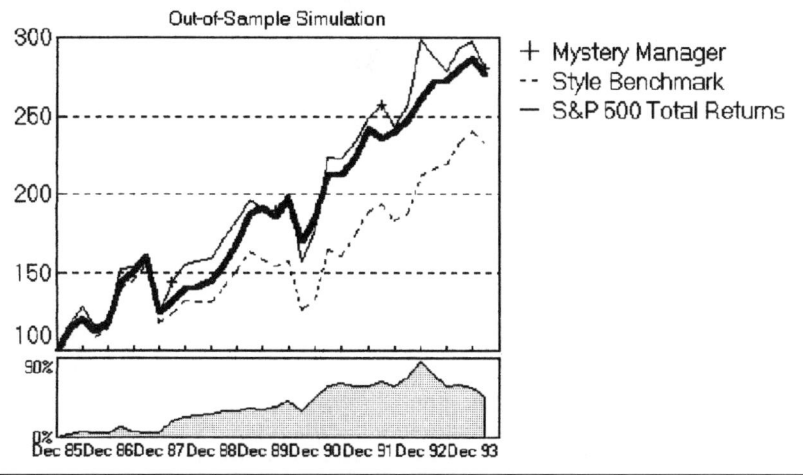

Exhibit 6: Out-of-Sample Performance/Cumulative Excess Return

(Out-of-Sample Simulation chart, Dec 85 – Dec 93, showing Mystery Manager, Style Benchmark, and S&P 500 Total Returns)

One word of caution. Our discussion so far assumes that most managers have a fairly consistent style. If changes in style happen, they are usually fairly subtle and occur gradually. To the extent that this is true, the type of style analysis we have described can work very well. A small minority of managers, however, attempt to get their value added from rotating among sectors and styles, and predicting what particular sector or style will do well in the future. In this case, a manager's skill may lie more in the prediction of style or sector returns than in stock selection. Our style analysis and benchmark creation may not be suitable for analyzing such a manager. For true sector or style rotators, a more appropriate benchmark would be a broad-based benchmark such as the S&P 500 or the Russell 3000.

Our style analysis will spot a true sector rotator very quickly. First, the history of style points will fall all over the style graph, instead of clustering in one area as the mystery manager did. Second, the R^2 calculated to determine the validity of the benchmark will be low, particularly when calculated out-of-sample. In other words, it should be almost impossible to predict the future on the basis of the past because the manager's style is not consistent, and there will also be a very high turnover in the benchmark. The calculation of the benchmark is dynamic, since it is always based on the past 12 quarters of data. The typical annualized turnover in the style benchmark averages about 20% to 30% for a manager whose style is reasonably consistent, while the turnover for a true sector rotator will be much higher (typically over 100%).

I've noticed that a number of managers who call themselves sector rotators still tend to cluster in one particular style. To the degree that the manager's style can be predicted accurately out-of-sample, this approach is still relevant. It boils down to ignoring what managers call themselves and simply looking to see what they have been and are doing. Since most institutional pension plan sponsors hire specialty style managers, this concern over sector rotators should not be great.

TESTING STYLE BENCHMARKS

So far our discussion of this methodology has been anecdotal. I have taken one real manager's returns to demonstrate that we can identify a manager's asset class and investment style. But is this approach valid enough to work on a large number of managers? More specifically:

1. Can we predict a manager's future style by looking at the manager's past style?
2. Can we build customized style benchmarks out-of-sample that capture more information and are better than a broad-based generic benchmark such as the S&P 500?

To answer these questions, I conducted a study using the Mobius Database, which is a commercial database that includes quarterly returns for over 1,200 domestic equity managers. I include only those managers who had quarterly returns for the last eight years, thereby creating a universe of 869 managers. Using a 12-quarter window, I do an out-of-sample style analysis and build a benchmark each quarter for five years. I do this for each manager.

I do not include the performance for the in-sample portion of data, which constitutes the first 12 quarters. Therefore, all of the returns for the benchmarks and style points are created out-of-sample. The first 12 quarters are used to predict what the style and the benchmark will be for the 13th quarter. Then the 12th-quarter window must move one quarter, so that quarters 2 through 13 are used to predict the 14th quarter. This process is continued for each of the 869 managers for a total of 20 predictions per manager. The accuracy of the predictions and the quality of the benchmarks can be determined by looking at the out-of-sample R^2s of the benchmarks to each of the manager's actual returns.

Exhibit 7 shows a scatter diagram for each of the 869 managers. The R^2 of the style benchmark is measured on the horizontal axis and the R^2 of the S&P 500 on the vertical axis. If there were little difference between the style R^2s and the market R^2s, the points on the graph would generally fall along the 45° diagonal line. Note that the great majority of managers fall below the diagonal line, which indicates that the style R^2s are higher than the market R^2s. The average R^2 to the style benchmark for all of the managers is 83.7%; the average R^2 to the S&P 500 is only 76.43%. Since there are a number of extreme outliners that could skew the data, we also looked at the median R^2s, which are 87.25% and 80.61%, respectively, for the style benchmarks and the S&P 500.

In short, this study demonstrates that manager styles can be predicted on the basis of historical returns and that, for manager performance, custom-blended style benchmarks are superior to the S&P 500.

Exhibit 7: Style Benchmarks Versus S&P 500 Out-of-Sample R^2s for 869 Managers

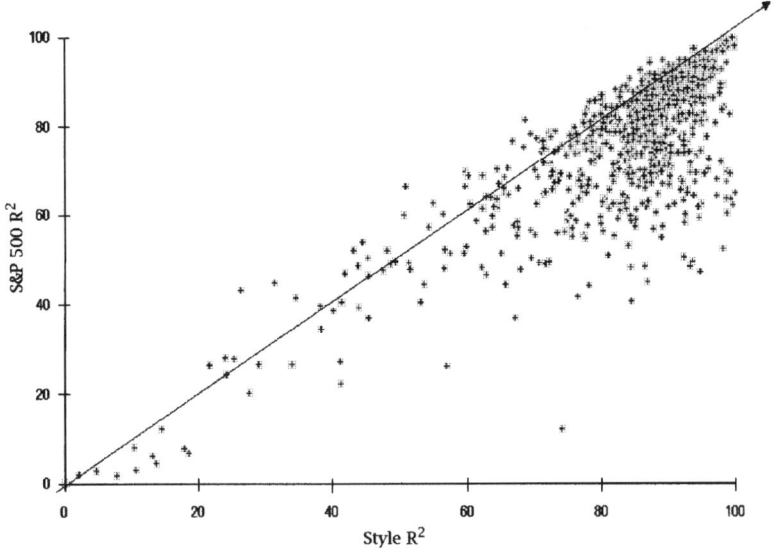

STYLE ANALYSIS FOR THE TOTAL EQUITY FUND

Plan sponsors typically hire a number of managers for each asset class. For large funds, it is not uncommon to find a number of managers for each domestic equity style. When a plan has a dozen or more domestic equity managers, how does one determine the style of the total equity portfolio? This is done by simply aggregating the equity managers' styles in their respective weights and performing a style analysis for the total fund. The style of the total equity fund can then be compared to the style of the plan sponsor's overall benchmark, which is generally a market benchmark such as the S&P 500 or Russell 3000.

Any deviation in style away from the market benchmark represents a "bet" by the plan sponsor. That plan sponsor "bet," whether intentional or not, is determined by the kind or style of managers hired and the amount of money allocated among them.

Exhibit 8 shows the style point for a total domestic equity portfolio (the circle). In this case, the plan sponsor hired only large growth equity managers. The benchmark for the total equity fund is the Russell 3000 (the cross). In this example, the plan sponsor has made a big bet toward large growth. The Style Advisor software program determines the optimum portfolio, in terms of style, that the plan sponsor should invest in to remove this bet. In other words, investing in this portfolio would bring the style point of the plan sponsor's equity portfolio as close to the style point of the benchmark (the Russell 3000) as possible.

Exhibit 8: Total Domestic Equity Portfolio Manager Style
March 1994

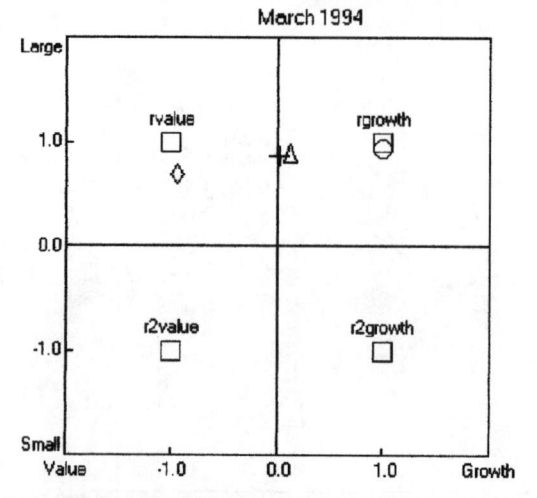

```
Large |                    |
      |   rvalue      rgrowth
  1.0 |     □      +△   ◙
      |     ◊            
  0.0 |--------------------
      |                    
      |   r2value     r2growth
 -1.0 |     □           □
      |                    
Small |_____
Value    -1.0   0.0   1.0   Growth
```

+ Russell 3000 Index-Total Return
○ Total Domestic Equity Portfolio (LG)
▲ 50% in Custom Core
◊ Custom Core Portfolio (50%)
□ Russell Style Portfolios

This new portfolio, which we call a *custom core portfolio* (also referred to as a completeness fund in Chapter 14), is represented by the diamond and is primarily all large value. This is a simple and extreme example, but it does demonstrate how the style of a fund can be analyzed and how a style bias can be removed if desired.

At first blush, it may seem as if the plan sponsor is just converting its total fund into one big index fund. But this is not the case. Remember, each particular active manager is expected to add value by beating a specific benchmark. If the managers in the aggregate are successful in accomplishing this goal, and the plan sponsor makes no significant bet away from the market benchmark, then, by definition, the total equity fund will outperform the market benchmark.

Any style bias represents a risk, and risk represents an opportunity for extra return. Sponsors who feel they have skill in predicting what investment styles will do well in the future can make such bets just as easily as they can move away from them. Whether a plan sponsor wants to make a style bet or remove a style bet, return-based style analysis as described here can be an extremely useful tool.

The style bets of plan sponsors can have dramatic return implications for the total fund. Many plan sponsors who choose not to make such bets do so because they believe that, over time, investment style return differences will even out, and that any good or bad total performance should be attributed to the managers. Although it is true that investment styles tend to smooth out over time, the length of time is beyond the threshold that most plan sponsors use when evaluating managers. This rationale has led to the somewhat common practice of changing managers every four to five years.

Exhibit 9: Annualized Rates of Return(%) for Rolling 4-Year Periods Using Russell Style Indexes

4-Year Period Ending	SmGro	SmVal	LgGro	LgVal	S&P 500
June 83	30.80	28.94	20.15	18.32	19.17
June 84	13.13	23.76	9.73	14.45	13.13
June 85	5.99	19.33	11.55	17.89	15.50
June 86	23.45	31.14	26.94	29.76	28.56
June 87	4.51	15.05	16.41	21.63	20.68
June 88	10.37	16.00	17.57	21.29	19.98
June 89	8.91	13.50	15.91	17.32	17.53
June 90	3.21	5.40	11.72	11.64	13.10
June 91	1.82	3.07	9.55	7.47	8.85
June 92	6.93	8.33	16.51	11.83	14.36
June 93	9.32	11.83	13.62	12.28	12.68
June 94	7.30	14.63	7.94	10.92	8.84
June 95	13.48	18.05	12.69	14.69	13.30
June 96	17.93	18.24	16.05	16.78	16.32

Exhibit 9 shows the annualized returns for the four investment styles measured over rolling four-year periods. Suppose a plan sponsor hired a small-cap growth manager in June 1983, gave that manager four years to perform, and evaluated the performance after June 1987. Let's assume that the small-cap growth manager's annualized performance was 8%. If the plan sponsor compares that to the S&P 500 (which was 20.68%), he might conclude that the manager is a poor performer. Yet Exhibit 9 shows us that the annualized return for small-cap growth during that period was only 4.5%. Hence, the small-cap growth manager who provided 8% annualized return was probably in the top quartile of the universe of small-cap growth managers for the period. Does it make sense to fire a manager simply because that manager's style is out of favor, even though the manager has demonstrated skill within a style?

Let's take another example. Suppose the plan sponsor hires a small value manager in June 1980, and then four years later realizes that the manager has provided an average annual return of 20% during this period. Compared to the S&P 500, with only 13.13% annualized return, this manager looks like a genius. Compared to the Russell Small Value Index (which returned 23.76%), however, the performance looks quite different; the manager beat the market, but did not demonstrate skill within the style. This manager would be a much better candidate for replacement than the small-cap growth manager in the first example.

One of the primary purposes of using appropriate benchmarks to measure managers is to keep plan sponsors from making the mistake that so many have made in the past of firing good managers and hiring or holding onto mediocre or poor-performing managers.

RETURN-BASED ANALYSIS FOR INTERNATIONAL MANAGERS

Doing style analysis on separate country portfolios is no different than doing style analysis on domestic equity funds. Boston International Advisors (BIA) has created style indexes (large value, large growth, small value, small growth) for 21 separate countries and 7 regions. Parametric Portfolio Associates has also created a similar set of international style indexes. Exhibit 10 shows a style analysis done on a Japanese manager using the four BIA Japanese style indexes.

Exhibit 11 shows a similar analysis for a manger that invests only in European stocks. In this example the BIA European style indexes were used.

Doing style analysis for multi-country, multi-regional managers is a bit more complicated. You will want to keep the number of style indexes you use to a minimum and at the same time, see if the managers style is consistent across countries. One way to do this analysis is to have the manager break his/her returns out by country and do a single country analysis for each set of returns. If this is not practical, a second option is to do the analysis using some of the regional style indexes.

Exhibit 12 shows an analysis of a multi-country international manager. For this analysis, we selected the BIA EuroPacific × Japan large value, large growth, small value, and small growth and the four BIA Japanese style indexes. By using separate indexes for Japan, we have avoided the problem that occurs when you use a benchmark such as EAFE, where Japan has such a large weight because of its capitalization. In this case, we will create a benchmark that will be a more normal portfolio for the manager by providing a weighting in Japan that represents the managers historical Japanese weighting. These style benchmarks have a much higher correlation to the managers actual returns than EAFE.

In January 1995 we selected all the international managers in the Mobius database that had at least four years performance. We did the same thing with all the international mutual funds in Morningstar. This left us with 125 diversified international managers from Mobius, and 50 international mutual funds. We did a style analysis and created a style benchmark using the regional and Japanese BIA style indexes as described above. These benchmarks were created out-of-sample. For each manager, we calculated the out-of-sample R^2 to the style benchmark and the R^2 to the EAFE index.

Exhibits 13 and 14 show the scatter diagrams for the managers. The R^2 for each manager to EAFE is on the vertical axis and the R^2 to the style benchmark is on the horizontal axis. If the R^2s were similar most of the dots would fall close to the 45° diagonal line. If the R^2s were higher using EAFE, the dots would fall above the line, and if they were better using the style benchmarks, they would fall below the line as they did. Exhibit 15 shows the median and mean R^2 using the style indexes versus EAFE for both Mobius and Morningstar. The weight of the evidence suggests that the style benchmarks do better than the EAFE index in predicting manager returns.

Chapter 3 67

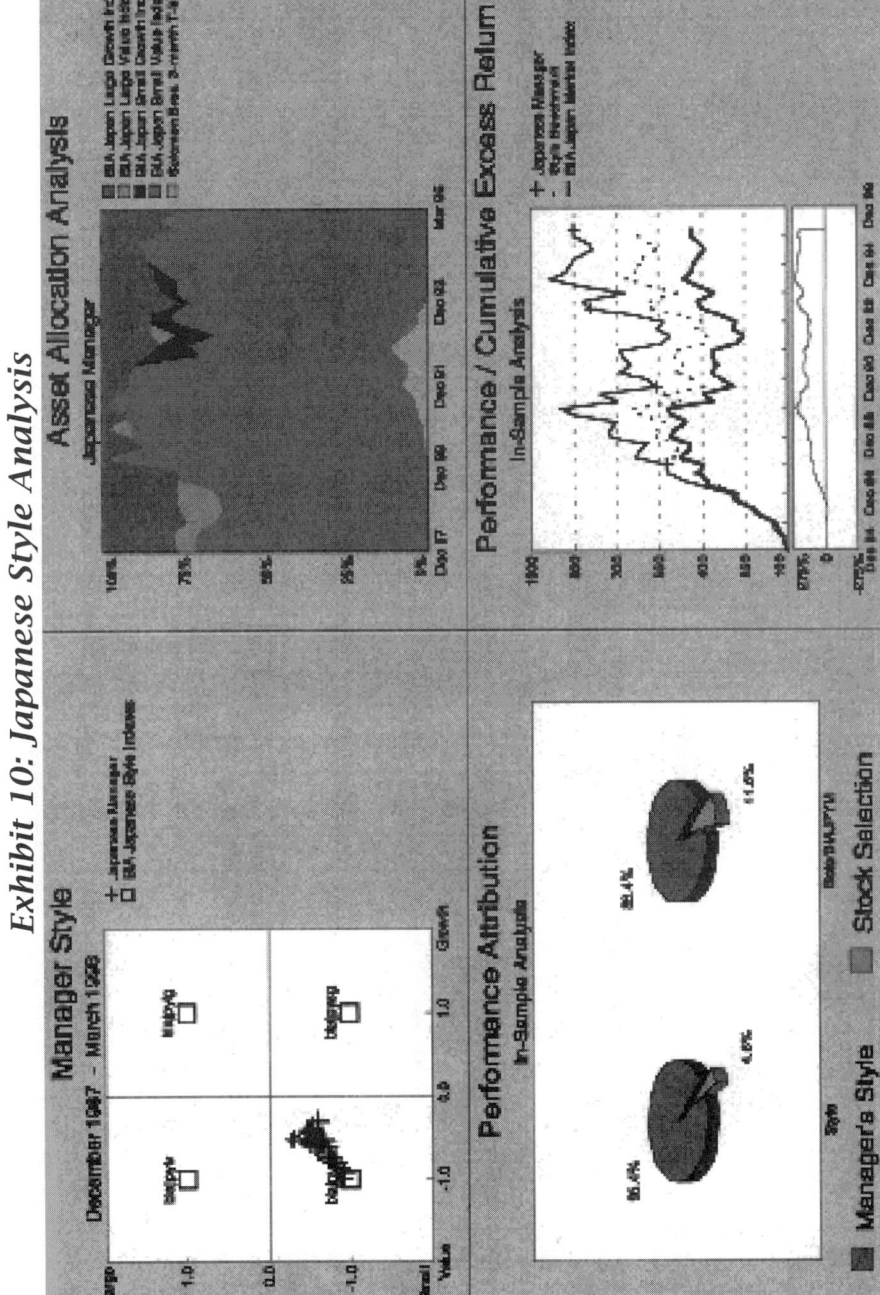

Exhibit 10: Japanese Style Analysis

68 Return-Based Style Analysis

Exhibit 11: European Style Analysis

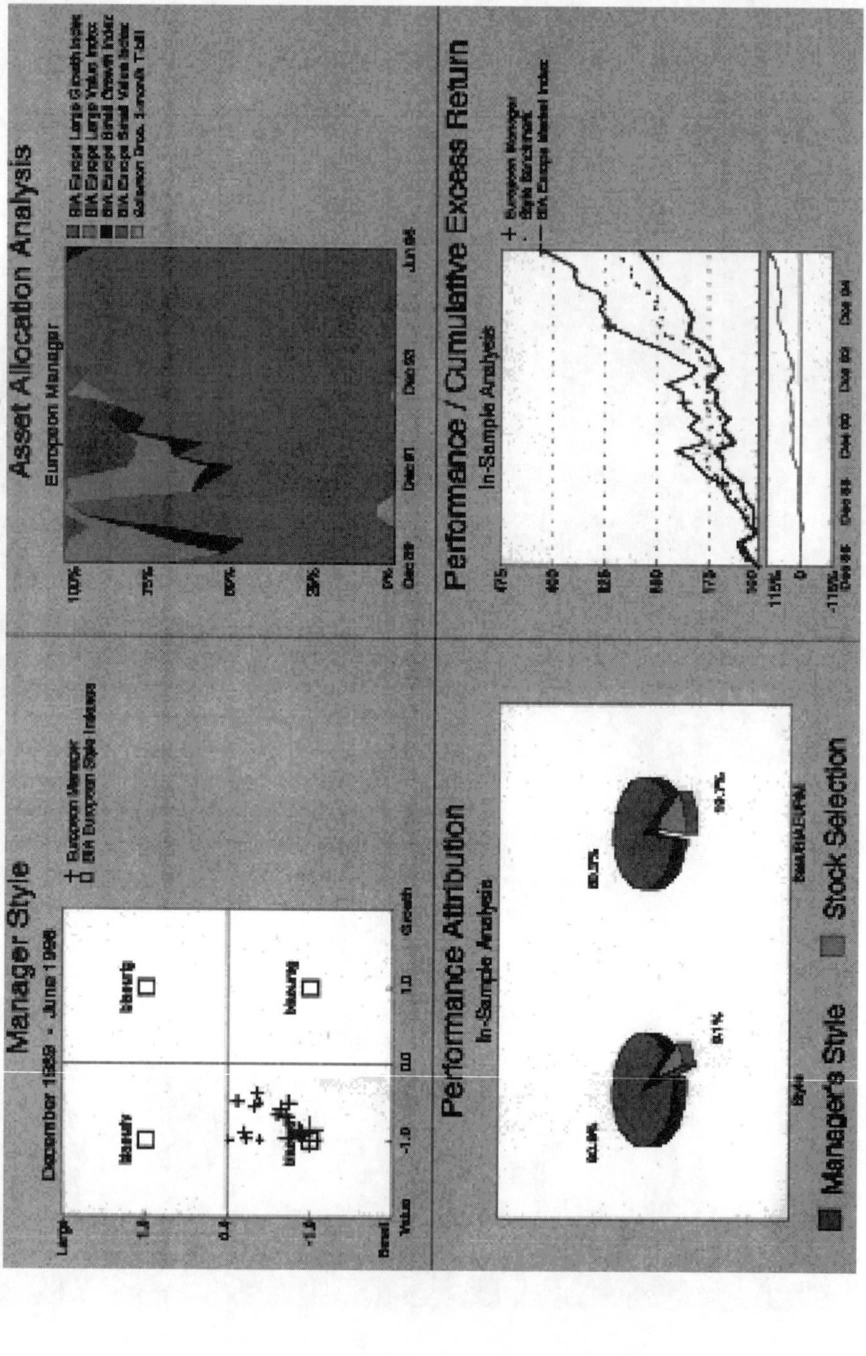

Chapter 3   69

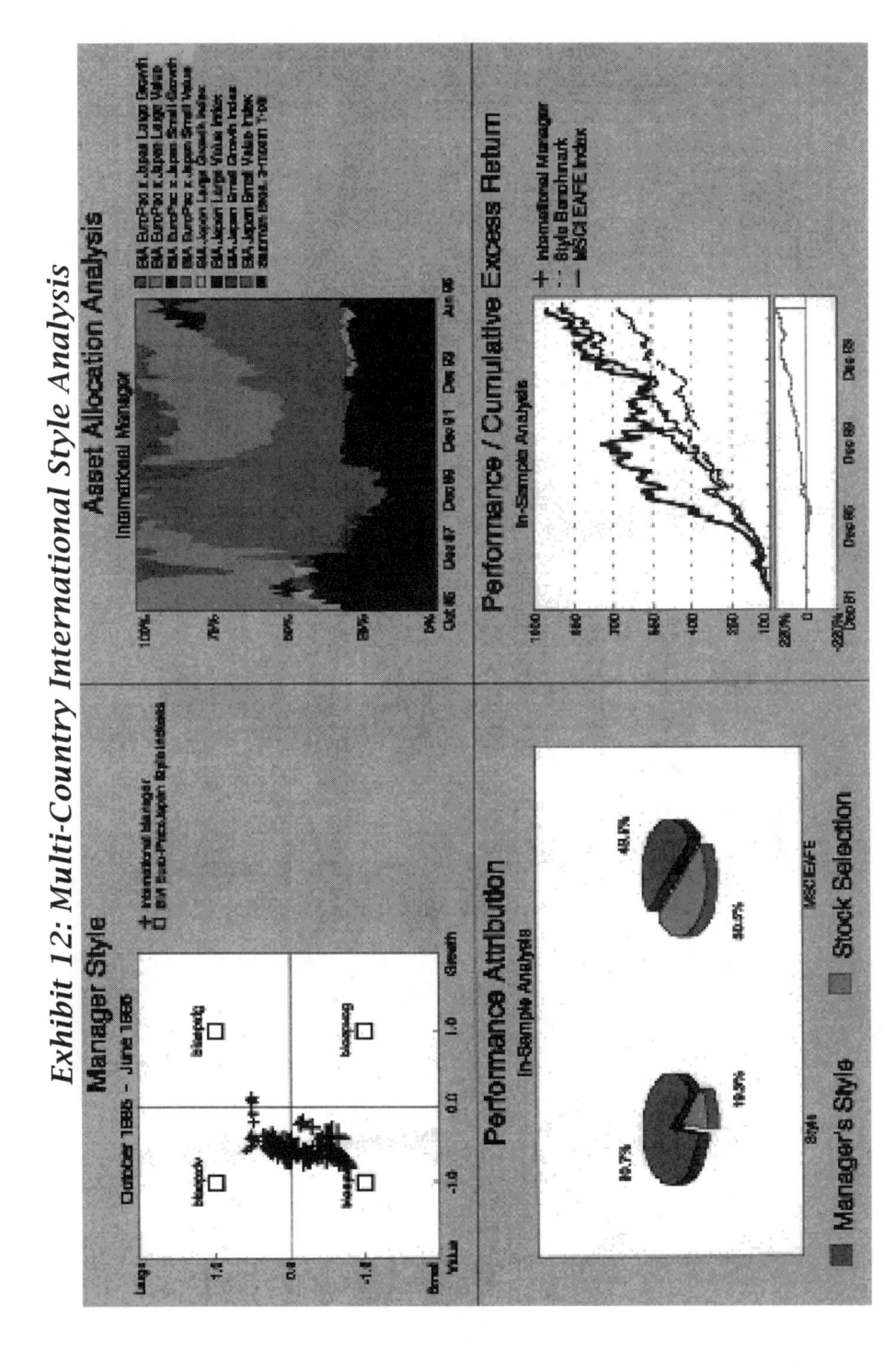

Exhibit 12: Multi-Country International Style Analysis

**Exhibit 13: Style Benchmarks versus EAFE R^2
International Managers in Mobius**

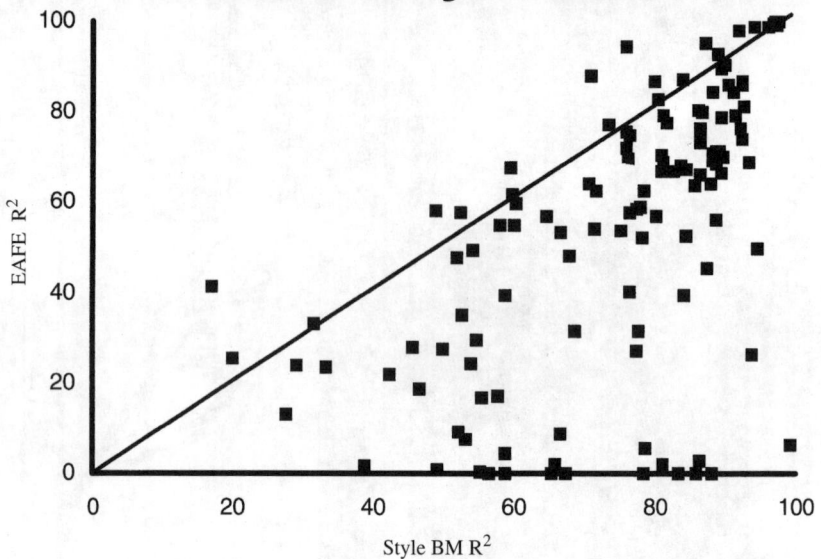

**Exhibit 14: Style Benchmarks versus EAFE R^2
International Mutual Funds**

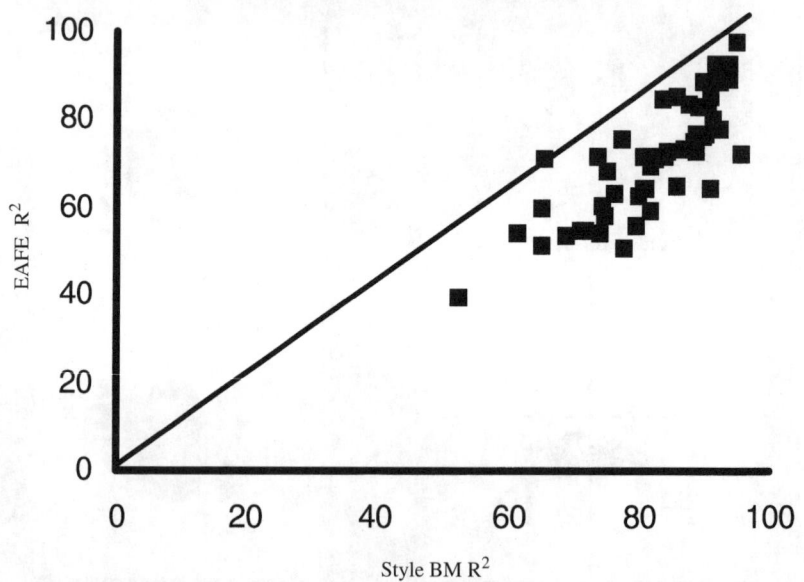

Exhibit 15: Median R^2 of Style Indices versus EAFE

Mobius	Median R^2	Mean R^2
Euro/Pac × Japan Styles	79.11	74.12
EAFE	59.36	53.33
Morningstar		
Euro/Pac × Japan Styles	82.44	81.42
EAFE	71.52	70.38

CONCLUSION

I believe return-based style analysis has revolutionized and will continue to revolutionize the way plan sponsors analyze their existing and potential money managers. For years, it has been a laborious and expensive process to analyze a manager's style, reconstruct the manager's style history, and build a customized style benchmark. The task was typically done by an outside consultant, who had to analyze portfolio holdings for a number of periods. In fact, because of the labor intensity and sophistication of this process, few consultants attempted to build customized benchmarks for managers. Instead, they chose simply to use a market benchmark such as the S&P 500. I submit that this unsophisticated approach resulted in many unnecessary manager changes and cost plan sponsors millions of dollars in terms of additional and unnecessary expenses.

With the sophisticated software and manager databases currently available, a plan sponsor can apply return-based style analysis to any number of managers and build customized style benchmarks in a matter of minutes. A plan sponsor can also scan a database of over 1,000 managers and quickly isolate those with the necessary style who have demonstrated skill within that style. Plan sponsors can also analyze the style of their total fund to be sure they have not taken any unwanted style bets because of the kinds of managers selected.

The idea started with William Sharpe. The technology that allows plan sponsors to take advantage of Sharpe's work has been developed by others. These innovations are recent, and the possibilities have only begun to be realized.

Chapter 4
Fundamental Factors in Equity Style Classification

David R. Borger, CFA
Director of Research
Wilshire Asset Management

INTRODUCTION

In recent years the term "style" has been prominent among equity practitioners in the areas of performance evaluation, manager selection, and product description. This usage gives just recognition to the well-known fact that certain categories of stocks perform differently than others, often over extended time periods. Within the last decade it has also been recognized that a manager who is hired to invest within the bounds of a particular category should not be reviewed favorably (unfavorably) if his returns exceed (fall short of) an arbitrary benchmark, the characteristics of which differ meaningfully from that of the type of portfolio that the manager can be expected to hold. To do so is unfair to both the manager and the sponsor and regardless of whether the manager's performance is made to look better or worse than a fair benchmark would make it appear, the resulting biased evaluation is likely to lead to an incorrect judgment on the part of the sponsor or consultant and an inappropriate feeling of satisfaction or dismay on the part of the manager. This can lead to a perverse system of rewards and punishments wherein a manager who has performed well but is perceived — by himself, his organization, the consultant and the sponsor — to have performed poorly is motivated to change a system which is, in fact, living up to expectations; at the same time a poorly performing but well perceived manager may well be rewarded with additional funds.

There are a number of ways of categorizing stocks, of course, but the paradigm which has gained greatest acceptance is a two-dimensional view in which size represents one dimension and some measure or measures of growth and value represent the second. There is some ambiguity in the terminology used to describe this breakdown. On the one hand, in describing the two dimensions it is common to refer to them as "size" and "style," the latter referring to the growth-value continuum. On the other hand, one also hears of the entire two dimensional approach as being "style" investing. As an example of the latter, below we shall make reference to the Large Growth "style" of investing. Clearly this refers to a management approach which focuses on companies with above average market capitalization — the size dimension — and which have a growth orientation — the former use of the term "style." While this situation is perhaps unfortunate, it has emerged as somewhat standard and the reader is advised to let the context determine the proper interpretation. (In this chapter when we feel it is necessary to emphasize or clarify the second meaning we will use the terms "style/size" or "size/style.")

Looking at the universe of equity investments through the lens of size and style we see at least four possible investment categories: Large Growth, Large Value, Small Growth and Small Value. Of course, one may choose to have finer subdivisions and include, perhaps, Mid Cap Growth and Mid Cap Value; or a neutral area between growth and value. Alternatively, sometimes it will be useful to aggregate these categories along one dimension, considering, for example, Large Growth and Large Value together as Large or Large Value and Small Value as "Value."

THE SIZE DIMENSION

What remains is to specify the criteria for membership in each of these categories. The easiest partition is the size partition. While there are numerous differences among the practitioners in the specifics of this division, the variable universally used to determine size breakpoints is market capitalization. One way of making the large/small split is to insist that the total market capitalization of each size category be the same (or as close to the same as is possible without having a single stock split between the two groups) as of a particular date.

The approach we took was somewhat different. First of all, we decided to focus our efforts on the largest 2,500 stocks from within the Wilshire 5000 Index. This subgroup represents about 97% of the market capitalization of the full index and we felt it was more representative of the type of stocks found in most institutional portfolios. It has the additional advantage of being more liquid and the stocks in the Top 2500, as we call it, are more likely to have complete and reliable financial data than are their micro cap brethren.

Since capitalization levels change over time, we decided to let our definition of "large" be reflective of this. Accordingly we defined "large" to mean the largest 750 stocks (Top 750) from the Top 2500 Index. We chose the largest 750 stocks to represent our large company universe because of a series of studies produced over the years by Wilshire's Institutional Services/Equity Division analyzing the performance profile by market capitalization over several market cycles. It was between the 700 and 800th stocks that we typically saw substantially different performance and since performance distinction by styles was a prime motivation for this endeavor, we felt this was an appropriate way to make the size cut. The remaining stocks in the Top 2500 were designated as small (Next 1750).

Subsequent to the initial creation of Wilshire's style indexes, an interest began to develop among some in the money management community in a Mid Cap category. Standard & Poor's Corporation was probably as responsible as anyone for fueling this interest when they introduced their Mid Cap 400. Perhaps the most natural way to define Mid Cap would be to divide the investment universe into three categories by using two breakpoints rather than a single one. Simply because we already had a vested interest in the Top 750/Next 1750 demarcation, we chose to approach Mid Cap as an overlay of our existing size categories. So for us Mid Cap consists of the 250 smallest stocks in the Top 750 and the 500 largest in the Next 1750.

DEFINING GROWTH AND VALUE

What makes a growth manager a growth manager? A reasonable and clearly intuitive answer would be: A growth stock manager is one who owns primarily growth stocks. What, then, is a growth stock? A growth stock is a stock which a growth stock manager would consider for purchase. This frustratingly circular attempt at defining growth illustrates the difficulty in trying to become specific about a term which has been used extensively, yet vaguely, and about which different investors have different ideas. Nonetheless, it does provide a helpful starting point if we try to focus on what is common among these alternate points of view and at the same time not try to satisfy everyone 100%. In particular, it should be kept in mind that there are different reasons investors may have in mind in the creation of style categories. Some, for example, may primarily be interested in the creation of a style index; others may be looking for a benchmark for performance measurement or performance attribution; still others may be primarily concerned with developing a disciplined model for investment management. These different perspectives may result in somewhat different approaches to one's definition of "style."

Expectations

In practice most equity managers, whether their orientation is to growth or value, construct their buy and sell lists based in part on expectations — either their own, consensus expectations, or the expectations of others. Even managers with relatively passive approaches occasionally design products which incorporate consensus earnings expectations. In our work with style we have chosen to base our models entirely on historically reported fundamental data. This approach is rooted in the belief that the historical ratios and growth rates correspond more closely with classic definitions or interpretations of growth and value. Furthermore, while all accounting numbers include a degree of subjectivity as well as noncomparability across time and possibly across industries, we believe that all of these problems exist to a greater extent with consensus forecasts and are still more problematic with specifically sourced (i.e., other than consensus) forecasts. But all this having been said and realizing, as mentioned above, that different investors may have different reasons for and different uses of style analysis, there is no reason why one could not legitimately include expectational data as part of a style model.

Growth

To determine what kind of stocks a growth stock manager might purchase, we can either examine the stocks that show up in growth stock portfolios or we can look at the process the growth stock manager uses to create his portfolio. The former approach does have the appeal of directness. However, the ability to get representative manager holdings data across a broad range of firms on a timely basis makes whatever analysis would result from this approach difficult to apply on a prospective basis. It also leaves unanswered the question of determining which managers are growth managers whose holdings should be considered representative of growth stocks in general. Not all managers who describe their approach as growth hold stocks which upon cursory review appear to be growth stocks. This is born out by Morningstar's recent decision to adopt a new fund classification scheme based on what managers actually own rather than on how they choose to describe their process. Additionally managers' styles drift overtime. Most likely the primary cause of this is performance pressure coupled with short time horizons. The result is a tendency to chase the style in favor and in the process move from a consistent style exposure.

Looking at what a growth manager does can also be said to suffer from the same lack of definition in the determination of who is a growth manager and who is not and hence whose actions it is that we should monitor. When Wilshire Asset Management created its style indexes in 1987, this was part of the dilemma we faced. How should we define "growth," whether we're talking about growth stocks or growth managers? There simply was no standardized definition. (A decade later there is still no standard but now the cause is an abundance of alternative definitions.) We chose to approach the problem in reverse — what is *not* a growth stock?

Consider the following thought experiment: Suppose you have been funded with an initial investment of $100 million and directed to start up an investment organization to actively manage this money in domestic equities in a manner consistent with an active, fundamental, large growth philosophy. You are given the financial resources (within reason) to hire whatever staff and purchase whatever support-ware you feel is necessary to profitably create and manage this organization. What is your game plan for allocating these resources? Consider that there are approximately 7,000 companies with U.S. headquarters which trade in the United States, either on one of the major exchanges or over-the-counter, for which daily prices are readily available — this being the definition used to include stocks in the Wilshire 5000 Index. Certainly it does not make sense to turn your analytical staff loose investigating all of these. Since we are interested in large company growth stocks, you decide to begin by setting a capitalization range within which you will work. There are some exciting opportunities in small growth stocks and some of your analysts may have a keen interest in some of them, but your mandate is large company growth and so you exclude these companies from consideration. For purposes of illustration, we will assume that you decide on the Wilshire Top 750 Index as your large company universe.

Similarly we want to eliminate stocks which, because of their fundamental characteristics, are unlikely to be considered growth stocks. Note the shift in perspective here: Instead of trying to define what growth is, we are trying to specify what it probably is not. We might conclude, for example, that a growth company is unlikely to pay out more than half of its earnings as dividends. If a company is a growth company, we expect it to have numerous opportunities to invest in projects which will produce high returns and, as a result, earnings growth well above that of the average company. Such a company will likely choose to retain most of its earnings for investment in such projects rather than pay them out as dividends. So, as our next screen we eliminate from our large company list all stocks with five-year average payout ratios greater than 50%.

Several things should be clear here. First, we are not asserting that every company with less than a 50% payout ratio is a growth company. We intend to further screen this list to zero in on a more growth-oriented group of companies. Second, we do not claim that it is impossible to find companies that most analysts would agree are growth companies yet which just happen to have payout ratios greater than 50%. Rather we believe that we lose little in our attempt to construct a quality portfolio of large company growth stocks if we restrict our analysis to companies with lower payout ratios and gain to the extent that our efforts are directed at a segment of the market more likely to contain the type of securities we seek. And finally, we do not assert that there is anything magic about the choice of 50% as a threshold. It is simply a convenient and, we believe, reasonable cutoff point in our definition of growth.

We can continue in this fashion eliminating stocks based on criteria which are thought not to be associated with growth. It will be clear as we proceed that the choice of some specific factors rather than others as well as the cutoff level for each is a matter of individual taste and reflects the creator's own biases with respect to a particular definition of growth within the guidelines just described. With regard to our biases, when we defined large growth we were thinking of an "established growth" kind of growth rather than either cyclical growth or turnaround growth. As a result we included as our next screen measures of the historic five-year average earnings growth and variability. Stocks which lagged relative to their peers were eliminated. We also screened on five-year average sales growth and five-year average return on equity. While the exact fashion in which these screens interact and the parameters used in the screening process are proprietary, they certainly are not unique in their ability to represent style. In fact it is our position that most growth managers have been or continually go through similar exercises with their own set of criteria. As indicated by the structure of this exercise, our goal is simply to produce a *working* list similar to that produced by an active manager — or, in this case, an active manager with a large company growth mandate.

It is our contention that such an active manager could take our list in place of his and through the application of his various methodologies and analyses generate performance consistent with the validity and current status of the approach he used. That is, if his large company growth methodology "works" and is currently "in favor" then this should be apparent in above average returns when applied to the large company growth index we intend to produce. Nor should there, over time, be any indication that these methods worked less well simply because they were applied to this specific index rather than another which might have been created at the time the model was run and the portfolio created. This exercise is realistic in that most managers already are creating lists in similar ways. Ours is an attempt to represent what is common among them.

Small Growth When building the value categories below, we use a single set of criteria for both large stocks and small. In the case of growth, however, we found it necessary to take a slightly different approach. Because in our design of the large company growth model our focus was on established growth, we required that a company have enough history to compute certain five-year average rates and ratios. The mere fact that a company had four or five years worth of history lent some credibility to the notion of "established." When looking at small company stocks, however, such a rigid requirement seemed inappropriate, particularly in recent years with the emergence of a plethora of new companies many of which became immediately perceived as growth companies. Despite the rapidly rising enthusiasm for many of these, we felt that it was necessary to demand some evidence that real earnings and real growth were possible. So we modeled the small company growth criteria as much as possible after the large, adjusting primarily for the likely limited availability of historic data.

One additional point. Those who are tempted to include expectational data in their style definitions might find this an appropriate place to take the plunge. The very short fundamental history of many of the companies in this capitalization range makes a purely quantitative judgment riskier than with larger companies. Of course, because of the size and newness of many of these firms, the availability of expectational data — at least on a consensus basis — may also be limited.

Value Stocks

We next go through a similar exercise for value. Here we are looking for fundamental factors which those who manage according to a value approach would likely evaluate in the construction of their portfolios or which those who hire value managers would expect to find well represented in their portfolios. Note at this point that very few self-proclaimed value managers would consider their universe of stocks to be simply anything which was not selected by a growth manager. Rather they would develop their own set of criteria based on their own understanding and interpretation of the term "value."

As was the case with growth, there is a range of opinion on just what constitutes value. Some investors think of value in terms of income and expect a value portfolio to consist primarily of high yielding stocks. Others think in terms of standard measures of cheapness such as relatively high earnings/price (E/P), book/price (B/P) or cash flow/price (CF/P) ratios, while still others are expectations driven and consider a stock to be attractive if its expected growth justifies its price.

This latter definition has intuitive appeal and has been in use for some time. Investors who follow this approach would argue that regardless of how low a stock's E/P ratio might be, if the expected growth rate is high enough, the stock is attractive. This approach is sometimes called "growth at a reasonable price." Such an approach, if faithfully and consistently implemented, need not reflect any selection biases relative to any specific fundamental factor. In other words, assuming that the inputs to the model for technology stocks are consistent with and comparable to those for bank stocks, there is no reason to suppose that technology stocks will be ranked favorably more often than bank stocks; or that low E/P stocks will be selected more or less often than stocks with high E/P's; and so on for every factor or classification system that one might consider.[1]

Models of this type (dividend discount models, for example) are used by many managers with a great deal of success. These models may lack in the ability to precisely time entry and exit points, but over the long run many, supported by a strong research staff capable of providing the required inputs, have been quite successful. Our reason for not using this definition of value was based not as much on the fact that, as indicated above, we have taken an overall approach to style based only on historic data — one which does not rely on expectational inputs, but rather in the lack of bias in the outputs just described. This lack of bias by its very nature makes it impossible to categorize such stocks into distinct groups. Lack of bias implies lack of discrimination and in this case our goal is in fact to distinguish between two types of stocks/managers which we feel are in some sense quite different and are able to serve two vary distinct roles in a sponsor's aggregate portfolio.

Some may object to this on the grounds that the valuation approach just described does offer a very clear classification of stocks — namely "overvalued" and "undervalued" (and throw in "neutral" if you like). Again without intending

---

[1] The terms "comparable" and "consistent" as used above to describe the technology and bank inputs are not intended to imply that there should be no difference in the inputs or that one can't be more optimistic about the growth prospect for technology stocks that for bank stocks. Rather we wish to factor out those situations where an analyst for one industry may be significantly more optimistic/pessimistic than his peers. This fact alone will cause that analyst's stocks to rank inappropriately high/low. We assume in this discussion the ideal situation where this is not the case.

to disparage managers who follow this approach, this is not the type of distinction which meets the needs of a true style paradigm as we have outlined it. According to this paradigm, we wish to classify stocks in such a way that each category (with the exception of the "other" category — the category of leftovers) is a potential working list or could be reasonably used as a working list for some group of equity managers. We have perhaps prejudiced the discussion by identifying these early on as growth managers and value managers; deconstructing things a bit more we might have (or might still) come up with other divisions. Nonetheless, there is not likely to be a group of managers whose *intended* strategy or "style" is to invest in overvalued stocks.

In identifying value candidates, we have taken an exclusionary approach similar to that taken for growth. While it may be the case that there are some stocks which it may be reasonably argued are underpriced or are value stocks in some other sense but which also have relatively low E/P ratios, we doubt if a classic value manager will have difficulty building a value portfolio *without* these names. Similarly for B/P and yield. Also, as was the case with growth, there will be some who will choose other factors than the ones which we chose and which will combine them in different ways. They will, of course, come up with a different list of stocks which will in turn have a different performance profile and different overall characteristics. Again, however, we have no reason to believe that a value manager would have difficulty working from our list or from any of a number of similarly constructed lists.

In the case of growth stocks, there was an explicit requirement that to be included in the growth index corresponding to the stock's capitalization range that some minimum amount of history be available. Any such seasoning requirement in value is only implicitly stated. The key elements in our value model are the latest 12 months of earnings (hence an implicit requirement of at least 12 months and perhaps a bit more to allow for reporting lags); book value (this is a point in time number and its existence does not guarantee any back history for the company — in fact a company has a book value as soon as it comes into being); dividend (again, point in time); and price (current data only). Furthermore in the case of our value models the exact same screening criteria are used for both large and small companies.

The "Other" Category

The process which we have just described for classifying stocks as growth or value is not guaranteed to assign every stock in our universe into one of these two categories. In fact a substantial number are not so classified based on the variables and parameters which we used. An acceptance of this fact is tantamount to an acceptance of the premise that, indeed, not all stocks are either growth or value. If it is agreed that the terms "growth" and "value" have some natural meaning within the investment community, both among practitioners and consumers, then this state of affairs should not only not be surprising, it should be expected. This is certainly consistent with the decision above not to define value as simply being non-growth.

There are a number of reasons why a stock might not be considered as either growth or value. The first of these is negative earnings. We classify a stock as value in part because of a relatively high earnings/price ratio, where "earnings" is the latest 12 months reported earnings and price is the price as of the date of the creation of the value list. Since stocks with negative earnings will rank low in an E/P ranking, it is unlikely that such stocks would be considered value stocks according to our criteria.[2] Furthermore, a stock with negative earnings for the last 12 months is unlikely to be ranked among the top growing companies over the last five years. And there is a good chance that it will also fail the earnings stability screen.[3] Given this perspective, it is difficult to see why a company should be forced into either of these style categories.

A second reason is the differential performance profile we see in using our criteria — differences in both return and risk. Our creation of style indexes and style funds was in large part motivated by the belief that managers which follow growth approaches perform differently from those who follow value approaches — that at any point in time one style may be in favor and the other out, and that neutral or biased benchmarks can distort not only performance evaluation but also the manager selection process. In order to address this issue we set two goals: we wanted our indexes to be broad enough to serve as reasonable working lists for managers with clear style orientation and we wanted to be sufficiently focused so that the stocks selected by our models were *clearly* representative of the indicated style. We considered it *a priori* possible that all stocks would be classified into one of our style categories; however, we did not feel that this was necessary. In fact, we find it somewhat satisfying that they are not, given our intuition, commented on elsewhere, that value and growth are different investment approaches and that managers who adhere to one or the other approach their jobs differently. This being the case, we were not prepared to *force* all stocks into one category or the other.

Stocks which are Value and Growth

Because the criteria used for growth and value are distinct and because the construction rules for these stocks rely on a completely different set of variables, there is no reason to suppose that there will be no overlap between growth and value. While it is unlikely that a stock with a high historic growth rate and which passes all of the other growth screens will also have a high E/P and pass the various value criteria, it is certainly not impossible. In fact we have found typically that somewhere in the range of six to eight companies will be classified as both growth and value. We have also examined the performance of these stocks thinking that perhaps we have found some rare jewels, namely cheap growth stocks. Unfortunately, there does not seem to be any advantage to owning this particular group of stocks.

---

[2] Others, however, may seek out exactly this type of stock as a turnaround/value stock.

[3] Again, this is based on our approach; others could legitimately choose to include cyclical growth stocks — which could well have negative earnings — in their growth indexes. We chose not to.

Others have suggested that all stocks are part growth and part value and carry out their analysis of style from this point of view. We certainly agree with the hypothesis and, in fact, the style metric which we discuss below is based on this belief. However, as discussed in the previous section, at times it is useful to focus the analysis on those stocks which are clearly identifiable as belonging to one category or the other. Either starting point is possible and from either one can get to the other. The approach which we favor starts with a discrete categorization of stocks by size and style and develops a continuous measure (the style metric) from that. The other starts with a continuous measure and, by the selection of appropriate ranges, can be used to classify stocks into discrete style classes.

Weighting, Re-Weighting, and Other Issues

At this point we have proposed a methodology for screening a universe of stocks based on fundamental factors normally associated with growth and value styles. We have suggested that the criteria we used, while not the only criteria available, are relatively non-controversial. We would further expect that the result of the thought experiment described above, if applied by a large number of investors or investment organizations, would result in a wide range of specific rules and the use of a number of different variables and parameters. We do not expect that the end results would differ widely, nor that any of the differences would be perceived as beyond compromise.

Having built one such list we are now confronted with the issue of maintenance. In particular, how frequently do we run our model? While much of the data used change only quarterly, some, especially price data, change daily. Since even the data which changes quarterly may become available on any random day during the quarter, an argument can certainly be made for running the model on a daily basis. However, our intent in developing a style model was to enable us to manage style portfolios. As a result we were interested in selecting a rebalancing frequency which reached a modest balance between accurately reflecting current information and avoiding unnecessary turnover. We felt that a quarterly rebalancing frequency (at calendar quarter-ends) was appropriate for the inclusion of new fundamental data while an annual adjustment to the definition of "large" and "small" would properly avoid the marginal turnover which would result in the frequent reclassification of stocks as large or small simply due to short-term price fluctuation. As a result, our institutional universe, consisting of the largest 2,500 stocks by market capitalization, is reconstructed each June 30 and split into large and small based on the market capitalization of its constituents as of that same date.

Regardless of the applications one may have in mind for the development of a style categorization, one of the outputs of the process will undoubtedly be a time series of returns for each style. This effectively requires that a paper portfolio be created and that some attention be given to the issue of the weighting methodology and frequency. The most common approach here is to capitalization weight the lists as of each rebalance interval, in our case quarterly. On occasion one might see reference to equal-weighted returns, but the sensitivity to the rebalance period generally limits the usefulness of such series. There is also the issue of what shares should be used in the calculation of market capitalization. The various approaches to this, however, transcend the issue of style and so will not be discussed in detail here. Suffice it to say that a seemingly simple data item such as shares outstanding means different things to different people. Naturally these difference will have an impact on the performance of a benchmark or index. Capitalization weighting also aids in the management of a fund intended to track the index. Since larger capitalization names *tend* to be more liquid than smaller names, we will tend to own larger shares of companies for which it is easier to acquire larger amounts.

Sector Representation

When viewing the style categories individually, particularly after the component securities have been capitalization weighted, there are clear sector over- and underweightings present compared with the universe of all equities or even with the subuniverses of securities of comparable size. Historically, these sector bets are more prominent in the value indexes than in the growth indexes. Of course, it is not surprising that some of the factors which are strong style determinants are also correlated with industry membership. We expect, for example, that more technology stocks will be classified as growth than as value — particularly among small companies — and that more banks and utilities will show up as value.

The issue at hand is whether to attempt to neutralize these sector bets or not. The answer again depends on the use one wants to make of the resulting index. If the indexes are intended to be used as benchmarks for the purpose of performance based incentive fees, then the creator of the index should be careful not to include in the structure of the index characteristics which will motivate the manager to perform in an undesirable fashion. It has not been uncommon, for example, for the Wilshire Small Value Index to have a combined weight in the Finance and Utility sectors of 60% or more. It is unlikely that a sponsor or consultant would want to set that as a target for all small value managers.

Our purpose, on the other hand, was to design indexes with a very focused exposure to a particular style as represented by what we believe to be classic style factors. The industry and sector profiles which emerge from this tell us something about how these factors appear in various segments of the market. We would not propose that any sponsor invest all of his money in any of these indexes or the corresponding portfolios. Rather they can serve as extremely useful tools for diversification. Because of their focus, it requires less of an investment in one of these indexes to move one's aggregate portfolio toward a desired style/size exposure. We would also argue — whether with regard to style management or portfolio management in general — that if each manager a sponsor hires individually attempts to diversify his own portfolio, then the sponsor's aggregate portfolio will be overdiversified. Better that each manager design a portfolio which represents his own best efforts in the style he manages and then the sponsor/consultant diversify among managers (as they already are attempting to do).

The Multifactor Approach

The minimum requirement for a factor-based style classification is a factor which one is willing to claim represents style. One can then rank stocks according to that factor and insert any number of breakpoints according to whatever rule one deems appropriate and claim to have created style categories.[4] But, in part, because the categories of growth and value have evolved over the years to mean different things to different investors, it seems unlikely to find a single, simple variable which will meet this need.

The consideration of multiple style factors proceeds in two directions. The first of these considers whether or not a single factor — or even a single group of factors — can be used for both growth and value. Below, where we discuss the development of the style metric, we will appear to answer this question in the affirmative. However, note that in that case we have really taken a somewhat different approach in developing a single variable which is itself a mathematical combination of several others, some of which are intended to represent growth and others to represent value. The variable itself, the "style metric," is not a naturally occurring or commonly used investment variable. Note too that the weighting scheme changes over time to reflect the predictive contribution of each of these factors and also that the weights are selected *ex post* to optimally represent an *ex ante* classification based on separate growth and value variables.

The notion of a single, "natural" variable, particularly an accounting-based one, which can distinguish between growth and value is an attractive one, but one which is probably counterintuitive to most managers as well as most plan sponsors. Growth managers and value managers have different approaches to stock selection as well as portfolio construction. Each of these uses a combination of variables/factors to evaluate the stocks in their universes and while there may be some overlap, it is unlikely that any of these managers would be comfortable reducing their process to the examination of a single variable, much less explaining or justifying the composition of their working lists in these terms. Our choice of different factors for growth and value stemmed from the desire to create indexes in much the same way as an active manager would create such a working list, using those variables normally associated with each particular style. It was not clear as we proceeded with our initial work that the end result of this process would be the creation of indexes/portfolios which differed not only in their composition but also in their return profile. As we will see below, the latter turned out to be the case.

---

[4] Of course, one would hope that there was some rationale — either statistical or otherwise — for the selection of this factor and that the classes which resulted had some natural association with common investment classes.

Amongst those who nonetheless favor using a single variable, probably the most popular candidate is the book-to-price ratio (B/P), based in large measure on the work done by Fama and French.[5] We, too, have found B/P to be a very useful discriminator of *value* stocks, though we must admit to having some difficulty seeing why stocks with low B/P's should be considered growth. In addition to B/P, we also use E/P as mentioned above. As one might expect, selecting stocks by B/P and alternatively selecting by E/P often produces a similar list. Often, but not always. There are times when the B/P effect is stronger and times when the E/P effect dominates and, to be sure, there are times when it is a toss up as to which one is the more important. Since each works well in identifying value candidates and because sometimes one works better than the other, we have chosen to include both (along with yield) in our value model and to include them in such a way that this complex interaction is reflected.

Having argued for the need for multiple variables (in our case three) to represent value, we observe that the style classification scheme would in some sense be simplified if we were able to find a way to identify growth stocks using the same variables. Unfortunately there does not seem to be any clear path to that end. While it is true that a classic growth portfolio, including our growth indexes, will on average have low E/P, low B/P, and low yield — the exact opposite of what one expects in a value portfolio, these are not the defining characteristics of growth. After all, such portfolios typically have other common characteristics as well. These factors are simply not the basis of growth stock selection by growth managers. Growth stock managers are more likely to look at direct measures of growth, either historic or projected, and if they have to tolerate low E/P's and B/P's, so be it; if they can find growth candidates with higher valuation ratios, so much the better.

The Performance Profile

It is one thing to create a classification system for stocks and another to establish that such a classification is meaningful. One could, for example, have classified stocks somehow based on the first letter of their ticker symbols or the age of their CEO, but one would not expect such schemes to have any useful application. Our selection of the variables which we used to define growth and value was admittedly based on preconceived notions of what these terms meant and clearly reflect some author's license in their selection and interaction. Others have created other factor based approaches which they aggressively defend. Some of the methodologies they use have been discussed above. Different investors will respond differently to the various rationales and explanations for each of these different style models. And the different models will suit different investors' various needs better or worse than others.

---

[5] Eugene F. Fama and Kenneth R. French, "Common Risk Factors in the Returns on Stocks and Bonds," *Journal of Financial Economics*, 33 (1993), pp. 3-56, and "The Cross-Section of Expected Stock Returns," *Journal of Finance* (June 1992), pp. 427-465.

Exhibit 1: Equity Style Performance Profile
1978-1996/Q3

Period	Growth Return (%)	Value Return (%)	Wilshire 5000 Return (%)
1978-80	28.7	13.7	22.4
1981-88	10.7	19.5	13.1
1989-91	24.2	13.2	17.6
1992-1993	4.6	15.1	10.1
1994-1996/Q3	20.4	14.9	17.2

Having reviewed the construction process of factor based classification models and the reasonableness of referring to these as "growth" and "value," it remains to be shown that this breakdown is significant and should be viewed as such by managers and sponsors. The key issue here is performance. Do these two groups of stocks perform differently in any way which would be useful to a plan sponsor, a money manager, or a consultant? As Exhibit 1 shows, the answer is clearly, "yes." During the period for which we have constructed the style categories, there have been several easily discernible style trends. Such trends are of course best seen in hindsight, once one can determine whether a small reversal will develop into a total change of course or whether the old trend will resume shortly. Also, the meaning of the term "trend" changes depending on one's time horizon. It is quite possible that some will choose to look within the periods listed in Exhibit 1 to identify other, shorter term trends, while others will combine some or all of these into longer periods. With that caveat, Exhibit 1 presents one breakdown of the time period over which we have investigated style.

Exhibit 1 clearly shows that style, as represented by the factors used to define the Wilshire Style Indexes, has been a significant factor in the determination of performance over the last two decades. The compound annual return for switching to the best performing style in each of these time periods was 21.3%, compared with 11.5% for being in the worst performing style and 15.5% for staying in the Wilshire 5000 Index. Of course, this reflects perfect hindsight and does not include the transaction costs of implementing such a strategy. These returns are presented solely to illustrate the potential significance of style to total equity performance.

The implications for performance measurement are dramatic and have been reflected in the way that consultants measure and evaluate managers compared with a decade ago. Imagine being a growth manager in 1992-1993 and being benchmarked against the Wilshire 5000. You would have had to be very good or very lucky just to meet your benchmark. Stocks with classic growth characteristics simply did not perform well in that period. Of course, if you were a growth manager of another sort with less exposure to these factors than the Wilshire Growth Indexes, this, too, would have impacted your performance, for better or worse.

Or if you were a classic growth manager as characterized by these indexes but saw the strengthening performance of value stocks and as a result shifted your portfolio in that direction, you probably would have generated returns better than your peers in growth. Whether or not you were fulfilling your responsibility to your client who hired you to deliver growth, is another matter. This departure from style purity in response to external events is referred to as "style drift." Here, we should emphasize, we are referring to drift along both the size and style dimensions. It is not uncommon for managers with small company mandates to bump up the limits on their definition of "small" when mid cap and large companies seem to be taking the lead.

A STYLE METRIC

The methods outlined above for the creation of style categories have proven useful in a number of areas, including the development and management of style oriented portfolios as well as style related performance attribution. However, after managing style portfolios for a while, it became clear that it would be useful to have a continuous measure of style orientation rather than the discrete classifications we were working with. As things stood, any security in our universe was classified as either growth, value, or other. There was no way to determining whether a value stock was just barely a value stock or whether an "other" stock just missed being classified as growth. For some applications this did not cause a problem, but for real-life portfolio management where trading costs are an important component of return — particularly with small stock applications — we would like to avoid buying a stock which is only slightly value and at the same time selling one which just barely failed our screens. Ironically, it is our use of a multifactor model, which we feel is important for an accurate specification of style, which complicates the situation.

While in certain trivial cases it is possible to "eye ball" the model output to determine whether a passing stock passed with flying colors or not, in general this is not practical. Suppose a stock which shows up as a small value stock would not have if the E/P ratio had been slightly lower and another would have failed if the B/P had been slightly lower. Should these two cases be considered identical? Suppose a stock which failed would have passed if its E/P ratio had been slightly higher but has a B/P ratio which was in the top half of the universe. If this stock is currently held, should it be sold to purchase one of the previous two? What guidelines can be offered to assist in making these trade-offs? Any attempt to answer these questions is further complicated by the observation above that the relative importance of the model's factors is not constant over time.

To address these questions, Wilshire developed a style metric — a single measure of style which allows us to distinguish, based on fundamental data, those stocks which are most growth-like and those which are most value-like. The statistical technique used to accomplish this is discriminant analysis — a procedure for classification of objects based on properties of these objects and of similar objects whose proper classification is known. The original work in this area was done early in the century by Fisher who wanted to develop a methodology for classifying iris plants in general based on physical measurements on individual iris plants. He was able to accomplish this by taking a series of such measurements on plants whose classification was already known and through a Baysian strategy, discriminant analysis, to develop a linear weighting of the variables which was optimal in the sense of being able to classify the known plants properly with highest possible success rate of any such weighting. Another benefit of this methodology, which is particularly important in the development of the style metric, is the fact that the linear model produces a monotonic, continuous result, so as an individual's score toward a particular category increases, it is more and more likely to be a member of that category.

The application to style classification and the shortcomings of our discrete model are clear. We can use the fundamental variables from the original style classification as the measurements and the results of that classification as the basis for estimating the model. Understand that we are not changing the construction of our existing indexes; nor are we proposing a methodology which could be used as an alternative. The style metric is based entirely on the style indexes as we have already described them and relies on their existence for its computation. With these (or comparable) indexes in hand, we can calculate, using standard statistical software, for any security for which the requisite fundamental data are available, what the probability is that stock is a growth stock or a value stock. When we apply this computation to the stocks which have already been assigned to one of these two categories, we find that the "hit" rate — the number of stocks which are mapped to the proper category — is quite high. Of course this is not surprising since the nature of the discriminant model is that it will find the linear model of the input variables which produces the greatest number of "hits."

Suppose, for example, we select a stock at random from the union of our Large Company Growth and Large Company Value indexes. In other words, we know that the company has already been selected by either our growth model or our value model; however, we do not know which model is the reason for its inclusion in the union. (For simplicity sake we will rule out the possibility that it was selected by both.) We do, however, have available a complete listing of the stock's fundamental characteristics as well as those same characteristics (mean values and standard deviations) for the two indexes. Consider the two style indexes in Exhibit 2.

Now suppose that the stock which we selected had an E/P of 0.08. Is it a growth stock or a value stock? Admittedly this is very little information to go on and whatever our answer we will certainly have a limited amount of confidence in it. But that having been said, most people would probably say it is a value stock or that is more likely to be a value stock than a growth stock. If we were to select another random stock which happened to have an E/P of 0.10, most people would probably conclude that this is a value stock as well; and that it is more value like than the first, or perhaps that they have a higher degree of confidence that the second stock is a value stock.

Exhibit 2: Sample Characteristics of Wilshire Style Indexes

	E/P	B/P	Five Year EPS Growth (%)	Five-Year Return on Equity (%)
Large Growth				
Mean	0.047	0.23	15.9	21.3
Standard Deviation	0.018	0.22	13.8	19.4
Large Value				
Mean	0.072	0.54	10.7	13.4
Standard Deviation	0.072	0.51	8.3	12.5

Now suppose we add another variable, say B/P, and reconsider the first stock we picked. If it were to turn out that this stock had a B/P of 0.60, this would serve to reinforce our belief that the stock is a value stock, giving us a higher degree of confidence or causing us to assign a higher (subjective) probability to its being a value stock. However, what if the stock had a B/P of 0.40? That's not quite as value-like and might add to any doubts we might have had about this really being in the value index. Still it does have a B/P more like a value stock than a growth stock, so we'll stick with our original answer. But what if the stock had a B/P of 0.20? If this were all the information we had, we would call it a growth stock. But since it also has a value-like E/P, we're caught in the middle. Is one factor more important than the other? Are the answer to these questions valid always or just with this particular data set? If we add in five or six more variables and a few hundred securities, the problem becomes completely intractable using only *ad hoc* tools.

This is exactly the type of classification problem the discriminant model was designed to deal with and does so in the following ways: (1) normalize each stock's exposure to each factor so that we are dealing in units of standard deviations from the respective means; (2) for each stock compute a score which is a weighted average of the above exposures; (3) rank the stocks by this score and call the stocks ranked in the top half "growth-like" and the bottom half "value-like;" (4) calculate the percentage of stocks that are properly classified — i.e., growth-like stocks are in fact in the growth index; and, (5) determine the weighting scheme so that the percentage of correct classifications in step 4 is maximized.

The discriminant model is structured in such a way that the scores in step 2 above are in fact probabilities — namely the probability that any given stock is a growth stock. (We could equally well have specified the model in terms of value stocks.) So a score of 0.75 means that there is a 75% chance that the stock is a growth stock. Step 3 then selects all stocks with a better than 50% chance of being a growth stocks and calls them "growth-like." The scoring system — that is the weighting scheme — which does the best job of classifying stocks consistent with their membership in the growth and value indexes is the one which is used.

Since the results of the discriminant models are probabilities, it follows that they can be interpreted as a continuous measure of style orientation and since we have only two classifications (growth and value) in our sample, if a high (low) score represents growth then a low (high) score will represent value. We have scaled our style scores so that the equal-weighted average score for a stock previously identified as a value stock is −100 while the average growth stock has a score of +100.[6]

The Style Metric and Portfolio Comparisons

In addition to aiding in the reduction of turnover and transaction costs by providing a means for avoiding marginal trades, the style metric is also useful in evaluating portfolios, both individual and aggregate. Because the style model is linear, the style score of a portfolio is simply the market value weighted average style score of the individual securities. Similarly the style score of a group of portfolios is the weighted average score of the components. This provides a useful measure of the style orientation of individual managers or groups of managers. It also provides a means of evaluating the consistency of a manager's style exposure over time or the consistency of the management of purportedly similar portfolios within an organization.

The style metric also yields itself readily to graphic representation. One graphic tool which has proven quite popular is the so-called "style map," a two dimensional plot which presents size on the vertical axis and style on the horizontal. Individual securities, portfolios, and indexes can then be graphed — either separately or in combination. By using such a map to view the style profile of their existing managers as well as their aggregate portfolio, a plan sponsor can quickly determine the net style bets that are being taken. By overlaying this graph with a plot of alternative investment managers or by hypothetically adding, deleting or re-weighting managers, the sponsor can easily see which actions would most easily address whatever style deficiencies exist.

Over time we have had the chance to review the results of the style metric model with investment managers as well as plan sponsors. The reception from each has been encouraging. Managers are frequently concerned with the consistency of results across accounts managed by different portfolio managers. Our metric analysis allowed us to view the exposure of these managers to style/size and to evaluate their resulting performance variability. In those cases where there were outliers, our analysis was supported by comments from these firms of the idiosyncrasies of the highlighted managers.

We were also able to show managers how the style exposure of their funds changed over time. Of course, with some managers there was a high degree of consistency — a fact which should be pleasing to their clients. Others, however, did show some variability, either a trend from a base style toward the other

---

[6] This is a convention which we chose to give us a measure of comparability across time and a standard scoring system with which to describe a stock's or a portfolio's growth exposure. Some who have adopted this overall approach have chosen different scaling parameters, including forcing the style axes through a prespecified point, such as the Wilshire 5000.

or a steady exposure to one style and then a rapid, perhaps temporary, jump to the other. Again, these moves were validated in discussions with these managers as they reflected on their changing strategies over this time.

ADVANTAGES OF THE FACTOR APPROACH TO STYLE

There are at least two major approaches to identifying equity style: the returns-based approach and the factor- (or portfolio-) based approach. Each of these has its proponents and each has its strong and weak points. Among the advantages of the factor-based approach is that it directly focuses on the very characteristics that the style-oriented manager focuses on in the construction and maintenance of his portfolio. This aids the manager in seeing where he might be taking bets relative to his style before the bets are taken. It also makes it possible for a manager to understand the reason for the over- or underperformance that comes out of an attribution analysis.

Another way of looking at this is that factor-based equity style analysis is security oriented — any portfolio level conclusions or observations flow directly from the aggregation of the security based results. There is total comparability between the interpretation of style at the security, portfolio or aggregate level, and it is straight forward to determine how one impacts the other. If a portfolio is not as value oriented as one would like, a candidate list of stocks and an optimizer — or for that matter any structured portfolio construction tool — could be used to create a portfolio with any target value profile, even subject to a wide range of construction constraints.

A second benefit of the factor-based style approach is that it is easier to determine style drift. A returns-based approach, requiring as it does some meaningful amount of history to compute its correlations, will not necessarily catch near-term composition changes which some managers will make in an attempt to profit by reacting to short-term trends. Factor-based style classification always focuses on the characteristics of the stocks which the manager holds right now, those which will impact future performance, not those which may have influenced the past. If the manager continues to hold stocks which no longer fit the desired style profile or begins to purchase "hot" stocks outside of his normal style, this will immediately become apparent using a factor-based model.

Finally, regression based models of style are subject to one of the potential flaws of any regression based model, namely misspecification. One popular way of measuring a portfolio's style orientation is to regress the portfolio's returns over some time period against the corresponding return of a set of style indexes.[7] If, in fact, all managers fall into one of the styles included in the regression, such an approach will show which managers' returns have been most corre-

---

[7] It is also common practice to constrain the coefficients to sum to one.

lated with which style. That of course is just what the regression does. The question then is how one interprets these results. In one of the early applications of this approach, one consultant attempted to classify the Wilshire Style Indexes. Because at that time there was no acknowledgement of small value as a separate category and because as a result it was not included in the regression model, our Small Company Value Index showed up with heavy exposure to Japanese equities, of which it held none.

Another way that this can happen is due to an individual manager's alpha. Suppose over the time period used in the regression a particular large value manager had a significant positive alpha, while remaining strict in his adherence to a value discipline. Suppose, too, that during this period large growth stocks outperformed large value. Depending on a number of other factors (such as the volatility and correlation of the individual indexes over this specific time period) it could appear that this very strict value manager could be classified as growth based on a regression approach. (This is a real life observation, not a hypothetical.)

SUMMARY

Style is more than a fad. Ten years ago no one talked about portfolio construction or performance measurement in terms of style. Now you can't talk equities to a consultant without the term "style" popping up in the conversation. Style managers exist because stocks with different fundamental characteristics have different performance profiles. Sometimes one style is in favor, sometimes another. There are those investors who prefer to permanently position themselves in one size/style quadrant or another in a belief that that style will outperform the others on a secular basis. Despite fairly long-term studies which support some of these strategies, that view of the market could well change in the future. It could well be that a century from now when all of our databases are overflowing with information and our time series encompass dozens of market cycles, that the very long-term performance results will show no difference in the performance of these styles "over the long run." But surely the patterns that we have seen over the shorter term will continue: namely, that the classic fundamental factors distinguish among stocks as well as among managers and that these will generate their own unique performance patterns into the future. So regardless of what apparent anomalies have or continue to exist, the need for diversification among equity styles will persist, and the successful investor will employ the various style tools in his stock/manager selection and review process.

Chapter 5

Style Return Differentials: Illusions, Risk Premiums, or Investment Opportunities

Richard Roll, Ph.D.
Allstate Professor of Finance
Anderson Graduate School of Management
University of California, Los Angeles
and Co-Chairman
Roll and Ross Asset Management Corporation

POSSIBLE EXPLANATIONS FOR INVESTMENT STYLE RETURNS

For both the investor and the finance researcher, the single most important unanswered question about equity style investing is the origin of historically observed differential returns. There seem to be at least three possibilities:

1. Return differentials across investment styles are statistical aberrations. They do not reflect differences in *expected* returns and are thus not likely to be repeated.
2. Return differentials are risk premiums. They *do* reflect differences in expected returns, but this is compensation for risk.

The author thanks Laura Field, Stephen A. Ross, and Ivo Welch for constructive comments and suggestions and Ken Mayne for expert assistance.

3. Return differentials represent market opportunities. Not only are they statistically significant, but they occur above and beyond any measurable risk. Investing according to style can thus be expected to earn extra return without bringing any additional exposure to loss.

These explanations are not mutually exclusive; each one could have some degree of empirical relevance.

Many empirical studies of style investing, including other chapters in this volume, have uncovered seemingly significant statistical differences in the returns of portfolios classified by price/earnings ratio, market capitalization, book/market ratio, and other indicia of style. Yet the first explanation above is not completely moribund. Taken individually, each empirical study employs sound econometric methods and draws scrupulously correct inferences from the data. But taken as an aggregate, the studies are far from independent investigations.

The historical record of observed returns is limited, and there are more professional data miners than data points. Just by chance, all this mining over the years could have uncovered fool's gold. This view is championed persuasively by Fischer Black.[1] Unfortunately, it is difficult to know whether data mining can completely explain style-specific results and what, if anything, we can do to correct the problem.

Beyond the data-mining issue, various studies have argued that the empirical results may be tainted by selection bias or by aberrations in the data. For instance, Kothari, Shanken, and Sloan find evidence that survivorship bias in COMPUSTAT data, the usual source of accounting information, may affect subsequent returns, particularly among small firms.[2] Brown, et. al. argue that survivorship histories of individual firms can bias performance studies; they apply this to mutual fund performance, but the effect is more generally applicable.[3]

If we are willing to assume that style investment results are not simply statistical aberrations, then the second and third possible explanations listed above can be subjected to empirical enquiry. By assuming some rational model of risk and return, and deriving empirical measures of risk, it is conceptually straightforward to ascertain whether risk premiums account totally for return differences across investment styles, conditional on the validity of the assumed risk/return model.

The purpose of this chapter is to present such an investigation in the context of Ross's Arbitrage Pricing Theory (APT) of risk and return.[4] The APT has

---

[1] Fischer Black, "Return and Beta," *Journal of Portfolio Management* (Fall 1993), pp. 8-18.
[2] S. P. Kothari, Jay Shanken, and Richard G. Sloan, "Another Look at the Cross-section of Expected Stock Returns," Working Paper, William E. Simon Graduate School of Business Administration, University of Rochester (December 1992).
[3] Stephen J. Brown, William Goetzmann, Roger G. Ibbotson, and Stephen A. Ross, "Survivorship Bias in Performance Studies," *The Review of Financial Studies* (1992, Number 4), pp. 553-580.
[4] Stephen A. Ross, "The Arbitrage Theory of Capital Asset Pricing," *Journal of Economic Theory* (December 1976), pp.341-360.

become one of the standard paradigms of risk/return finance in the sense that it now appears in most investments textbooks, is frequently cited in journal articles, and is employed in practice for portfolio selection and capital budgeting.

More important for our purpose here, the APT has the potential to explain investment style returns because it is a multi-factor theory. Many studies have found several distinct dimensions of style. For example, Fama and French document that both market capitalization (Size) and the ratio of book-to-market equity (B/M) are associated with cross-sectional differences in return.[5] They also find that the single-factor Capital Asset Pricing Model (CAPM) fails to explain any of the cross-sectional average return differences.[6]

Since portfolios classified along two style dimensions appear to have different expected returns (assuming this has not been produced by data-mining), a risk/return model with at least two risk premiums would seem *a priori* to have the greatest chance of empirical success.[7] Investment style literature mentions a number of possible dimensions; in addition to Size and B/M, earnings/price, leverage, sales growth, price momentum, and seasonals are among the suggested proxies for cross-sectional differences in returns.[8] Also, it seems reasonable to anticipate that still unknown styles may eventually be discovered, thereby adding to dimensionality burden of any rationally-based risk/return model.

Beyond Size and B/M, there is little agreement about the materiality of other indicia of style. Fama and French, for example, present evidence that earnings/price and leverage are unimportant when Size and B/M are taken into account.[9] Sharpe's method of return attribution based on investment styles has only two dimensions for *domestic* equities, Size and growth/value, the latter measured by B/M.[10] Sharpe gives other style dimensions for fixed-income assets and lists foreign equities as a separate style dimension for domestic U.S. investors. This is perfectly adequate for most U.S. investors, but one might wonder whether equities in non-U.S. markets display return differences across such attributes as Size and B/M, or whether other variables are more important.

Although it is a controversial conclusion, the empirical APT literature generally agrees that several distinct factors are associated with risk premiums.

---

[5] Eugene F. Fama and Kenneth R. French, "The Cross-Section of Expected Stock Returns," *Journal of Finance* (June 1992), pp.427-465.

[6] The Capital Asset Pricing Model was originated by William F. Sharpe, "Capital Asset Prices: A Theory of Market Equilibrium Under Conditions of Risk," *Journal of Finance* (September 1964), pp.425-442, and John Lintner, "The Valuation of Risk Assets and the Selection of Risky Investments in Stock Portfolios and Capital Budgets," *Review of Economics and Statistics* (February 1965), pp.13-37.

[7] Technically, a single risk premium model could explain the results, but only with a different parameterization than has previously been employed.

[8] The APT has already been used with some degree of success to explain the size anomaly. See K.C. Chan, Nai-Fu Chen, and David A. Hsieh, "An Exploratory Investigation of the Firm Size Effect," *Journal of Financial Economics* (September 1985), pp.451-471.

[9] *Op. cit.*

[10] William F. Sharpe, "Asset Allocation: Management Style and Performance Measurement," *Journal of Portfolio Management* (Winter 1992), pp.7-19.

Many studies provide evidence of between two and five factors, while others suggest fewer or more.[11] Given the preponderance of evidence in favor of five or fewer factors, this chapter simply *assumes* that five factors are relevant for domestic U.S. equities. The power of statistical tests will be reduced by an incorrect assumption about the true number of factors. Additionally, if there are actually *more* than five relevant factors, the tests will be biased in favor of concluding that the risk/return model (the APT) is inadequate; i.e., the tests will be biased in favor of the market inefficiency hypothesis. If there are five or fewer factors, however, no particular bias will occur.

THE EXPERIMENTAL DESIGN

Eight U.S. domestic equity portfolios were formed by classifying individual stocks along three style dimensions: large or small Size, high or low earnings per share/price (E/P), and high or low book equity/market equity (B/M). The first and third dimensions are known to produce material *ex post* return differences in past sample periods, and the second dimension is a popular focus of practical growth/value style investing.[12] In an effort to avoid using information not available to market participants, classification into style groups was accomplished using accounting data (B and E) pertaining to a period at least four months prior to the classification date.[13] All listed NYSE and AMEX and OTC stocks available from the CRSP database on the classification date were included in one of the eight portfolios.[14]

Every stock with available information was sorted by each of the three style dimensions, and then assigned to one of eight portfolios, depending on

---

[11] Supporting the presence of a single dominant factor is Charles Trzcinka, "On the Number of Factors in the Arbitrage Pricing Model," *Journal of Finance* (June 1986), pp.347-368. Trzcinka concludes that other factors may be present, but that the first factor is by far the most important. Supporting the presence of a limited number of factors, but more than one, are Stephen Brown and Mark Weinstein, "A New Approach to Testing Asset Pricing Models: The Bilinear Paradigm," *Journal of Finance* (June 1983), pp.711-743. Supporting a large number of factors are Phoebus J. Dhrymes, Irwin Friend, and N. Bulent Gultekin, "A Critical Re-examination of the Empirical Evidence on the Arbitrage Pricing Theory," *Journal of Finance* (June 1984), pp.323-346. Supporting the presence of just a single factor in some countries and several factors in other countries are John E. Hunter and T. Daniel Coggin, "The Correlation Structure of the Japanese Stock Market: A Cross-National Comparison," Working Paper, Investment Department, Virginia Retirement System (August 1994).

[12] In the practitioner literature, both B/M and E/P are considered indicators of "growth" versus "value" equities.

[13] The analysis was repeated using an eight-month lag, to make absolutely certain that no hindsight crept in; the results are qualitatively similar.

[14] Center for Research in Securities Prices, Graduate School of Business, University of Chicago. Subsequent to the latest available CRSP date (December 1992), the data were supplemented with the proprietary database of Roll and Ross Asset Management Corporation. Accounting data (for earnings and book equity) were also obtained from the latter source.

whether it was in the lowest or highest half of all stocks for that dimension. If Size, E/P, and B/M had been cross-sectionally uncorrelated, this would have resulted in an equal number of stocks in each portfolio. There was, however, some cross-sectional dependence among these indicia, so the eight style portfolios contain unequal numbers. Exhibit 1 shows the number of stocks per portfolio over the sample period, chosen rather arbitrarily to cover the latest available decade, April 1984 through March 1994.[15]

The plotting convention used in Exhibit 1 is followed throughout the chapter. Low (high) Size portfolios are represented by narrow (wide) lines, low (high) E/P portfolios by dashed (solid) lines, and low (high) B/M portfolios by grey (black) lines. Each portfolio is labeled with a three-character designator, where the first character is for Size, the second character is for E/P, and the third character is for B/M; in each case the character is "L" for low or "H" for high. For example, the HLH portfolio includes stocks in the half of all stocks with larger market capitalization, the half with lower earnings per share/price, and the half with higher book equity/market equity. As Exhibit 1 shows, even the portfolio with the smallest number of stocks included more than 100 individual issues in every period, and most portfolios had at least 200 most of the time.[16]

After all stocks were assigned to style portfolios, value-weighted averages of the three indicia of style were calculated for each portfolio at the beginning of each sample month.[17] These averages are plotted over the sample period in Exhibits 2, 3, and 4, for Size, E/P, and B/M, respectively.

The efficacy of the classification scheme can be observed in these exhibits. Ideally, all four portfolios in a given class for a particular dimension should have similar mean values for their common attribute and should differ markedly from the four portfolios in the other class. For instance, the four portfolios with low Size, but with high and low E/P and B/M, should have similar average market capitalization and materially different market capitalization than the four portfolios with high Size. Exhibit 2 shows this to be the case: The four portfolios LLL, LLH, LHL, and LHH all have average market capitalization in the $30 to $100 million range. Their average market cap is far from that of the four portfolios in the high group, whose average market cap hovers around $10 billion.

---

[15] Actually, there is some rationale for the choice of sample period. It was limited to ten years so that earlier data might constitute a hold-out sample should someone want to check the intertemporal robustness of results reported here. Also, the later part of the sample period here has not yet been used in other studies. For instance, the data period in Fama and French, *op. cit.*, ends in December 1990. Thus, more than three years of our sample is not subject to the charge that it has already been data-mined.

[16] Because of missing accounting information, not every stock with returns could be included in a portfolio. Also, stocks with negative earnings or negative book values in a given period were discarded from the sample in that period.

[17] That is, weighted averages were calculated for Size, E/P, and B/M, with the weights proportional to each stock's market capitalization at the beginning of the month.

Exhibit 1: Number of Stocks in Portfolios

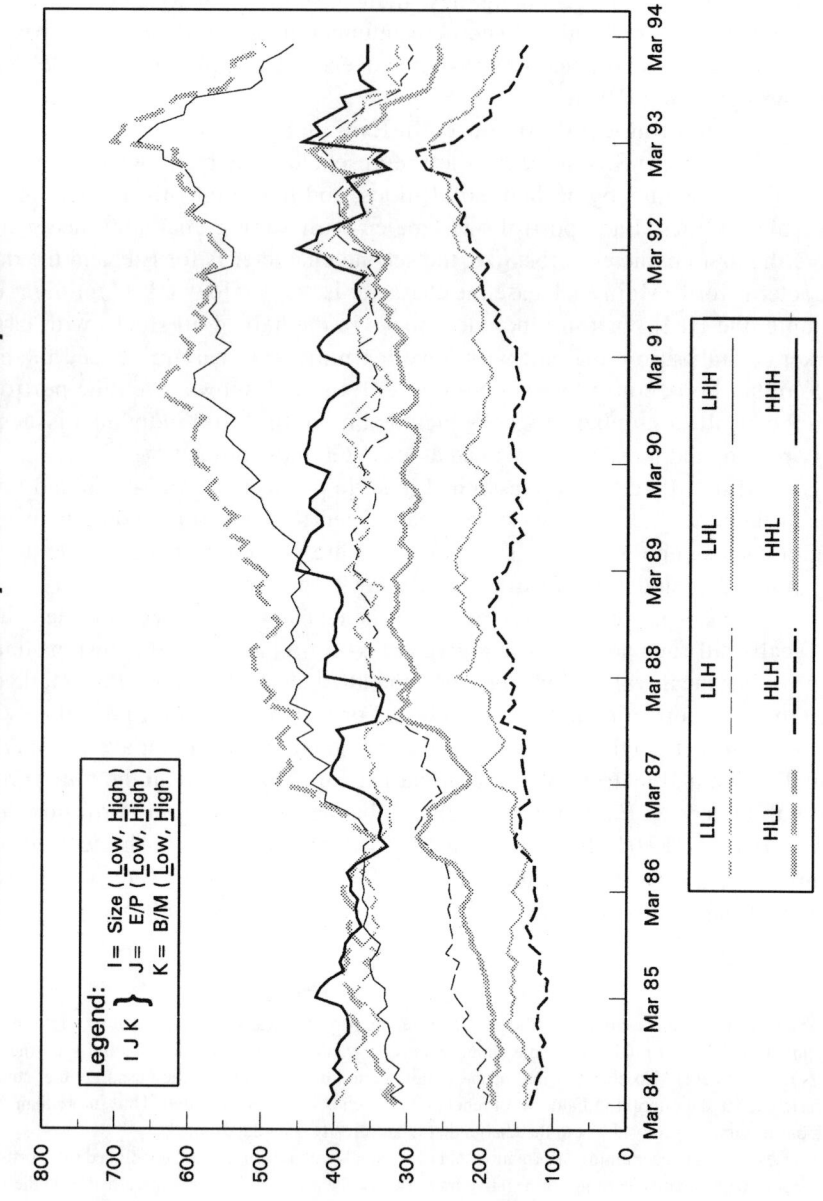

Legend:
I J K { I = Size (Low, High)
J = E/P (Low, High)
K = B/M (Low, High)

LLL   LLH   LHL   LHH
HLL   HLH   HHL   HHH

Chapter 5   99

Exhibit 2: Weighted Average Market Capitalization

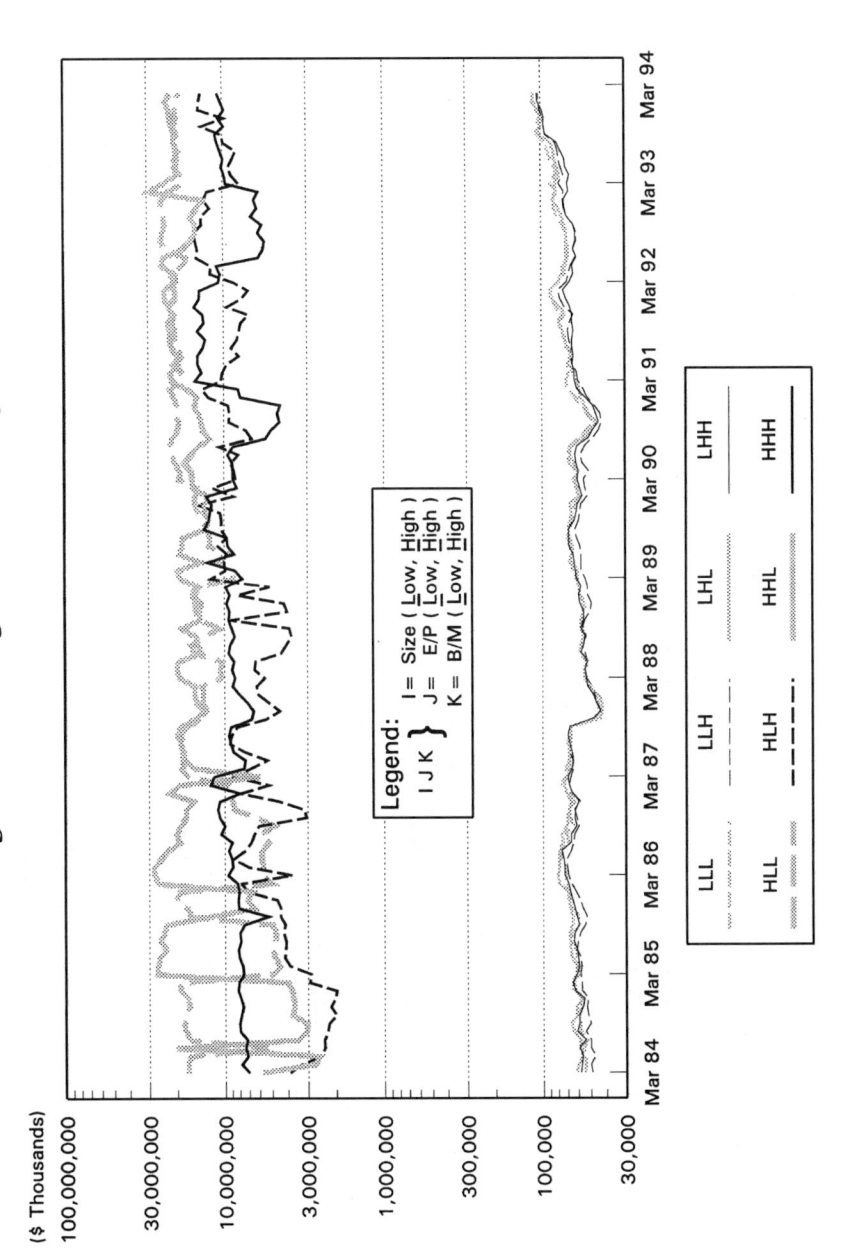

Legend:
I J K { I = Size (Low, High)
       J = E/P (Low, High)
       K = B/M (Low, High)

LLL   LLH   LHL   LHH
HLL   HLH   HHL   HHH

Exhibit 3: Mean Earnings/Price

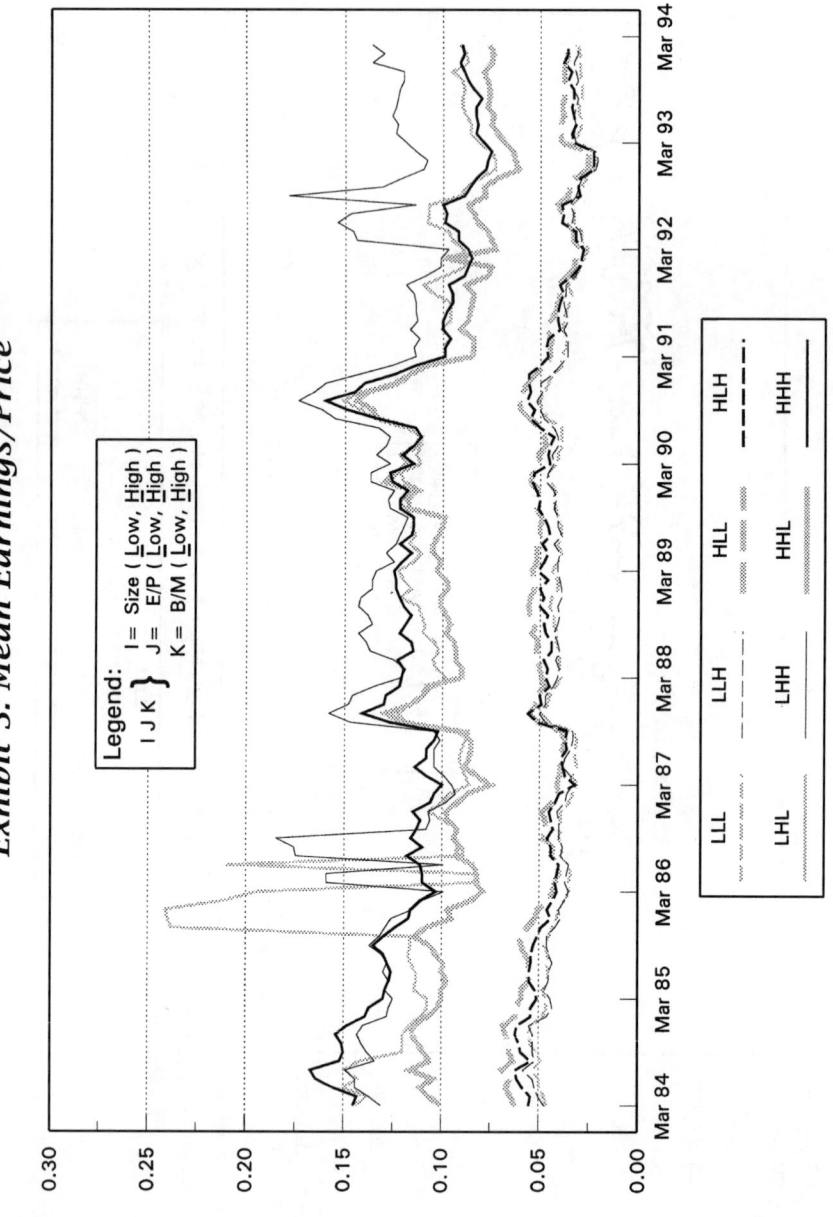

Exhibit 4: Mean Book/Market

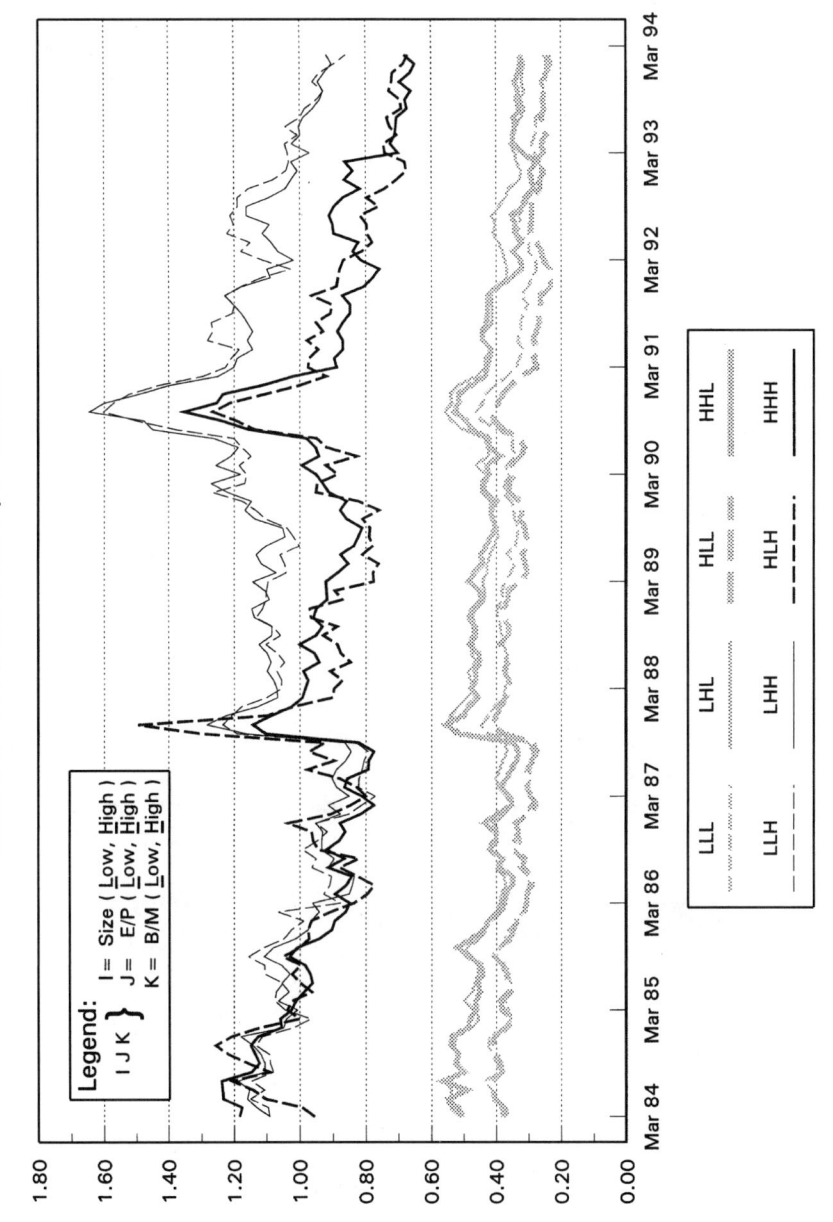

Similar clustering is apparent for E/P and B/M in Exhibits 3 and 4. The low E/P portfolios have average E/P values around 0.05 while the high E/P portfolios, although somewhat more diverse within their category, have average E/Ps around 0.10 to 0.15. Low B/M values are around 0.4, while high B/M values are between 0.8 and 1.20. One noticeable regularity in all cases is the greater dispersion in mean attribute values in the high groups, whether it be Size, E/P, or B/M. In the case of Size, this is probably attributable to one or two extremely large stocks moving from low to high E/P or from low to high B/M, or vice versa, as stocks are reassigned to portfolios month by month. In the cases of E/P and B/M, the cause is less apparent, but it might be due simply to greater price volatility in low-priced stocks.

STYLE PORTFOLIO INVESTMENT PERFORMANCE OVER THE PAST DECADE

Differences in Raw Returns

Value-weighted total returns for all eight portfolios were calculated over each month subsequent to a classification date. At the end of that month, stocks were reclassified and the portfolios were reformed. Total return investment levels, assuming reinvestment of cash dividends and other distributions, are plotted in Exhibit 5, along with the corresponding cumulative total return level for the S&P 500 Index, also including dividends.

During this decade, the best-performing portfolio was LHH: small market cap, high E/P, and high B/M. In conformance with other empirical reports, this is essentially a "value" portfolio, but one composed of small stocks. Small stocks per se, however, were not necessarily ideal investments during this decade; the worst-performing portfolio was LLL, small market cap, low E/P, and low B/M. Here are the relative rankings of the eight style portfolios and of the S&P 500:

Rank	Accumulated Value of One Dollar*	Style		
		Size	E/P	B/M
1	$6.85	Low	High	High
2	$5.34	High	High	High
3	$5.15	Low	High	Low
S&P 500	$3.96	—	—	—
4	$3.49	High	High	Low
5	$3.05	High	Low	Low
6	$2.76	High	Low	High
7	$2.02	Low	Low	High
8	$1.64	Low	Low	Low

*That is, a dollar invested on March 31, 1985, would have accumulated to this amount on March 31, 1994, assuming reinvestment of dividends.

Chapter 5 103

Exhibit 5: Style Portfolio Investment Value

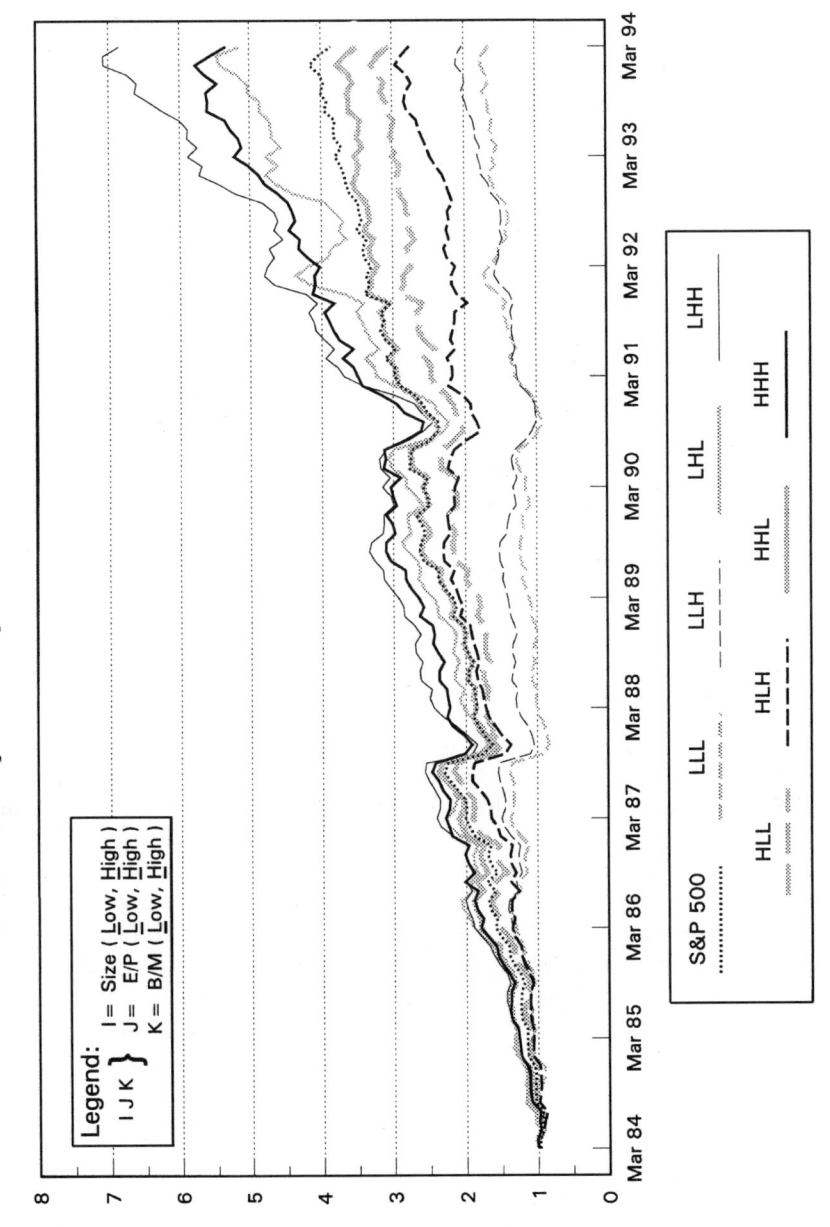

Legend:
I J K } I = Size (Low, High)
J = E/P (Low, High)
K = B/M (Low, High)

S&P 500   LLL   LLH   LHL   LHH
HLL   HLH   HHL   HHH

The numbers show a dramatic range of investment results, from a compound annual return of 5.07% for the worst portfolio to 21.2% for the best. The S&P's compound annual return was 14.8%. The three style portfolios that outperformed the S&P 500 were all in high earnings per share/price groups. Two of the three had small market cap, but so did the two lowest-ranked portfolios. The book equity/market equity style dimension displayed a middle ground of performance. Although the two best-performing portfolios had high B/M, so did portfolios that ranked sixth and seventh. For this particular sample period, these raw returns suggest a conclusion that the E/P style dimension was the most important.

Is Style Performance Significant?

Are differences in style portfolio investment returns statistically significant? If so, can they be ascribed to differences in risk? To answer both these questions, we shall implement a particularly tractable version of the statistical technique known as the *analysis of variance*. The technique employs a pooled time series/cross-section regression with appropriately chosen explanatory risk variables plus "dummy" variables used to classify the returns along style dimensions.[18] A "dummy" variable takes on the values zero or one depending on the class to which the dependent variable belongs. Thus, since we have three style dimensions, we shall employ three dummy variables; each dummy variable has the value zero or one, depending on whether the observed return is in the low or high group. For example, if an observed return were in a low Size, high E/P, and low B/M portfolio, the dummy variable triplet would be 0,1,0. The exact form of the regression equation is

$$R_{j,t} - R_{f,t} = \alpha_{LLL} + \alpha_{Size}D_{Size} + \alpha_{E/P}D_{E/P} + \alpha_{B/M}D_{B/M} + \varepsilon_{j,t} \qquad (1)$$

where $R_{j,t}$ is the return on style portfolio j in month t, $R_{f,t}$ is the riskless rate, D_i is the dummy variable for style dimension i, and $\varepsilon_{j,t}$ is a regression disturbance. Note that the regression intercept has subscript "LLL" (for low Size, low E/P, and low B/M). For this combination of styles, all three dummy variables are zero.

Our first regression pools the monthly excess returns[19] (for 120 months) on all eight style portfolios. These returns comprise the 960 observations of the dependent variable in the pooled regression. The explanatory variables are 960 dummy variable triplets, each one describing the particular style for the corresponding monthly portfolio return. Exhibit 6 presents the results.

The regression coefficients indicate the marginal contribution produced by having a high value of the style attribute, holding constant other style dimensions, in percent per month. The t-statistic measures whether the coefficient is reliably nonzero, a test of statistical significance. To be specific, the Size dummy's coeffi-

---

[18] For a general treatment of pooling time series and cross-sectional data using dummy variables, see George G. Judge, R. Carter Hill, William E. Griffiths, Helmut Lütkepohl, and Tsoung-Chao Lee, *Introduction to the Theory and Practice of Econometrics* (New York: John Wiley & Sons, 1988), Section 11.4, pp. 468-479.

[19] The excess return is the total monthly return on the portfolio less the return on a U.S. Treasury bill that had one month to maturity at the beginning of the month.

cient of 0.0177 indicates that an extra 1.77 basis points *per month* would have been earned in the sample decade simply by investing in large- rather than small-cap stocks, *ceteris paribus*. The *t*-statistic is only 0.0551, however; this indicates that the extra investment return of 1.77 basis points is not statistically significant.

Along the E/P dimension, the extra investment return was 65 basis points per month (!), and its t-statistic was 2.02. This indicates that the earnings/price style did produce reliably different returns, and they were sizable; 65 basis points per month implies an annual incremental return of approximately 7.80% simply from investing in stocks in the higher half of E/P ratios each month, holding constant other styles.

The results for B/M are less dramatic. The incremental return from buying high B/M stocks was 13.9 basis points per month. This is certainly nothing to ignore, but the t-statistic of 0.432 provides little assurance that differential return along this style dimension was statistically reliable.

Adjusting for Risk

The results in Exhibit 6 are based on raw returns; they are not risk-adjusted. Also, they are subject to a technical difficulty. The analysis of variance assumes that the observations are independent.[20] We know, however, that this is unlikely in our case because we have pooled monthly returns from eight portfolios observed over the same sample period. A glance at Exhibit 5 shows that the market values of these portfolios fluctuate together with considerable regularity. Most large diversified portfolio values correlate positively because they are subject to *common* factors, either a single market factor as in the CAPM or several macroeconomic factors, as predicted by the APT. To remove the dependencies among the style portfolios and thereby make our inferences more reliable, we ought to remove the sources of the dependence. It turns out that we can do this simultaneously with correcting for differences in risk across the portfolios.

Exhibit 6: Eight Style Portfolios on Style Dummy Variables
Pooled Time Series/Cross-Section Regressions
April 1984 – March 1994, Monthly

Intercept	Size	E/P	B/M
	Dummy Variables		
α_{LLL}	α_{Size}	$\alpha_{E/P}$	$\alpha_{B/M}$
0.25038	0.01771	0.65012	0.13867
(0.77930)	(0.05512)	(2.0235)	(0.43160)

Sample Size	960
Adjusted R^2	0.001337
F-statistic for Regression (3/956)	1.4280
Durbin-Watson	1.7046

Note: t-statistics in parentheses.

---

[20] If the observations are dependent, the regression is misspecified because the disturbances are not "spherical." This induces bias in the estimated standard errors and t-statistics, although not in the coefficients.

Our method is to include either a market factor or a set of APT factors as additional explanatory variables in the pooled time series/cross-sectional regressions, along with the dummy variables for style already reported. In addition, we shall include a set of cross-product terms between the dummy variables and the factors. These cross-product terms will effectively control for differences in risk.

To see how this works, let's first start in the context of the simplest model, a single-factor risk/return market model inspired by the CAPM. As an example, consider a portfolio with a particular style, say, LHL for low market cap, high E/P, and low B/M. We can write its single-factor market model as

$$R_{LHL,t} - R_{f,t} = \alpha_{LHL} + \beta_{LHL}(R_{M,t} - R_{f,t}) + \varepsilon_{LHL,t} \qquad (2)$$

where the subscript f denotes the riskless return, M denotes the single-factor market return, and ε is a regression disturbance.

Notice that both α, the intercept, and β, the slope coefficient, have subscripts denoting the portfolio's style. The style subscript on β signifies that a portfolio's style can conceivably influence its market risk. Since returns are measured in excess of the riskless rate, the style subscript on α signifies that style might provide an expected return *not* accounted for by risk, an "extra-risk" return. Differing values of β would support risk as the explanation of style investment returns, while differing values of α would support an investment opportunity such as pricing inefficiency as their source.

There is a potentially different equation such as (2) for each style portfolio; this is captured by interportfolio variation in the values of α and β. These values can be estimated directly from a pooled time series/cross-sectional regression by using the dummy variable method. We need both intercept and slope dummy variables. The complete regression equation with a single market factor is

$$\begin{aligned}R_{j,t} - R_{f,t} = &\alpha_{LLL} + \alpha_{Size}D_{Size} + \alpha_{E/P}D_{E/P} + \alpha_{B/M}D_{B/M} \\ &+ \beta_{LLL}(R_{M,t} - R_{f,t}) + \beta_{Size}D_{Size}(R_{M,t} - R_{f,t}) \\ &+ \beta_{E/P}D_{E/P}(R_{M,t} - R_{f,t}) + \beta_{B/M}D_{B/M}(R_{M,t} - R_{f,t}) + \varepsilon_{j,t}\end{aligned} \qquad (3)$$

Note that D_i is zero for each i with style dimension LLL (low Size, low E/P, and low B/M). For this combination of styles, only the intercept α_{LLL} and market factor excess return $[\beta_{LLL}(R_{M,t}-R_{f,t})]$ will appear with nonzero values. The incremental effect on risk (relative to LLL) of any other combination of styles will be empirically measured by the sum of βs whose subscripts bear the style description. Similarly, the extra-risk incremental return from a style combination different from LLL will be empirically measured by the corresponding αs with style-descriptive subscripts. The statistical significance, if any, of different styles can be measured directly by the t-statistics of these slope and intercept dummy variable coefficients. Finally, the validity of the inferences can be checked by examining the correlations of residuals across style portfolios.

Exhibit 7: Eight Style Portfolios on Single-Factor Market (S&P 500) Risk
Pooled Time Series/Cross-Section Regressions
April 1984 - March 1994, Monthly

	Base (LLL)	Size	E/P	B/M
		Dummy Variables		
Intercept α	−0.55014 (−3.5107)	0.02278 (0.14537)	0.68232 (4.3543)	0.24481 (1.5623)
Market Risk β	1.0609 (30.880)	−0.006721 (−0.19564)	−0.04267 (−1.2419)	−0.14067 (−4.0944)

Sample Size	960
Adjusted R^2	0.76894
F-statistic for Regression (7/952)	456.91
Durbin-Watson	1.7373

Note: t-statistics are in parentheses.

Exhibit 7 presents the empirical results from fitting Equation (3) using the eight style portfolios and a decade of monthly observations. The market factor is the total return on the S&P 500 index. The return units are percent per month. The market factor is highly significant, as would be expected in a time series model where the dependent variable is a well diversified portfolio. All three of the slope dummy coefficients are negative, although only $\beta_{B/M}$ is highly significant. This implies that higher book equity/market equity style portfolios have less market risk.

The intercept dummy variable coefficients have larger t-statistics than when Equation (1) was fit to the same data without a market factor. This is somewhat surprising, because a possible reason for the significance of style return differences in Equation (1) is differing market risks; thus, one might have predicted *a priori* that adjusting for risk would eliminate the significance. Yet the contrary is true. The intercept dummy coefficient, $\alpha_{E/P}$, has a similar magnitude in the two regressions, 65.0 versus 68.2 basis points in regressions (1) and (3), respectively; but it now has a considerably larger *t*-statistic, 4.35. This result indicates that style investing along the E/P dimension has been reliably profitable over the past decade, above and beyond single-factor market risk.

Regression model (3) explains more than three-quarters of the monthly variability in style portfolio returns across time and across the eight combinations of style. Most of the explained variability is attributable to the market factor. However, a single market risk factor may not be adequate to fully capture the multidimensional risks that may be underlying style investment returns. Can a multi-factor APT risk model do better?

Using the method of Connor and Korajczyk (hereafter CK), five factors were extracted from the entire data sample of individual equity excess returns.[21] The CK method has the great advantage of handling virtually any number of individual assets; the computations involve inversion of a covariance matrix with only as many rows and columns as the number of time series observations, in our case 120×120. The extracted factors have monthly observations that can be scaled in units equivalent to monthly rates of return. Connor and Korajczyk show that the first factor is similar to a large market index, although it is equal-weighted rather than value-weighted like the S&P 500. The second and higher CK factors are approximately unrelated to the first factor and to each other. They are constructed as combinations of systematic risks other than general market risk.

Once the time series of APT factor returns is available, we can employ the same procedure as before, but now we can be more precise about the possibility of multiple risks as sources of style portfolio returns. The pooled time series/cross-sectional regression will now have a total of 23 explanatory variables: 3 intercept dummy variables, the 5 APT factors, and 15 slope dummy variables (three for each of the five factors). The regression equation is

$$R_{j,t} - R_{f,t} = \alpha_{LLL} + \alpha_{Size} D_{Size} + \alpha_{E/P} D_{E/P} + \alpha_{B/M} D_{B/M}$$
$$+ \sum_k [\beta_{LLL,k} F_{k,t} + \beta_{Size,k} F_{k,t} + \beta_{E/P,k} D_{E/P} F_{k,t}$$
$$+ \beta_{B/M,k} D_{B/M} F_{k,t}] + \varepsilon_{j,t} \qquad (4)$$

where $F_{k,t}$ is the observed excess return on factor k in month t. The summation extends for $k=1,...,5$, over the five factors. All the slope coefficients, including those associated with slope dummy variables, must now have k subscripts to denote the factor with which they are associated. Exhibit 8 presents the results.

The explanatory power has increased substantially over the single-factor market model regression; the adjusted R-square is 0.914. Also, each of the five slope coefficients for style portfolio LLL (low size, low E/P, and low B/M), is statistically significant. Among the 15 dummy variable slope coefficients, 11 have t-statistics whose absolute values are greater than 2, the usual rule-of-thumb value for reliability. This implies that there are substantial and statistically significant differences in APT risks among style portfolios. The differences are not confined just to the first factor (which is like a single broad market factor); nine of the large t-statistics are associated with factors two through five. Thus, it seems reasonable to conclude that adding more factors gives us more ability to distinguish risk differences among investment styles.

---

[21] Gregory Connor and Robert A. Korajczyk, "Performance Measurement with the Arbitrage Pricing Theory: A New Framework for Analysis," *Journal of Financial Economics* (March 1986), pp.373-394. See also Gregory Connor and Robert A. Korajczyk, "Risk and Return in an Equilibrium APT: Application of a New Test Methodology," *Journal of Financial Economics* (September 1988), pp. 255-289.

Exhibit 8: Eight Style Portfolios on Five APT Risk Factors
Pooled Time Series/Cross-Section Regressions
April 1984 - March 1994, Monthly

	Base (LLL)	Size	E/P	B/M
		Dummy Variables		
Intercept α	−0.5348 (−5.4807)	−0.1323 (−1.3556)	0.6130 (6.2825)	0.2945 (3.0182)
APT Risks				
β_1	1.0136 (54.7160)	−0.1025 (−5.5314)	−0.0274 (−1.4815)	−0.1160 (−6.2605)
β_2	0.2863 (15.4570)	−0.3027 (−16.3400)	−0.0658 (−3.5526)	−0.0072 (−0.3908)
β_3	0.1158 (6.2549)	−0.2452 (−13.2430)	0.0696 (3.7619)	−0.0465 (−2.5104)
β_4	0.0576 (3.1093)	−0.1788 (−9.6569)	−0.0037 (−0.2016)	0.1468 (7.9268)
β_5	−0.0958 (−5.1762)	0.0563 (3.0397)	0.0391 (2.1103)	0.0365 (1.9705)

Sample Size 960
Adjusted R^2 0.91427
F-statistic for Regression (23/936) 445.64
Durbin-Watson 1.7053

Note: t-statistics are in parentheses.

Despite better ability to measure risk empirically, or, better said, *because* of this ability, the intercept dummy variable coefficients are now even more statistically significant. The intercept dummy variable for E/P has a coefficient of 0.613 (basis points of extra risk-adjusted return per month) with a *t*-statistic of 6.28. The intercept dummy for B/M has a coefficient of 0.295 with a *t*-statistic of 3.02. The coefficient for size, however, remains insignificant.

The inescapable conclusion: Controlling for multiple dimensions of risk by using a five-factor APT model does not eliminate return differences across investment styles. Indeed, it strengthens the effect. According to the empirical methods here, risk does vary substantially across investment styles, but risk alone does not explain differences in return. Higher values of both E/P and B/M are usually associated with "value" stocks as opposed to "growth" stocks. Value portfolios outperformed growth portfolios over the past decade, and the performance is not attributable to CAPM (single-factor) or APT (five-factor) risk.

Risk and Return Profiles for Style Portfolios

To get a feeling for risk and return differences across style portfolios, a simple expedient is to calculate their overall profiles from the dummy variable coefficients. Remember that we have eight style portfolios, denoted IJK, where I represents Size, J represents E/P, and K represents B/M. I, J, and K can be either low (L), or high (H) on the style attribute. For example, portfolio HLH has large (high) market capitalization stocks, low earnings per share/price stocks, and high book equity/market equity stocks. The dummy variables are 0 for L and 1 for H; thus, the dummy variable triplet corresponding to HLH is 1,0,1.

To obtain the estimated risk coefficient of portfolio HLH for, say, the first factor, multiply each coefficient by its dummy variable value and add it to the base coefficient, $\beta_{LLL,1}$; e.g., $\beta_{HLH,1}$=1.0136+1(−0.1025)+0(−0.0274)+1(−0.1160)=0.795.

Thus, the first factor risk coefficient for a portfolio with large-cap stocks, low E/P stocks, and high B/M stocks is considerably less than 1.0. This might have been partly anticipated because a coefficient of 1.0, given the Connor/Korajczyk factor method, would be the first factor coefficient for an equal-weighted portfolio and $\beta_{HLH,1}$ is for large-cap stocks. But notice in the adjustment above that a slightly greater contribution to the reduction in the coefficient comes from B/M than comes from Size. High B/M stocks also have lower first-factor risk.

The dummy variable slope coefficients in Exhibit 8 have an interesting pattern across the factors. For the Size slope dummies, the first four factors have negative and highly significant coefficients. Thus, large-market cap stocks have less APT risk on these four factors. For the fifth factor, the Size dummy coefficient is positive and significant, but this is swamped by the first four factors. As might have been anticipated, the overall volatility induced by systematic factors is greater for small than for large stocks.

Among the E/P slope dummies that are significant, factor 2 is negative, while factors 3 and 5 are positive. This mixed pattern makes it all the more surprising that the *intercept* dummy for E/P becomes so much more significant when going from a single-factor model to a multiple-factor model. Evidently, high E/P stocks are more susceptible to some risk sources and less susceptible to others compared to low E/P stocks. Although the overall difference in volatility is not particularly dramatic between low and high E/P portfolios[22], holding constant the other style dimensions, the ability to control for multiple risk sources substantially improves the ability to detect extra-risk performance.

---

[22] The sample standard deviations of returns, in percent per month, are as follows for the eight style portfolios (for ease of comparison, organized by matching pairs holding constant the other style dimensions):

Low Size		High Size		Low E/P		High E/P		Low B/M		High B/M	
LLL	5.84	HLL	4.82	LLL	5.84	LHL	5.67	LLL	5.84	LLH	4.92
LLH	4.92	HLH	4.63	LLH	4.92	LHH	4.73	LHL	5.67	LHH	4.73
LHL	5.67	HHL	4.61	HLL	4.82	HHL	4.61	HLL	4.82	HLH	4.63
LHH	4.73	HHH	4.21	HLH	4.63	HHH	4.21	HHL	4.61	HHH	4.21

The slope dummy coefficients corresponding to B/M are significantly negative for the first and third factors and positive for the fourth and fifth. The coefficient is insignificant for the second factor. Overall, high B/M stocks are somewhat less volatile; the volatility difference is more obvious than in the case of the E/P dimension. Again, as in the case of E/P, controlling for multiple risk sources renders the return difference along the B/M dimension more statistically reliable. Unlike E/P, risk control also increases the average return differential attributable to B/M.

Exhibit 9 presents a pictorial view of the risk coefficients and extra-risk returns across the eight style portfolios. The numbers depicted in Exhibit 9 consist of the base coefficient (α_{LLL} for the intercept and $\beta_{LLL,k}$ for the slope on factor k) plus the appropriate dummy variable coefficients. As can also be seen from the pattern of dummy variable coefficients in Exhibit 8, smaller Size is associated with algebraically larger risk coefficients on factors 1 through 4 and a smaller coefficient on factor 5. Larger E/P is associated with slightly smaller risk coefficients on the first and second factors and slightly larger coefficients on the third and fifth factors. Larger B/M is associated with smaller risk coefficients on the first and third factors and larger coefficients on the fourth and fifth factors. There is clearly a variety of APT risk profiles among the style portfolios, and the variation is statistically significant.

But perhaps the most striking chart is the bottom panel of Exhibit 9, which presents the extra-risk return of the eight style portfolios. Increasing either E/P or B/M had a monotonic impact on extra-risk return, holding Size constant. The largest extra-risk returns for either small- or large-cap stocks are in portfolios in the highest class of *both* E/P and B/M, while the worst-performing portfolios are in the lowest class of both these measures. The performance rankings by style are close to, but slightly different from, the rankings presented earlier based on raw returns. One notable departure concerns the lowest ranking portfolio in Exhibit 9, style HLL. On the basis of raw returns, it is ranked fifth out of eight. This is a bit puzzling because larger-cap stocks have *lower* risks on the first four factors.

Correcting for Cross-Sectional Dependence

In pooled time series/cross-section regressions, the standard errors of the estimated coefficients are affected by cross-sectional dependence in the regression disturbances. The regression residuals, sample estimates of the true but unobservable disturbances, display considerable dependence in Equation (1), the regression that makes no correction for risk. All the correlations in residuals across style portfolios are positive.[23] Their average value is 0.861, and eight of them exceed 0.9.

After correcting for single-factor market risk in regression (3), all these correlations are closer to zero, although six of them are still larger than 0.5, and the average is 0.287. After correcting for the five APT risk factors in regression (4), only three (of 28) exceed 0.4 and the average value is 0.115. This is the expected result; most of the cross-portfolio dependence is attributable to common factors.

---

[23] Among the 8 style portfolios there are 28 pairwise correlations.

Exhibit 9: Estimates from Pooled Time Series/Cross-Section Regression

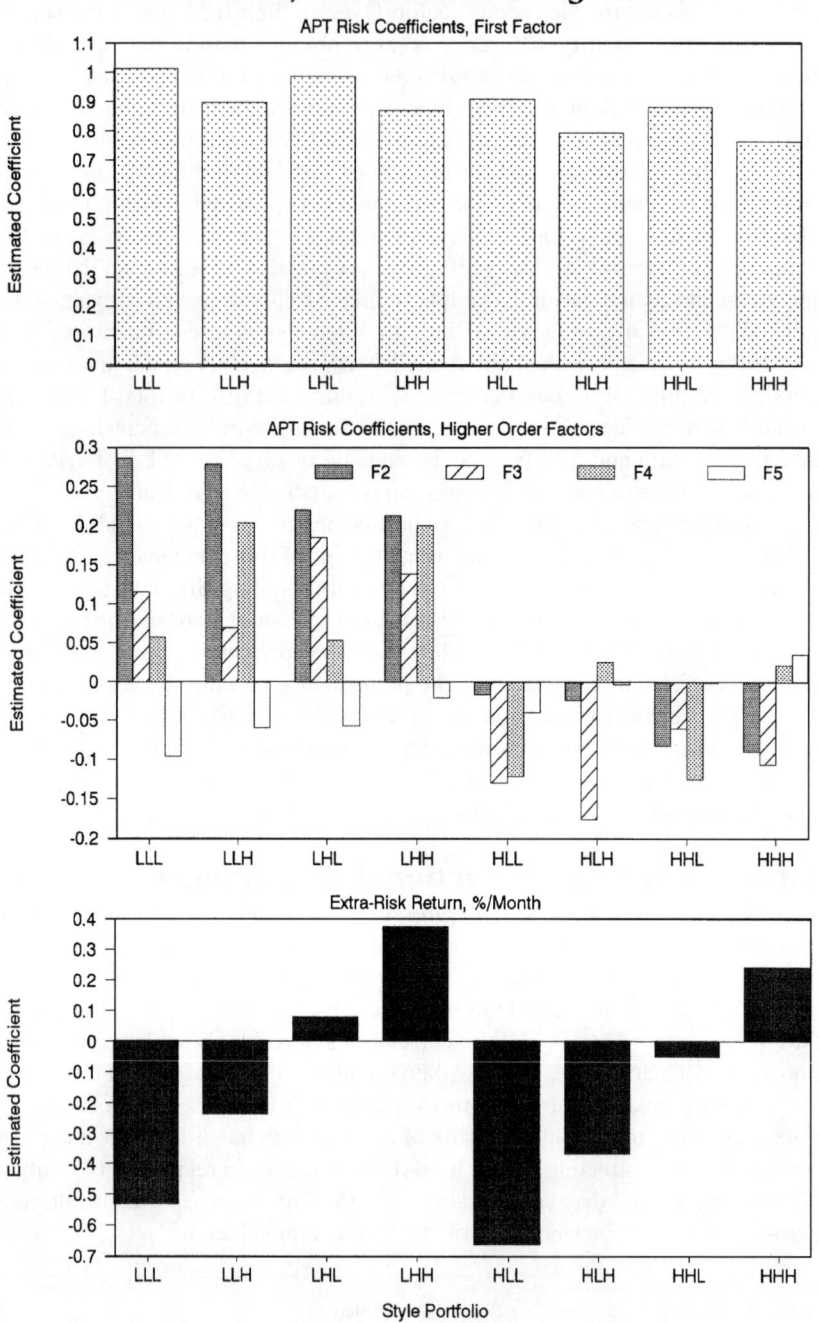

Even though the degree of cross-portfolio dependence is considerably reduced by removing systematic comovement, there could still remain enough dependence to bias inferences. A formal test of whether the 8 × 8 correlation matrix of the residuals from regression (4) is diagonal is rejected at the 0.001 significance level.[24] Although the correlations are small in magnitude, this test result implies that at least some of them are statistically significantly nonzero.

To be sure that the remaining cross-sectional dependence does not bias our inferences, we apply the "Seemingly-Unrelated Regressions" (SUR) method of Zellner to the eight style portfolio returns and the associated APT factors.[25] In SUR, a separate regression model, with possibly distinct coefficients, is estimated for each style portfolio; simultaneously, cross-regression dependence in the residuals is taken into account when computing standard errors and t-statistics.

The first step in SUR is simply to fit ordinary least squares (OLS) separately for a regression of the type:

$$R_{j,t} - R_{f,t} = \alpha_j \sum_k [\beta_{j,k} F_{k,t}] + \varepsilon_{j,t} \tag{5}$$

where j denotes the style portfolio, (j=LLL, LLH,...., HHH). There are eight separate regressions in this case, one for each style. Then an 8 × 8 cross-sectional covariance matrix is formed from the εs, the OLS residuals. The estimated covariance matrix is then employed in a generalized least squares *multivariate* regression, which provides revised estimates of the coefficients. A new set of residuals is then computed, and the process is repeated. Most of the time, there is little variation in the coefficient estimates after a few iterations.[26]

The results are tabulated in Exhibit 10 and the coefficients plotted in Exhibit 11. An "*" in Exhibit 11 signifies a coefficient that is statistically different from zero at the 1% level. The risk coefficients on the first factor have much more than this level of significance for all eight style portfolios; the smallest t-statistic is 27. Most of the higher-order risk factors also have significant coefficients. The extra-risk returns of five style portfolios, LLL, LLH, LHH, HLL, and HHL, differ from zero at the 1% level.

Comparing the SUR results in Exhibit 11 with the simpler pooled time series/cross-section results in Exhibit 9, we see that there is little material difference. The patterns among the risk coefficients are virtually identical, although there is some minor variability in the higher-order coefficients for large-cap portfolios.

---

[24] The test was derived by T. S. Breusch and A. R. Pagan, "The Lagrange Multiplier Test and its Applications to Model Specification in Econometrics," *Review of Economic Studies* (1980), pp.239-254. It is based on the asymptotic Chi-square distribution of the sum of the correlation coefficients.
[25] Arnold Zellner, "An Efficient Method of Estimating Seemingly Unrelated Regressions and Tests of Aggregation Bias," *Journal of the American Statistical Association* (1962), pp.348-368. A convenient discussion is in Judge, *et al., op. cit.*, Chapter 11.
[26] Three iterations and the SHAZAM econometrics software were used here. See *SHAZAM User's Reference Manual Version 7.0* (New York: McGraw-Hill), Chapter 25.

Exhibit 10: Eight Style Portfolios on Five APT Risk Factors
Seemingly-Unrelated Regressions, April 1984 - March 1994, Monthly

Style Portfolio
(IJK: I = Size, J = E/P, K = B/M, each one either *L*ow or *H*igh)

	LLL	LLH	LHL	LHH	HLL	HLH	HHL	HHH
Intercept								
α	−0.7268	−0.4085	0.2425	0.5687	−0.4093	−0.2700	−0.2840	0.1102
	(−3.938)	(−3.801)	(1.593)	(6.065)	(−3.524)	(−1.669)	(−2.588)	(1.194)
APT Risks								
β_1	1.0348	0.8738	1.0053	0.8536	0.8921	0.8168	0.8623	0.7865
	(29.53)	(42.82)	(34.79)	(47.95)	(40.45)	(26.60)	(41.38)	(44.88)
β_2	0.2554	0.2634	0.2703	0.2100	−0.0451	0.0518	−0.0723	−0.1458
	(7.290)	(12.91)	(9.354)	(11.80)	(−2.047)	(1.685)	(−3.469)	(−8.322)
β_3	0.1293	0.0605	0.1837	0.1361	−0.1065	−0.2034	−0.0944	−0.0669
	(3.693)	(2.965)	(6.359)	(7.650)	(−4.831)	(−6.627)	(−4.531)	(−3.821)
β_4	0.0852	0.1935	0.0711	0.1666	−0.1750	0.0625	−0.1161	0.0297
	(2.433)	(9.486)	(2.460)	(9.364)	(−7.938)	(2.037)	(−5.573)	(1.694)
β_5	−0.0418	−0.0832	−0.0775	−0.0297	−0.0486	−0.0243	−0.0247	0.0904
	(−1.194)	(−4.078)	(−2.684)	(−1.670)	(−2.203)	(−0.791)	(−1.187)	(5.163)
Explained Variation								
R^2	0.8890	0.9473	0.9196	0.9564	0.9349	0.8645	0.9364	0.9462

Note: Sample Size: 120 Months
t-statistics are in parentheses.

The extra-risk returns estimates, however, do differ between the two econometric methods in an interesting way: estimates from SUR display a wider disparity across styles among the four portfolios of small-cap stocks but less of a disparity for large-cap stocks. By accommodating cross-sectional dependence, the SUR method produces estimates that appear to be even more intuitively consistent with an inefficient markets explanation: If investment styles really do account for differing *extra-risk* expected returns, one would anticipate the effect to be more pronounced among smaller and thus less well-analyzed stocks.

Finally, the SUR method provides a convenient method of testing hypotheses across equations. We are particularly interested here in testing whether the intercepts in all eight regressions with the eight style portfolios are *jointly* and significantly different from zero.[27] Of course, from Exhibit 10, we can already observe that five of the eight intercept coefficients have t-statistics in excess of levels usually considered significant, so a joint test is likely to provide a similar inference. It does. The joint test of the hypothesis that all eight intercepts are really zero produces a Chi-square statistic of 123.1 with 8 degrees of freedom. If the hypothesis were true, the probability of observing such a value is zero to more than five significant digits!

---

[27] A similar procedure is developed for tests of the CAPM in Michael R. Gibbons, "Multivariate Tests of Financial Models: A New Approach," *Journal of Financial Economics* (March 1982), pp.3-27.

Exhibit 11: Estimates from Seemingly Unrelated Regressions

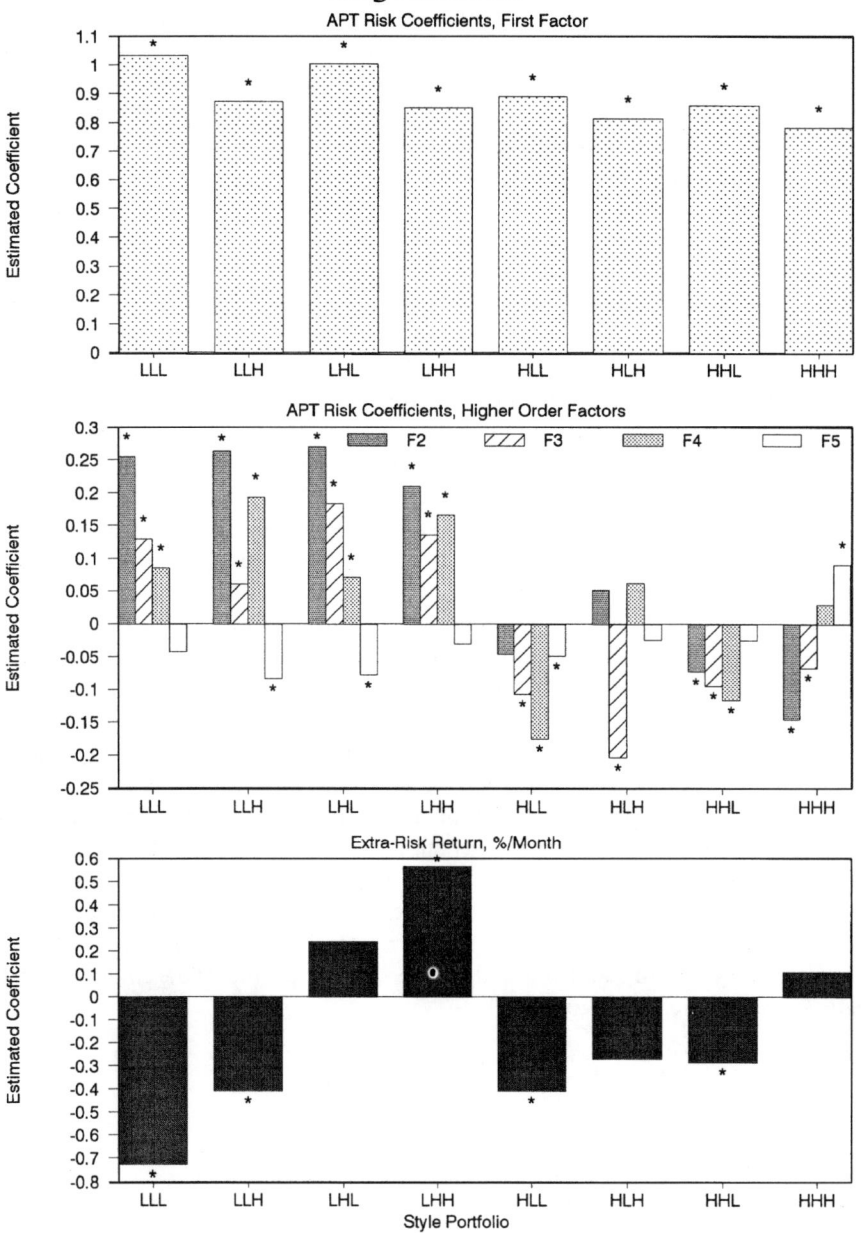

Non-Stationarity in Extra-Risk Return

One of the most puzzling empirical results in this paper, at least to the author, concerns the estimated relative importance of the three style dimensions, particularly with respect to estimated extra-risk return. In every test, the earnings per share/price (E/P) dimension is the most important. Although book equity/market equity (B/M) does finally appear as a significant style dimension after accounting for multi-factor risk with the APT, it has a smaller impact than E/P. Market capitalization has no significant effect in any of the tests.

These findings are puzzling because they seem to conflict with earlier results. Size, for example, is perhaps the earliest style dimension documented by rigorous research to yield extra-risk return (relative to a single risk factor).[28] The more recent Fama/French article also presents evidence that Size is inversely cross-sectionally related to average return, although its influence was somewhat larger before 1977.[29] Fama/French conclude that E/P is not an important explanatory variable for average return after controlling for Size and B/M.

The data samples in previous research are of course drawn from an earlier period, and the empirical methods differ to some extent. It does not seem likely, however, that empirical methods could cause the differential results. In the sample decade of this paper, high E/P stocks performed better, whether or not returns are adjusted for risk. It is hard to believe that an alternative empirical method would make any difference.

If the results are chiefly sample period-specific, they represent just another level of the investment enigma: style may matter, and style investing may produce extra-risk return, but which particular style is most important *now*? If styles change rapidly, the practical investor may derive little benefit from knowing that styles even exist. If they change more slowly, there is hope that they can be tracked and exploited with appropriate analytics.

In a preliminary foray along this path, the simplest type of intertemporal model, a deterministic time trend, was appended to the intercept terms, and then Seemingly-Unrelated Regressions (SUR) were recomputed for the eight style portfolios. The idea was to estimate whether the extra-risk returns of any of the eight style portfolios, as measured by their intercepts, had a reliably different value at the beginning and the end of the sample period. The amended SUR regression for style portfolio *j* is

$$R_{j,t} - R_{f,t} = \alpha_{j,0} + \alpha_{j,\text{time}}\tau + \sum_{k}[\beta_{j,k}F_{k,t}] + \varepsilon_{j,t} \tag{6}$$

---

[28] See Rolf W. Banz, "The Relationship Between Return and Market Value of Common Stocks," *Journal of Financial Economics* (March 1981), pp.779-794.

[29] Black, op. cit., argues that the size effect was originally uncovered by data-mining. He notes: "In the period since the Banz study (1981-1990), they [Fama/French] find no size effect at all, whether or not they control for beta [single factor risk]....Lack of theory [about why there *should* be a relation between size and return] is a tip-off; watch out for data mining!" (p. 9, bracketed phrases added for clarification).

where τ is a linear time index.[30] Given the base intercept, $\alpha_{j,0}$, and the slope coefficient on time, $\alpha_{j,\text{time}}$, an estimate of the extra-risk return for portfolio j at any time τ is simply $\alpha_{j,0} + \alpha_{j,\text{time}}\tau$. Exhibit 12 presents values of the extra-risk returns for each of the eight style portfolios at three different points during the sample period, the beginning, middle, and end, from the SUR regressions.

The middle bars, those for April 1, 1989, are almost identical to the average extra-risk returns reported in Exhibits 10 and 11. But among the four small market capitalization style portfolios, on the left side of Exhibit 12, there is a substantial reduction in extra-risk return during the sample period. For each of the four small Size style portfolios, the estimated extra-risk return was closer to zero at the end than at the beginning of the decade. There is not such a clear pattern among the large Size portfolios.

However, the statistical significance of this nonstationarity is questionable. None of the t-statistics associated with $\alpha_{j,\text{time}}$ is large for any j; the largest in absolute value is only 1.46. A joint test that they are *all* zero produces a Chi-square statistic of 14.8 with 8 degrees of freedom. This implies a significance level of about 6%. The ex post odds are almost 20-to-1 that at least some of the eight coefficients are nonzero, but no particular coefficient can be singled out as responsible.

Exhibit 12: Estimated Trends in Extra-Risk Return From Seemingly-Unrelated Regressions With Deterministic Time Trend Intercepts

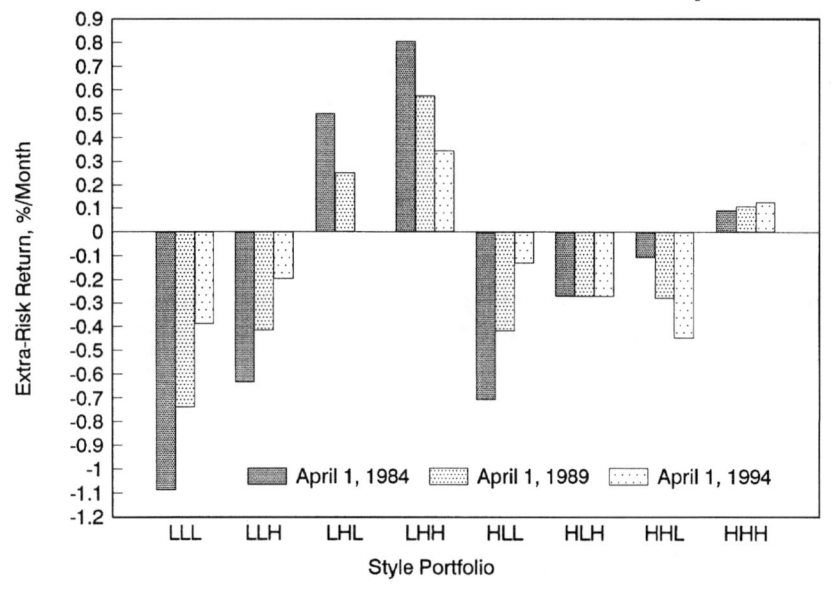

[30] For convenience, $\tau = t/120$ for the tth month of the sample period.

Thus, there is marginally significant evidence that style-specific returns are nonstationary. A model more sophisticated than a simple deterministic time trend may provide interesting details about the extent and form of the nonstationarity.

A Caveat About Risk Adjustment and Pricing Efficiency

Any risk adjustment model that employs factor portfolios is subject to a technical problem: If the risk factors cannot be combined linearly to produce an *ex ante* mean-variance efficient portfolio, expected returns *cannot* be expressed as linear combinations of risk coefficients.[31] This implies that the intercept terms in our regressions could differ significantly across style portfolios without necessarily implying pricing inefficiency. In the context of a single-factor model, Roll and Ross show that even minor departures of the index from mean-variance efficiency can allow room for considerable cross-sectional variation in what appears to be "extra-risk" return.[32]

As a consequence, the evidence that risk models do not eliminate significant investment performance variation across styles is consistent not only with pricing inefficiency but also with a technical failure of the risk factors to be mean-variance efficient portfolios. From a practical investment viewpoint, however, this has virtually no operational relevance. If an investor had structured a portfolio during the past decade to have larger investments in high E/P and B/M stocks while holding risk at the same level as either the S&P 500 or at the same multiple levels as every one of five APT factors, the performance results would have been splendid. The portfolio would have outperformed benchmarks with equivalent single-factor or multiple-factor risk profiles without displaying any greater total volatility. Whether this result was induced by market inefficiency or simply because the structured portfolio was closer to the true efficient frontier might be an interesting issue for the scholar; but the investor enjoying surplus wealth could probably care less!

SUMMARY

Using U.S. domestic equity returns over the past decade, from early 1984 through early 1994, stocks were classified by three indicia of investment style: market capitalization (Size), earnings per share/price (E/P), and book equity/market equity (B/M). At the beginning of each sample month, all listed and OTC stocks in the upper and lower halves of these variables were assigned to separate groups, thereby creating eight style portfolios. The subsequent monthly return was then observed for each portfolio.

---

[31] This result was emphasized about previous single-factor CAPM tests in Richard Roll, "A Critique of the Asset Pricing Theory's Tests," *Journal of Financial Economics* (March 1977), pp.129-176.

[32] Richard Roll and Stephen A. Ross, "On the Cross-Sectional Relation Between Expected Return and Betas," *Journal of Finance* (March 1994), pp.101-121.

Style portfolios had dramatically different performance over the decade. The best portfolio (LHH, for low Size, high E/P, and high B/M) outperformed the worst portfolio, LLL, by more than 15% *annually*. Using pooled time series/cross-section regressions with dummy variables for investment style, the raw return differences were found to be statistically significant.

Both the single-factor CAPM (with the S&P 500 as the factor) and the multi-factor APT (with five factors) were employed in an effort to determine whether style performance could be attributed to risk. Style portfolios *do* differ markedly in their risk profiles. There is substantial statistical evidence that all three style dimensions are associated with diverse sensitivities to various risk factors, a broad market factor *and* higher-order factors.

Yet, the risk models used here do not fully explain style performance. There is statistically significant evidence in this empirical sample that style is associated with extra-risk return. Specifically, a high E/P portfolio returned more than 60 basis points *per month* in extra performance over the decade, holding constant both multi-factor APT risks and other dimensions of style. The estimated t-statistic for this effect was 6.3. Similarly, a high B/M portfolio returned about 30 basis points per month in extra performance with a t-statistic of 3.0. Size is the style exception; it was associated with no significant difference in returns.

Various specification tests were conducted to assure that econometric difficulties were not responsible for the results. The Seemingly-Unrelated Regressions method was employed to ascertain the impact, if any, of cross-sectional dependence in the pooled time series/cross-section model. Although there is evidence of minor cross-sectional dependence, correcting it with SUR actually strengthens the conclusions about extra-risk return to E/P and B/M, particularly in the small size group of style portfolios.

The three style dimensions are ranked differently here from previously published research, a fact that raises the specter of nonstationarity. A cursory empirical investigation was initiated into whether style returns change substantially over time. Using a very simple model, a deterministic time trend in extra-risk returns, there is marginally significant evidence that styles have changed in comparative importance over the decade. In general, extra-risk return appeared to diminish among smaller firms. A more sophisticated intertemporal model might well produce more meaningful and significant nonstationary effects and better investment performance.

Chapter 6
Style Betas: An Approach to Measuring Style at the Security Level

Keith Quinton, CFA
Senior Vice President
Putnam Investments

INTRODUCTION

Style investing and style benchmarks are a natural evolution from the concepts of assets and asset benchmarks. The most critical decision in any investment process is the asset allocation: how much in stocks and bonds, in a two-asset world for example. Once the asset allocation decision is made, performance can now be measured not in absolute returns, but in returns relative to the benchmarks that define the assets: often the S&P 500 for stocks and the 20-year Treasury bond for bonds. The investor is now focused on the critical variable (i.e., asset allocation) and has a measuring rod (i.e., returns relative to the benchmarks).

Style investing is the next level of detail down from asset allocation. Rather than lump all stocks together, we split them up into "sub" asset classes: value, growth, large, small, for example. Then we focus on allocating across these groups and measure performance relative to the representative benchmarks. Once again the investor is focused on the bigger picture, and also has a way to measure manager or portfolio performance.

WHY STYLE?

There is some debate as to whether style classifications represent different asset classes or not. Clearly, value, growth, large, and small stocks are not as different as stocks and bonds, but there appears to be meaningful differences in the returns on a monthly basis. Allocation across growth, value, large, and small can add value to the asset allocation process, since the returns are not perfectly correlated.

There are different views regarding whether or not benchmarking managers to a style index is fair from a performance perspective, since the sponsor may raise the bar that the manager has to jump over to exhibit skill in investing. Conversely, some sponsors may feel that the manager has a lower bar to clear during prolonged periods of weak style performance. Appropriately selected, style benchmarks are fairer comparison standards, not better or worse, easier or harder. They eliminate the systematic return bias in a style portfolio, allowing a manager's stock picking ability to be revealed.

In addition to its role in asset allocation and performance evaluation, style investing can also be used as a tool for performance attribution in a stock portfolio that is not indexed to a specific style. Some important questions result. Does a portfolio's return come from a higher or lower than market exposure to various styles? Is the style consistent over time? How much of the portfolio's return comes from stock selection skills versus systematic bets?

Finally, style investing can also be a source of excess return, by either identifying a style category that *regularly* experiences excess return, or by developing a methodology that episodically identifies when a style is going to outperform. In summary, there is an important role for style in a modern investment process at many levels in a variety of ways.

STYLE DEFINED

Most current style benchmarks identify a starting universe of stocks of interest and then develop criteria that classify these stocks into style categories. Several problems with this process surface when we use its results to analyze other portfolios or managers. First of all, what do we do with outsiders such as stocks that were not a part of the original universe? One commonly used set of value and growth benchmarks, developed by BARRA and Standard & Poor's, begins with the 500 stocks that make up the S&P 500. How do we classify a stock outside the S&P?

A second problem results from weaknesses in the underlying data for any given stock. The previously mentioned set of style benchmarks also uses book-to-price ratios to differentiate between growth and value: a "high" B/P ratio indicating a value stock; a "low" B/P ratio indicating a growth stock. Some companies have distorted book values because of acquisitions, restructurings, and changes in accounting rules, and the book to price ratio may not capture the true essence of the company. By implication, if there are problems at the stock level, style measurement at the portfolio or manager level may also be suspect. What is needed is a clean, intuitively, and theoretically appealing method of classifying any stock and a portfolio of stocks according to style.

STYLE BETAS

The stock market is filled with uncertainty and unclear data: future prospects for companies, accounting treatment of income statement and balance sheet items, and so forth. Some of the cleanest stock data available includes end of day prices and actual dividends paid. Both are widely reported and usually undisputed. A methodology that classifies stocks on the basis of their price data would be subject to little question or dispute. Methodologies that classify stocks according to some accounting-based or market measure — book-to-price or market capitalization for example — may be suspect at the stock level, but acceptable in aggregate. For example, S&P/BARRA's book/price methodology may misclassify an individual stock, but the aggregated Value and Growth Indices may be acceptable since the large number of stocks in each index tends to cancel out individual problems, preserving the overall style effect.

Developing a measure of a stock's price change relative to an aggregate index by regressing monthly stock returns against the index returns combines these two acceptable data sources to generate *style betas*. Just as a market beta identifies a stock's sensitivity to market moves, a style beta identifies a stock's sensitivity to value, growth, large, or small. This approach eliminates the problem of outsiders; any stock that trades can be classified according to its style sensitivity. It is intuitively appealing in that it is price driven. It identifies which stocks act like growth stocks, which stocks act like value stocks, which stocks act like big stocks, and which stocks act like small stocks, regardless of their accounting-based measures of growth and value and observed market capitalization. Essentially, we should judge a stock's style by the company it keeps.

THE MATHEMATICS

The approach is as follows. Take 60 consecutive observations of monthly total return (5 years total) for a given stock and regress them against the monthly market and style index total returns for the same time period to generate style betas. These betas measure a stock's systematic sensitivity or exposure to growth-value and size. Equation (1) shows one potential approach:

$$R_{stock} = Alpha + Beta_{market} \times R_{market} + Beta_{value} \times R_{value} + Beta_{growth} \times R_{growth} + Beta_{large} \times R_{large} + Beta_{small} \times R_{small} \quad (1)$$

where:

R_{stock} = the monthly return of a given stock
$Alpha$ = the unexplained or stock specific return
$Beta_{market}$ = the sensitivity of a given stock's return to the overall market

R_{market} = the monthly return on the market (S&P 500)
$Beta_{value}$ = the sensitivity of a given stock's return to the value index (S&P/BARRA)
R_{value} = the monthly return of the value index (S&P/BARRA)
$Beta_{growth}$ = the sensitivity of a given stock's return to the growth index (S&P/BARRA)
R_{growth} = the monthly return of the growth index (S&P/BARRA)
$Beta_{large}$ = the sensitivity of a given stock's return to the large index (Russell 1000)
R_{large} = the monthly return of the large index (Russell 1000)
$Beta_{small}$ = the sensitivity of a given stock's return to the small index (Russell 2000)
R_{small} = the monthly return of the growth index (Russell 2000)

Solving for the alpha and beta estimates individual stock sensitivities to value, growth, large, and small. Unfortunately, regression analysis leads to very unstable coefficients when the independent variables are highly correlated. For example, from January 1981 through December 1993, I calculated the following correlations:

	S&P 500	Value	Growth	Large	Small
S&P 500	1.00	0.97	0.98	1.00	0.86
Value	0.97	1.00	0.91	0.97	0.84
Growth	0.98	0.91	1.00	0.98	0.84
Large	1.00	0.97	0.98	1.00	0.88
Small	0.86	0.84	0.84	0.88	1.00

The correlations of the independent variables shown here are too high to be acceptable in a multiple regression environment. Equation (2) shows a needed modification:

$$R_{stock} = Alpha + Beta_{market} \times R_{market} + Beta_{g-v} \times R_{growth-value} + Beta_{l-s} \times R_{large-small} \qquad (2)$$

where:

R_{stock} = the monthly return of a given stock
$Alpha$ = the unexplained or stock specific return
$Beta_{market}$ = the sensitivity of a given stock's return to the overall market
R_{market} = the monthly return on the market (S&P 500)
$Beta_{g-v}$ = the sensitivity of a given stock's return to the difference between the growth index and the value index (S&P/BARRA)
$R_{growth-value}$ = the monthly return of the growth index minus the value index (S&P/BARRA)
$Beta_{l-s}$ = the sensitivity of a given stock's return to the difference between the large index and the small index (Russell)

$R_{\text{large-small}}$ = the monthly return of the large index minus the small index (Russell)

The cross-correlation problem is mitigated by using the difference in return between the growth and the value indices and the large and the small indices. The independent variables are still correlated, but significantly less than the indices themselves. Solving for the alpha and betas here results in truer, more stable measures of a stock's growth-value sensitivity and large-small sensitivity. Exhibit 1 shows a detailed example of the results for IBM.

Exhibit 1: Sample Calculation of Style Betas for IBM

Date	IBM	S&P 500	L-S	G-V
12/31/95	−5.4	1.9	1.1	1.6
11/30/95	−0.4	4.4	0.3	−1.6
10/31/95	2.9	−0.4	4.0	2.4
9/30/95	−8.6	4.2	2.3	1.5
8/31/95	−4.8	0.3	−1.3	−1.2
7/31/95	13.4	3.3	−1.9	−0.3
6/30/95	3.2	2.4	−2.5	3.1
5/31/95	−1.5	4.0	2.1	−0.9
4/30/95	15.2	2.9	0.4	−0.7
3/31/95	9.1	3.0	0.9	0.4
2/28/95	4.7	3.9	−0.1	0.0
1/31/95	−1.9	2.6	3.8	−0.2
12/31/94	3.9	1.5	−1.3	0.5
11/30/94	−4.7	−3.7	0.4	0.8
10/31/94	7.0	2.3	2.3	0.2
9/30/94	1.6	−2.4	−2.0	2.1
8/31/94	11.1	4.1	−1.3	2.5
7/31/94	5.3	3.3	1.6	−0.2
6/30/94	−6.7	−2.5	0.7	0.6
5/31/94	10.0	1.6	2.5	0.0
4/30/94	5.3	1.3	0.6	−1.7
3/31/94	3.3	−4.4	1.0	−0.5
2/28/94	−6.0	−2.7	−2.3	1.8
1/31/94	0.0	3.4	−0.1	−2.5
12/31/93	4.9	1.2	−1.6	−1.0
11/30/93	17.7	−0.9	1.9	1.7
10/31/93	9.5	2.0	−1.3	3.2
9/30/93	−8.2	−0.7	−3.1	−1.5
8/31/93	3.4	3.8	−0.5	−0.3
7/31/93	−9.9	−0.5	−1.7	−3.3

Exhibit 1: (Continued)

Date	IBM	S&P 500	L-S	G-V
6/30/93	−6.4	0.3	0.0	−2.2
5/31/93	9.6	2.7	−1.7	1.7
4/30/93	−4.4	−2.4	0.1	−4.2
3/31/93	−6.4	2.2	−0.8	−1.3
2/38/93	6.6	1.4	3.2	−4.3
1/31/93	2.2	0.7	−2.6	−3.8
12/31/92	−26.2	1.3	−1.8	−1.2
11/30/92	3.9	3.4	−3.8	1.3
10/31/92	−17.2	0.4	−2.3	2.3
9/30/92	−6.8	1.2	−1.0	0.1
8/31/92	−7.3	−2.0	0.7	1.7
7/31/92	−3.2	4.0	0.7	0.9
6/30/92	7.9	−1.4	3.1	−1.3
5/31/92	1.3	0.5	−0.7	0.5
4/30/92	8.7	2.9	5.9	−3.8
3/31/92	−3.9	−2.0	1.3	−0.8
2/29/92	-2.1	1.3	−1.7	−1.4
1/31/92	1.1	−1.9	−9.3	−3.5
12/31/91	−3.8	11.4	3.4	5.6
11/30/91	−4.6	−4.0	0.8	3.0
10/31/91	−5.2	1.3	−1.0	-0.2
9/30/91	7.0	−1.6	−2.0	−1.1
8/31/91	−3.1	2.3	−1.1	1.8
7/31/91	4.2	4.7	1.3	1.4
6/30/91	−8.5	−4.6	1.3	0.8
5/31/91	4.2	4.3	−0.7	−1.0
4/30/91	−9.5	0.3	0.4	−1.0
3/31/91	−11.6	2.4	−4.3	2.9
2/28/91	2.5	7.2	−3.9	1.2
1/31/91	12.2	4.4	−4.2	−0.6

Regression results:

Alpha	0.00

	Beta
S&P 500	0.64
L-S	0.42
G-V	−0.21

The growth-value beta that comes out of the regression is a measure of the sensitivity of a given stock to the relative performance of growth versus value. Stocks with positive growth-value betas are growth stocks: they have done well when growth outperformed value. Stocks with negative growth-value betas are value stocks: they historically have done poorly when growth outperformed value, i.e., done well when value outperforms growth. For example, if XYZ stock has a growth-value beta of 0.61, it is a growth stock. The regression equation predicts a positive relationship between the growth-value differential and XYZ's return: for every 1% that growth outperforms value, XYZ is forecast to have a 0.61% return.

Similarly, the large-small beta that comes out of the regression is a measure of the sensitivity of a given stock to the relative performance of large versus small. Stocks with positive large-small betas are large stocks: they have done well when large outperformed small. Stocks with negative large-small betas are small stocks: they historically have done poorly when large outperformed small, i.e., done well when small outperforms large. For example, if XYZ stock has a large-small beta of −1.5, it is a small stock. The regression equation predicts a negative relationship between the large-small spread and XYZ's return: for every 1% that large outperforms small, XYZ is forecast to have a −1.5% return.

This approach develops Arbitrage Pricing Theory(APT)-type multi-factor betas: a stock's return is a function of its market beta, growth-value beta, large-small beta, and some stock specific return. Another benefit of this approach is that it quantifies a stock's exposure exactly. Style classifications are not all or nothing — shades of gray exist on the continuum of growth-value and large-small. The style betas capture this range of sensitivities, allowing stocks to be extremely sensitive to the differentials (either positively or negatively), somewhat sensitive, or not at all sensitive. Exhibit 2 shows style betas for selected companies as of year-end 1995.

USES OF STYLE BETAS

Portfolio Analysis
Now that the sensitivity of any stock to styles is known by computing its style betas, it is possible to compute a portfolio-weighted average sensitivity to styles. In this way it is possible to estimate how a portfolio may potentially do over time in various market environments or a given manager's style exposure.

Misclassification
The style betas can also be used to flush out "masqueraders" — stocks that (based on book to price ratios) may be classified as value stocks, but have actually behaved like growth stocks, or stocks that have a large capitalization but behave like small stocks.

Exhibit 2: Style Betas for Selected Companies as of 12/95

Symbol	Name	G-V Beta	L-S Beta
ABT	Abbott Laboratories	0.53	0.38
AIG	American International G	−0.19	0.11
AIT	Ameritech Corporation	−0.71	0.41
AN	Amoco Corporation	−0.62	0.60
T	AT&T Corporation	−0.33	0.23
BLS	Bellsouth Corporation	−0.64	0.70
BMY	Bristol-Meyers Squibb Co.	0.71	0.16
CHV	Chevron Corporation	−1.01	0.28
KO	Coca-Cola Company (The)	0.83	0.04
DD	Du Pont (E.I.) De Nemour	−0.90	0.32
XON	Exxon Corporation	−0.34	0.44
GE	General Electric Company	−0.21	−0.14
GM	General Motors Corp	−2.10	−0.69
GTE	GTE Corporation	0.01	0.57
HWP	Hewlett-Packard Company	0.66	−0.87
INTC	Intel Corporation	−0.08	−0.79
JNJ	Johnson & Johnson	1.49	0.31
LLY	Lilly (Eli) and Company	0.99	0.15
MCD	McDonald's Corporation	0.02	−0.12
MRK	Merck & Co., Inc.	1.00	0.28
MSFT	Microsoft Corporation	1.01	−0.76
MOB	Mobil Corporation	−0.70	0.44
MOT	Motorola, Inc.	−0.74	−0.61
PEP	Pepsico, Inc.	0.48	0.11
PFE	Pfizer Incorporated	1.18	0.44
MO	Philip Morris Companies	1.31	−0.01
PG	Procter & Gamble Company	0.49	0.09
RD	Royal Dutch Pet-NY Reg	−0.54	0.64
SBC	SBC Communications Inc.	0.03	0.58
WMT	Wal-Mart Stores, Inc.	1.29	0.09

Company Evolution

Style betas can also be used to study the evolution of companies — how their style changes over time. Style shift is one of the more critical facts regarding understanding a company's fundamentals and the style betas can help highlight these changes by identifying companies and industries that are evolving. Exhibit 3 shows the evolution of IBM's style exposure over time.

Exhibit 3: Style Beta Evolution (IBM: 1986-1995)

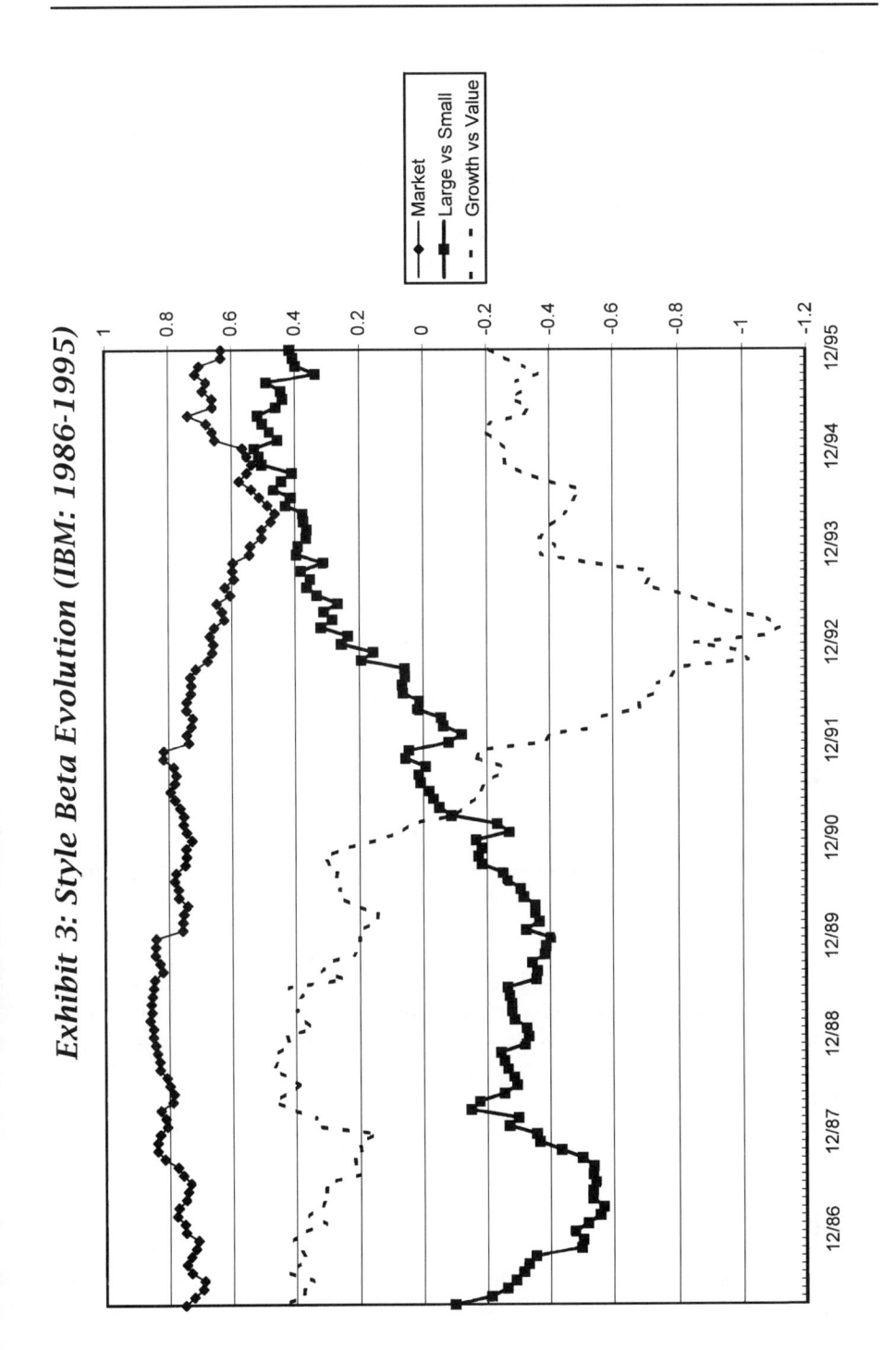

Pairs Identification

Traditional pairs analysis and trading begins with the identification of pairs of stocks that are essentially equivalent from a systematic risk perspective. Once identified, the short-term performance of these pairs is tracked. In the absence of any stock-specific information that would lead to relative performance, pairs trading assumes that any short-term relative performance will be reversed, as a pair of stocks have the same exposures to the broad forces that drive performance in the stock market.

Pairs trading can be implemented as a pure arbitrage strategy, where the expensive half of the pair is sold short and the cheap half is purchased. In a more traditional long-only portfolio, pairs trading can be used to switch out of the expensive half of the pair in the portfolio and purchase the cheap half, thus keeping the overall systematic exposure of the portfolio to the market and style the same, while potentially picking up some short-term relative performance. Style betas can be used in this pairs definition process by identifying pairs of stocks that have similar market and style betas.

Research Focus

It is also possible to find many stocks with essentially zero market and style betas. These are stocks that tend to move solely on the basis of stock specific events — they have little or no systematic exposure. Their return is largely driven by fundamental happenings at the company level — they are independent of the broad forces that drive most stocks. As such, these stocks are good candidates for in-depth analyst research and are also good diversifying holdings in a portfolio.

Excess Return

Finally, style betas are a potential source of excess return. Book/price and size are two of the most commonly used tilts in portfolio construction. Historically, high book/price stocks have outperformed low book/price stocks and small companies have outperformed large companies. Negative growth-value betas correspond to high book/price companies, but in a purer form. Negative large-small betas correspond to small stocks, but also in a purer form. As such, they can potentially identify cheap stocks.

Furthermore, the alpha that comes out of Equation (2) can be thought of as the residual return; the "Y-intercept" of the regression or the excess return after removing market and style effects. Research has shown that a stock's subsequent performance tends to be negatively correlated with its trailing excess return in the short term: the so-called residual reversal effect. The alpha that comes out of the style beta regressions is one measure of residual return. Hence residual reversal practitioners could use it as a potential source of alpha.

CONCLUSION

Clearly there is a role for style in the investment process. However there are inherent weaknesses in accounting-based and market-based style classification methodologies. Style betas are a price-based method of classification that can lend insight into individual stocks, portfolios, and managers by giving a clearer picture of the growth-value and large-small dimensions of style.

Chapter 7

Value-Based Equity Strategies

Gary G. Schlarbaum
Partner
Miller, Anderson & Sherrerd, LLP

INTRODUCTION

As equity investors, we have certain bedrock beliefs that guide our investment decisions. These beliefs are based on our experience, that of our predecessors, and on findings from continuing research. In fact, one of our bedrock beliefs is that careful research is a major contributor to investment success.[1] To test our long-held belief that focusing on measures of value is very important in the investment process, we measured value using price/earnings ratios (P/E's). We also looked at the importance of near-term business dynamics, as measured by earnings-estimate revisions, and how those might affect the performance of value stocks. Then we looked at a combination of the two to see how that would have worked. As it turned out, a combination of the two — a value score — worked better than either by itself.

Our research has practical application. When we construct equity portfolios, we begin by looking for stocks with low expectations — measured by low-P/E's. Second, we look for stocks that have rising expectations — measured by positive earnings-estimate revisions.[2] Third, we subject the resulting candidate stocks to rigorous fundamental analysis by our experienced analysts and portfolio managers.

---

[1] The research reported in this chapter was conducted at Miller, Anderson & Sherrerd in the fall of 1994. It is best viewed as an extension of research that was conducted by Paul Miller and Jay Sherrerd (two of our founding partners) back in the mid-1960's — even before our firm began. This work was continued by Robert Hagin, who did extensive work on value investing in the 1980's. Our 1994 results show, as did the earlier work, that investing in value stocks gives an investor an important edge, reaffirming one of the basic principles that lie at the heart of our equity-investment process.

[2] It is, of course, preferable to detect stocks for which expectations are about to rise by thoroughly analyzing inexpensive stocks. Our analysts spend much of their time looking for such stocks.

Finally, we build diversified portfolios — in keeping with our experience that broadly diversified value portfolios are less volatile but provide comparable excess returns. This is a continuing process. We screen our database every week in search of inexpensive stocks whose fundamentals are turning. Screening is central to our stock-selection process.

Our research focused on the 500 largest U.S. companies over the period 1977 through 1994. We formed various 100-stock portfolios and examined the market-relative returns of those portfolios. The market-relative return is the difference between the return on a particular portfolio and the average return on the universe. For the purpose of this research, we assumed that we rebalanced those portfolios quarterly. We developed results for portfolios of various types — equal-weighted, value-weighted, diversified, and nondiversified. The best results were obtained from equal-weighted diversified portfolios.

The results for portfolios formed using P/E ratios are reported first. Results for portfolios formed using estimate revisions and value scores are presented in the subsequent two sections. An examination of results within individual economic sectors is then presented. Finally, we look at the differences in results between diversified and nondiversified portfolios.

RETURNS FOR PORTFOLIOS CONSTRUCTED USING P/E RATIOS

We have long believed that value is the central consideration in a sensible investment process. Although the P/E ratio is not the only possible measure of value, we believe it is the most effective. We have not undertaken a comparative evaluation of different measures of value in this study. Rather, we have focused on P/E ratios. We have found them to be a very effective tool for selecting stock portfolios over the period of the study.[3]

The effectiveness of value investing reflects the mispricing of financial assets at either end of the spectrum. Investors overvalue the prospects of the stocks they consider to be the best and undervalue the prospects of those they view as the worst. There is a tendency to project positive or negative developments of the past into the future. As a result, prices are pushed too far in the direction of recent events. Ultimately, however, there is reversion to the mean as the perceptions of investors change. The reversion to the mean can be more or less rapid, but overvalued (high-P/E) securities will tend to underperform on average, while undervalued (low-P/E) securities will, on average, deliver superior returns. The implosion of stock price when a high-multiple stock misses the consensus estimate by a penny or two in the reporting of quarterly results is a vivid example of a rapid change in perception and movement toward the mean.

---

[3] The findings are consistent with those developed by Paul Miller and Jay Sherrerd in the 1960's and with those obtained by various academic researchers in later years.

Exhibit 1: P/E Strategy — Using Sector-Neutral Equal-Weighted Portfolios*

	P/E Quintile	Annual Rate of Return (%)	Market-Relative Return (%)	Quarters of Outperformance
Lowest	1	17.6	3.1	46
	2	16.3	1.8	43
	3	14.0	-0.4	35
	4	12.6	-1.8	29
Highest	5	11.2	-3.3	25
Universe:		14.4		

* Period included 69 calendar quarters from the first quarter of 1977 through the third quarter of 1994.

Exhibit 2: P/E Strategy — Using Sector-Neutral Equal-Weighted Portfolios

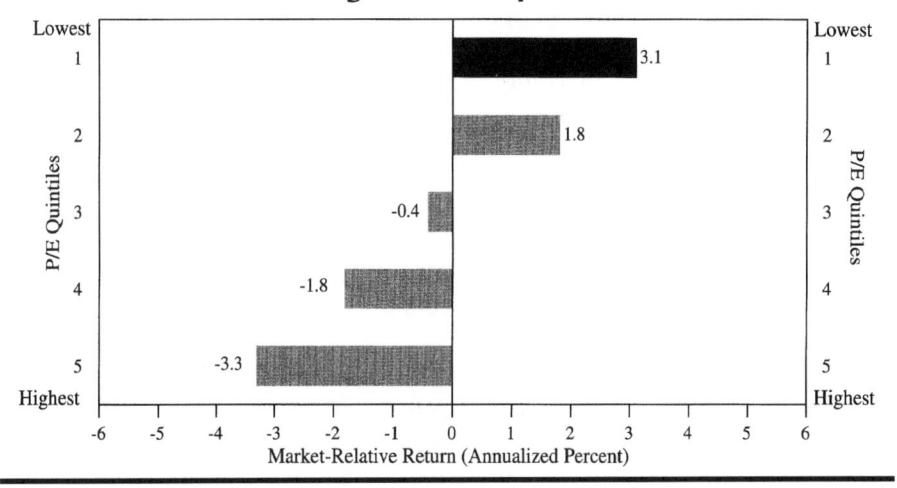

P/E Quintile	Market-Relative Return (Annualized Percent)
1 (Lowest)	3.1
2	1.8
3	-0.4
4	-1.8
5 (Highest)	-3.3

The price/earnings ratios used to form portfolios for this study were based on current price and consensus estimates of earnings for the next 12 months. This choice is based on our view that the market focuses on and capitalizes earnings 12 months ahead. We did not do any tests to determine whether estimates of future earnings provide better results than trailing earnings. We consider estimates of future earnings preferable from a conceptual point of view. Furthermore, the estimates are clean and not clouded by extraordinary items.

Absolute returns, market-relative returns, and a count of the number of the quarters of outperformance are shown for five portfolios in Exhibit 1. The market-relative returns are depicted in Exhibit 2 as well. The results for the lowest-P/E portfolio are shown on the top line of the table, those for the second-lowest-P/E portfolio are shown on the second line, etc. The bars in Exhibit 2 are shown in the same order.

The results included in Exhibits 1 and 2 are for equal-weighted, sector-neutral portfolios. The portfolios were formed in two steps. First, the stocks were grouped into 12 economic sectors. Then the lowest quintile of P/E's from each sector was selected for inclusion in the low-P/E portfolio. The same procedure with the appropriate quintiles was used to form the rest of the portfolios. The returns, then, are those of very well diversified value-based portfolios. (A comparison of the results for diversified and nondiversified portfolios is contained in a later section of this chapter.)

We found that, over this period, being sector neutral and picking the lowest-P/E portfolio from each economic sector led to 3.1% a year additional return relative to the 14.4% return for the universe. In contrast, the high-P/E portfolio had an annual return of 3.3% below that of the universe. Moreover, the low-P/E portfolio outperformed in 46 out of 69 quarters included in the study while the high-P/E portfolio outperformed in only 25 of the quarters. In other words, the low-P/E portfolio outperformed two thirds of the time, and the high-P/E portfolio underperformed about two thirds of the time.

The results reported in this section are consistent with our belief that value is the central consideration in a well designed investment process. P/E ratios were very effective tools for selecting stocks over the period studied here. Concentrating on low-P/E stocks and avoiding high-P/E stocks provided an important advantage for investors. We believe that focus on stocks with low expectations as measured by P/E ratios will continue to provide an advantage.

RETURNS FOR PORTFOLIOS CONSTRUCTED USING ESTIMATE REVISIONS

Stock prices are driven by the earnings generated by the underlying businesses. The question posed here is whether changes in expectations about earnings, as measured by analysts' estimate revisions, are useful in selecting a portfolio of common stocks.[4] Estimate revisions are important as representations of the near-term business dynamics of the companies being considered. We used 3-month smoothed revisions for the purposes of this study. More weighting is assigned to the most recent month in computing the estimate revision used for ranking stocks.

Estimate revisions provide a measure of the direction and magnitude of change in expectations about a company's earnings. The assumption is that rising expectations are associated with above-average stock returns and falling expectations are associated with below-average returns. Revisions tend to be positively serially correlated. Positive revisions tend to be followed by positive revisions, and negative revisions tend to be followed by negative revisions. It is difficult for

---

[4] I/B/E/S collects the earnings estimates of analysts and, in addition to reporting them, aggregates the estimates into summary measures such as the mean and median. A revision is a change in the mean estimate for a company. Changes for the three most recent months are combined to obtain the measure of estimate revisions used here.

analysts to judge how far a positive or negative trend may go once it has begun. Recent academic studies have shown that investors and analysts tend to respond sluggishly to new information (i.e., that markets are not totally efficient). Analysts react slowly to a change in the direction of the underlying fundamentals because of a natural unwillingness to believe the change. These studies opine that the effect may be stronger on the downside because of the reluctance of analysts to make negative comments about companies with which they have investment-banking relationships. As a result, the analysts issue frequent, minor revisions instead of marking their estimates down all at once.

There is also a strong relationship between estimate revisions and earnings surprises.[5] Positive estimate revisions are frequently followed by a positive earnings surprise. The positive earnings surprise will often be followed by subsequent positive estimate revisions. There is a kind of virtuous cycle when the fundamentals of a company are improving. Of course, the opposite is true when the underlying fundamentals are deteriorating. Disappointing earnings lead to negative revisions, which are followed by more disappointments, and so on.

We again formed five portfolios of 100 stocks each to ascertain the relationship between returns and estimate revisions. The stocks were grouped into 12 economic sectors. Then the stocks were divided into quintiles within the sectors on the basis of estimate revisions. The stocks from the highest quintile within each economic sector formed the first portfolio. The same procedures with the appropriate quintiles were used to form the rest of the portfolios.

Absolute returns, market-relative returns, and a count of the number of quarters of outperformance are shown for the five portfolios in Exhibit 3. Market-relative returns are also shown in Exhibit 4. The results for the best-revision portfolio are shown in the top line of the table, those for the second-best-revision portfolio are shown in the second line, and so on. The bars in Exhibit 4 are shown in the same order.

Exhibit 3: Estimate-Revision Strategy — Using Sector-Neutral Equal-Weighted Portfolios*

	Estimate-Revision Quintile	Annual Rate of Return (%)	Market-Relative Return (%)	Quarters of Outperformance
Best	1	18.6	4.2	51
	2	15.8	1.4	39
	3	14.7	0.3	36
	4	11.9	−2.5	28
Worst	5	10.2	−4.3	23
Universe:		14.4		

* Period included 69 calendar quarters from the first quarter of 1977 through the third quarter of 1994.

[5] An earnings surprise is the difference between the actual quarterly earnings of a company and the consensus estimate at the time of the report.

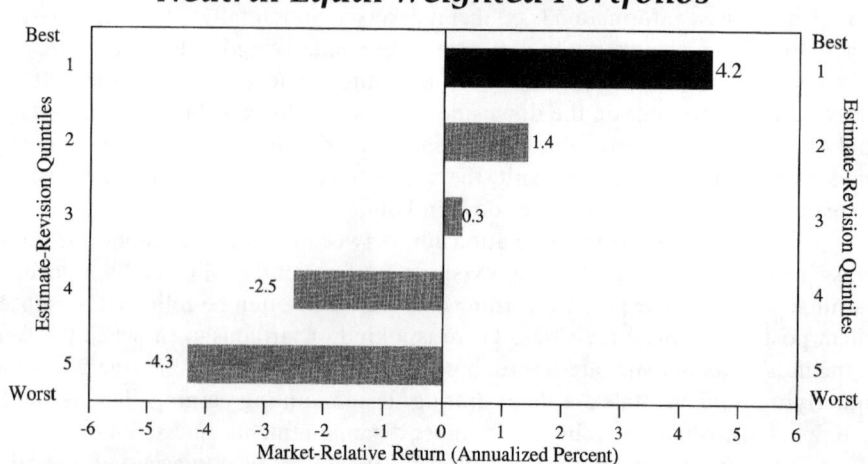

Exhibit 4: Estimate Revision Strategy — Using Sector-Neutral Equal-Weighted Portfolios

Estimate-Revision Quintiles	Market-Relative Return (Annualized Percent)
1 (Best)	4.2
2	1.4
3	0.3
4	-2.5
5 (Worst)	-4.3

The sector-neutral portfolios with the best-revision stocks provided an extra 4.2% a year relative to the 14.4% return for the universe. The worst-revision portfolio, on the other hand, underperformed the universe by 4.3%. The returns were perfectly rank ordered by the revisions. Moreover, the best-revision portfolio outperformed the universe in 51 out of 69 quarters — nearly 75% of the time. Meanwhile, the worst-revision portfolio was nearly as consistent, trailing in 46 of 69 quarters.

These results show the strong relationship between near-term business dynamics and equity returns. The results are consistent and powerful. (We should note that the extra returns based on near-term business dynamics are harder to capture than those based on measures of value because of the greater trading activity required.) It is clear that the direction of expectations is a powerful influence on stock performance.

We saw in the previous section that portfolios of low-expectation stocks outperform. This section demonstrated that portfolios of stocks with rising expectations also outperform.

RETURNS FOR PORTFOLIOS CONSTRUCTED USING VALUE SCORES

We have demonstrated in the previous two sections that both value as measured by P/E and fundamental business dynamics as measured by estimate revisions are effective as portfolio selectors. Stocks with low expectations, on average, outperform the market. Stocks with high expectations lag. Stocks with rising expectations, on average, outperform the market. Stocks with falling expectations lag. Seemingly a combination of good value and positive dynamics would be more powerful than either by itself in forming a portfolio. The question addressed in this section is whether this is in fact the case.

Each stock in the universe of the largest 500 stocks was assigned a percentile ranking based on P/E and a percentile ranking based on estimate revision. A value score was then computed for each stock by determining a weighted average of the percentile rankings. We assigned 70% of the weight to P/E and 30% to estimate revision. This was the only set of weightings that we tried. In fact, other combinations are undoubtedly very effective as well; investors with a stronger growth orientation might well choose to place more weight on estimate revisions.

We again formed five portfolios of 100 stocks each to discern the relationship between returns and value scores (combinations of P/E and estimate revisions). Stocks were divided among 12 economic sectors and ordered from high to low on the basis of the value scores. Those with the best (highest) value scores were assigned to the first portfolio, and those with the worst (lowest) value scores were assigned to the fifth portfolio. Equal weightings were used in forming the portfolios. The results shown below are, as a result, for equal-weighted sector-neutral portfolios.

Absolute returns, market-relative returns, and a count of the number of quarters of outperformance are shown for the five portfolios in Exhibit 5. Market-relative returns are shown again in Exhibit 6. The results for the best-value-score portfolio are shown in the top line of Exhibit 5. Those for the second-best-value-score portfolio are shown in the second line, and so on. The bars in Exhibit 6 are shown in the same order. The sector-neutral portfolio of stocks with the best value scores earned an extra 4.6% a year relative to the universe. The sector-neutral portfolio of the lowest-value-score stocks lagged the universe by 5.4%. The portfolio returns were perfectly rank-ordered. The best-value-score portfolio consistently outperformed the universe; the count was 49 out of 69 quarters, more than 70% of the time. The worst-value-score portfolio was even more consistent, lagging in 55 of 69 quarters.

A comparison of the results included in this section with those in the previous two reveals that the value score is a better selector than either P/E or estimate revision. The top-quintile portfolio's relative return was more than one and a half percent higher than that of the top-quintile-P/E portfolio and moderately higher than that of the top-quintile-estimate-revision portfolio. At the opposite end of the spectrum, the bottom-quintile-value-score portfolio lagged the universe by 5.4%, whereas the bottom-quintile-estimate-revision portfolio trailed by 4.3% and the worst-quintile-P/E portfolio by 3.3%. The advantage of the value score is most pronounced at the least attractive end of the range. Simply avoiding stocks in the fifth quintile of the value scores should significantly enhance performance. The comparisons of top- and bottom-quintile performance for the three selectors is shown in Exhibit 7.

Exhibit 5: Value Score Strategy — Using Sector-Neutral Equal-Weighted Portfolios*

	Value Score Quintile	Annual Rate of Return (%)	Market-Relative Return (%)	Quarters of Outperformance
Best	1	19.0	4.6	49
	2	16.3	1.9	45
	3	14.5	0.0	34
	4	12.8	-1.6	25
Worst	5	9.0	-5.4	14
Universe:		14.4		

* Period included 69 calendar quarters from the first quarter of 1977 through the third quarter of 1994.

Exhibit 6: Value Score Strategy — Using Sector-Neutral Equal-Weighted Portfolios

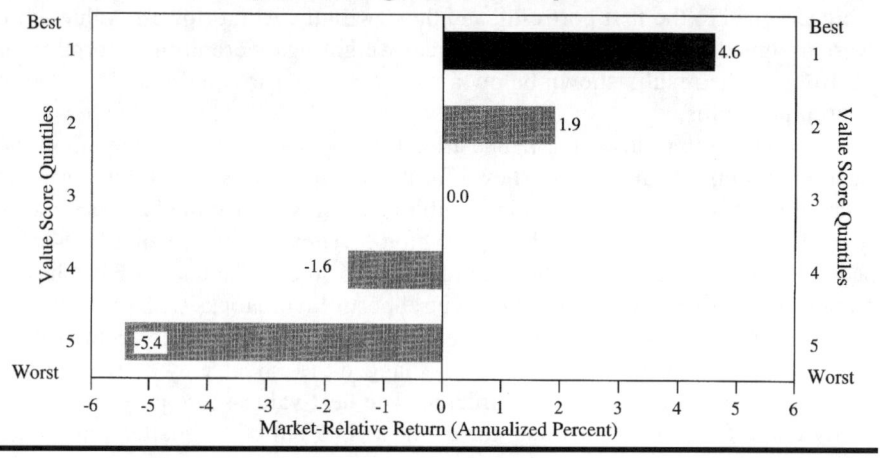

Value Score Quintile	Market-Relative Return (Annualized Percent)
Best 1	4.6
2	1.9
3	0.0
4	-1.6
Worst 5	-5.4

The results presented in this section (and the previous sections) do not take trading costs into account. The impact of trading costs is to mitigate the positive excess returns obtained by investing in the most attractive stocks. The question is by how much. The answer depends on both the cost of trading and the amount of portfolio turnover required to be continuously invested in the more attractive stocks.

The cost of trading will depend on trading skills and on the kind of stock deemed attractive by the selector. It is reasonable to presume that both turnover and trading costs would be higher for an approach based on estimate revisions than for one based on P/E ratios. It is also reasonable to conclude that the value-score approach combining the two would fall somewhere in between. As long as the last statement is true, the value-score approach will be better than an approach based on revisions alone because of the superior discrimination power and lower trading costs of the value-score system. The value-score approach would be superior to one based on P/E ratios unless the turnover were much higher for the former.

Exhibit 7: Performance Comparisons Using Three Strategies

P/E
- Quintile 1: 3.1
- Quintile 5: -3.3

Market-Relative Return (Annualized Percent)

Estimate Revisions
- Quintile 1: 4.2
- Quintile 5: -4.3

Market-Relative Return (Annualized Percent)

Value Score
- Quintile 1: 4.6
- Quintile 5: -5.4

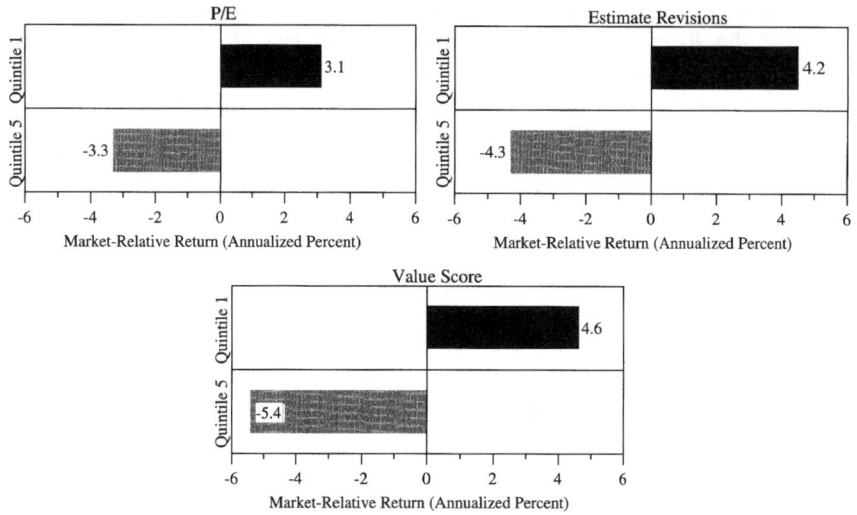

Market-Relative Return (Annualized Percent)

Exhibit 8: Quarterly Turnover Using the Value Score

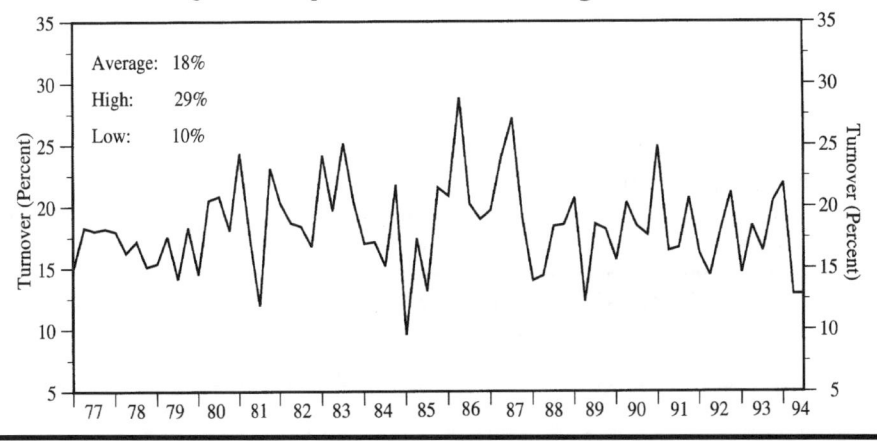

Average: 18%
High: 29%
Low: 10%

We have examined turnover percentages for the value-score approach for the entire period of our study. Quarterly turnover percentages for a strategy that involved buying quintile-one stocks and holding them until they became quintile-three stocks are shown in Exhibit 8. Using the value-score, the average quarterly turnover was 18%. The highest turnover for any quarter was 29%, and the lowest was 10%. The average of 18% implies an annual turnover of 72%. This is not an extraordinarily high turnover ratio for an active manager. And the strategy should allow the investor to capture a combination of quintile-one and quintile-two returns with an emphasis on the quintile-one stocks.

142 Value-Based Equity Strategies

The turnover ratio for the low-P/E approach was 12% — implying a 48% annual turnover. Assuming that transaction costs amount to two percent for a round trip, the difference in turnover ratios between the value-score approach and the low-P/E approach reduces the advantage of the value-score approach by 48 basis points — just about one half of 1%. This reduces the advantage from approximately 1.5% to 1.0% for first-quintile stocks. Nonetheless, the value-score approach retains a significant advantage. And it retains that advantage so long as round-trip costs are 6% or less.

COMPARISON OF SELECTION STRATEGIES ON A SECTOR-BY-SECTOR BASIS

This section focuses on how well the three selectors considered in this study — P/E ratio, estimate revision, and value score (a combination of P/E's and revisions) — work within each of the 12 economic sectors employed in the study. Previous results cause us to expect that the value score will work most effectively in most sectors. However, there is no reason to believe that the same selector will work best in every sector. Furthermore, there is no reason for an investor to use the same approach in every sector of the stock market.

The within-sector relative returns for all quintiles for each selection are shown in Exhibit 9. Each chart in the exhibit shows the results for one of the 12 economic sectors. Review of the charts suggests that the value score was the most effective selector in eight of the twelve economic sectors while estimate revision was best in three and P/E was best in one. In most cases, the conclusions seem obvious, but there are several sectors in which performance of two of the selectors is very close. Note that the vertical scales in Chart 6 were selected to illustrate the return differences within each economic sector.

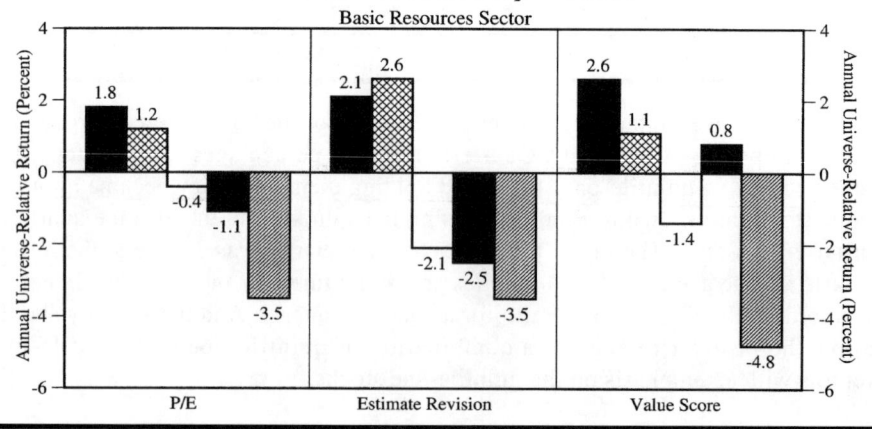

Exhibit 9: Comparisons of Universe — Relative Returns by Sector

Basic Resources Sector

P/E	Estimate Revision	Value Score
1.8, 1.2, -0.4, -1.1, -3.5	2.1, 2.6, -2.1, -2.5, -3.5	2.6, 1.1, 0.8, -1.4, -4.8

Exhibit 9: (Continued)

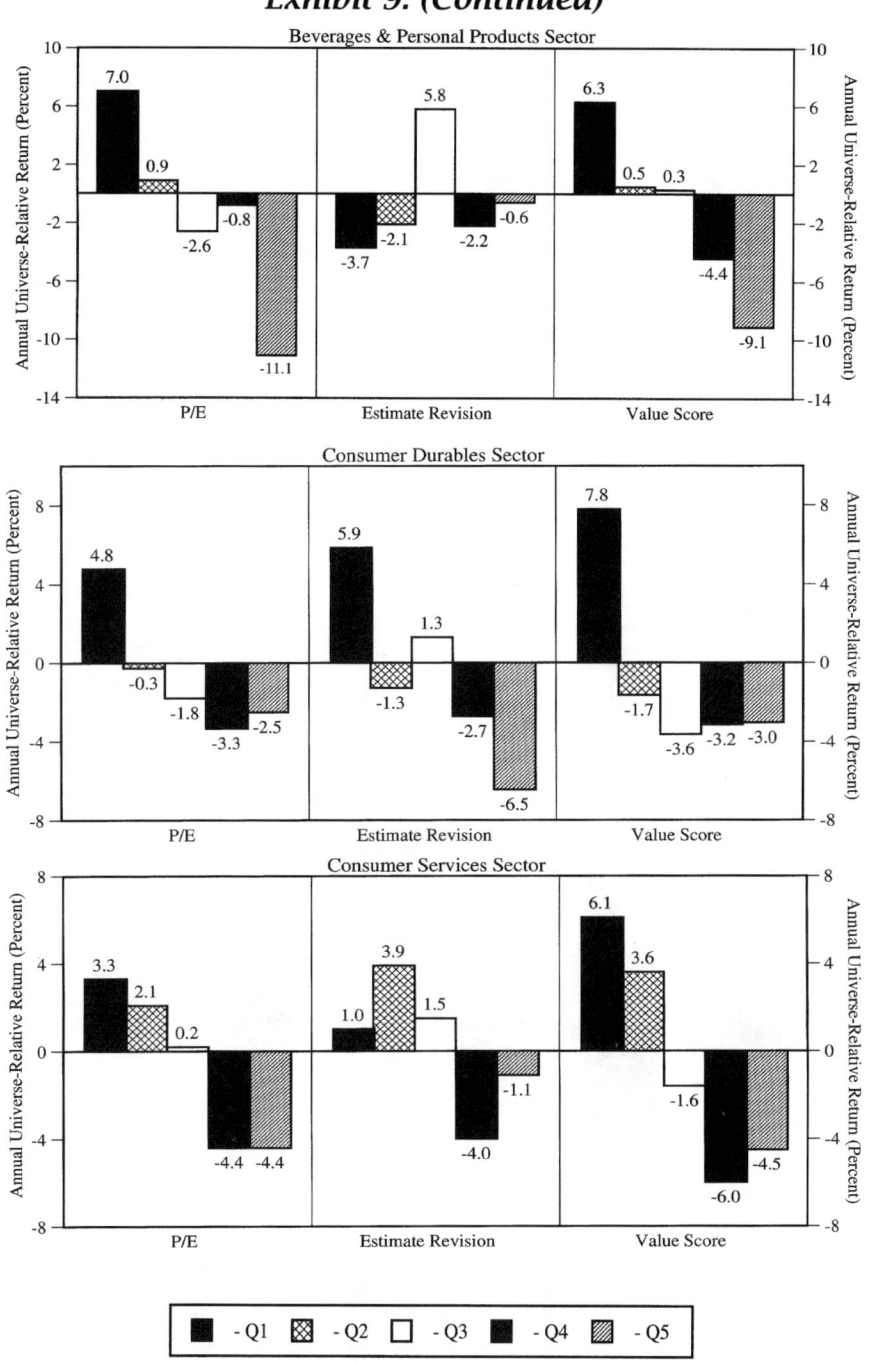

Beverages & Personal Products Sector

P/E: Q1 7.0, Q2 0.9, Q3 -2.6, Q4 -0.8, Q5 -11.1

Estimate Revision: Q1 -3.7, Q2 -2.1, Q3 5.8, Q4 -2.2, Q5 -0.6

Value Score: Q1 6.3, Q2 0.5, Q3 0.3, Q4 -4.4, Q5 -9.1

Consumer Durables Sector

P/E: Q1 4.8, Q2 -0.3, Q3 -1.8, Q4 -3.3, Q5 -2.5

Estimate Revision: Q1 5.9, Q2 -1.3, Q3 1.3, Q4 -2.7, Q5 -6.5

Value Score: Q1 7.8, Q2 -1.7, Q3 -3.6, Q4 -3.2, Q5 -3.0

Consumer Services Sector

P/E: Q1 3.3, Q2 2.1, Q3 0.2, Q4 -4.4, Q5 -4.4

Estimate Revision: Q1 1.0, Q2 3.9, Q3 1.5, Q4 -4.0, Q5 -1.1

Value Score: Q1 6.1, Q2 3.6, Q3 -1.6, Q4 -6.0, Q5 -4.5

■ - Q1   ▩ - Q2   □ - Q3   ■ - Q4   ▨ - Q5

144 Value-Based Equity Strategies

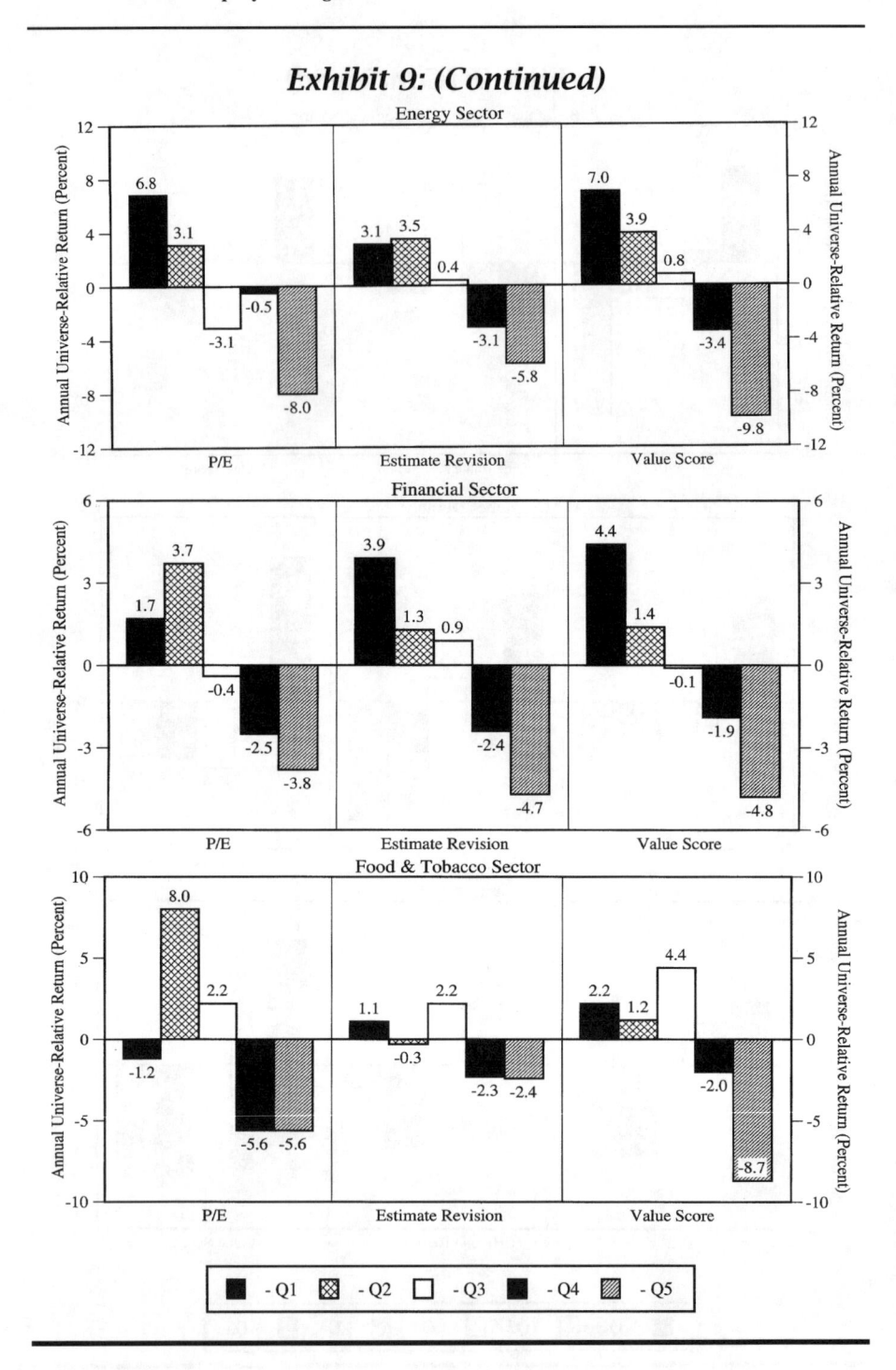

Exhibit 9: (Continued)

Energy Sector

P/E: Q1 6.8, Q2 3.1, Q3 -3.1, Q4 -0.5, Q5 -8.0
Estimate Revision: Q1 3.1, Q2 3.5, Q3 0.4, Q4 -3.1, Q5 -5.8
Value Score: Q1 7.0, Q2 3.9, Q3 0.8, Q4 -3.4, Q5 -9.8

Financial Sector

P/E: Q1 1.7, Q2 3.7, Q3 -0.4, Q4 -2.5, Q5 -3.8
Estimate Revision: Q1 3.9, Q2 1.3, Q3 0.9, Q4 -2.4, Q5 -4.7
Value Score: Q1 4.4, Q2 1.4, Q3 -0.1, Q4 -1.9, Q5 -4.8

Food & Tobacco Sector

P/E: Q1 -1.2, Q2 8.0, Q3 2.2, Q4 -5.6, Q5 -5.6
Estimate Revision: Q1 1.1, Q2 -0.3, Q3 2.2, Q4 -2.3, Q5 -2.4
Value Score: Q1 2.2, Q2 1.2, Q3 4.4, Q4 -2.0, Q5 -8.7

Legend: ■ - Q1 ▨ - Q2 □ - Q3 ■ - Q4 ▨ - Q5

Chapter 7 **145**

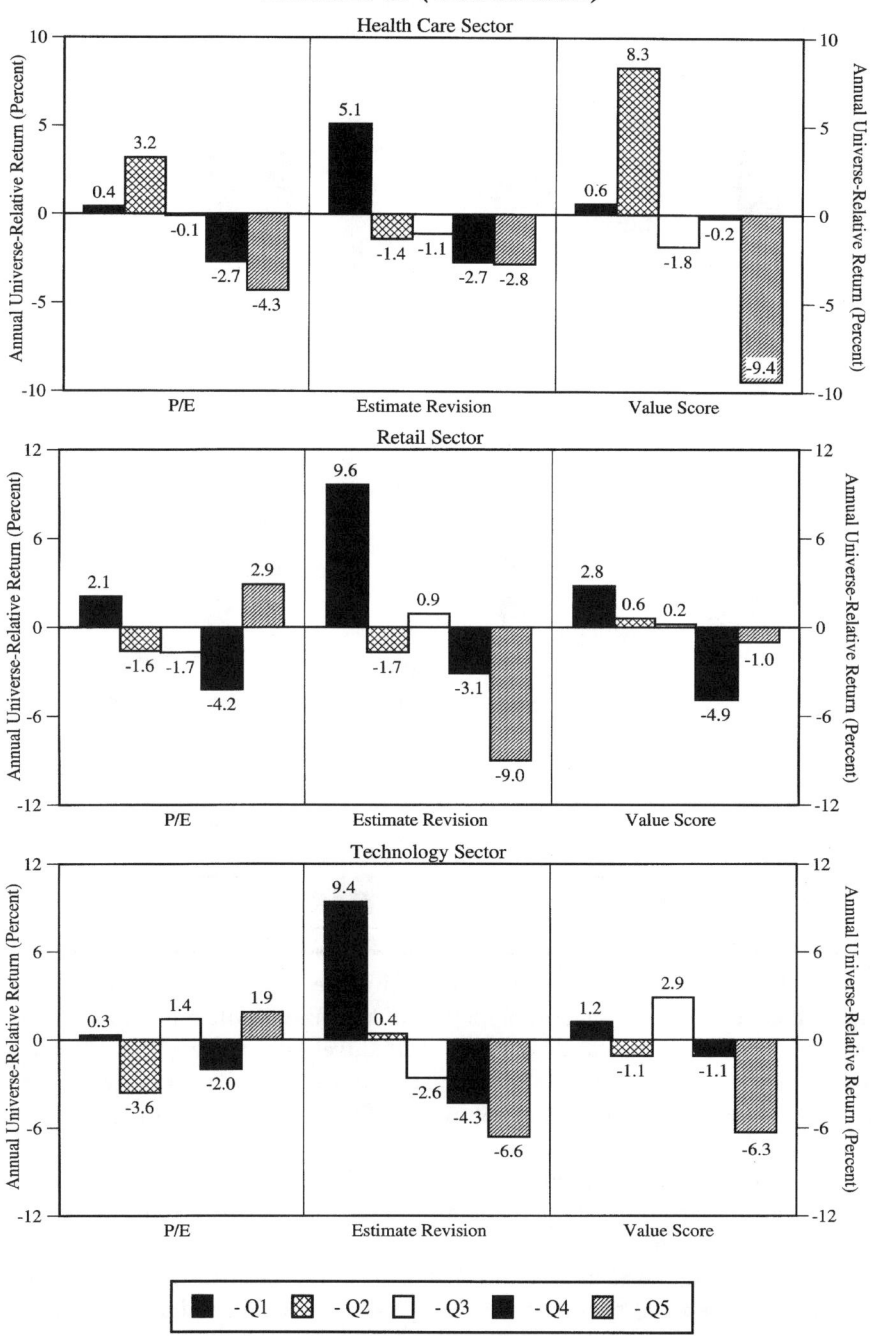

Exhibit 9: (Continued)

Health Care Sector

P/E: Q1 0.4, Q2 3.2, Q3 -0.1, Q4 -2.7, Q5 -4.3
Estimate Revision: Q1 5.1, Q2 -1.4, Q3 -1.1, Q4 -2.7, Q5 -2.8
Value Score: Q1 0.6, Q2 8.3, Q3 -1.8, Q4 -0.2, Q5 -9.4

Retail Sector

P/E: Q1 2.1, Q2 -1.6, Q3 -1.7, Q4 -4.2, Q5 2.9
Estimate Revision: Q1 9.6, Q2 -1.7, Q3 0.9, Q4 -3.1, Q5 -9.0
Value Score: Q1 2.8, Q2 0.6, Q3 0.2, Q4 -4.9, Q5 -1.0

Technology Sector

P/E: Q1 0.3, Q2 -3.6, Q3 1.4, Q4 -2.0, Q5 1.9
Estimate Revision: Q1 9.4, Q2 0.4, Q3 -2.6, Q4 -4.3, Q5 -6.6
Value Score: Q1 1.2, Q2 -1.1, Q3 2.9, Q4 -1.1, Q5 -6.3

■ - Q1   ▧ - Q2   □ - Q3   ■ - Q4   ▨ - Q5

Exhibit 9: (Continued)

Transportation Sector

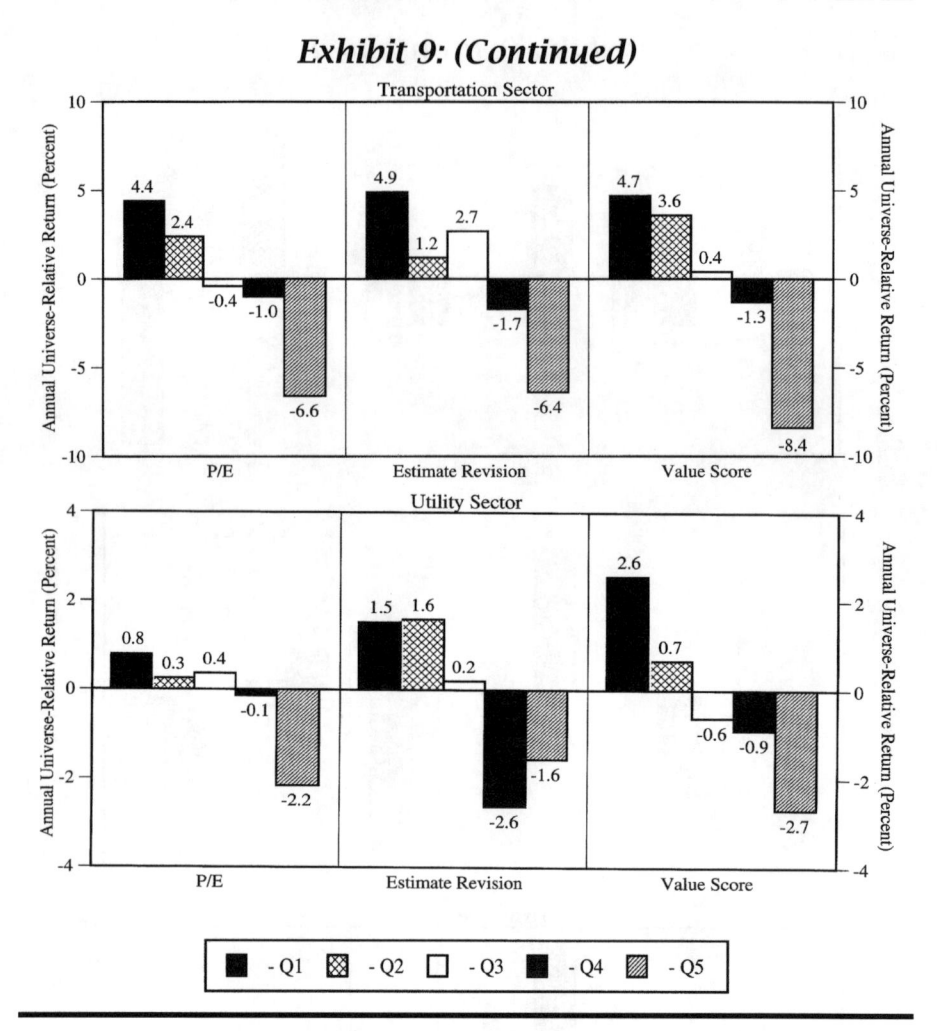

	P/E	Estimate Revision	Value Score
Q1	4.4	4.9	4.7
Q2	2.4	1.2	3.6
Q3	-0.4	2.7	0.4
Q4	-1.0	-1.7	-1.3
Q5	-6.6	-6.4	-8.4

Utility Sector

	P/E	Estimate Revision	Value Score
Q1	0.8	1.5	2.6
Q2	0.3	1.6	0.7
Q3	0.4	0.2	-0.6
Q4	-0.1	-1.6	-0.9
Q5	-2.2	-2.6	-2.7

■ - Q1   ▨ - Q2   □ - Q3   ■ - Q4   ▨ - Q5

In those cases in which the first-quintile returns for a selector were higher than those for the others *and* in which the fifth-quintile returns were lower, the selector in question was deemed most effective. For example, the value score was clearly the most effective in the energy sector. The first quintile of value-score stocks produced a relative return of 7.0% while the first quintile of P/E stocks provided 6.8% and the first quintile of estimate-revision stocks only 3.4%. At the same time, the fifth quintile based on value score lagged the universe by 9.8% while P/E and estimate-revision fifth-quintile stocks lagged the universe by 8.0% and 5.8%, respectively.

If we use the relative performance of first- and fifth-quintile stocks as criteria, P/E's worked best in the Beverage and Personal Products sector. Estimate revisions dominated in the Retail sector and the Technology sector. The value score was clearly most effective in Basic Resources, Consumer Services, Energy, Financials, Food and Tobacco, Transportation, and Utilities sectors. The Consumer Durables sector yielded mixed results; the value score was most effective on the upside, but revisions were relatively close on the upside and clearly were most effective in identifying laggards. On balance, we conclude that estimate revisions are most effective. The other controversial sector is Health Care. Estimate revisions best identified superior performers. But the value score was clearly dominant in identifying laggards. This fact — and the good performance of the first two quintiles based on value score — led to the conclusion that the value score is most effective.

Caution is warranted in interpreting the results contained in this section of the chapter. Too much weight should not be placed on empirical results for a specific period of time. One could argue, for example, that value scores should be used in all sectors because of their conceptual soundness and the power of the overall cross-sectional results. We have, in fact, chosen to sort stocks into quintiles by value score in 10 of the 12 sectors in our continuing analytical work on the stock market. Nonetheless, we do place more emphasis on estimate revisions in the Retail and Technology Sectors. The empirical results supporting this decision are very strong, as shown above.

Moreover, there are sound conceptual reasons for believing that near-term business dynamics will dominate in determining the winners and losers in the Retail and Technology sectors. Value is elusive in both cases. Take Technology, for example. The rate of change and obsolescence in Technology is very rapid. Once a product is obsolete, the equipment used to produce it has little, if any, value. As a result, stocks in the technology sector that appear cheap are not necessarily inexpensive at all. Often the companies are simply in a declining stage, and the usual measures of value provide no help in determining where stock prices might go. In Retail, too, it is not so much the value of the fixtures and physical space as the concept that counts. When a concept is working, the fundamentals move in a positive direction. When it is not, a decline in price and an apparently attractive measure of value do not mean that the stock is likely to do well in the future. Rather, when a concept is not working, the fundamentals move in a negative direction; that is the signal to avoid the stock.

DIVERSIFIED VERSUS NONDIVERSIFIED PORTFOLIOS

Throughout this chapter, we have presented returns from diversified portfolios. The purpose of this section is to compare the returns and risks of *diversified* portfolios and *nondiversified* portfolios. Each portfolio contains 100 securities. Diversified portfolios, are those that are spread across economic sectors so that the weighting of each economic sector in the portfolio is the same as the weighting of the sector in the universe. These portfolios are "sector-neutral." For example, the low-P/E diversified portfolio includes the low-P/E quintile of stocks *from each economic sector.*

Nondiversified portfolios are formed without regard to economic sector membership. The low-P/E, nondiversified portfolio contains the 100 stocks with the lowest P/E ratios in the whole universe. This low-P/E portfolio would typically have a larger weight in banks and utilities than the universe.

The focus of our attention is always the best portfolio — the top-quintile portfolio. We examined returns and risks for the best diversified and the best nondiversified portfolio in every instance. We found that diversified portfolios provided higher relative returns on average, and, at the same time, protected the investor on the downside in those instances in which the returns from the best portfolios lagged those of the universe. This was true regardless of the selector used in forming the portfolios.

The average relative returns and the worst annual relative return for diversified and nondiversified portfolios are shown in Exhibits 10, 11, and 12. Exhibit 10 shows the results for portfolios based on P/E ratios; Exhibit 11 shows the results for estimate revisions; and Exhibit 12 shows the results for the value score. The average relative return was always higher for the diversified portfolios' and it was nearly one percent higher in the case of the value-score portfolios. Similarly, the worst annual return was always lower for nondiversified portfolios than for diversified portfolios. The difference was not large in the case of the estimate-revision portfolios. But it was dramatic for the low-P/E portfolios and the value-score portfolios; in each case the difference was over 16%.

The results reported in this section suggest that a diversified value approach is preferable to one that is highly concentrated. Diversifying across economic sectors does not reduce the extra returns provided by value portfolios. In fact, over the period of this study, diversification actually enhanced returns. More importantly, diversified portfolios provided significant protection against years of dramatic underperformance.[6] Clients may question their commitment to value investing after a year in which their portfolio trailed the universe by 1,000 basis points. It is easier to maintain their commitment after a year in which performance lagged by 100 to 200 basis points.

---

[6] We believe that broad diversification is desirable much of the time. Furthermore, we believe that systematic approaches must work within sectors to be effective overall. Nonetheless, these results do not imply that it is not possible to add value through making sector overweighting and underweighting decisions. In fact, our own experience has shown that it is possible to augment returns through sector-weighting decisions. Our results suggest that either (1) other tools are more valuable for making sector decisions than the selectors used to pick stocks within sectors here or (2) there were few opportunities to add value through sector selection over the time period of the study because sectors were fairly priced relative to one another most of the time. There is probably a degree of truth in both of these possibilities.

Exhibit 10: Lowest P/E Strategy

Average All Quarters (Average Annual Market-Relative Return, Percent)
- Diversified Portfolios: 3.1
- Non-Diversified Portfolios: 3.2

Worst Four Quarter Returns (Average Annual Market-Relative Return, Percent)
- Diversified Portfolios: -6.1
- Non-Diversified Portfolios: -18.6

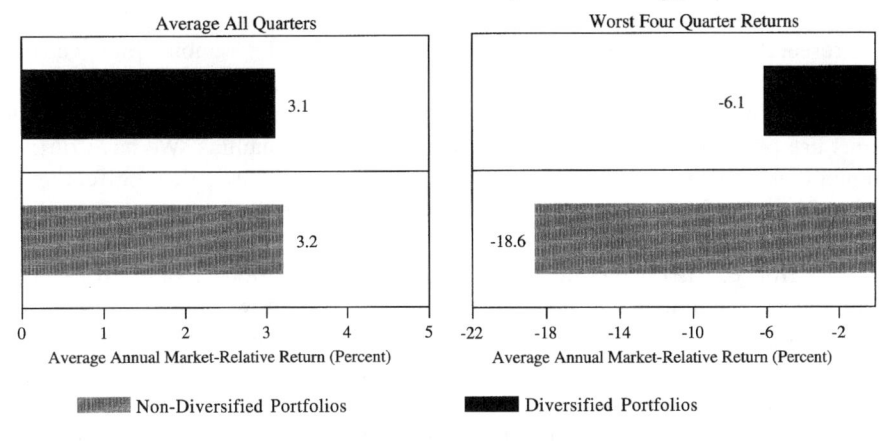

Exhibit 11: Highest Estimate-Revision Strategy

Average All Quarters (Average Annual Market-Relative Return, Percent)
- Diversified Portfolios: 4.2
- Non-Diversified Portfolios: 3.6

Worst Four Quarter Returns (Average Annual Market-Relative Return, Percent)
- Diversified Portfolios: -3.8
- Non-Diversified Portfolios: -8.2

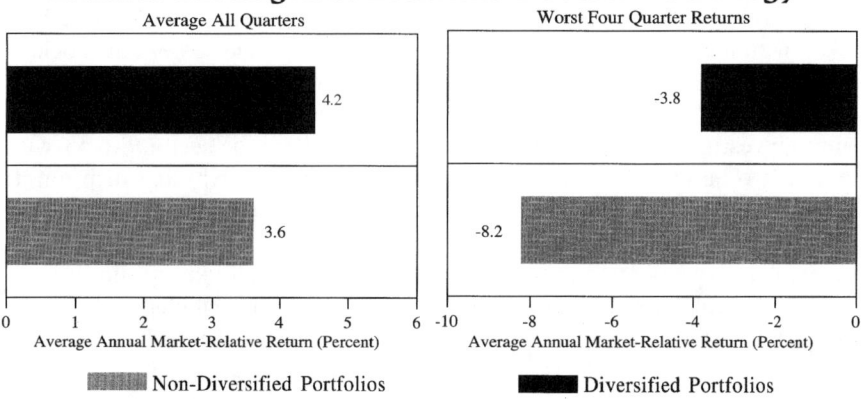

Exhibit 12: Highest Value-Score Strategy

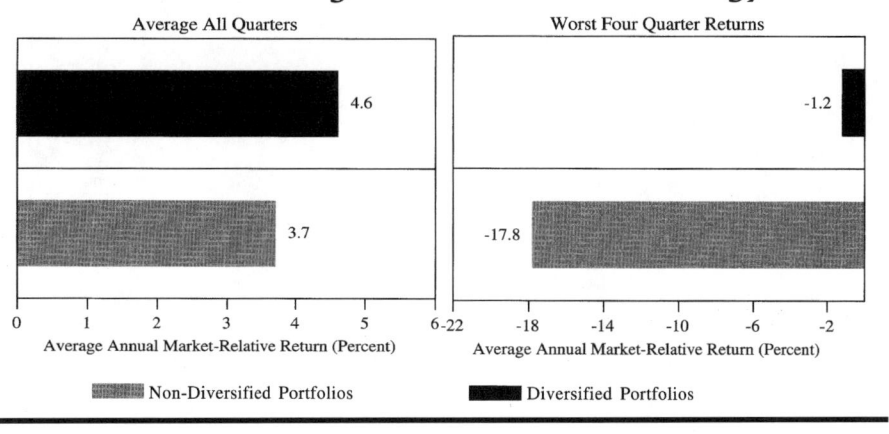

Average All Quarters (Average Annual Market-Relative Return, Percent)
- Diversified Portfolios: 4.6
- Non-Diversified Portfolios: 3.7

Worst Four Quarter Returns (Average Annual Market-Relative Return, Percent)
- Diversified Portfolios: -1.2
- Non-Diversified Portfolios: -17.8

CONCLUSION

The research reported here has confirmed the bedrock beliefs upon which we construct equity portfolios. We have once again found that value investing leads to higher returns. We have shown that a value approach can be enhanced by judicious use of a measure of the underlying business's dynamics. We have further shown that a diversified approach to value investing is particularly effective at controlling portfolio risk — while not detracting from the benefit of the value-only approach.

Hence, when we build equity portfolios, we begin by looking for stocks with low expectations — measured by low-P/E's. Second, we look for stocks that have rising expectations — measured by positive earnings-estimate revisions. Third, we subject the resulting candidate stocks to rigorous fundamental analysis by our experienced analysts and portfolio managers. Finally, we build diversified portfolios — in keeping with our research findings that broadly diversified value portfolios are less volatile but provide comparable excess returns.

Our approach employs a systematic component wherein stocks are ranked within each economic sector according to our value score. The stocks are sorted into quintiles. Each economic-sector portfolio is the responsibility of a portfolio manager who devotes his research time and the research resources of his team to investigating those stocks ranked highest within the sector. Stocks within the first two quintiles are selected for the portfolios. Fourth- and fifth-quintile stocks are eliminated. In the end, we believe, the systematic elements of our approach, combined with the judgment of our experienced portfolio managers, constitute a very attractive approach to managing large equity portfolios.

We believe that a focused approach to stock selection built around this effective ranking system will produce superior investment results over the long haul.

Chapter 8

Investment Styles, Stock Market Cycles, Investor Expectations, and Portfolio Performance

W. Scott Bauman, DBA, CFA
Professor of Finance
Northern Illinois University

Robert E. Miller, Ph.D.
Safety-Kleen Professor of Finance
Northern Illinois University

INTRODUCTION

Many investors consider one of the most important decisions they make to be the selection of portfolio policies or investment styles. Naturally, investors prefer to choose a style that results in a superior portfolio performance. As a prelude to making that choice, many investors study the past performance of different styles; however, their research frequently fails to take into account major exogenous variables that affect performance. Several such variables consist of stock market cycles, traditional portfolio policy constraints, market illiquidity, and investor psychological behavior.

In this chapter, we will review our research on the performance of pension funds and mutual funds that pursue different investment styles. We will also examine the performance of empirically constructed growth stock portfolios and value stock portfolios. Based on this analysis, we address these questions: Does investment style make a difference in portfolio performance? Is the ranking of past performance of portfolios based on style useful in predicting future performance rankings? If there is a difference in portfolio performance based on style, what accounts for this difference?

RANKING PORTFOLIO PERFORMANCE BY STYLE

Investors generally prefer a portfolio style that consistently performs above the average of other styles. Yet, style performance rankings are rather volatile over time, such that a particular portfolio style that ranks above other styles in one period, subsequently ranks lower in the next period. If so, past rankings can be misleading indicators of future performance. In comparing the performance of portfolios over different time periods, many studies fail to take into account effects caused by economic and stock market cycles. If these variables are taken into account, major differences in the performance of portfolio styles diminish. The reason is that aggressive or riskier styles tend to perform better in rising markets while more conservative styles tend to perform relatively better in contracting markets.

To test this concept, Callan Associates, Inc. furnished a database for the period from December 1972 through September 1991, consisting of a large number of pension fund and mutual fund portfolios. Portfolio performance was tracked over complete stock market cycles, defined as a period commencing with a market peak, followed by a trough, and ending with a subsequent market peak, as determined by the S&P 500 Index. Five complete market cycles were identified, with quarterly peaks occurring on December 1972, December 1976, March 1981, June 1983, September 1987, and September 1991. The portfolios were identified according to the following five major styles: (1) general policy (multistyle), (2) growth, (3) value, (4) core (index tilt), and (5) income/yield. The general policy group does not consistently or predominantly employ any single, specific investment style. Portfolios in the core policy group use broad diversification, similar to a stock index, but frequently tilt the portfolio toward stocks with specific investment characteristics.

Exhibit 1 shows the average portfolio performance of each of the five style groups over the five stock market cycles (numbered 1 to 5).[1] We will focus attention on the last three cycles which represent a larger sample of portfolios. The return is the annualized return for the average portfolio in the group. The betas measure the sensitivity of the quarterly return of the average portfolio in the group to the return of the S&P 500 Index. Sigma is the annualized standard deviation of the quarterly returns of the average portfolio.

---

[1] See Bauman, W. Scott and Robert E. Miller, "Portfolio Performance Rankings in Stock Market Cycles," *Financial Analyst Journal* (March-April 1995), pp. 79-87.

Exhibit 1: Mean Portfolio Performance by Type of Portfolio Policy Style

Type of Portfolio Policy		Time Period					Average 3, 4, 5
		1	2	3	4	5	
(1)		(2)	(3)	(4)	(5)	(6)	(7)
General	Number	11	11	180	286	212	
	Return	6.8	22.6	19.5	19.3	9.5	16.1
	Beta	0.85	1.11	0.95	0.95	0.96	
	Sigma	23.3	9.8	19.0	15.7	19.0	
Growth	Number	65	65	123	140	136	
	Return	−1.6	21.6	20.9	16.6	8.6	15.4
	Beta	1.11	1.18	1.10	1.12	1.05	
	Sigma	29.1	16.8	22.0	18.0	20.5	
Value	Number	2	2	58	86	76	
	Return	7.6	16.6	19.8	20.3	8.1	16.1
	Beta	0.72	0.94	0.85	0.86	0.91	
	Sigma	20.2	13.8	16.8	13.9	17.5	
Core	Number	3	3	18	24	17	
	Return	4.3	12.5	17.6	18.9	9.1	15.2
	Beta	0.87	0.85	0.90	0.99	0.97	
	Sigma	21.3	11.5	17.4	15.6	18.4	
Yield	Number	0	0	10	21	18	
	Return	—	—	19.8	21.3	8.4	16.5
	Beta	—	—	0.80	0.75	0.82	
	Sigma	—	—	15.9	12.4	15.9	

In comparing the five style groups, the growth group had the highest return in period 3, but the lowest return in period 4. This indicates that differences in performance between styles can rotate from one market cycle to the next. The yield group had the highest return in period 4 and the highest return on average over the combined periods of 3, 4, and 5; the active style portfolio managers appeared to add value inasmuch as the more passive core group had the lowest average return. The maximum spread between the group with the highest return and the group with the lowest return in each cycle ranged between 470 basis points in the 4th period down to 140 basis points in the 5th period. When the returns by group are averaged over the last three periods, the maximum spread narrows to only 130 basis points. This suggests that the returns among style groups tend to converge when the time period is extended. The two groups with the lowest risks (yield and value) as measured by beta and sigma, paradoxically had the highest average returns over the combined periods 3, 4, and 5. The yield and value groups together with the general group had the highest reward-to-risk ratios (risk-adjusted returns). Because the value and yield type stocks have higher dividend yields, their total rates of return would tend to be more stable. By contrast, the growth group had a much higher volatility as might be expected, yet had a comparatively lower return, thus resulting in the lowest reward-to-risk ratio among the five style groups. Relative difference in volatility of quarterly returns among the style groups, as measured by sigma, tend to be consistent over time, and hence easier to predict.

An analysis of variance was also conducted to measure for differences in portfolio returns between types of portfolio styles. The results are presented in Exhibit 2. Among the 40 cells or possible group pairs, only 15 were statistically different, but in no instance was the return from one specific style group superior to another single style group in more than two out of four time periods. In addition, the value and yield groups had no statistical difference, consistent with observations made in Exhibit 1. These results suggest that comparing the performance of portfolios with different styles over complete stock market cycles tends to create a "level playing field" for evaluation purposes; that is, differences in performance resulting from an investment style tend to be offset or neutralized when returns are measured over several market cycles.

RANKING PORTFOLIO PERFORMANCE WITHIN STYLE GROUPS

Using historical return data, it appears easier to predict the performance rankings of portfolios in some style groups than in others. The portfolios within each style group were ranked and assigned to quartiles in each market cycle period based on their relative rates of return. Their return rankings were then compared and correlated to their return rankings in the next market cycle period. These comparisons were done three times over the time periods 3, 4, and 5. The portfolios were ranked and assigned to quartiles in period 2 and their returns were measured over period 3 in the same original quartile. This ranking was repeated in periods 3 and 4, with returns correlated in periods 4 and 5, respectively.

Exhibit 3 combines the results for the three market cycles for the five style groups. The general policy group (in column 2) had the most predictable relative performance over the three periods. For this group, the average returns in all four quartiles were positively related to their quartile returns in the subsequent time periods; in fact, the return spread between quartiles 1 and 4, 400 basis points, was the largest of any group. In addition, Spearman and chi-square statistics were significant in two out of three periods. The growth style group in column 3 and the value group in column 5 had the next most predictable returns with a spread between quartiles 1 and 4 of 220 and 180 basis points, respectively. The other two smaller portfolio groups, the core and yield styles frequently had inconsistent quartile returns, had statistically insignificant return rankings, and in the case of the yield group, a negative 90 basis point spread between quartiles 1 and 4.

Exhibit 2: Analysis of Variance Matrix of the Differences in Portfolio Returns Between Types of Portfolio Policies in Time Periods 2, 3, 4, and 5[1]

Type of Portfolio Policy	Time Period	Number of Portfolios	Average Return	Standard Deviation	Statistical Differences in Portfolio Returns[2]			
					Growth	Value	Core	Yield
General	2	206	14.6%	5.8%	↑***	--	--	n.a.
	3	372	21.3	8.0	--	--	←***	--
	4	374	19.5	4.2	←***	↑***	--	**
	5	333	9.6	3.6	←**	←***	--	--
		Average	16.3					
Growth	2	123	19.7	7.7		←***	←***	n.a.
	3	149	21.3	6.6		--	←***	--
	4	158	16.6	4.1		↑***	↑***	↑***
	5	160	8.5	3.3		--	--	--
		Average	16.5					
Value	2	58	15.6	5.7			←***	n.a.
	3	91	20.5	4.9			←**	--
	4	96	20.4	2.6			--	--
	5	79	8.0	2.2			--	--
		Average	16.1					
Core	2	18	12.6	2.5				n.a.
	3	26	17.1	3.2				--
	4	26	19.3	2.5				--
	5	21	9.0	1.6				--
		Average	14.5					
Yield	2	10	11.7	3.2				
	3	21	20.1	3.3				
	4	24	20.9	2.5				
	5	22	8.6	1.6				
		Average	15.3					

1. At least one or more groups have returns that are statistically different from that of other groups at the 1% level in time periods 2 and 4, at the 5% level in time period 5, and at the 10% level in time period 3, based on ANOVA.
2. ***Portfolio returns are statistically different between the two groups at the 1% level.
   **Portfolio returns are statistically different between the two groups at the 5% level.
   *Portfolio returns are statistically different between the two groups at the 10% level.
   --Portfolio returns are not statistically different.
   The arrows point to the style that has the higher return.

Exhibit 3: Average Annual Returns over the Three Periods from April 1981 Through September 1991, Based on the Quartile Return Rankings in the Previous Time Period: with Portfolios Classified by Type of Portfolio Style

Previous Quartile Ranking	Annual Portfolio Returns Over Time Periods 3, 4, and 5				
	General	Growth	Core	Value	Yield
(1)	(2)	(3)	(4)	(5)	(6)
1st	18.4%	16.3%	15.1%	17.1%	16.6%
2nd	16.1	15.3	15.5	16.1	16.6
3rd	15.2	15.8	15.8	15.8	15.8
4th	14.4	14.1	14.4	15.3	17.5
% Return Spread between Q1 and Q4	4.0	2.2	0.7	1.8	–0.9
Frequency of Significant Chi-Square Values[*]	2	1	n.a.	n.a.	n.a.
Frequency of Significant Spearman Rank Correlation Coefficient*	2	1	0	1	0
Range of Portfolios	180-286	123-140	17-24	58-86	10-21

n.a. = not applicable, small sample size
* This indicates the number of cycles out of a total of three that the relative returns were consistently significant.

Therefore, relative performance was more predictable for some portfolio style groups than others. The most predictable, in descending order, are the general policy groups, followed by the growth and value style groups; the return rankings of portfolios in the core and yield groups were relatively unreliable for purposes of predicting relative performance. It is not surprising that differences in the quartile returns are so small for the core group inasmuch as the portfolios are expected to share many of the same securities. Conclusions regarding the yield style group are somewhat limited by the small number of portfolios represented in the sample.

CONCLUSIONS REGARDING THE FIVE STYLES

Compared with other studies, the ranking of performance of portfolios is relatively more predictable when the time periods encompass a complete stock market cycle rather than being confined to calendar years. The portfolio return rank correlations were meaningful. The portfolios in the first quartile usually outperformed those in the fourth quartile over the entire three market cycles. We found that portfolio performance characteristics are associated with different types of portfolio policies or styles.

The performance rankings of the general-policy group and the growth group were relatively consistent over time. The general-policy group's performance was so consistent that the portfolios historically ranked in the first quartile produced the highest average return of any group during the study period. Why would an undefined portfolio style group produce such consistent results? Perhaps because those managers are using a blend of styles and a pragmatic approach to the selection of stock groups. In any event, the rankings were the most reliable for the general-policy group, and the rankings for the yield, the value, and the core groups were generally undependable.

One surprising observation was that the average returns for the different portfolio style groups tended to cluster together when returns were measured over several market cycles. This suggests that long-term investors may achieve similar returns with different investment styles. The value and yield style groups, however, had decidedly the lowest risk levels as measured by betas and sigmas and, as a result, had the highest reward-to-risk performance ratios of any style.

GROWTH STYLE VERSUS VALUE STYLE

The growth style and the value style have received much attention in recent years. The growth style, commonly associated with stocks with high earnings per share (EPS) growth rates and high price-earning (PE) ratios, has been a popular portfolio strategy over the past 50 years, especially during times of strong economic growth. In recent years, however, the value style has received considerable attention together with the contrarian approach, considered a subset of this style. The value style is commonly associated with stocks with low market prices in relation to EPS, to cash flow per share, to book value per share, or low recent EPS growth rates. Many studies observe that value stocks with low PE ratios, low EPS growth rates, and low price to cash flow per share, outperform growth stocks that have the opposite characteristics. This difference in performance appears to be explained at least in part by the *adaptive expectations hypothesis*. This hypothesis asserts that forecasters rely too heavily on past trends when formulating expectations about the future. If so, investors will be inclined to overestimate expected EPS of stocks with high past growth rates and underestimate the expected EPS of stocks with low past growth rates; this is especially so if the EPS growth rate of companies experiences a mean reversion tendency over time. Because the expected EPS is a determinant of the present value of a stock, the market price would reflect such expectations. Consequently, when reported EPS are subsequently compared to biased expected EPS, the resulting surprises will understandably lead to market price adjustments.

TEST OF THE ADAPTIVE EXPECTATIONS HYPOTHESIS

In order to test the adaptive expectation hypothesis, the EPS consensus forecasts of securities research analysts in brokerage firms, furnished by Zacks Investment

Research, are used to proxy expectations of investors. The forecasts were made as of March 31 for the EPS in the then current year; this process was repeated for a total of 14 times covering the years 1980 through 1993. The sample of stocks consisted of all the stocks with the necessary financial data in the Compustat Research files and the rates of return in the CRSP NYSE/AMEX and NASDAQ data files. On the basis of a specified criteria, portfolios of stocks were formed into quartiles as of March 31 in each of the 14 years.[2]

Price-Earnings (PE) Ratio as a Criterion

Exhibit 4 presents the performance of the portfolios formed on the basis of PE ratios (PER). Commencing with the first year studied in 1980, PE ratios are determined based on the market price at the end of March in 1980 divided by EPS reported for 1979. Portfolio A, considered to consist of value stocks, represents one-fourth of the sample with the lowest PE ratios, portfolio B represents one-fourth of the sample with the next higher PE ratios, etc., and portfolio D represents one-fourth of the stocks with the highest PE ratios. Portfolio D is considered to be composed of growth stocks because of the above average PE ratios. The portfolios were formed in this manner in each of the 14 years. Annual returns for each portfolio were measured as the equally-weighted annual returns of the stocks from the end of March in the year the portfolios were formed to the end of March in the following year.

Portfolio A, the value stock portfolio, outperformed portfolio D, the growth stock portfolio, in eight out of 14 years, in which the difference was statistically significant (column 8) at the 1% level in 5 years and at the 10% level in one year. By contrast, portfolio D outperformed portfolio A in the other six years in which the difference was statistically significant at the 1% level in only two years, at the 5% level in one year, and at the 10% level in two years. The annual compound (geometric mean) return over the total period for portfolio A was 19.3% or 310 basis points greater than for portfolio D (16.2%). The standard deviation of annual returns for portfolio A at 19.3% is moderately lower than for portfolio D at 20.2%. Therefore, the risk-adjusted return, measured as the return-to-risk ratio (the arithmetic mean return to the standard deviation) for portfolio A at 1.05 is substantially higher than for portfolio D at 0.87. Although the relative performance on an annual basis between portfolios A and D follows an irregular pattern, a strong central tendency emerges over the longer term, which favors portfolio A over portfolio D on both a total return basis and on a risk-adjusted basis. Over the 14 years, portfolio A consisted of 2,311 annual stock returns with a mean return of 19.0%, and portfolio D consisted of 2,272 stocks with a mean return of 16.8%. The difference in returns between these two portfolios was statistically significant at the 0.044 level. These results generally confirm prior studies regarding the low PER anomaly. The median PER over the 14-year period for the four portfolios show a substantial difference between portfolio A at 7.2 and portfolio D at 27.1.

---

[2] See Bauman, W. Scott and Robert E. Miller, "Investor Expectations and the Performance of Value Stocks Versus Growth Stocks," *Journal of Portfolio Management*, forthcoming (Spring 1997).

Exhibit 4: Annual Returns for Price/Earnings Ratio Portfolios

Year Beginning 3/31- (1)	Number of Stocks (2)	Price/Earnings Ratio Portfolios (%)				Total Sample Return (%) (7)	Difference Between A&D[1] (8)	Market Index Return[2] (%) (9)
		A (Low) (3)	B (4)	C (5)	D (High) (6)			
1980	347	52.7	41.4	43.8	50.0	47.0	+2.7	43.8%
1981	539	2.7	−7.2	−14.2	−16.6	−8.8	+19.3***	−12.9
1982	666	49.6	49.0	44.1	61.1	50.9	−11.5*	44.8
1983	620	18.4	14.1	9.7	4.9	11.8	+13.5***	7.9
1984	646	31.4	26.2	19.0	12.1	22.2	+19.3***	18.2
1985	671	43.2	42.7	35.5	31.2	38.2	+12.0***	36.9
1986	637	17.4	17.8	19.6	24.3	19.8	−6.9*	23.0
1987	630	−9.3	−6.4	−2.9	−6.6	−6.3	−2.7	−8.3
1988	750	15.1	15.7	12.1	14.8	14.4	+0.3	16.7
1989	784	6.1	10.1	14.0	15.3	11.4	−9.2***	18.0
1990	771	1.5	8.4	9.2	9.4	7.1	−7.9**	12.7
1991	733	26.4	22.3	14.9	13.1	19.2	+13.3***	11.7
1992	634	28.6	22.8	17.1	22.0	22.6	+6.6*	15.2
1993[3]	690	0.8	3.7	3.2	9.4	4.3	−8.6***	6.0
Geometric Mean		19.3	17.8	15.3	16.2	17.2		15.9
Arithmetic Mean		20.3	18.6	16.1	17.5	18.1		16.7
Standard Deviation		19.3	17.2	16.4	20.2	17.7		16.9
Return to Risk Ratio		1.05	1.08	0.98	0.87	1.02		0.99
Median PER		7.2	10.6	14.7	27.1	12.7		

[1] *** Significant at the 1% level.
** Significant at the 5% level.
* Significant at the 10% level.
[2] CRSP Value-Weighted.
[3] 9-month return through December 31, 1993.

Price-Earnings Ratio Criterion and Earnings Surprises

The next step in testing the hypothesis is to measure the expectations of investors and determine the existence, if any, of forecast bias. A proxy for investor expectations is the consensus forecast of EPS for each stock in each year. This forecast is the mean of the individual analyst forecasts for year t made in March of study year t. The existence of any systematic forecast bias is indicated by the *earnings surprise* for a stock, which is measured as the difference between reported EPS and the consensus forecast; this difference is divided by a normalization factor, which is the standard deviation of the individual analyst forecasts. The EPS of some stocks are more difficult to forecast as reflected by a large diversity of forecasts among analysts. In such instances, we would expect a larger divergence in forecasts to be associated with a correspondingly larger difference between reported EPS and the consensus forecast. To adjust for differences in the uncertainty of expectations among stocks, the normalization factor is applied as the denominator to the forecast error that is in the numerator. The earnings surprise for a stock is calculated as:

$$ES_i = \frac{A_i - F_i}{SD_i}$$

Where:

- ES_i = earnings surprise indicator for stock i.
- A_i = reported (actual) EPS in year t for stock i.
- F_i = consensus forecast of EPS for year t made in March of year t for stock i.
- SD_i = standard deviation of the individual analyst forecasts in reference to the consensus EPS forecast for stock i.

The earnings surprise indicators, ES_p, for portfolios is the mean of the ES indicators for the stocks in the respective portfolios:

$$ES_p = \frac{\sum_{i=1}^{n} ES_i}{n}$$

The earnings surprises for the respective PE ratio portfolios A through D are presented in Exhibit 5. With but few exceptions, the earnings surprises become progressively more disappointing as the PER increases from portfolio A to B, to C, and to D. Portfolio A, the value portfolio, had the fewest earnings disappointments (three negative values) and the most positive (eleven) earnings surprises. By contrast, portfolio D, the growth portfolio, experienced earnings disappointments in every year and the most negative earning surprises in each year as compared to all the other portfolios.

The difference in the ES indicator between portfolios A and D is statistically different in every year — at the 1% level in 11 years and at the 5% level in the other three years. These results strongly suggest that a major explanation for differences in performance between low PER stocks and high PER stocks is EPS forecasting errors. Over the 14 years as a whole, portfolio A is the only one with an average positive earnings surprise indicator (0.99), which means that this portfolio is the only one in which the analysts consistently underestimated EPS. By contrast, portfolio D had the largest average negative earnings surprise indicator, at −3.40. Over the 14 years, portfolio A was represented by 2,311 EPS forecasts and portfolio D had 2,272; the difference in ES indicators between these two groups was significant at the 0.0001 level. In terms of performance, once investors realize the earnings disappointments with the stocks in portfolio D, returns appear impeded and more volatile as revealed in Exhibit 1. In the case of portfolio A, however, returns appear to be enhanced as favorable earnings surprises become apparent to investors. Among the 9,118 EPS forecasts in the aggregate, the average ES for the total sample was −1.21, which means the average analyst forecast appears to have an optimistic bias.

Earnings Per Share (EPS) Growth Rates

To test the adaptive expectations hypothesis as applied to common stock earnings surprises, we next examine the relationship between historical trends in EPS and earnings surprises in order to determine whether investor and analyst expectations rely too heavily on past EPS trends. The past EPS trend for a stock in study year t was computed as the log-linear annual growth rate over the previous four years, $t-4$ through $t-1$ ($t-5$ was the base year). So the past growth rate for the 1980 study year, for example, was the growth rate for EPS in the years 1976 through 1979 (1975 was the base year).

Portfolios were formed into quartiles as of the end of March in each of the 14 years studied on the basis of the past EPS growth rates. Portfolio A, considered to be composed of value stocks, consisted of one-fourth of the sample with the lowest past growth, while portfolio D, the growth stock portfolio, consisted of the one-fourth with the highest past growth. The average annual performance of these portfolios over the 14-year period is shown in Exhibit 6. Portfolio D tended to have the lowest return and had the highest standard deviation in returns (21.2%) as compared to the other portfolios. Portfolio A had the lowest standard deviation (15.2%) and the highest return-to-risk ratio (1.18), while portfolio D had the lowest (0.83).

Exhibit 5: Earnings Surprises for Price/Earnings Ratio Portfolios (Arithmetic Means)

Year Beginning 3/31- (1)	Number of Stocks (2)	Price/Earnings Ratio Portfolios				Total Sample (7)	Difference Between A&D[1] (8)
		A (Low) (3)	B (4)	C (5)	D (High) (6)		
1980	347	2.73	0.87	−1.01	−1.39	0.31	4.12**
1981	539	0.83	−1.53	−0.54	−1.01	−0.55	1.84**
1982	666	0.76	−0.04	−1.88	−2.87	−1.00	3.63***
1983	620	−1.64	−2.65	−3.84	−4.08	−3.05	2.44***
1984	646	0.99	−0.15	−0.82	−1.80	−0.44	2.79***
1985	671	1.99	−0.25	−1.63	−3.01	−0.72	5.00***
1986	637	0.47	−1.50	−2.30	−4.75	−2.03	5.22***
1987	630	−0.12	−1.11	−0.27	−3.70	−1.30	3.58***
1988	750	−0.86	−0.66	−1.02	−4.13	−1.21	3.27***
1989	784	2.12	0.37	−1.07	−2.77	−0.32	4.89***
1990	771	0.47	−0.99	−1.53	−4.39	−1.60	4.86***
1991	733	1.36	−2.06	−3.47	−3.50	−1.90	4.86**
1992	634	1.33	0.51	−2.42	−4.92	−1.37	6.25***
1993[2]	690	2.05	−1.50	−1.28	−3.77	−1.09	5.82***
Average	9,118	0.99	−0.80	−1.68	−3.40	−1.21	4.39

[1] *** Significant at the 1% level.
    ** Significant at the 5% level.
    * Significant at the 10% level.
[2] 9-month return through December 31, 1993.

Exhibit 6: Annual Returns for 5-Year Growth Rate Portfolios
March 31, 1980 to December 31, 1993

	Five-Year Growth Rate Portfolios				Total Sample Return	Difference Between A & D	Market Index Return[1]
	A (Low)	B	C	D (High)			
	(3)	(4)	(5)	(6)	(7)	(8)	(9)
Geometric Mean	17.4%	17.3%	17.2%	16.1%	17.1%	+1.3	15.9%
Arithmetic Mean	18.0	18.0	18.4	17.5	18.0	+0.5	16.7
Standard Deviation	15.2	16.1	19.4	21.2	17.7	−6.0	16.9
Return to Risk Ratio	1.18	1.12	0.95	0.83	1.02	+0.35	0.99

[1] CRSP Value-Weighted

Exhibit 7: Earnings Surprises for 5-Year Growth Rate Portfolios (Arithmetic Means)

Year Beginning 3/31-	Number of Stocks	Five-Year Growth Rate Portfolios				Total Sample	Difference Between A & D[1]
		A (Low)	B	C	D (High)		
(1)	(2)	(3)	(4)	(5)	(6)	(7)	(8)
1980	329	2.18	0.44	0.47	−1.81	0.31	3.99**
1981	510	0.13	−1.16	−0.82	−1.10	−0.74	1.23
1982	611	−0.85	−0.92	−0.77	−1.48	−1.00	0.63
1983	556	−2.10	−2.79	−3.58	−4.09	−3.14	1.99***
1984	550	0.12	0.01	−0.90	−1.15	−0.48	1.27***
1985	534	−0.97	−1.30	0.05	−0.56	−0.70	−0.41
1986	507	−2.05	−2.27	−1.48	−2.07	−1.97	0.02
1987	475	−2.18	−1.90	−1.37	−1.53	−1.75	−0.65
1988	492	−0.51	−2.07	−2.11	−1.91	−1.65	1.40
1989	505	−1.99	−0.60	−0.13	−0.08	−0.70	−1.91**
1990	492	−1.97	−2.90	−2.43	−1.85	−2.79	−0.12
1991	451	−2.36	−3.83	−2.77	−2.87	−2.96	0.51
1992	413	−1.47	−2.06	−3.44	−2.84	−2.45	1.37*
1993[2]	425	−0.82	−1.72	−2.03	−1.14	−1.43	0.32
Average	6,850	−1.12	−1.66	−1.52	−1.73	−1.51	0.39

[1] *** Significant at the 1% level.
** Significant at the 5% level.
* Significant at the 10% level.
[2] 9-month return through December 31, 1993.

Exhibit 7 presents the earning surprise indicators for the four portfolios. The EPS of stocks in portfolio D tended to be overestimated to a greater extent than in the other portfolios, and were more greatly overestimated on average in ten out of 14 years as compared to portfolio A. The EPS for portfolio A was underestimated in three years (1980, 1981, and 1984) and, in general, tended to be the least overestimated. In a cross sectional, time series correlation analysis of the

6,850 stock earnings surprises with respect to their past growth rates, the correlation was -0.04, which was significant at the 0.001 level. This evidence supports the adaptive expectation hypothesis inasmuch as analysts appeared to overestimate EPS to a greater extent (produce a larger negative ES indicator) for stocks with higher past growth rates than for stocks with lower past growth rates.

Changes in annual EPS tend to resemble a random walk. To test for existence of this phenomenon in our sample, we conducted a cross sectional, time series correlation analysis of the 6,850 past four-year EPS growth rates with their respective current year (year t) growth rates. The resulting correlation coefficient was −0.03, which was significant at the 0.012 level. This negative relationship suggests that EPS growth rates have a mean reversion tendency.

The above evidence suggests that analyst and investor expectations and current price-earnings ratios tend to reflect past EPS growth rates. When expectations are derived by a tendency to extrapolate past growth rates into the future, and by pursuing a growth stock policy defined as owning stocks with high PER ratios and high historic EPS growth rates, such a policy appears to lead to greater disappointments in expected EPS and in lower risk-adjusted portfolio returns. By contrast, investors who pursue a contrarian, value-type policy by owning stocks with low PER ratios and with lower historic EPS growth rates, appear to experience relatively more favorable EPS surprises and higher risk-adjusted portfolio returns.

Size of Firms

The performance from the value style is distinct from the small firm investment style. The portfolios previously formed as quartiles in each year, designated as portfolios A, B, C, and D, were subdivided into four groups on the basis of capitalization size so that a total of 16 portfolio groups were formed. Capitalization size of a stock in each year is measured as the market price at the end of March times the number of shares outstanding. The annual returns of the stocks in these 16 groups were then averaged over the 14 years.

Exhibit 8 presents the average annual performance for the PE ratio portfolios subdivided by cap size. Reading the columns vertically, the small firm effect tends to exist in which the smallest size group, group 1, had the highest average return (19.0%) as shown in column 6, while the largest size group, group 4, had the lowest average return (15.5%). However, the low PER affect is also reflected by reading the rows horizontally. In the last row of column (2), portfolio A, with the lowest PER, had the highest return (19.0%), while portfolio D in column (5), with the highest PER, had a lower return (16.8%). In general, the groups with the highest returns were those stocks with lower PER and smaller capitalizations. However, one major exception was portfolio D-1, composed of the smallest stocks with the highest PER, which had the highest return, 21.2%. This group may include value stocks with EPS in year $t–1$ that were cyclically depressed, or had nonrecurring accounting adjustments such as starting-up expenses or write-offs. The annual return on this group was also very volatile with a standard deviation of 26.6% and a return to risk ratio of only 0.85.

Exhibit 8: Average Annual Returns for Price/Earnings Ratio Portfolios Divided into Quartiles by Firm Size
March 31, 1980 to December 31, 1993

Firm Size Group (1)	Price/Earnings Ratio Portfolios (%)								Total	
	A (Low) (2)		B (3)		C (4)		D (High) (5)		(6)	
Smallest 1	21.1	(163.6)	18.2	(168.7)	15.2	(158.2)	21.2	(150.4)	19.0	(160.2)
2	20.2	(504.3)	18.5	(492.7)	17.6	(487.4)	16.0	(486.9)	18.1	(493.0)
3	17.8	(1328.6)	18.7	(1281.6)	16.4	(1340.2)	13.7	(1246.5)	16.7	(1300.9)
Largest 4	16.9	(5681.1)	16.6	(7443.2)	12.8	(7416.5)	15.8	(7708.5)	15.5	(7072.7)
TOTAL	19.0	(1885.4)	18.0	(2221.7)	15.4	(2458.0)	16.8	(2486.9)	17.3	(2261.3)

( ) denotes the average capitalization in millions of dollars.

Persistence of EPS Forecast Bias

Why do the differences in earnings expectations between value stocks and growth stocks persist over an extended period of time? First, it is observed that the earnings surprise indicator for our total sample was negative in each year except in 1980. Therefore, analysts tend to have expectations that are optimistically biased, except for the sample quartile with the lowest PER. Why do these biases persist? One explanation is that investors and analysts can become psychologically attached to their industries and companies, especially if they have had a favorable recent performance; and may tend to extrapolate past EPS growth rates too far into the future as suggested by the adaptive expectations hypothesis. If the pattern of successive annual EPS growth rates reflect a random walk or a reversion to the mean, then growth stocks with high past EPS growth rates will tend to have PE ratios that are too high and earnings expectations that are too optimistic.

Second, companies with a recent record of low EPS growth or adverse performance, tend to appear less popular and frequently have low PER. Because most sell-side analysts are ultimately compensated on the basis of brokerage commissions generated, analysts have an incentive to sell stocks to customers. It is easier for analysts to present an enthusiastic and persuasive argument for the purchase of a stock of a company that has been performing well and which is supported by a favorable EPS growth rate forecast. Likewise, it is easier for a portfolio manager to justify the purchase of such a stock, especially for portfolio managers who are under pressure from clients to produce superior short-term performance. If the EPS are subsequently disappointing, the analyst and portfolio manager may merely explain that the performance of the company changed unexpectedly. Conversely, it is more difficult to justify a less popular stock of a company with a poor recent performance. In this instance, the analyst needs to build the case that the future for the company will be better than its past. The fear among analysts and portfolio managers, who recommend and purchase such a stock, of course, is that if the performance of the company fails to improve, they have the awkward burden of explaining why they recommended a company at the time it had a mediocre performance. Therefore, such stocks may become too neglected and their PE ratios fall to an abnormally low level. It is interesting to note that some prominent portfolio managers who have successfully pursued a value style, appear individualistic and independent-minded, and have a loyal clientele who do not question their short-term performance.

Hypothetical Portfolios Versus Actual Portfolios

It should be noted that in the analyses discussed here, as well as in those by others, the difference in performance between styles largely depends on whether actual portfolios or hypothetically constructed portfolios are used. When actual portfolios are used, the difference in average returns between the value style and growth style was only 70 basis points (bp) in Exhibit 1 (column 7), and only 40 bp in Exhibit 2; but in the hypothetical portfolios A and D, the difference in the geometric mean returns between the portfolios was 310 bp in Exhibit 4. In all three instances, however, the risk as measured by sigma or standard deviation is higher for the growth style, such that the value style groups clearly had the highest reward-to-risk ratios.

Nevertheless, the quite narrow spread in performance between the actual portfolios can be puzzling. Several plausible explanations are offered. One is that most portfolios have policy constraints. Portfolios typically require a minimum level of diversification which limit the proportion of funds that can be invested in any one economic sector, industry, or company (such as a maximum of 3% in the stock of any one company). Our hypothetical portfolios invest in all the stocks that meet the specified quantitative filter regardless of the number of stocks that come from the same industry. Consequently, a value style portfolio can easily be considered to be imprudently concentrated in a few industries at times, such as the finance, utility, or capital goods industries. Another constraint is the limit on ownership (such as a maximum of 5%) of a total stock issue for liquidity or regulatory reasons. This constraint is particularly relevant to large portfolios and for ownership of smaller cap stocks. Consequently, value portfolios, especially larger ones, are restrained from using the asset weights employed by hypothetical portfolios, particularly among value-type medium and smaller cap stocks, which are frequently the higher performing ones.

Another major difference can be transaction costs and market liquidity. No allowance was made for transaction costs in the performance of the hypothetical portfolios. It is possible that some of the value stocks, as compared to the growth stock, trade in thinner markets. If so, value portfolio managers may be incurring larger transaction costs which reduce net performance, while other managers may avoid investing in the less liquid value stock issues in order to avoid these large costs. In still other instances, managers may take a longer period of time to accumulate or to liquidate a less liquid issue in order to minimize the market price impact; but meanwhile, over this longer period of time, competing investors have more time to exploit this same research information that triggered the initial transaction.

A third explanation for the narrower difference in performance between the actual portfolios is that many of these portfolios may not strictly represent a pure style. Consequently, some of the value portfolios may include stocks that also possess growth characteristics and some growth portfolios may include stocks that possess the undervaluation characteristics of value stocks. To the extent that some of these portfolios in the style groups represent a blend of style characteristics, then the differences in the performance of these styles will become blurred.

SUMMARY

Several major conclusions can be drawn from this chapter. First, when comparing portfolios based on different investment styles, the spread in portfolio returns narrows considerably when the time period used is extended over several market cycles. Second, relative rankings of performance among portfolios within style groups were reasonably consistent over complete stock market cycles for the growth, value and general policy style groups. However, the rankings for the core and yield style groups were relatively uncorrelated from one market cycle to another. Third, value stocks appeared to outperform growth stocks due in part to biased earnings forecasts made by security analysts. Specifically, earnings were consistently underestimated for the lowest PE stocks and consistently overestimated for the highest PE stocks. These biased forecasts may be explained by the adaptive expectations hypothesis, in which the forecasters rely too heavily on recent past trends in formulating future projections. Analysts appear to be extrapolating past trends in EPS into the future, while the true pattern in the normal growth rate of earnings tends to resemble either a random walk or mean reversion.

Chapter 9

Analyzing the Performance of Equity Managers: A Note on Value versus Growth

T. Daniel Coggin, Ph.D.
Director of Research
Gerber/Taylor Associates

Charles Trzcinka, Ph.D.
Professor of Finance
State University of New York at Buffalo

INTRODUCTION

A continuing debate in the investment community centers on a single question: Does active equity management add value?[1] Like religion and politics, there are those who know the answer, and no amount of contrary evidence will shake their convictions. A study by Coggin, Fabozzi, and Rahman analyzed the performance of a sample of 71 U.S. equity pension fund managers from the Frank Russell Company investment manager database. In that study, equity pension fund managers were defined as institutional money mangers who have been hired by pension funds to manage equity portfolios. The major findings are: (1) regardless of

---

[1] For a discussion of the various forms of active equity management, see T. Daniel Coggin, "Active Equity Management" Chapter 4 in Frank J. Fabozzi (ed.), *Portfolio & Investment Management* (Chicago: Probus Publishing, 1989).

the choice of benchmark portfolio or estimation model, the mean selectivity measure (alpha) is positive and the mean market timing measure is negative for the full sample; and (2) when managers are classified by equity style, the choice of a benchmark portfolio for estimating selectivity and timing does matter.[2] That study is still one of only a very few studies of equity *pension fund managers*. The vast majority of the previous work in this area has analyzed the performance of equity *mutual fund managers*.

The authors of this chapter came to this issue from two different backgrounds and perspectives. One of us is a finance professor who teaches his students the *efficient market hypothesis*, and thus is skeptical of the existence of sustained outperformance on the part of equity fund managers. The other author has worked in the investment profession for a number of years and thus is skeptical of the validity of the efficient market hypothesis. After a number of discussions, we decided to collaborate on a larger study of the performance of equity pension fund managers. This chapter summarizes our findings on one important aspect of that larger study. The focus of this chapter is on the difference in performance between value and growth managers in our sample of equity pension fund mangers. Specifically, we found that growth managers did significantly better than value managers relative to their benchmark portfolios in our data. The following chapter by Robert Haugen offers an explanation for this result.

DATA AND METHODOLOGY

Data

The data for our study were obtained from Mobius Group, Inc. (Research Triangle Park, NC).[3] Mobius Group currently collects data from over 2,000 equity pension funds and provides those data (along with analytical software) to subscribers for a fee. There are 502 equity pension fund portfolios in our study, representing 340 equity managers. In order to be included in our sample, a portfolio (or composite portfolio) had to be U.S. domestic equity, have at least three years of quarterly returns, and include deleted accounts in composites. All returns are gross of management fees. The time period of our study is March 1979 through June of 1993. The actual range for the number of quarters of data for portfolios in our sample spans the interval $16 \leq Q \leq 58$, with a mean of 41. Only active equity managers are included (i.e., no index funds).

---

[2] T. Daniel Coggin, Frank J. Fabozzi, and Shafiqur Rahman, "The Investment Performance of U.S. Equity Pension Fund Managers: An Empirical Investigation," *Journal of Finance* (July 1993), pp. 1039-1055. The paper was originally presented at the 1993 annual meeting of the American Finance Association. The discussant for the paper was Charles Trzcinka.

[3] At this point, we note that the conclusions reached in this chapter are ours alone and not necessarily those of the Mobius Group.

Methodology

We used three investment performance models to estimate alphas for our sample of equity manager portfolios. The Market Model (using the S&P 500 as the market portfolio) is:

$$R_P - R_f = \alpha + \beta (S\&P500 - R_f) + e \tag{1}$$

The Market Model is the classic equity performance measurement model and needs no further explanation here.

The (modified) Elton-Gruber-Das-Hlavka Model is:[4]

$$R_P - R_f = \alpha + \beta_1 (S\&P500 - R_f) + \beta_2 (Russell2000 - R_f) + \beta_3 (LBGC - R_f) + e \tag{2}$$

where LBGC is the Lehman Brothers Government/Corporate Bond Index, and the S&P500 and the Russell2000 stock indexes were orthogonalized to mitigate the problem of multicollinearity. The E-G-D-H Model was developed to correct the Market Model for its failure to specifically include small stocks and bonds. The E-G-D-H and Market Models were applied to all 502 portfolios.

The Equity Style Model is:

$$R_P - R_f = \alpha + \beta (Russell1000Value - R_f) + e \tag{3}$$

for value managers or

$$R_P - R_f = \alpha + \beta (Russell1000Growth - R_f) + e \tag{4}$$

for growth managers.

The Equity Style Model is included here to reflect the recent focus by academics and practitioners (and *this book*) on the concept of *equity style*. That is, there is a growing awareness that an equity manager should be compared to a benchmark portfolio that reflects his/her style of investing (i.e., value/growth and small/large). For the Equity Style Model, portfolios were assigned to the value or growth category on the basis of the manager's self-description of the portfolio. Thus there are 170 value and 141 growth portfolios in our sample.[5]

In each of these models, α is the *risk-adjusted excess return* on the portfolio for the period. All three models were estimated using ordinary least squares time series regression.

---

[4] Edwin J. Elton, Martin J. Gruber, Sanjiv Das, and Matthew Hlavka, "Efficiency with Costly Information: A Reinterpretation of Evidence for Managed Portfolios," *Review of Financial Studies* (Spring 1993), pp. 1-22.
[5] The reader has no doubt noticed that we are using the *large cap* Russell value and growth indexes (i.e., the R1000V and the R1000G indexes) in the Style Index Model. For this reason, managers who call themselves "small value" or "small growth" (or "market oriented") were not classified as value or growth for the purpose of estimating this model. We note that there were not many small value or growth managers in our sample.

Exhibit 1: Mean Alphas for Three Investment Performance Models

Investment Model	Mean Alpha	No. Positive	No. Negative
Market Model	0.56%/Quarter	413	89
E-G-D-H Model	1.40%/Quarter	469	33
Style Model-Value	0.24%/Quarter	110	60
Style Model-Growth	1.01%/Quarter	130	11

RESULTS

Our results using the three models are presented in Exhibit 1. It is interesting to note that no matter which model we use, the mean alpha is positive. This runs contrary to the conventional wisdom concerning the performance of equity managers and supports the findings of the study by Coggin, Fabozzi, and Rahman.[6] While Exhibit 1 clearly shows evidence of some skill on the part of the mangers in our sample, there are two factors which would reduce the magnitude of these alphas. One, as noted above, our observed quarterly returns are *gross of fees*. Therefore, subtracting fees would lower managers' alphas. Two, there is no doubt an element of *survivor bias* in our results as well. It is well known that survivor bias can distort equity performance measures in favor of detecting skill (i.e., positive alphas).[7]

We focus here on the large disparity in the mean alphas for value and growth portfolios using the Equity Style Model (i.e., 0.24% versus 1.01% per quarter). To our knowledge, this has not been specifically documented before. That is, we know of no previous study which documents the observation that it is *more difficult for value managers than for growth managers to outperform their benchmark portfolio*. We currently do not have an explanation for this finding. However, we are happy to note that Robert Haugen does. He has spent a significant amount of his time in the past few years investigating the performance of value stocks/managers versus growth stocks/managers. After hearing of our results, he agreed to offer his own explanation for our finding. That explanation is presented in the next chapter.

---

[6] Coggin, Fabozzi, and Rahman, "The Investment Performance of U.S. Equity Pension Fund Managers: An Empirical Investigation."

[7] For more on the subject of survivor bias, see Stephen J. Brown, William N. Goetzmann, Roger G. Ibbotson, and Stephen A. Ross, "Survivorship Bias in Performance Studies," *Review of Financial Studies* (Winter 1992), pp. 553-580; and Edwin J. Elton, Martin J. Gruber, and Christopher R. Blake, "Survivorship Bias and Mutual Fund Performance," forthcoming in the *Review of Financial Studies*.

Chapter 10

The Effects of Imprecision and Bias on the Abilities of Growth and Value Managers to Out-Perform their Respective Benchmarks

Robert A. Haugen, Ph.D.
Professor of Finance
University of California — Irvine

INTRODUCTION

The previous chapter by Coggin and Trzcinka shows disparity in the performance of growth and value managers relative to their respective stylized benchmarks. This chapter presents a framework for understanding why this is likely to be the general case.

Let's begin by considering the manner in which the stylized benchmarks are constructed. The Russell Value Index begins with the population of stocks in the Russell 1000 Stock Index. This index is capitalization-weighted and contains roughly the 1000 largest (based on market capitalization) U.S. equities. Russell ranks the 1000 stocks on the basis of the ratio of book equity-to-market price (an indicator of cheapness). Beginning with the stock with the highest ratio, Russell goes down the list until it reaches the half-way point in terms of total market capitalization. That is, the total market capitalization of the stocks in the top-side is equal to the total market capitalization of the stocks in the bottom-side of the list. The stocks in the top-side go in the Russell Value Index, and the stock in the bottom-side go in the Russell Growth Index. Both indices are then capitalization-weighted.[1]

---

[1] The weighting is actually based on the fraction of the capitalization that is publicly traded not privately held.

As seen in the previous chapter, when the risk-premiums of growth managers are regressed on the risk premiums of the Russell Growth Stock Index, the average, annualized alpha is roughly 4% with 130 out of 141 managers showing positive performance. But the value managers show less than 1% annualized value added relative to their index, with only 110 out of 170 out-performing.

While the record of the value managers is good, it pales relative to the apparent performance of the growth managers. Why? If the market were efficient, both styles should show neutral performance. The fact that both styles out-perform can be taken as evidence that the market is not efficient.[2] As we shall see below, the *differential* in their performance can be taken as a product of the *nature of the market's inefficiencies*.

IMPRECISION

Most of us learned the concept of normal profit in the introductory economics course. Given a firm's capital investment, the real rate of interest, and the risk associated with that investment, the firm, as an investor, deserves to earn a reasonable rate of return. We also learned that, in competitive lines of business, in the short-run, firms may earn abnormal profits — greater or less than what is reasonable.

Call the risk-adjusted present value of the abnormal profits a firm is expected to earn over the period of short-run, *Abnormal Profit*. Growth stocks are defined here to have positive Abnormal Profits. The Abnormal Profits of value stocks are negative.

Now consider two estimates of Abnormal Profit. The first is the *best estimate*. This estimate considers all relevant available information. This information is processed and analyzed using the best available technology. The best estimate is not necessarily highly accurate, but it is unbiased, and it is the most accurate estimate available. Call this estimate *True Abnormal Profit*.

The second is the *market's estimate*. This is the estimate that's reflected in the market price for the stocks. Call this estimate *Priced Abnormal Profit*.

Indicators of Priced Abnormal Profit measure the cheapness or dearness in the price of the stock. They are ratios indicating the magnitude of the market price relative to the current cash flows produced from operations. These indicators include sales-to-price, cash flow-to-price, earnings-to-price, as well as the indicator used to construct the Russell Growth and Value Indexes, book-to-price.

Exhibit 1 plots True Abnormal Profit against Priced Abnormal Profit. Growth stocks are above the horizontal line; value stocks are below. The dots in the exhibit represent individual stocks. With the exception of the two larger dots, all are priced efficiently. For these stocks the abnormal profit reflected in the price

---

[2] This conclusion must be tempered by the fact that there is survival bias in the test of Coggin and Trzcinka. However, unless there is a clear difference in the relative turnover between growth and value managers, the clear differential in their performance speaks to inefficiency in the market.

is equal to the best estimate. For these stocks Priced Abnormal Profit is equal to True Abnormal Profit, and they are all plotted on the 45 degree line. Call this line the *Efficient Market Line*.

The stock that is positioned above the Efficient Market Line is under-priced. It's true Abnormal Profit is greater than what is reflected in its market price. As such, it will produce an abnormally large return for investors who buy it at that bargain price. Similarly, the stock positioned below the Efficient Market Line is over-priced. It is a value stock, and it is priced as such, but its price is not low enough. The True Abnormal Profit of this stock is very low. The market price should be much lower than it actually is. Investors who buy the over-valued stock will receive abnormally low rates of return in the future. An efficient market wouldn't allow over- or under-pricing of stocks. In a perfectly efficient market, all stocks would be positioned on the Efficient Market Line. However, few would argue that, for the real stock market, we are dealing with a *line*. Surely we must have a *band*. The controversy, then, is over the *width* of the band.

The market prices with *imprecision*. It assigns the same price to stocks with different True Abnormal Profits, as indicated by the vertical arrow of Exhibit 2. It assigns different prices to stocks with the same abnormal profit as indicated by the horizontal arrow.

Later I will cite evidence that makes a convincing case for the contention that the band depicted in Exhibit 2 is very wide. Grant me that assumption for the moment.

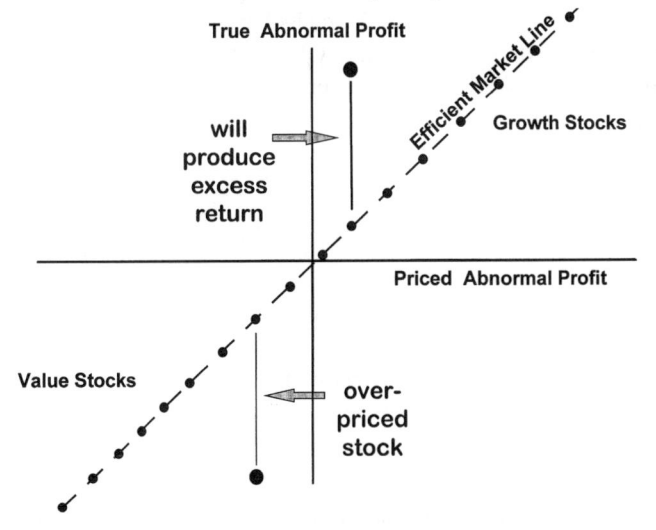

Exhibit 1: *The Position of Portfolios in Abnormal Profit Space*

Exhibit 2: The Position of Portfolios in Abnormal Profit Space

(Figure: Abnormal Profit Space diagram showing True Abnormal Profit on vertical axis and Priced Abnormal Profit on horizontal axis, with the Efficient Market Line running diagonally through a shaded band of available assets. Annotation reads: "IMPRECISION: Stocks with the same price have different TRUE abnormal profit.")

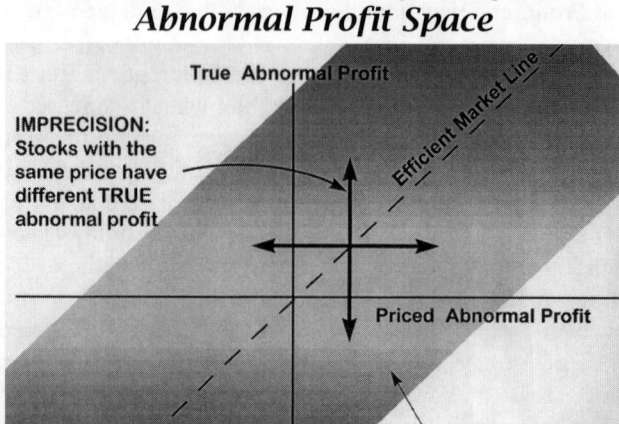

In a market that is merely imprecise, managers who base their strategy on buying "cheap" stocks won't add value. If you rank stocks based on some measure of cheapness, say book-to-price, you move the left in Exhibit 2, but your expected position within the gray area is in the middle — on the Efficient Market Line. Consequently, if the market were merely imprecise, we wouldn't see the results of Fama and French,[3] where stocks with relatively large book-to-price ratios tend to subsequently produce relatively high returns.

In the same sense, if you rank stocks based on some measure that may be correlated with True Abnormal Profit, say the firm's rate of return on total assets, you wouldn't expect to add value either. This time you move to the north in Exhibit 2, but your expected position is, once again in the middle of the shaded area, again on the Efficient Market Line.

BIAS

In Exhibit 3 we have a market that is both *imprecise* and *biased* in its pricing. How biased?

The market is biased in its assessment of the length of the short-run — the period over which the firm can be expected to earn abnormal profits.[4] The market depicted in Exhibit 3 over-estimates the length of the short-run. If a firm is

---

[3] E. Fama and K. French, "The Cross-section of Expected Stock Returns," *Journal of Finance* (June 1992).
[4] For the collective evidence that the market is truly biased in this way, see R. Haugen, *The New Finance: The Case Against Efficient Markets* (Englewood Cliffs, NJ: Prentice Hall, 1995).

earning positive abnormal profits now, the market projects prosperity to continue for too long. It under-estimates the power of competitive entry, which will drive profits to normal levels in a line of business.[5]

In a market that prices stocks with this bias, the band will tilt downward, positioning itself below the Efficient Market Line to the right and above it to the left. Firms that are earning positive abnormal profits now (growth stocks) tend to become over-priced. They tend to be positioned below the Efficient Market Line. And the more profitable they are now, the more over-priced they tend to be.

Conversely, unprofitable firms (value stocks) tend to be under-priced. The market projects their lack of success to continue for too long. The reality is that competitors will leave their lines of business, re-inventing themselves and moving elsewhere. Those that remain in the line will now be able to raise prices and enjoy greater market share. Both those that leave and those that remain will likely see their profits rise to normal levels.

The market of Exhibit 3 over-reacts to success and failure. It is biased. Now, in this market, consider the relative merits of growth and value investing. Suppose you rank stocks based on some measure of Priced Abnormal Profit — say, once again, book-to-price. As you move to the left in the exhibit, you expect to be positioned above the Efficient Market Line, in the vicinity of the point marked "Pure Value." At this position, you would expect to add value. On the other hand, as you move to the right, in the direction of more expensive stocks, you expect to under-perform.

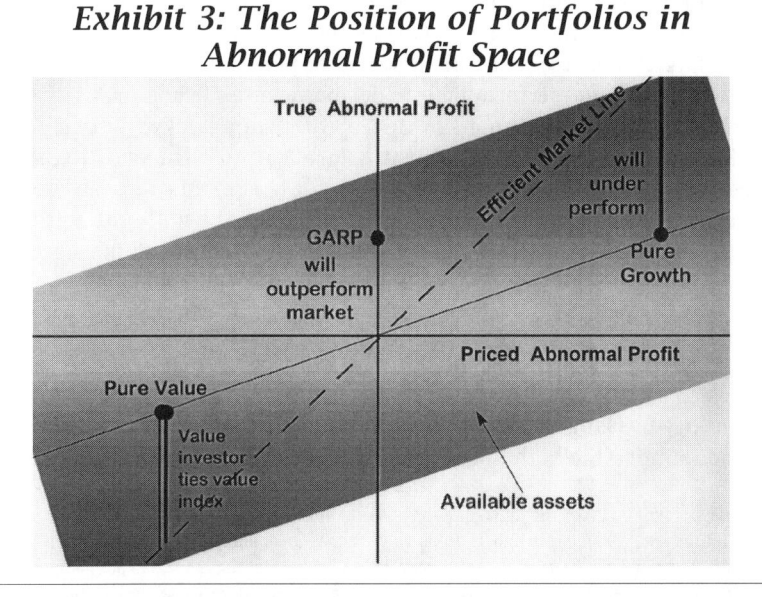

Exhibit 3: The Position of Portfolios in Abnormal Profit Space

---

[5] The speed of competitive entry differs from line to line. However, there will be an average speed, or length of the short-run, over all lines. The market of Exhibit 3 has under-estimated that average.

In the market of Exhibit 3, *value managers attempt to move to the west.* They generally rank stocks based on some measure of cheapness, and they buy relatively cheap stocks. They tend to stress discipline in their investing. They tell some version of the story related to the market's tendency to over-estimate the length of the short-run. *They are taking advantage of the market's bias.*

On the other hand, *growth managers attempt to move to the north.* They look for profitable companies with bright prospects for earning Abnormal Profits. However, growth managers *who simply do this* are looking for trouble. If you rank stocks on the basis of indicators of True Abnormal Profit, and simply buy the best looking stocks, you can expect to position yourself in the vicinity of the point marked "Pure Growth," under the efficient Market Line. You can expect to under-perform.

This does not mean that growth managers, as a group, cannot add value.

Growth managers who look for companies with bright prospects at reasonable prices can be expected to be positioned in the vicinity of the point labeled "GARP" (Growth At a Reasonable Price). Managers like these are positioned above the Efficient Market Line, and can be expected to add value.

In moving to the north, while avoiding a significant move toward the east, *growth managers are taking advantage of the market's imprecision.* In the context of Exhibit 3, the relative merit of growth and value investing is measured by their relative distances above the Efficient Market Line. In the exhibit, I have assumed that growth and value investors are equally meritorious. However, consider how they will perform relative to their stylized benchmarks.

The growth benchmark, constructed to contain expensive stocks, can be expected to be positioned near the point labeled "Pure Growth." The Benchmark, being under the Efficient Market Line, can be expected to under-perform. On the other had, GARP managers can be expected to beat not only the general market, but they will easily out-perform their under-performing benchmark.

But the value benchmark, made up of cheap stocks, will be positioned above the Efficient Market Line near "Pure Value." Since it, itself, can be expected to out-perform, this will be a difficult benchmark to beat. Those value managers who beat it will do so by investing in stocks with good prospects in spite of the fact that they are selling cheap.[6] This is why growth managers have an easier time out-performing their benchmarks than do value managers.[7]

SUPER STOCKS

In a recent paper, Haugen and Baker (HB) show that it is possible[8] to create portfolios of common stocks that are, at the same time, very cheap and very profit-

---

[6] These managers will be taking advantage of the market's imprecision *and* bias in pricing.
[7] Note that in, the study by Coggin and Trzinka, value managers actually out-performed their benchmarks, although by not as much as the growth managers. This indicates that the managers are taking advantage of both bias and imprecision, moving to the north of the point labeled "Pure Value" in Exhibit 3.
[8] R. Haugen and N. Baker, "Commonality in the Determinants of Expected Stock Returns," *Journal of Financial Economics* (July 1996).

able. HB estimate the expected returns of stocks by estimating the expected payoffs related to firm characteristics. By interfacing these projected payoffs with the contemporary set of firm characteristics, they estimate the expected returns to different stocks. HB then rank stocks based on these expected returns and form into deciles. The high return decile not only out-performs consistently, it is characterized by a very interesting profile.

As an aggregate, the stocks in the decile are low-risk, big, liquid highly profitable and very cheap. The stocks in the low-return decile (Decile I) have the opposite profile.

In Abnormal Profit space, the deciles are positioned as in Exhibit 4. I have labeled decile 10 as "Super Stocks," given their outstanding character. *The Super Stock portfolio takes maximum advantage of the market's imprecision and bias in pricing.* It is positioned well over the Efficient Market Line. The fact that such extreme portfolios can be created stands in testimony to the great width of the band.

However, Super Stock portfolios can't be formed using commonly employed hierarchical screening techniques. That's because there are no individual stocks that have the complete profile of a Super Stock profile. If you merely try to screen stocks, so that each is characterized by a set of attributes, you will never approach the position of Super Stocks in Exhibit 4.

To get to the Super Stock position, you must build your portfolio with regard to the nature of the portfolio as an aggregate. *You can't require each of its members to have the character of the aggregate portfolio itself.*

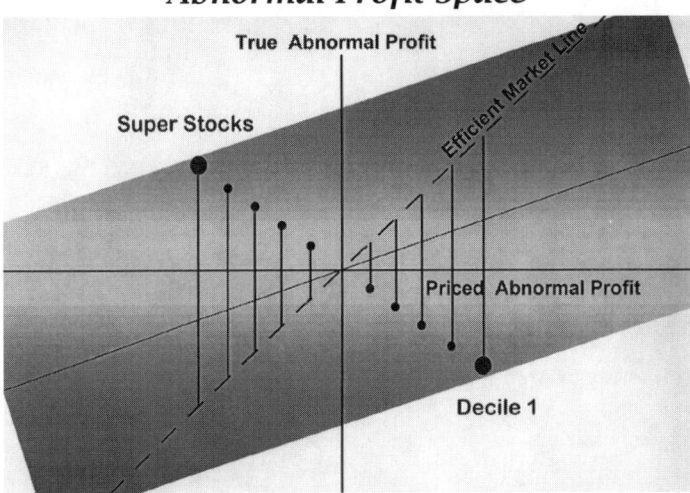

Exhibit 4: The Position of Portfolios in Abnormal Profit Space

SUMMARY

The market is both biased and imprecise in its pricing. The market's bias is a product of its propensity to over-estimate the length of the short-run. Its imprecision results from its propensity to assign different prices to stocks with the same true prospects for earning Abnormal Profit and the same prices to stocks with different true prospects. Value managers take advantage of the market's bias in buying cheap stocks. Growth stock managers take advantage of the market's imprecision in buying stocks with good prospects at reasonable prices. Because of the market's bias, growth stock benchmarks, made up of expensive stocks, can, themselves be expected to under-perform. Conversely, value stock benchmarks, made up of cheap stocks, can be expected to over-perform, making it more difficult for value managers to beat their stylized benchmarks.

Chapter 11

The Many Sides of Equity Style: Quantitative Management of Core, Value, and Growth Portfolios

David J. Leinweber, Ph.D.
Managing Director
First Quadrant, L.P.

Robert D. Arnott
President and Chief Executive Officer
First Quadrant, L.P.

Christopher G. Luck
Director
First Quadrant, L.P.

INTRODUCTION

Equity style is a central issue in institutional equity portfolio management. Yet institutional investors have different views of the role of equity style in structuring their holdings. Even seemingly basic concepts, such as the definition of style, are not uniformly agreed upon by all managers and sponsors.

The following people have worked on the strategies described in this chapter: John Chiu, David Krider, Lisa Plaxco, Peter Swank, Peyjen Wu, Daniel Xystus, and Jia Ye. We gratefully appreciate their contributions.

Once a suitable style definition is chosen, institutional investors' use of style varies widely. Many choose to maintain a style neutral stance and seek to add value within each style classification. Others look to add value by actively managing style tilts. They allow a significant portion of the equity portfolio to have an active style bet. The type of active style management appropriate to a particular investor will depend on both the definition of style used and the chosen role for style in the portfolio.

In this chapter, we try to sort out some of these issues, clarify the ways the idea of style is used in institutional management, and explain the basics of a quantitative approach to active style management.

DEFINITIONS OF STYLE

The basic view of equity style is often explained using the chart seen in Exhibit 1.[1] This resembles a yield sign during hunting season, but it is actually a schematic showing how the equity world is divided into growth stocks and value stocks using a simple recipe:

- Pick a universe of stocks (e.g., the S&P 500)
- Calculate the price-to-book (P/B) ratio for each one
- Sort the stocks, with the lowest P/B ratios on top
- Pick stocks from the top of the pile until you have 50% of the total capitalization, these are the value stocks
- The rest are the growth stocks
- If you're inclined, you can split them again by capitalization into large/medium/small cap value and growth

This has the distinct advantage of being nice and simple. All stocks are classified, all the time. There are no grey areas.

This classic definition has the virtue of simplicity, but there are some arbitrary and unappealing aspects to it. There is almost no difference between the last value stock and the first growth stock. They will have nearly identical P/B ratios. At the border between growth and value stocks, this type of style definition is not especially meaningful.

The simplest style indices are constructed using this basic single variable P/B definition. The best known are the S&P/BARRA style indices. The starting universe is the S&P 500. The P/B ratios are calculated (with adjustments for FAS 106 post-retirement health care cost), and the index constituents are re-determined every six months.

---

[1] The exhibit is based on W.F. Sharpe, "Asset Allocation: Management Style and Performance Measurement," *Journal of Portfolio Management* (Winter 1992).

Exhibit 1: Equity Style: The Plain Vanilla Definition

```
                Growth           Value
   High    ●───────────────────────●
   Cap      \                     /
             \                   /
   Mid        \       ●         /
   Cap         \     /
                \   /
   Low           \ /
   Cap            ●
            Low B/P         High B/P
                   Median
                   Book/Price
```

Source: W.F. Sharpe, "Asset Allocation: Management Style and Performance Measurement," *Journal of Portfolio Management* (Winter 1992).

A style switching active management strategy based purely on a simple definition like this would be something of a churner, with lots of trading signifying nothing. If the value and growth futures develop a liquid market, the costs of making these pure style bets would drop substantially. However, this hasn't happened.[2]

Better Style Definitions

The simple price-to-book split seemed too coarse. Some kind of refinement to the basic style definition was needed. Many academicians and practitioners jumped in to provide it. Soon there were many elaborations to this basic definition of style. These were based on some of the many other variables that can be used to classify equities. A selection of these are seen in Exhibit 2.

Up until 1995, the Frank Russell 1000 style indices were defined using a two variable deterministic split. Each stock in the full universe of 1,000 was ranked using a composite of a book-to-price ratio (adjusted for FAS 106 and 109 write-offs) and the IBES long-term growth forecast.[3] These two variables are combined to give each stock a "value score." All stocks with scores greater than the capitalization-weighted median go into the Value index, and the rest in the Growth index, so the two style indices will each comprise half the market cap of

---

[2] After years of talk and anticipation, trading in S&P/BARRA Value and Growth futures began in November of 1995. Unfortunately, there was much more talk and anticipation than trading. The open interest in these contracts has been very low, averaging less than 400 contracts at month-end in 1996 through September. The future of these futures is murky, even though they have significant and diverse potential applications. The contracts are discussed in Chapter 19.

[3] All information on the construction of the Russell indices are from the Frank Russell white papers, "Russell Equity Indices: Index Construction and Methodology," dated July 8, 1994, and September 6, 1995.

the Russell 1000. This two variable classification may have less of the "jitter" at the Value/Growth boundary, but there will still be stocks that are shifted from one index to the other in response to small changes in the classification variables. This jitter problem cannot be cured if we insist that every stock, without exception, must fall into one of two categories based on a rigorously quantified rule. Many stocks must barely fall into one category or the other, and can easily fall out once they have fallen in.

All of this led to much more complicated and creative classification rules, and more complicated and creative problems. In some schemes, a single stock could fall into multiple classifications, while others might be unclassified. All style definitions involving rules with fixed cutoffs have problems of this sort.

This is a problem crying out for a probabilistic (we mean fuzzy) interpretation, and it got one. Actually, it got several. When the Russell 2000 style indices were put together, they used the same two ingredients used for the pre-1995 Russell 1000 (B/P and IBES Growth), but combined them using a different recipe, this time with a pinch of probabilistic fuzz. The universe of 2,000 stocks is ranked using a composite value score, just as was done before with the 1,000 stocks. Instead of picking the median value score and defining all stocks above the line as value, the 2,000 stocks are broken into three equal cap groups, strong value stocks, with the highest third of value scores, strong growth stocks, with the lowest third and "hmmmm...fuzzy" stocks in the middle. These middle stocks are given a probability of belonging in value and a probability of belonging in growth based on how close their scores are to the "pure" value and growth zones. After 1995, this probabilistic method was used for both the Russell 1000 and 2000 style indices.

This is a fine and sensible way to put together style indices. Companies don't make odd transitions based on minuscule changes in their own (or other firms') ratios. Stocks "on the edge" are held, at less than their full market-cap weight, in both portfolios. So the small changes that are problematic for simpler indices show up as small changes in portfolio weights, rather than a headlong rush for the exit to the complementary style, followed by a rush in the opposite direction.

Exhibit 2: Alternate Style Definitions

Based on more than just Book/Price
- Earnings/Price ratios
- Dividend Yields
- Return on Equity
- Earnings Growth Estimates (e.g. IBES)
- Earnings Variability
- Return correlations with extreme G/V indices

Exhibit 3: Salomon Brothers Style Probability Ranking

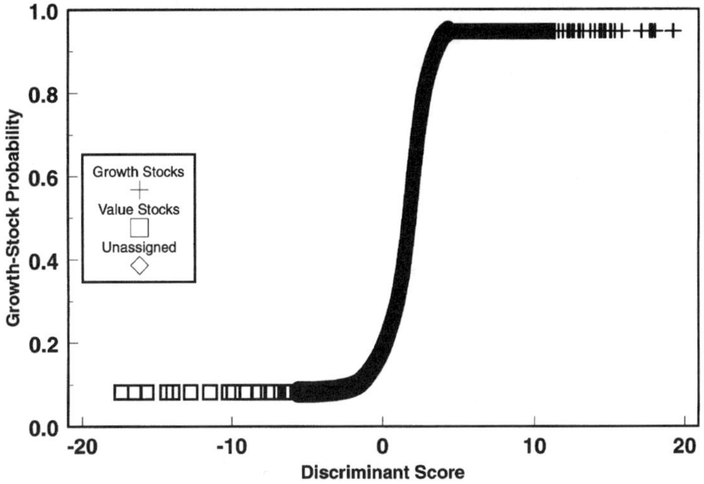

Source: S. Bienstock and E. Sorenson, "Segregating Growth from Value: It's Not Always Either/Or," *Salomon Brother Report* (July 1992), p. 6.

Multifactor Probabilistic Style Definitions

There is no reason to limit style scoring to two variables. Salomon Brothers has developed a sophisticated probabilistic style classification technique.[4] In addition to the P/B and earnings variables, the Salomon Brothers classification technique includes variables derived from P/E ratios, dividend yields, and the relationships of a stock's historical returns to concentrated growth and value indices.

A multiple regression technique is used to combine these factors into a style probability. This is the likelihood that a stock is growth or value. The factors determine the weights for each stock in the style index portfolio. These probabilities are nicely illustrated in a Salomon chart reproduced in Exhibit 3.

While these definitions may seem complex, they are more intuitively appealing in many ways than the blunt instrument P/B ratio method. "Extreme" value or growth stocks are classified in the same way by both methods. But those pesky middle-of the-style-road stocks turn out to have roughly a 50% chance of being value or growth, which makes sense. An active style switching or tilting strategy based on these ideas would do much less trading.

Multifactor Style Models and Multifactor Models: Generalized Style

The factors included in the most elaborate style definitions, and the regression techniques used to combine these factors, are suggestive of sophisticated multifactor mod-

---

[4] This is described in S. Bienstock and E. Sorensen, "Segregating Growth From Value: It's Not Always Either/Or," *Salomon Brothers Report*, July 1992.

els of equity risk and return. These models can viewed as generalizing the notion of style. Factor models are also the basis for an important set of portfolio optimization tools that are useful in a wide range of quantitative style management strategies. This topic will be discussed in more depth in the next section of this chapter, which deals with active management viewed in the context of the many definitions of style.

APPROACHES TO STYLE MANAGEMENT

The first decision a sponsor makes is the choice of a suitable style definition for assets at the fund level. The next decision is whether to make or avoid deliberate style bets under the chosen definition. Either approach has the potential to add value over a passive benchmark. Because different managers may well be using different definitions of style, there can be a fair amount of work involved for a sponsor in analyzing various manager holdings and/or returns using a consistent definition of style.

Determining Manager Style by Assets or by Returns

When there was one simple P/B style split, it was easy to characterize a manager as value or growth by looking at the stocks in their investment universe. Value managers picked from the value stocks and vice versa. It gets fuzzier when this analysis utilizes one of the probabilistic definitions we've just discussed. A particular stock will often be classified with different style probabilities by different formulas, so the old value manager/growth manager split may not mean as much as it once did. An asset based classification of managers based on the style of the stocks they choose (or don't choose) is greatly complicated by all these new style definitions.

One reasonable, and widely used approach is to use returns based style classification.[5] This was first suggested by William Sharpe[6] and now embodied in several classification systems. These ignore the style of underlying assets and classify managers on the basis of the correlations of their returns with whatever set of style indices the sponsor chooses.

After selecting a style definition and developing the capacity to classify managers using this definition, a sponsor can then move on to the question of making or avoiding explicit style tilts.

Motivation for Style Tilts: Historical Returns to Value and Growth

There are several issues to consider in regard to style tilts. Are they valuable enough to overcome the costs of implementing them? If so, on what time scale should these tilts be made? Are they applicable in international equity markets?

---

[5] Returns based style analyzers are a form of factor model themselves. In this case the single market return factor is replaced by several style return factors. These models are intermediate in complexity between the simple CAPM and the complex BARRA multifactor models.

[6] W.F. Sharpe, "Determining a Fund's Effective Asset Mix," *Investment Management Review* (November/ December 1988), pp. 59-69

Exhibit 4: Growth of $1 in S&P500 Value and Growth

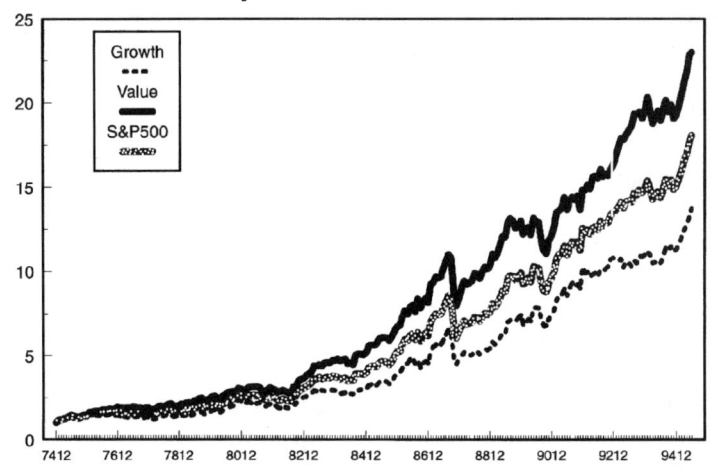

Exhibit 5: Cumulative Returns: S&P500 Value – Growth

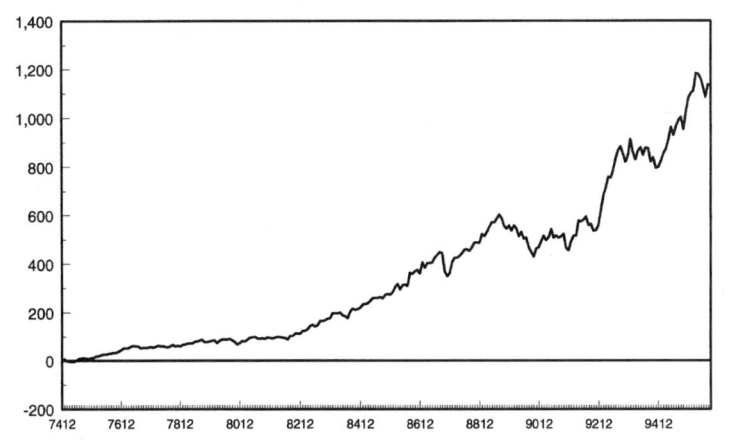

The starting point to answer these questions is to look at the historical returns to value and growth.[7] For the United States, over long periods, value stocks have outperformed growth stocks. As seen in Exhibit 4, a dollar invested in U.S. value stocks in January 1975 would have grown to $23 by June of 1995, while a dollar invested in growth stocks would be worth only $14, and a dollar in the S&P 500 would have grown to $18 over the same period.

Another way of showing this is to look at the cumulative returns to a value portfolio minus the returns to a growth portfolio. For the United States, this is shown in Exhibit 5. While it is obvious that over the full period value has been

---

[7] All the style returns discussed in this section are based on the simple P/B definitions.

a better investment, there are multi-year periods where the opposite is true. On a monthly scale, growth does better than value over 45% of the time. This suggests that an effective style switching discipline could be a very lucrative strategy.

Perfect Foresight Style Switching

Consider an imaginary active manager, with perfect foresight one month ahead of which style would do best in that month. One dollar invested in this (unrealizable) strategy in January 1975 would have grown to $42 by June 1995, with 1% trading costs charged for each style switch. This is the appeal of style switching strategies. However, the turnover for this strategy is enormous, often in excess of 1000% per year, so if the forecasts are less than perfect, as they will always be, the trading costs can easily drag the performance down.

International Style Returns and Style Switching

Capaul, Rowley, and Sharpe examined returns to international value and growth stocks, and discovered a remarkably similar pattern to what is observed in the United States.[8] Exhibits 6, 7, 8, and 9 extend their analysis over a longer period,[9] from January 1975 to June 1995, for Japan, the United Kingdom, Canada, and Germany. As was done for the United States in Exhibit 5, the charts show the cumulative return to value minus growth. The results are strikingly similar. In each country, value does significantly better over the full period, but there are periods ranging up to five years where this is not the case.

Exhibit 6: Cumulative Returns: Japan Value - Growth

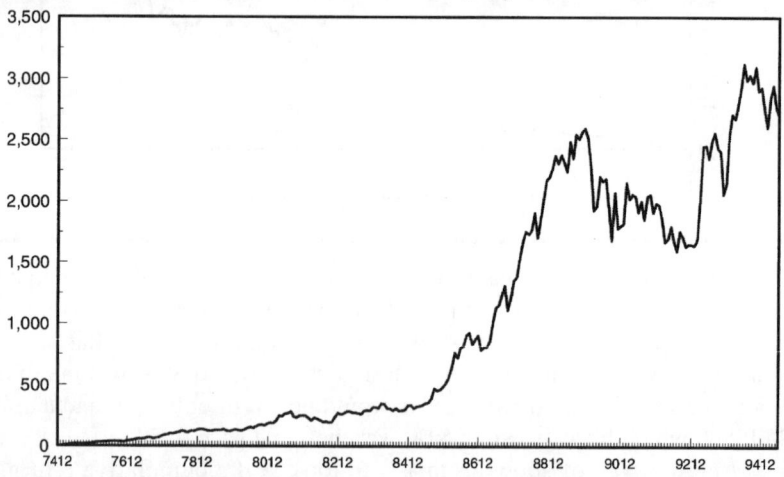

[8] C. Capaul, I. Rowley, and W.F. Sharpe, "International Value and Growth Stock Returns," *Financial Analysts Journal* (January/February 1993), pp. 27-36.

[9] These international growth and value indices are created by International Investment Associates, based on a simple equal-capitalization P/B split. For a discussion of these indices, see Chapter 13.

Exhibit 7: Cumulative Returns: U.K. Value – Growth

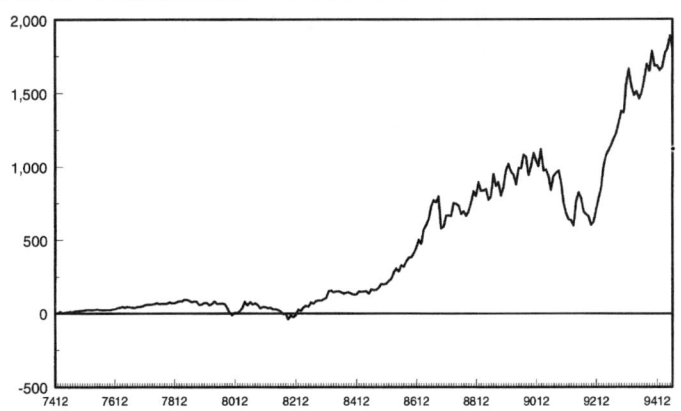

Exhibit 8: Cumulative Returns: Canada Value – Growth

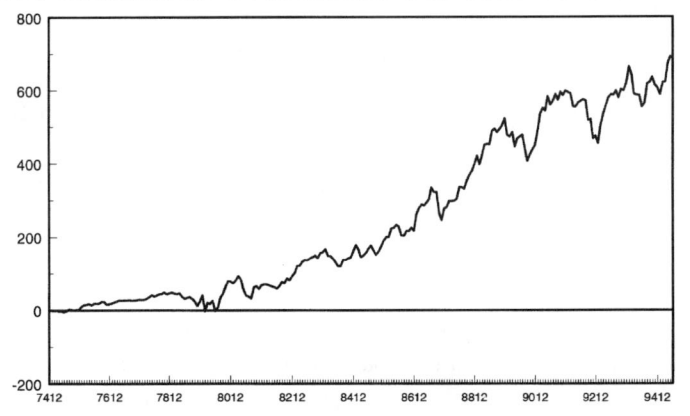

Exhibit 9: Cumulative Returns: Germany Value – Growth

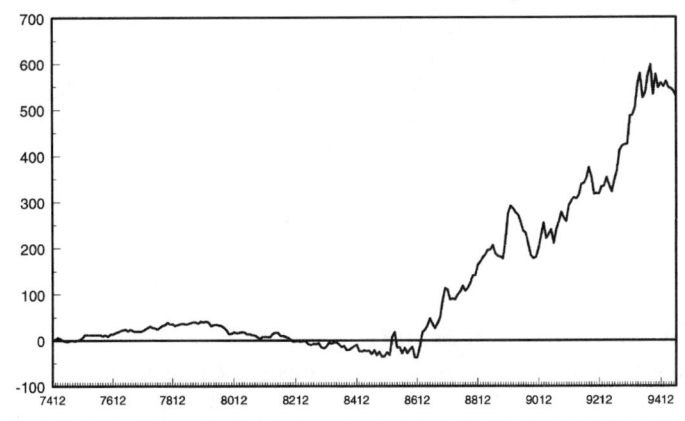

Exhibit 10: The Motivation for an Active Style Switching Strategy

Country	$1 in Value after 20 years	$1 in Growth after 20 years	$1 in Best of Value-or-Growth, each month, after 20 years	Portion of monthly returns when Growth>Value
US	$23	$14	$42	45%
UK	$42	$24	$82	44%
Japan	$37	$10	$89	39%
Canada	$12	$5	$31	39%
Germany	$14	$9	$30	45%

The first three columns of Exhibit 10 show the growth of one dollar invested in value, growth and a perfect foresight style switching strategy. The last column shows the portion of months in which growth outperforms value. These results are surprisingly similar. In all of these countries (and in nearly all others) there is a strong incentive for developing a means to accurately forecast returns to styles.

Implementing Style Tilts and Switching Strategies

Perfect style forecasts are impossible to achieve, so a real style switching strategy would often incur the high costs of trading completely in and out of large equity positions, without earning the returns to offset these costs. There are a number of less extreme ways of implementing a less aggressive, less risky version of a style tilt strategy. These can be used separately or in combination.

- The amount of trading can be reduced by restricting the size of the style bets, for example, allowing only a 60%/40% mix, rather than the 100%/0% illustrated above. Reducing the size of the active bet, so only a portion of the value stocks are sold off and replaced with growth stocks when growth is forecast to outperform and vice versa, will reduce the cost (and risk) of a style switching strategy.
- Use a probabilistic style definition to concentrate trading on the strongest value or growth stocks, leaving the grey zone stocks in the middle pretty much alone. This concentrates trading in names most likely to provide the desired exposure, further reducing transaction costs.
- Extend the time horizon for style forecasts. If trading only occurs when a style is expected to outperform for a longer period, there is much less churning. By looking ahead for a sufficiently long period of time, a sponsor can implement style bets by means of manager allocation or selection.

Long-Term Style Forecasts

In our own work, we have provided these long horizon forecasts to our clients. We have developed two types of style forecasting models. Top-down style forecasting models employ the same methods we have used in analyzing broad equity and bond markets in domestic and global tactical asset allocation strategies.[10] The same mathematical techniques, and the same sorts of market, macroeconomic and sentiment indicators employed are used to forecast returns to style indices.

The second type of style forecaster is based on the analysis of the BARRA multifactor model framework used for our active equity strategies. This is described in more detail later in this chapter. These models use a bottom-up approach to form style forecasts by summing the forecast returns to factors weighted by the exposure of the style index portfolios to those factors.

It is noteworthy, that, despite the difference in these two approaches to forecasting style returns, they produce remarkably similar results, as seen in Exhibit 11. These models have proven quite useful, with information coefficients (correlations between forecast and actual outcomes) of approximately 0.3. This exhibit shows the S&P500 Growth/Value return spreads predicted by the top-down and bottom-up models described in the text. Due to data limitations, there is a shorter history for the bottom up model.

Exhibit 11: Forecast U.S. Style Returns: S&P 500 Growth - Value

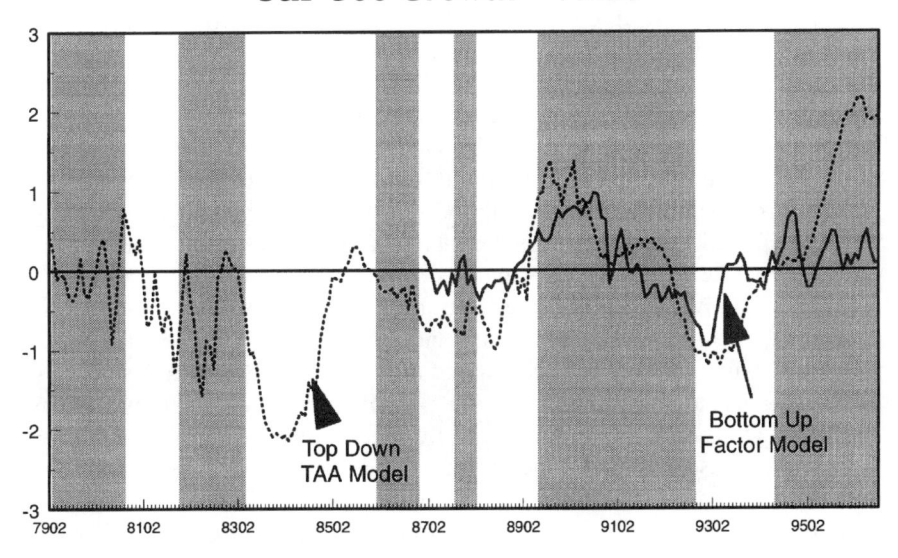

Note: Shaded regions are periods in which growth outperformed value, on a trailing 12 month return basis.

---

[10] See R. Arnott and J. von Germeten, "Systematic Asset Allocation," *Financial Analysts Journal* (November/December 1983); R. Arnott and W. Copeland, "The Business Cycle and Security Selection," *Financial Analysts Journal* (March/April 1985); and, R. Arnott and F.J. Fabozzi (eds.), *Active Asset Allocation* (Chicago: Probus Publishing, 1992).

Values above zero are forecasts that growth will outperform value, and negative values correspond to forecasts that value will outperform growth. The shaded areas represent periods in which growth has actually outperformed value; non-shaded areas represent periods in which value has outperformed growth. These are shown on a trailing 12-month return basis.

These models are remarkably consistent with each other and both capture the longer trends. They tended to favor value through most of the 1980s, with several periods of relative neutrality. In 1989 to 1992 growth was favored, with a return to value from 1992 to 1994, and a recent moderate growth bias. The model was only incorrect in the relatively short growth cycle of 1982 and the six-month growth surge after the October 1987 crash. Both of these signals change very slowly, with quarterly serial correlations in excess of 90%, and for this reason, they will tend to generate infrequent trades.

Adding Value Using Refined Style Techniques

The simplest types of active style management, as described above, are simple tilts toward one style and away from another. These strategies can be implemented based entirely on simple P/B style definitions, or by using probabilistic definitions to increase the magnitude of the active style bet made relative to the trading costs that are incurred to make these bets. There is a single control variable in all of these strategies, which is just the degree of tilt toward value or growth, in an effort to add value over a broad core equity benchmark.

The complexity of the data going into the more elaborate style definitions suggests a much richer family of active quantitative style management strategies. Expanding the range of control variables available for these active strategies has several beneficial consequences. It provides more chances to be correct than a single style tilt. It improves the likelihood that value can be added over a broad equity benchmark. It also allows these methods to be used to add value over style segregated value or growth benchmarks as well. The key to introducing these more refined active strategies is the relationship between the more elaborate style models and factor models of equity risk and return.

A striking aspect of probabilistic models is that the variables going into them have substantial overlap with another set of probabilistic models that explain patterns in equity risk and return. These are fundamental factor models. There are lots of these in use, the most popular being the BARRA models. Exhibit 12 shows the common factors used in the BARRA models. In the exhibit, those factors which are also used in probabilistic style definitions are shown in italics. This overlap does not mean that these models are the same. It does suggest that much of the same data used for style classification can also be used in a more general way, for both producing value added and controlling risk, in the context of a factor based approach to quantitative equity management. Users of factor models and users of quantitative style models are dancing around the same tree. While there are mathematical differences, it clear that there is a great deal of commonality here.

Exhibit 12: Common Factors in BARRA U.S. Equity Model: Substantial Overlap with Style Variables

- Variability in markets
- Success
- *Size**
- Trading activity
- *Growth**
- *Earnings/price**
- *Book/price**
- *Earnings variability**
- Financial leverage
- Foreign income
- Labor intensity
- *Yield**
- *Locap**

* Italicized factors match elements of general style definitions.

Factor Models and Style Management

Factor models of equity risk and return are a central element of modern quantitative equity analysis. The first equity factor model was the Capital Asset Pricing Model (CAPM). The CAPM used the single market factor, beta, to explain much of the variation in a stock's returns.

In the 1970s, Barr Rosenberg and others extended the CAPM to include factors other than the single market factor. The intuition behind this was that there were other common factors that influence equity returns in addition to the market factor. Interest rates are a good example of an additional factor. Returns to stocks of companies with heavy debt will be more affected by interest rate changes than those to stocks of debt-free companies. Another intuitively appealing factor is exposure to foreign exchange rates. Companies with a high proportion of foreign income will be more sensitive to foreign exchange rate movements than those with only domestic income. Industry group membership is another readily quantifiable regularity in equity risk and return used to define factors in these models.

These generalizations of the CAPM led to the development of a number of Multifactor Models (MFMs). There are many variations on this theme. The most widely used MFMs are the BARRA models, produced and maintained by the company Barr Rosenberg founded for this purpose. An extensive discussion of factor models is beyond the scope of this chapter. Good theoretical discussions of MFMs in general can be found in finance texts and journals. Details specific to the BARRA approach are found in BARRA's publications.[11]

The more elaborate style definitions use statistical methods to categorize the style of a particular stock based on a number of factors particular to the company. An active strategy based on these ideas would forecast the returns to the outputs (the style variables). The success of these strategies depends on the ability to forecast returns to styles.

The multifactor models, constructed using much of the same data, directly forecast the expected return to a stock in terms of its sensitivity to the

---

[11] See "The United States Equity Model," Chapter 4 in *The BARRA Handbook*.

factors and the returns to those factors. Up to this point, we've tried to keep this discussion non-mathematical, but this idea is worth looking at as an equation, even for the algebraically challenged.

The following equation is the mathematical formulation of multifactor models:

$$R_s - R_{rf} = \sum_f \beta_f (R_f - R_{rf}) + \tilde{\varepsilon}$$

where

R_s = the return on the stock
R_{rf} = the risk-free return
R_f = return to the factor
β_f = stock's exposure to factor f
$\tilde{\varepsilon}$ = portion of return not explained by the factors

The difference between the return on the stock and the risk-free return is called the *excess return to the stock*. The model tells us that the excess return to the stock is the sum of the product of the stock's exposure to a factor and the return to the factor plus the portion of the return not explained by all the factors.

In CAPM, the single factor model, there would be no summation. In that case, the beta is just the sensitivity of the stock to the broad market, and the return to the factor is just the market return. Multifactor models generalize this idea by including more factors. In fundamental MFMs, such as BARRA's, the betas are calculated from fundamental data. For example, in calculating exposure (beta) to the factor "size," stocks would be ranked by market capitalization. The average stock would be defined as having an exposure of zero. A stock one standard deviation larger than average would have a size exposure of +1, a stock one standard deviation below average size would have an exposure of −1. This process is repeated for all the common factors. Industry factors are set at zero or one, to indicate which industry group a company belongs to. Companies in more than one industry can have multiple positive industry exposures adding up to one.

The returns on the left hand side of the equation are easy to determine. They are just the monthly returns to each stock, less the risk-free rate. Knowing both the factor exposures for each stock, from fundamental considerations, as well as the stock returns, makes it simple to calculate the factor returns (R_f) and asset specific returns (ε) each month by regression techniques.

Factor Returns and Active Management

These factor returns are the key element in an MFM-based approach to active style management. The factors provide the larger number of control variables for active strategies discussed earlier. They generalize and extend the notion of style returns.

We can ask the same questions about factor returns in evaluating the potential value of these strategies as we asked about style returns in a similar context. How much would it be worth to know these returns? Are they worth forecasting? Is there enough variation in factor returns from month to month for them to be useful in an active strategy? Can we forecast these returns?

Are Factor Returns Worth Forecasting?

We can answer the question about whether it is worth forecasting factor returns by looking at the returns to a perfect foresight factor return strategy. At the end of the month, the factor returns are known. An active strategy based on these ideas requires forecasts of these returns to be made at the beginning of the month. Let's assume that we had perfect factor forecasting models. What would these be worth?

Looking back at the basic BARRA equation, we see that the return to each stock is broken into two parts: (1) the summation of factor exposures and factor returns and (2) the asset specific portion not explained by factors. If the asset specific portion of returns swamps the portion explained by the factors, there would not be much point in worrying about the factors.

Use of Portfolio Optimization

In order to do this evaluation, we need to use the primary investment management tool derived from factor models, a portfolio optimizer. We can't go out and buy factors, like we can buy stocks. An optimizer provides a means to select a portfolio of stocks which gives us the mix of factor exposures we desire, i.e., positive exposures to those factors with positive forecast returns, and negative exposures for those with negative forecasts. We tell the optimizer about our factor preferences by putting in a set of forecasts for the monthly factor returns. We can do the same thing on an asset specific level by using a set of monthly stock forecasts. When the optimizer is used without any forecasts, it produces an index fund that tracks the specified benchmark.

By specifying constraints for the optimization, the optimizer also provides a means to control risk and turnover. Risk control constraints can be expressed as limits on the tracking error of the portfolio relative to the benchmark (i.e., the standard deviation of the difference in returns to the two portfolios), or as explicit limits on the size of allowed deviations from index weights on a stock or industry basis.

Long-Short and Market Neutral Portfolios

So far, we have been discussing optimization to produce equity portfolios designed to add value over an index by holding only long positions. The optimizer can also produce portfolios which include short positions. If the short side of a long-short portfolio has a value and market beta approximately equal and opposite to the long side, then the portfolio is market neutral. Since market neutral portfolios have no net exposure to the market index, their performance is generally measured relative to Treasury bills. Market neutral portfolios are extremely useful for both theoretical and practical reasons.[12]

---

[12] For a detailed discussion of market neutral investing, see John S. Brush, "Comparisons and Combinations of Long and Long-Short Strategies," *Financial Analysts Journal* (March/April 1997).

Exhibit 13: Reasons for Using Portfolio Optimization in a Quantitative Style Management Discipline

- Acheive desired style/factor tilts
- Incorporate asset specific alpha sources
- Control risk
  - Risk Measure: Tracking error relative to benchmark
  - Control Parameters
    - Active stock and sector weightings
- Constrain turnover
- Two types of portfolios produced
  - Long
  - Market Neutral

In a theoretical sense, market neutral portfolios provide an extraordinarily good way to test the value of an investment idea. Long-only portfolios are diluted expressions of investment ideas in two important ways:

- A risk controlled long-only portfolio designed to add value over an equity index must include substantial holdings in the index constituents for benchmark exposure. These are essentially passive investments. Only the deviations from index exposure contribute to the active return.
- Negative active bets on a stock in a long-only portfolio are limited to the stocks index weight. You can't hold less than a zero position in any stock, irrespective of the strength of a negative return expectation.

These (and other) advantages associated with portfolio optimization are summarized in Exhibit 13. Optimization is the means by which multifactor models are used in practice.

Perfect Foresight Tests of Factor Returns

Now that we have a firm grasp on the ideas of factor returns, optimization and market neutral portfolios, we are now ready to do the perfect foresight tests. Constraints are set to hold turnover and tracking error at prudent limits appropriate to institutional portfolios. No leverage is used. We start with cash in January of 1987. The actual realized subsequent monthly factor returns are put in as our factor forecasts, which are the forecasts we would have made if our models were perfect. In each simulated month, we rebalance the long and market neutral portfolios, pay our simulated transaction costs, and roll the calendar forward one month. What kind of returns do we see?

Both the long equity and market neutral portfolios do extraordinarily well. Exhibit 14 shows the rolling 12-month value added for U.S. long and market neutral portfolios. The long portfolio has returns averaging more than 55% above the S&P 500. In its worst 12-month period, the portfolio outperformed the S&P by 39%; in its best, by 82%.

As explained in the preceding section, a market neutral strategy is a particularly pure way of testing the strength of an investment idea. The market neutral perfect factor foresight portfolio returns averaged more than 138% over U.S. Treasury bills, again on a rolling 12-month basis. Its worst 12-month period saw 75% value added, and its best a remarkable 195%.

These results are not unique to the United States. When we run similar tests in international markets, we see similar results, as shown in Exhibit 15. Long returns are well over 70% above the index in each international market analyzed, and market neutral returns more than 120% above the Treasury bill equivalents.

Exhibit 14: Perfect Foresight Tests of U.S. BARRA Factor Returns
Rolling 12-Month Value Added

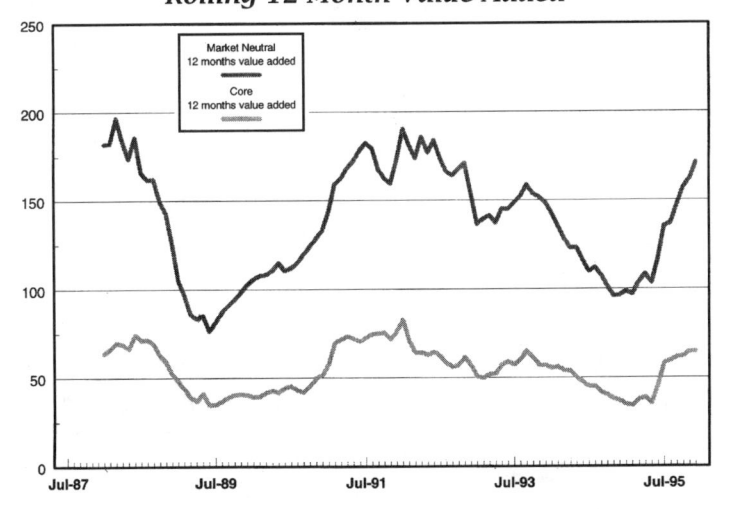

Exhibit 15: Perfect Foresight Summary
Market Neutral Strategies: 12-Month Rolling Value Added (%)

	High	Low	Average
US	195	75	138
UK	326	50	155
Japan	236	66	121

Long Core Strategies: 12-Month Rolling Value Added (%)

	High	Low	Average
US	82	39	55
UK	131	52	82
Japan	106	56	74
Canada	91	63	77

These perfect foresight tests establish the factor returns as a valuable resource in equity management strategies. If the numbers had been small, there would be little point in expending much effort in developing the ability to forecast factor returns. No forecasting model will be perfect, or even nearly so. Real models will be able to capture only a portion of the these potential returns, but the potential is so large, that this is worth pursuing.

Variability of Factor Returns

There is another aspect of factor returns we should examine. Are they relatively constant from month to month, or is there significant variability? This is analogous to looking at the month to month variations in returns to styles in considering the potential for a style switching strategy. If, for example, value *always* outperformed growth, there wouldn't be much point in attempting to switch styles in a timely manner. (In any remotely efficient market, an obvious and persistent inefficiency such as this would fade as the price of value stocks was bid up.)

When we look at monthly factor returns, what we hope to find is substantial variation, hopefully variation in sign, that can form the basis for an active management decision that can be made profitably every month. One way to do this is to compare the average value of each monthly factor return to its standard deviation. This comparison is shown for U.S. factors in Exhibit 16. We see that in every case the standard deviations are much larger than the means, and in many cases by an order of magnitude or more. Monthly factor returns will vary in sign nearly half the time. This is exactly the situation we want in order for them to be useful in an active strategy.

Exhibit 16: Monthly Variation in U.S. Factor Returns: Standard Deviations Much Greater than Means

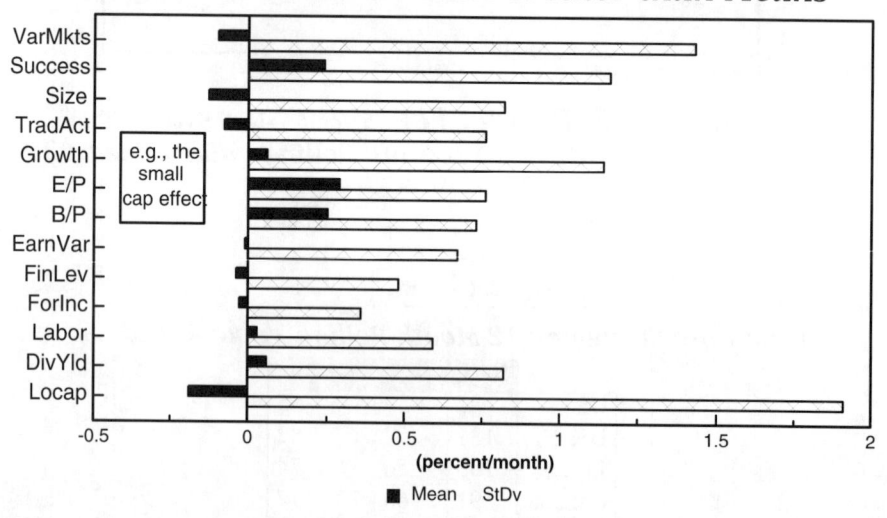

Exhibit 17: Monthly Variation in Japan Factor Returns: Standard Deviations Much Greater than Means

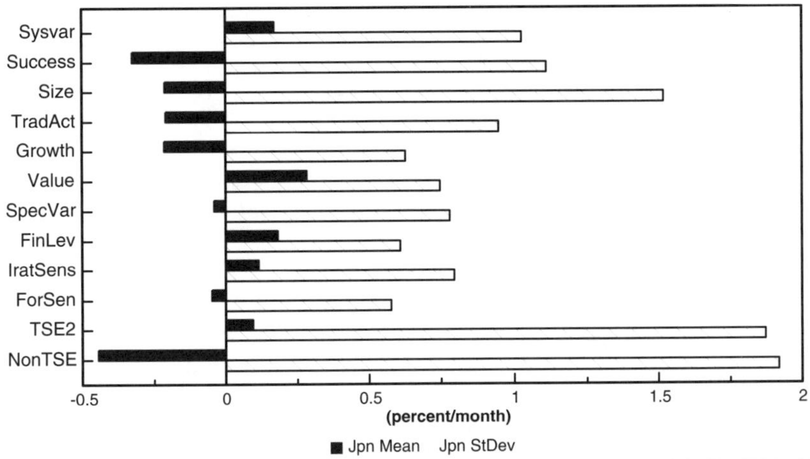

[Bar chart showing Jpn Mean and Jpn StDev for factors: Sysvar, Success, Size, TradAct, Growth, Value, SpecVar, FinLev, IratSens, ForSen, TSE2, NonTSE; x-axis in percent/month from -0.5 to 2]

The darker bars in Exhibit 16 show the mean monthly return to each factor, in percent per month. This is easy to understand by looking at one example in the exhibit. The mean return to the factor "size" is negative, −0.2% per month. This means that a stock with a market capitalization one standard deviation larger than the average stock has underperformed average size stocks by that amount. Smaller stocks, for example those one standard deviation below the average size, have outperformed average size by an opposite amount. This is just a quantitative expression of the well known small stock effect.

The same situation is found when we look at factor returns for international markets. Exhibits 17, 18, and 19 show means and standard deviations for monthly factor returns in Japan, the U.K. and Canada, respectively. In each country, we again observe that the standard deviations are much larger than the means, indicating that factor returns are suitable for an active quantitative approach to equity style management.

Forecasting Factor Returns

What do we know about factors so far? From the perfect foresight tests, we know that they explain a sufficiently large portion of equity returns. Hence, knowing them would be extremely valuable, so that forecasting them with a reasonable precision would be valuable as well. From our examination of the variability of factor returns we know that there is an active bet that can be made each month, with a potential payoff much larger than a simple tilt based on long-term averages.

All this is good news, but we have to be able to actually forecast factor returns to use them in an active strategy. In any prediction problem, there are two broad decisions to make:

- *What* to predict with, choosing information to use in making predictions.
- *How* to predict, choosing a forecasting technique suitable to the problem.

Exhibit 18: Monthly Variation in U.K. Factor Returns: Standard Deviations Much Greater than Means

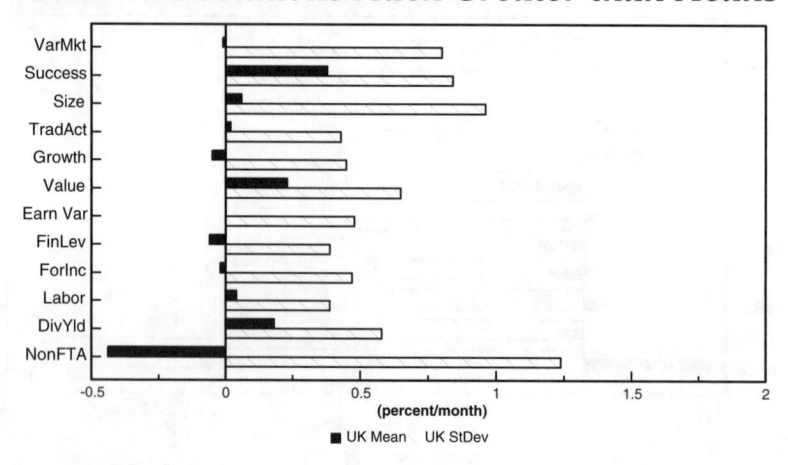

[Bar chart showing UK Mean and UK StDev for factors: VarMkt, Success, Size, TradAct, Growth, Value, Earn Var, FinLev, ForInc, Labor, DivYld, NonFTA; x-axis in percent/month from -0.5 to 2]

Exhibit 19: Monthly Variation in Canada Factor Returns: Standard Deviations Much Greater than Means

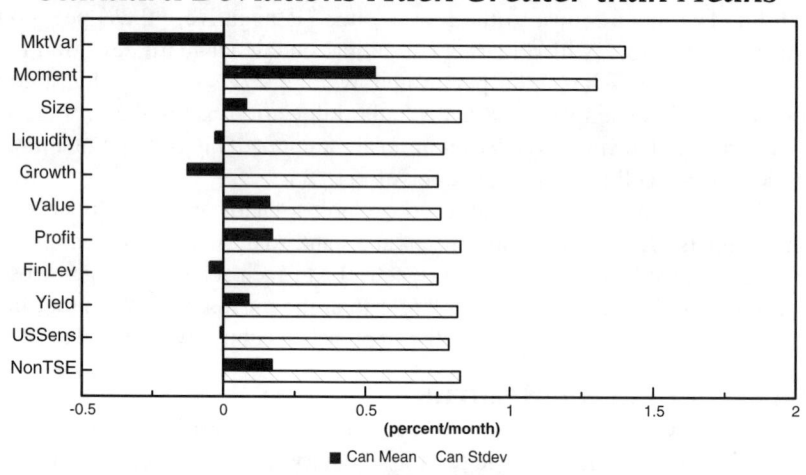

[Bar chart showing Can Mean and Can Stdev for factors: MktVar, Moment, Size, Liquidity, Growth, Value, Profit, FinLev, Yield, USSens, NonTSE; x-axis in percent/month from -0.5 to 2]

What to Predict With There are three broad classes of variables we use to forecast factor returns, summarized in Exhibit 20. The first class is just the factor returns themselves. These data capture the univariate time series properties of the factor returns, serial correlations, cyclicality, moving average, and autoregressive properties. Cross-factor relationships can also prove valuable.

The second class of predictive variables is based on market data. This includes index and sub-index returns, yield curve information, dividend yields, price-earnings ratio, commodity prices, and foreign exchange rates. The third class of variables includes macroeconomic data (such as unemployment), inflation measures, and industrial production.

For all these possible predictors, there are many plausible transforms and types of measurements that are worth considering. In many cases, it is more useful to consider changes, relative changes, rates of change, and unanticipated changes than the raw data alone. For each of these transforms, there are additional decisions to be made about the intervals over which to measure changes, rates of change or other measurements. For example, it is reasonable to think of looking at a change from month to month, quarter to quarter, year to year, month to the same month a year ago, and so on. With a large number of raw variables to start with, and so many plausible measurement variations, the number of combinations becomes truly huge. We mean big, really big, comparable to the number of atoms in the universe. It is a classic example of a combinatoric explosion.

This space of transformed variables is so large that many conventional search techniques are totally inadequate to deal with it. This is an area where we apply the genetic algorithm (GA), a relatively new form of machine learning which performs an iterative parallel, goal directed search of large spaces. We initially employed the GA in our asset allocation process and have since expanded its use significantly.[13]

Exhibit 20: Forecasting Returns to Factors

What we forecast with:
- Factor Variables, e.g.
  - Cyclicality
  - Cross relationships
- Market Variables, e.g.
  - Index returns and ratios
  - Yields
  - F/X and commodity prices
- Macroeconomic Variables
  - Inflation
  - Production
  - Unemployment

How we forecast:
- Non linear transforms of raw variables
- A variety of underlying forecast methods
- Expanding and moving windows

---

[13] The motivation for our use of this technique is described in D. Leinweber and R. Arnott, "Quantitative and Computational Innovation in Investment Management," *Journal of Portfolio Management* (Winter 1995). A good technical introduction to the GA is provided in J. Holland, "Genetic Algorithms," *Scientific American* (July 1992).

How to Predict There is also a wide selection of choices for a method of predicting. The tried-and-true, golden oldie is the expanding window, ex-ante regression. This is similar to ordinary regression, but as each new month passes, the new slice of data becomes part of the history, and the model coefficients are recalculated using the new expanded data set. This new model is then used to forecast the next period's factor return. One obvious problem with a pure expanding window strategy is that each new month's data has less weight in the model than the one before. After a long time has passed, a new month can make almost no difference. Similarly, there is no distinction between the oldest and newest data. A 20-year old time slice has the same weight as the most current observations, even if substantial changes have occurred.

There are many variations on this theme which seek to remedy some of these problems. They range from simple modifications — such as moving or weighted windows — to more complex mathematical and econometric techniques — such as robust regressions, seemingly unrelated regressions, kernel estimation, GARCH, Kalman filters, artificial neural networks, and many others. Some of these techniques do improve on the "keep it simple stupid" regressions. However, they do so at great computational cost and impose the engineering trade-off of devoting always finite computational resources to more extensive specification searching of the space of what we can predict with, or searching less, but using potentially more powerful methods. Throughout this process, it is important to maintain precautions against excessive data mining — torturing the data until it tells us whatever we want to hear.

Character and Performance of Factor Return Forecasters

Despite the complexity, relationships in the factor return forecasters that emerge from the research process are sensible in a financial and economic sense. Many of them are just quantitative expressions of very fundamental ideas. Many relationships recur from country to country.

Some of these are summarized in Exhibit 21. For example, returns to the "financial leverage" factor, go down as interest rates rise. Rising interest rates are also associated with lower returns to companies with highly variable earnings, exactly as one would expect from a Dividend Discount Model. Returns to the "foreign income" factor, high for companies with high income earned in foreign currencies, are reduced by unfavorable changes in exchange rates.[14]

Cyclicality in industry returns reflects the nature of the industry. The barriers to entry in trucking are very low. All you have to do is go rent a truck. Cycles are short. The opposite is true for utilities. It can take a decade for a new power plant to be designed, sited, approved, constructed, and inspected. Utility cycles are corresponding slow.

Cross-border influences are found as one might expect. The Canadian market is strongly influenced by the U.S. market, while the Japanese market is not. Calendar effects attributable to tax regulations or business practices particular to one country also show up.

Exhibit 21: Similarities & Differences: Global Factor Models

- Many common effects
- Quantitative reflections of known fundamental relationships
- Examples:
  - Dividend Discounting
  - Financial Leverage
  - Interest Rates and Macro-surrogates
  - F/X
  - Cyclical Stock
- Differences
  - Regulatory and Governmental effects
  - Cross-border influences

We have been conducting research on modeling factor returns for over five years and continue to do so. There are many ways of measuring the effectiveness of these models. One important measurement is the information coefficient (IC), which is just the correlation between the forecast and actual returns. Exhibit 22 shows the ICs for common risk factor models for the United States, United Kingdom, and Japan. The "zone of profitability" is an approximate indication of the level of IC needed to cover transactions costs.

Having gone through the steps of establishing that factor returns are valuable, variable, and forecastable, we can now show how they are used in active style management.

---

[14] The factor return forecasting models often conform to intuitive notions, but this is not necessarily always true. This arises from the nature of multifactor models. Factor exposures in a fundamental model, such as BARRA's, will conform to intuition, since they are defined from fundamental company information. Large companies will always have high exposure to size and so on. However, there are approximately a dozen common factors, and more than 30 industry factors in each country, so when we go to do the regressions to calculate factor returns, the results may be non-intuitive. This can carry over into the next level of models, those used to forecast factor returns, particularly when multivariate relationships are used there.

A nearly non-mathematical example that may help clarify the seemingly counterintuitve nature of multivariable models is to consider building a simple model to forecast a person's weight from their height. We'd expect weight to be approximated by some positive coefficient multiplied by height, and this would turn out to be true, Similarly, if we were to build another model to estimate weight by inseam instead of height, we'd expect another model approximating weight by another positive coefficient times inseam, and this would also be true. But when we put these two together in a two variable model to estimate weight we discover that the coefficient on height is still positive, but the coefficient for inseam has changed sign to negative. This is due to the fact that all other things being equal, a person with longer legs and a larger inseam will weigh less than a shorter waisted person with more torso.

Extending these notions to, for example, a 68 variable world, such as the BARRA U.S. model, we should not be the least bit surprised to find nonobvious, and seemingly nonintuitve effects, when we look at a particular relationship in a multivariate context.

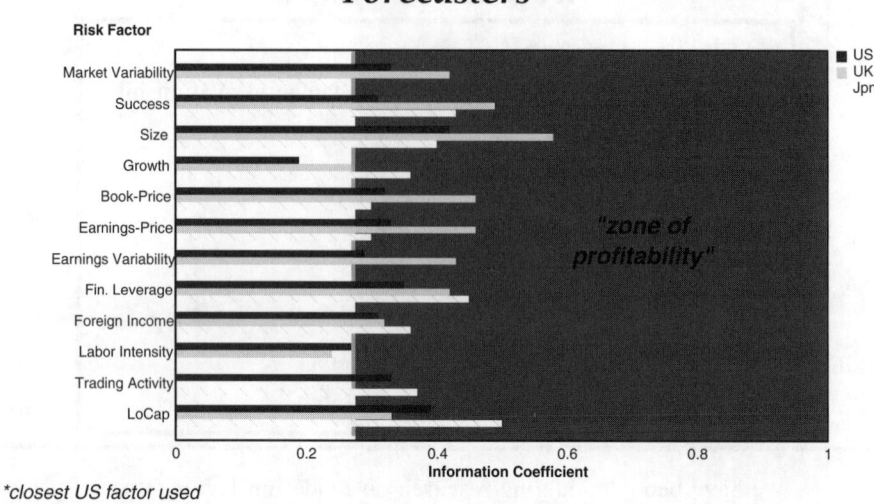

Exhibit 22: Predictive Power of Factor Return Forecasters

Risk factors (top to bottom): Market Variability, Success, Size, Growth, Book-Price, Earnings-Price, Earnings Variability, Fin. Leverage, Foreign Income, Labor Intensity, Trading Activity, LoCap. Bars show Information Coefficient (0 to 1) for US, UK, Jpn. "zone of profitability" annotated on chart.

*closest US factor used

Active Management Using Factors

The generalization of styles to factors provides for a wide range of active management techniques, applicable to the varied roles of style in institutional portfolios. There are core equity strategies, value and growth portfolio strategies, and market neutral strategies.

Core Long Equity Strategies The original and primary use is in core equity portfolios, to add value over a broad equity benchmark, by generalized style management. We have been doing this in the United States since 1990, on assets now totaling over $1.7 billion.[15] Average returns have been in excess of 260 basis points per year above the S&P 500 through September 30, 1996. Detailed historical performance is found in Exhibit 23.

The same ideas have been used, for a shorter period, in managing core portfolios totaling $137 million in the United Kingdom, Canada, and Japan. In each country, the strategy adds value over the core equity benchmark, by 60, 30, and 220 basis points per year (respectively trough September 30, 1996). Details for these strategies are found in Exhibits 24, 25, and 26.

Market Neutral Strategies In a preceding section we discussed the reasons why market neutral portfolios are more concentrated expressions of investment ideas. This was seen in the substantially larger value-added for perfect foresight market neutral portfolios. A similar boost is observed in real market neutral portfolios.

---

[15] $500 million of the U.S. core assets are in a lower risk enhanced index portfolio. Performance figures are for the standard core equity portfolios, which are targeted at a 4% tracking error.

Exhibit 23: U.S. Core Style Management

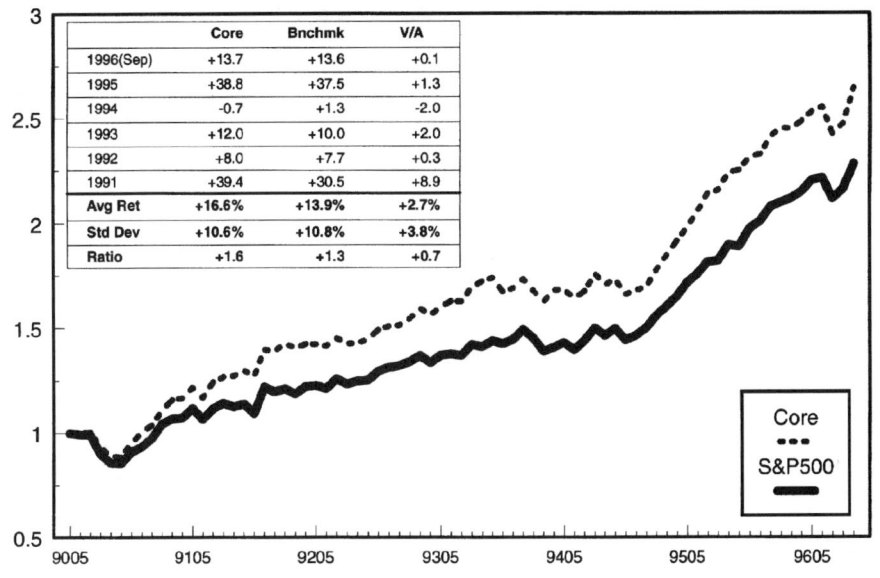

	Core	Bnchmk	V/A
1996(Sep)	+13.7	+13.6	+0.1
1995	+38.8	+37.5	+1.3
1994	-0.7	+1.3	-2.0
1993	+12.0	+10.0	+2.0
1992	+8.0	+7.7	+0.3
1991	+39.4	+30.5	+8.9
Avg Ret	+16.6%	+13.9%	+2.7%
Std Dev	+10.6%	+10.8%	+3.8%
Ratio	+1.6	+1.3	+0.7

Exhibit 24: U.K. Core Style Management

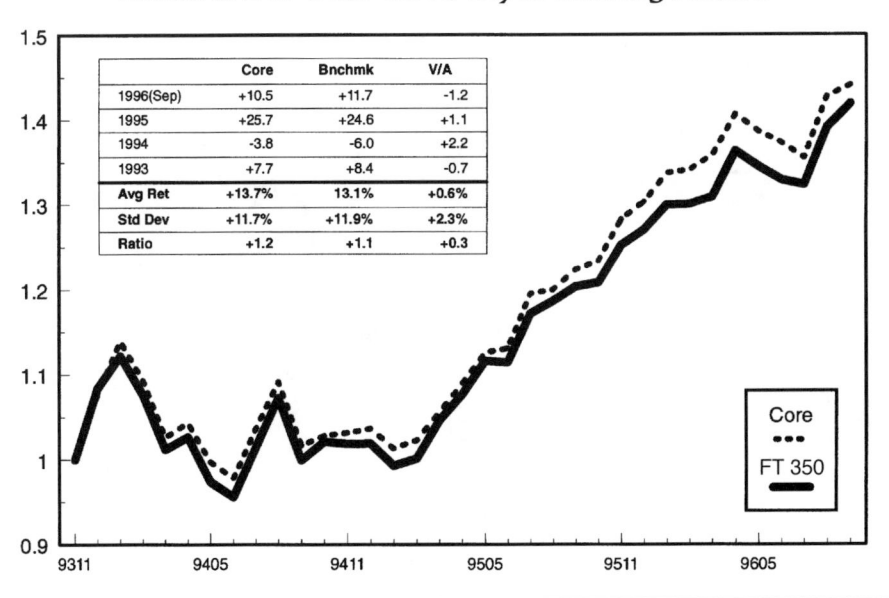

	Core	Bnchmk	V/A
1996(Sep)	+10.5	+11.7	-1.2
1995	+25.7	+24.6	+1.1
1994	-3.8	-6.0	+2.2
1993	+7.7	+8.4	-0.7
Avg Ret	+13.7%	13.1%	+0.6%
Std Dev	+11.7%	+11.9%	+2.3%
Ratio	+1.2	+1.1	+0.3

Exhibit 25: Canadian Core Style Management

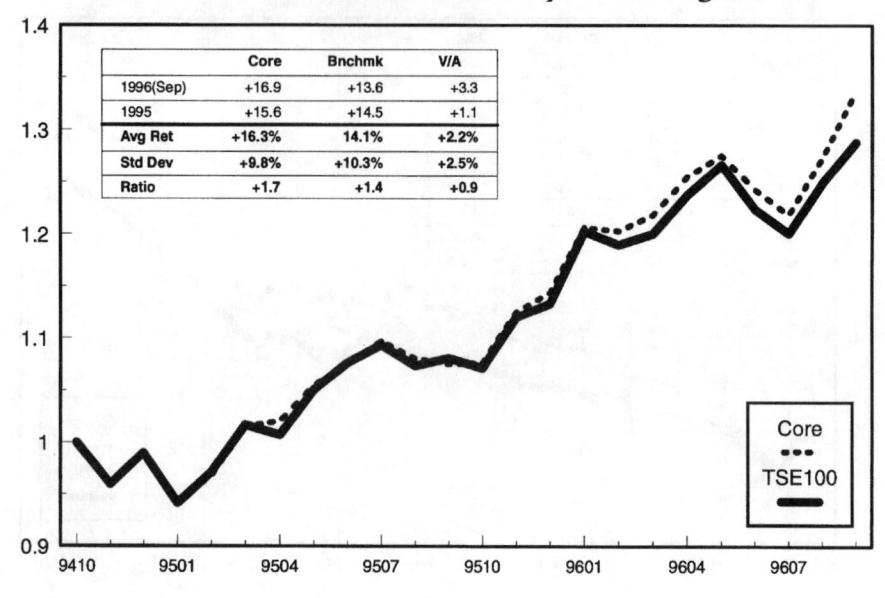

	Core	Bnchmk	V/A
1996(Sep)	+16.9	+13.6	+3.3
1995	+15.6	+14.5	+1.1
Avg Ret	+16.3%	14.1%	+2.2%
Std Dev	+9.8%	+10.3%	+2.5%
Ratio	+1.7	+1.4	+0.9

Exhibit 26: Japan Core Style Management

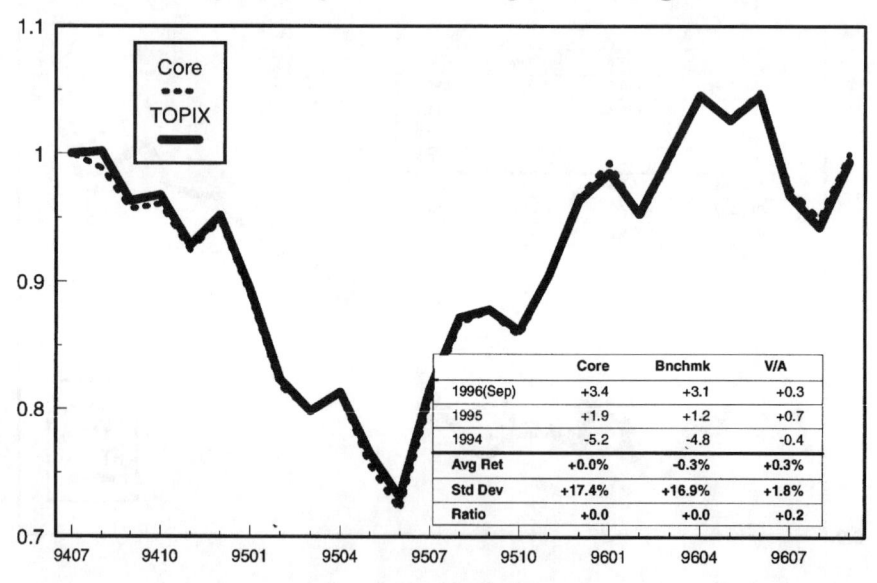

	Core	Bnchmk	V/A
1996(Sep)	+3.4	+3.1	+0.3
1995	+1.9	+1.2	+0.7
1994	-5.2	-4.8	-0.4
Avg Ret	+0.0%	-0.3%	+0.3%
Std Dev	+17.4%	+16.9%	+1.8%
Ratio	+0.0	+0.0	+0.2

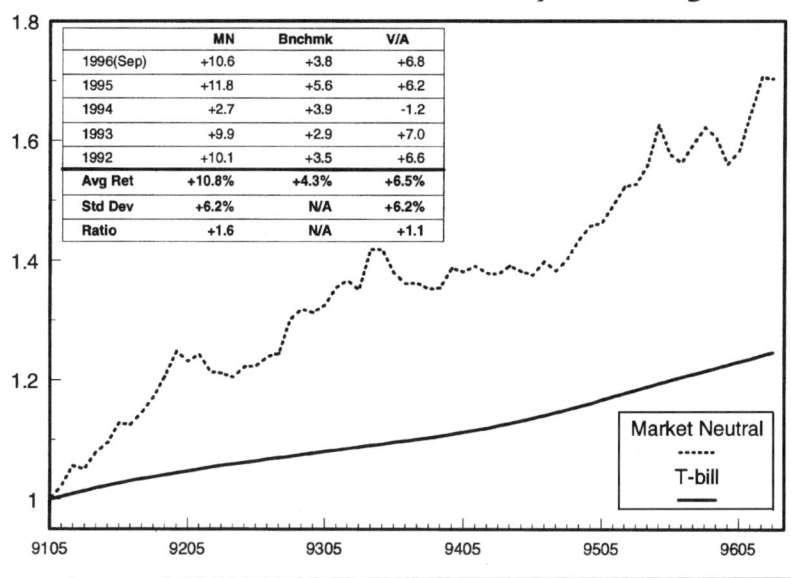

Exhibit 27: U.S. Market Neutral Style Management

	MN	Bnchmk	V/A
1996(Sep)	+10.6	+3.8	+6.8
1995	+11.8	+5.6	+6.2
1994	+2.7	+3.9	-1.2
1993	+9.9	+2.9	+7.0
1992	+10.1	+3.5	+6.6
Avg Ret	+10.8%	+4.3%	+6.5%
Std Dev	+6.2%	N/A	+6.2%
Ratio	+1.6	N/A	+1.1

Our U.S. market neutral strategy has been live since 1991, with assets now totaling over $1.1 billion. Average returns through September 1996 to these portfolios have been more than 660 basis points per year above the Treasury bill. Historical performance is found in Exhibit 27.

As we did for the core, we have developed similar market neutral strategies in the United Kingdom and Japan.[16] Again, in each country, the strategy adds value over the T-bill benchmark, by 7.4% and 4.6% per year (respectively through September 30, 1996). The performance histories for these strategies are found in Exhibits 28 and 29.

An important point about market neutral portfolios that we will only touch on briefly here is that their value added can be easily transported to any benchmark with a corresponding liquid futures contract. Most investors use this approach to equalize the market neutral returns, adding them to the market return for the corresponding equity market. In 1995, in the United States, this strategy returned 620 basis points above the S&P 500.

Finer Style Definitions Allow Management Within Broad Style Classes

This factor based approach to quantitative management can also be applied to a restricted universe of value or growth stocks (in contrast to the broad universe of value and growth stocks used for the core long portfolios). These portfolios are suitable for institutions seeking to add value within a particular style segment.

---

[16] These market neutral portfolios now total $135 million. There is no Canadian market neutral strategy due to limited short side liquidity in Canada.

Exhibit 28: U.K. Market Neutral Style Management

	MN	Bnchmk	V/A
1996(Sep)	+11.5	+4.4	+7.1
1995	+13.3	+5.4	+6.9
1994	+8.3	+3.8	+4.5
Avg Ret	+13.3%	+5.9%	+7.4%
Std Dev	+4.5%	N/A	+4.5%
Ratio	+3.0	N/A	+1.7

Market Neutral ···
T-bill ——

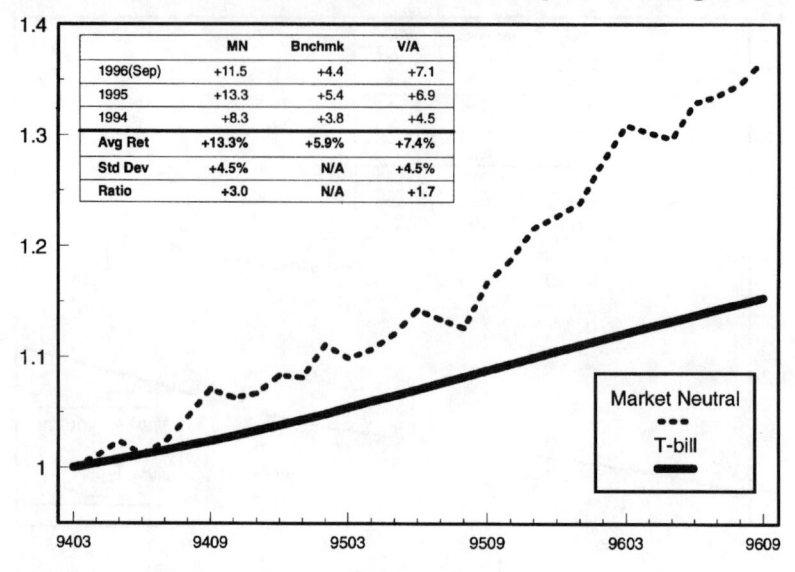

Exhibit 29: Japan Market Neutral Style Management

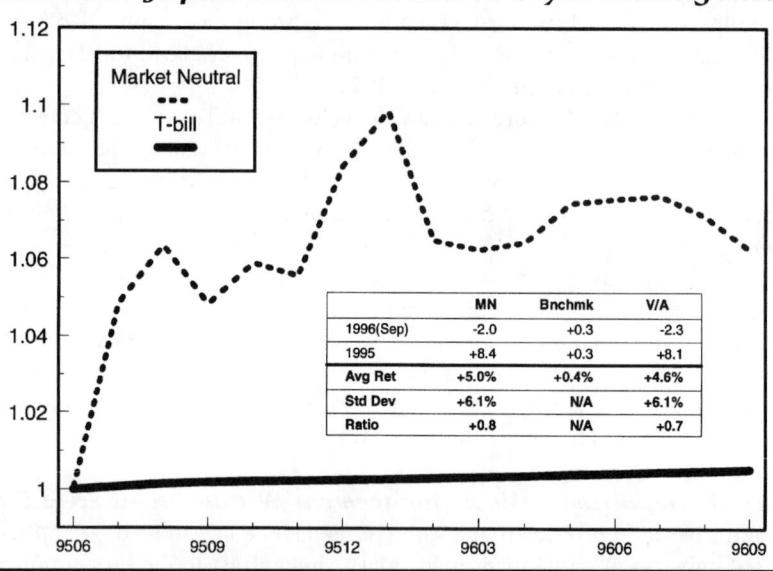

Market Neutral ···
T-bill ——

	MN	Bnchmk	V/A
1996(Sep)	-2.0	+0.3	-2.3
1995	+8.4	+0.3	+8.1
Avg Ret	+5.0%	+0.4%	+4.6%
Std Dev	+6.1%	N/A	+6.1%
Ratio	+0.8	N/A	+0.7

We have simulated the results when the same quantitative process used for our core strategies is applied to "style-segregated" value and growth portfolios. The sources of alpha and portfolio construction techniques of these portfolios are exactly the same as for the core portfolios. They differ in only two ways:

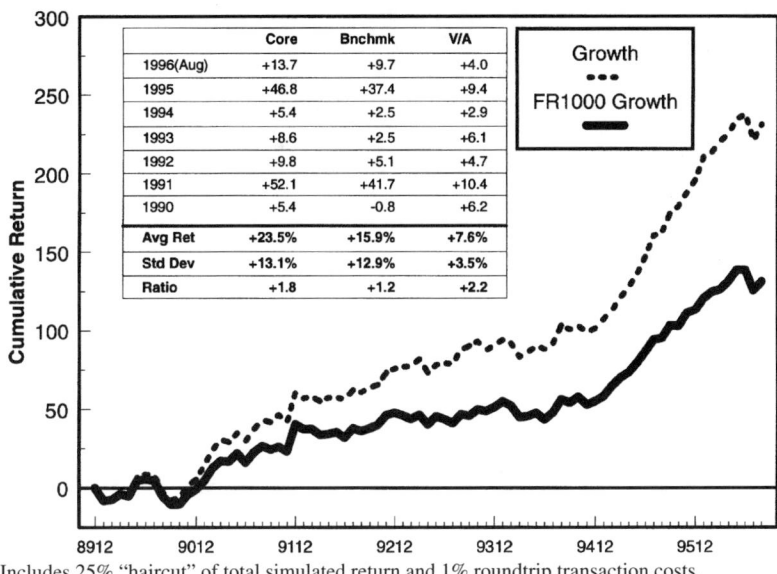

Exhibit 30: Growth Strategy Backtest August 1996

	Core	Bnchmk	V/A
1996(Aug)	+13.7	+9.7	+4.0
1995	+46.8	+37.4	+9.4
1994	+5.4	+2.5	+2.9
1993	+8.6	+2.5	+6.1
1992	+9.8	+5.1	+4.7
1991	+52.1	+41.7	+10.4
1990	+5.4	-0.8	+6.2
Avg Ret	+23.5%	+15.9%	+7.6%
Std Dev	+13.1%	+12.9%	+3.5%
Ratio	+1.8	+1.2	+2.2

Growth
- - -
FR1000 Growth

Note: Includes 25% "haircut" of total simulated return and 1% roundtrip transaction costs.

- *Investable Universe.* Only value or only growth stocks from the Russell 1000 Value and Growth indices are allowed in the managed value and growth portfolios.
- *Benchmark.* Each is benchmarked against the corresponding Russell 1000 style index, instead of the S&P 500.

We ran simulations using the same factor and asset alphas we have used for core portfolio management, but applied over an investable universe containing only value or only growth stocks. The results, after a 25% haircut and 1% round-trip transaction costs, are seen in Exhibits 30 and 31. The value added was 890 basis points over the value benchmark and 760 basis points over growth.

It appears that the same quantitative methods used over the core universe of all stocks work equally as well in the style restricted world. Simulations are just that, and the actual performance would be expected to be lower; however, these simulations are comparable to those for the existing core strategies. This bodes well for the prospect of realizing a substantial portion of the potential value added in real style-segregated portfolios.

SUMMARY

We set out to discuss the many definitions of style, the active strategies which flow from these definitions, and how they might be used for institutional asset management.

Exhibit 31: Value Strategy Backtest August 1996

	Core	Bnchmk	V/A
1996(Aug)	+9.0	+6.9	+2.1
1995	+46.0	+38.8	+7.2
1994	+5.3	-2.0	+7.3
1993	+24.1	+18.0	+6.1
1992	+25.6	+13.8	+11.8
1991	+38.7	+24.7	+14.0
1990	-5.3	-8.3	+3.0
Avg Ret	+23.9%	+15.0%	+8.9%
Std Dev	+12.4%	+11.2%	+2.7%
Ratio	+1.9	+1.3	+3.4

Value •••
FR1000 Value ——

Note: Includes 25% "haircut" of total simulated return and 1% roundtrip transaction costs.

Style tilts have the potential for adding value at a fund level, provided they are not done with a frequency that erodes their potential in trading costs. We have shown that broad style return forecasts can be useful in this regard for long-term decisions on style manager allocations.

More elaborate definitions provide a more fine-grained set of tools for active management. There is a conceptual convergence between the most complex style definitions and factor models of equity risk and return. A wide range of disciplined, quantitative, risk controlled strategies for core equities and market neutral investments were described.

Factors are appealing as the basis for active style management strategies for a variety of theoretical reasons, and have proven to be so in practice. We discussed seven real U.S. and international strategies which have demonstrated that these theoretical notions can be transformed into real value added for large institutional portfolios.

Chapter 12

Structuring Returns from Global Market Neutral Strategies

David J. Leinweber, Ph.D.
Managing Director
First Quadrant, L.P.

Christopher G. Luck
Director
First Quadrant, L.P.

Peter Swank, Ph.D.
Associate Director
First Quadrant, L.P.

INTRODUCTION

In the previous chapter we explained the motivation and methodology for a factor-based approach to equity style management. This methodology has been used for both long and market neutral portfolios in the United States and internationally since 1990. This chapter elaborates and expands on the discussion in the previous chapter by focusing on structuring returns from market neutral portfolios to fill a variety of institutional roles.

We begin with a review of the simple benefits of traditional long-only international equity investing, then look at market neutral, long-short portfolios.[1] Market neutral portfolios don't have any market return; the value they add is measured over the risk-free interest rate. We discuss how market returns can be restored by the passive technique of equitization using futures. The last portion of this chap-

---

[1] These will be referred to just as "market neutral" for the remainder of this chapter. All market neutral portfolios necessarily are also long-short, but the reverse is not true.

ter deals with the use of active market overlays to create multiple alpha strategies. Active asset allocation and active currency management decisions provide a means to add value above the alpha produced by the portfolios themselves. These strategies also enhance risk control, since the returns from their components are largely uncorrelated, they serve to diversify away a portion of the risk of each component.

INTERNATIONAL DIVERSIFICATION

Long international equity portfolios are constructed with specified index tracking error.[2] Consequently, their returns look like international index returns, plus some alpha. They provide a basic level of international diversification for a U.S. domestic investor. In contrast, market neutral portfolios are constructed with a tracking error measured relative to a Treasury bill benchmark. Without market exposure, they deliver an extraordinary level of diversification relative to equity indices. These "pure alpha" market neutral strategies are also uncorrelated with each other, and hence serve as an even more powerful diversification vehicle when several are used in combination.

Exhibit 1 shows the correlations of long and market neutral style portfolios with major equity indices. All are close to one. This is due to the tracking error constraint on the optimizer that produces these portfolios. They track the corresponding index on both a stock and industry scale, diverging only when significant gains may be achieved. The numbers in the first four columns of Exhibit 1 show the basic diversification value of international equity investments, with correlations (to the S&P 500) ranging from 0.34 to 0.77. This level of diversification can be realized with international index funds, or with tracking error constrained active equity portfolios, such as the style managed strategies we have described. Comparisons to other base countries, for example Canada, the U.K., and Japan, as seen in the exhibit show similar positive correlations.

The moderate diversification benefits of international investing are not news. A much higher degree of diversification is seen in the strikingly small correlations shown for the market neutral portfolios in the last three columns of Exhibit 1. These range from −0.16 to +0.18. These are remarkably low, essentially zero. Market-neutral portfolios have a much greater diversification value than long-only international equity portfolios. We can examine these correlations graphically as well. Exhibit 2 compares the returns of the FT All Share to the S&P 500. The correlation is 0.75.

Exhibit 1: Global Style as a Diversifying Element

	U.S.-L	U.K.-L	JPN-L	CAN-L	U.S.-LS	U.K.-LS	JPN-LS
S&P 500	*0.95*	0.75	0.34	0.77	*−0.10*	−0.14	0.13
FT All Share	0.62	*0.99*	0.36	0.65	0.01	*−0.16*	0.18
TOPIX	0.28	0.36	*0.98*	0.39	−0.08	−0.02	*0.11*
TSE 300	0.51	0.65	0.37	*0.99*	−0.05	−0.11	0.03

[2] "Index tracking error" is just the standard deviation of the difference in returns between the portfolio and the benchmark index. A portfolio with a tracking error of zero is an index fund.

Exhibit 2: Scatter Plot: S&P500 versus FTA
(Correlation 0.75)

[Scatter plot of S&P 500 Returns vs FT All-Shares Returns]

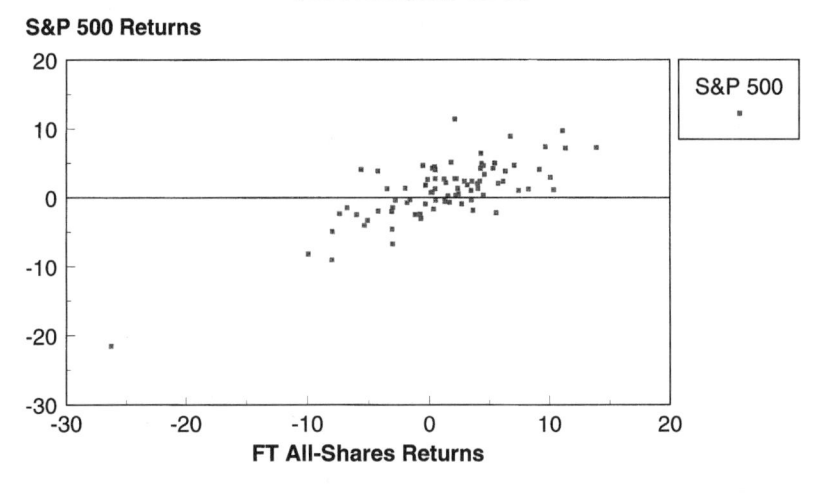

Exhibit 3: Diversification: Market Neutral Style versus the S&P 500

[Scatter plot of Long/Short Returns vs S&P 500 Returns for UK, Japan, Canada, USA]

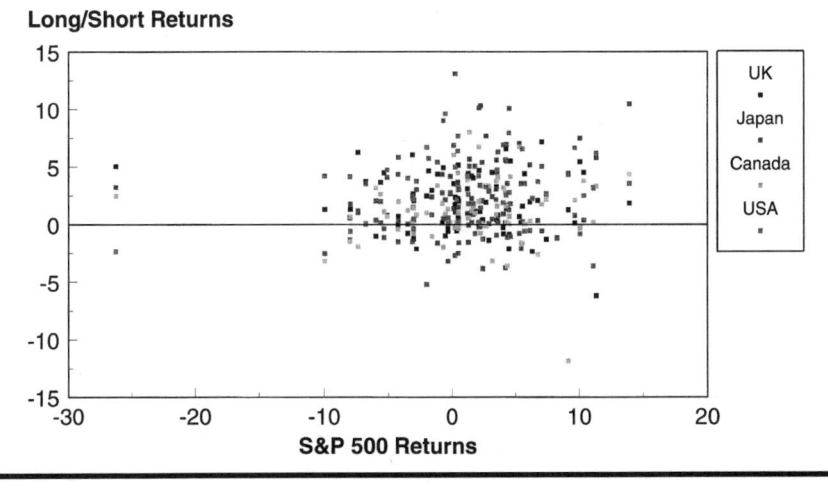

Exhibits 3, 4, and 5 demonstrate how low the index correlations for the market neutral portfolios are. These scatter plots show the monthly returns for the U.K., Japanese and Canadian, market neutral portfolios with the major equity indices: the S&P 500 (Exhibit 3), the FTA (Exhibit 4), the TOPIX (Exhibit 5), and the Canadian TSE 300 (Exhibit 6).[3] These correlations range from a low of –0.14 to a high of 0.10. Statistically, they are indistinguishable from zero.

---

[3] These scatterplots combine real and simulated performance.

Exhibit 4: Diversification: Market Neutral Style versus the FTA
(Correlation is close to Zero)

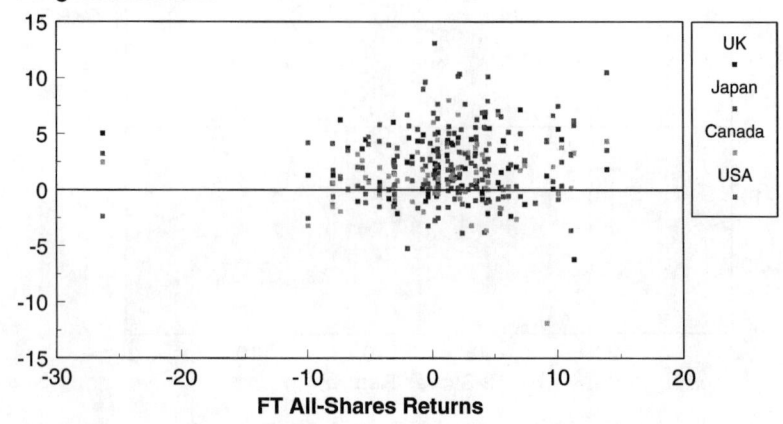

Long/Short Returns

[Scatter plot: Long/Short Returns (y-axis, -15 to 15) vs FT All-Shares Returns (x-axis, -30 to 20), with data points for UK, Japan, Canada, USA]

Exhibit 5: Diversification: Market Neutral Style versus the TOPIX

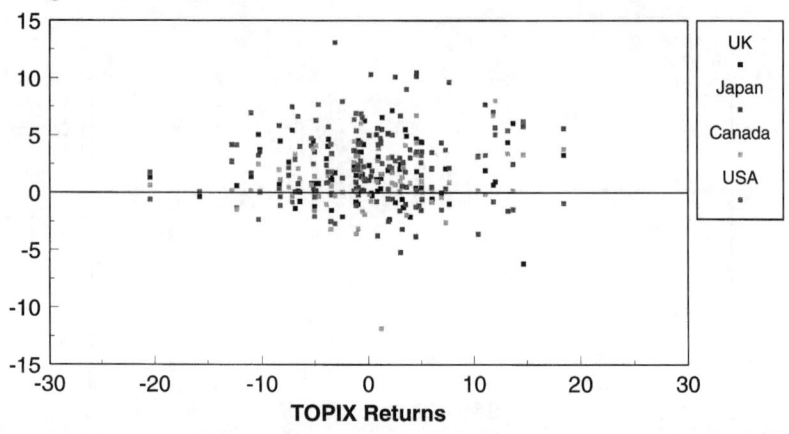

Long/Short Returns

[Scatter plot: Long/Short Returns (y-axis, -15 to 15) vs TOPIX Returns (x-axis, -30 to 30), with data points for UK, Japan, Canada, USA]

A noteworthy event visible in these plots is seen at the left of each exhibit. There are three points corresponding to large negative returns to each index in October 1987. Note that all three simulated market neutral portfolios had positive returns in October 1987. In Exhibit 5, the scatter plot against the Japanese TOPIX index, points on the left corresponding to the worst months for the index are not October 1987, but rather several months in 1991, when Japanese equity investors looked back on October 1987 as the good old days. All three market neutral portfolios, including Japan, had positive returns in these months as well.

Exhibit 6: Diversification: Market Neutral Style versus the TSE 300

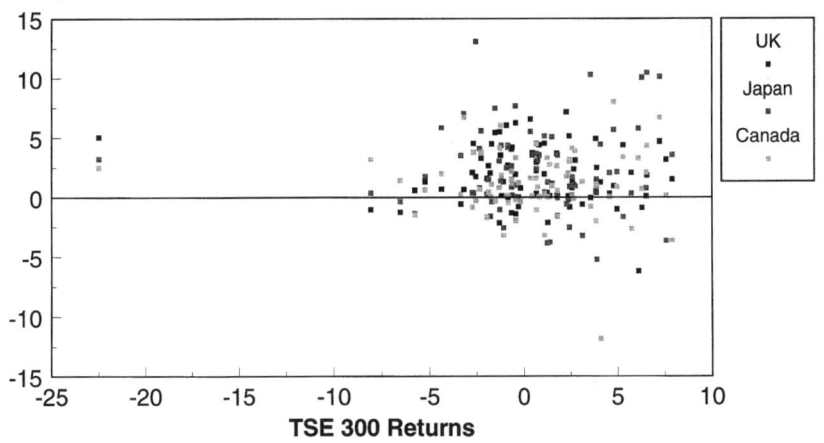

Long-Short Returns

[Scatter plot of Long-Short Returns (y-axis, -15 to 15) versus TSE 300 Returns (x-axis, -25 to 10) for UK, Japan, and Canada.]

Exhibit 7: Cross Correlations of Market Neutral Portfolios

	U.S.-LS	U.K.-LS	JPN-LS
U.S.-LS	1.00	−0.24	−0.29
U.K.-LS	−0.24	1.00	−0.07
JPN-LS	−0.29	−0.07	1.00

There is one important question remaining on the subject of diversification. While we have examined the correlations of these portfolios relative to equity indexes, it is worth asking whether they are diversifying investments with respect to each other. How much would be gained by placing assets in more than one market neutral portfolio?

The answer is seen in Exhibit 7, which shows the correlations of market neutral style portfolios for the U.S., U.K., and Japan, which are close to zero, with those largest in magnitude having a negative sign. These portfolios are among the most diversifying equity-based assets available to an institution today.

COMBINED MARKET NEUTRAL PORTFOLIOS

If one market neutral portfolio is a diversifying investment, what can we say about three? We have seen that the cross-correlations are very low. Now, we will look at an example of an equal weighted investment in all three market neutral strategies.

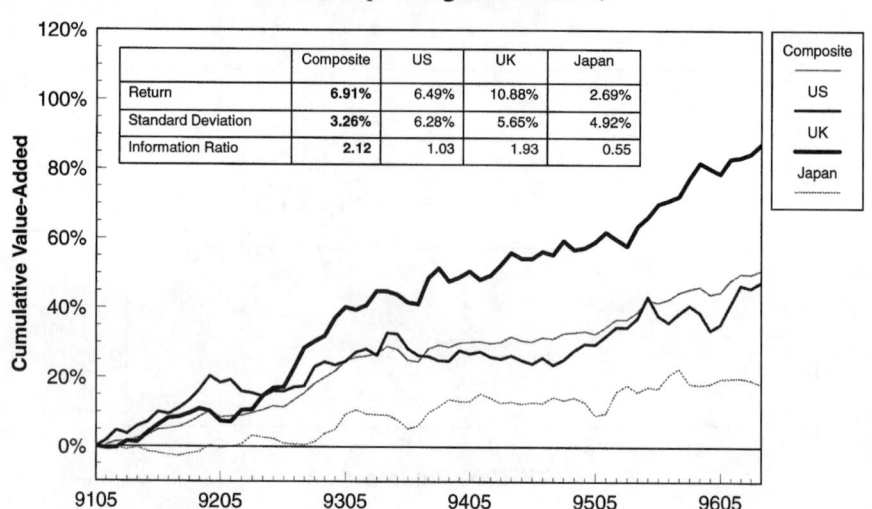

Exhibit 8: Three Country Market Neutral Portfolio
(Currency Hedged Returns)

	Composite	US	UK	Japan
Return	**6.91%**	6.49%	10.88%	2.69%
Standard Deviation	**3.26%**	6.28%	5.65%	4.92%
Information Ratio	**2.12**	1.03	1.93	0.55

As was the case for the previous examples, we use live returns when they are available, and simulations to fill the gaps. We have live U.S. performance for the whole period. U.K. and Japanese figures are a combination of simulated and actual performance as noted.[4]

Before we can look at the results, we have to decide how to treat the currency component of the international investments. There are three common passive answers to this question: to hedge fully, not to hedge at all, or to hedge 50% of the currency exposure. The last alternative is appealing in that it provides a useful central benchmark for evaluating active hedging strategies which will always move toward the fully hedged or unhedged alternatives.[5]

Exhibit 8 shows the performance of fully hedged three country market neutral portfolios, relative to a fully hedged benchmark. In the tabular portion of the exhibit, notice that although the return is the average of the three returns, the risk is lower. This is due to the lack of correlation between the strategies, reducing risk and increasing the information ratio. Exhibit 9 shows similar results for the unhedged currency exposure, with greater returns and greater volatility. Results for the 50% hedged benchmark are intermediate between the hedged and unhedged policies.

---

[4] The time period for this analysis is June 1991 - September 1996. Actual investment results from the U.S. were used for this full period, the U.K. for April 1994 - September 1996, and Japan for June 1995 - September 1996. Simulated results for the U.K. and Japan are used for other periods.

[5] Gary L. Gastineau, "The Currency Hedging Decision: A Search for Synthesis in Asset Allocation," *Financial Analysts Journal* (May/June 1995).

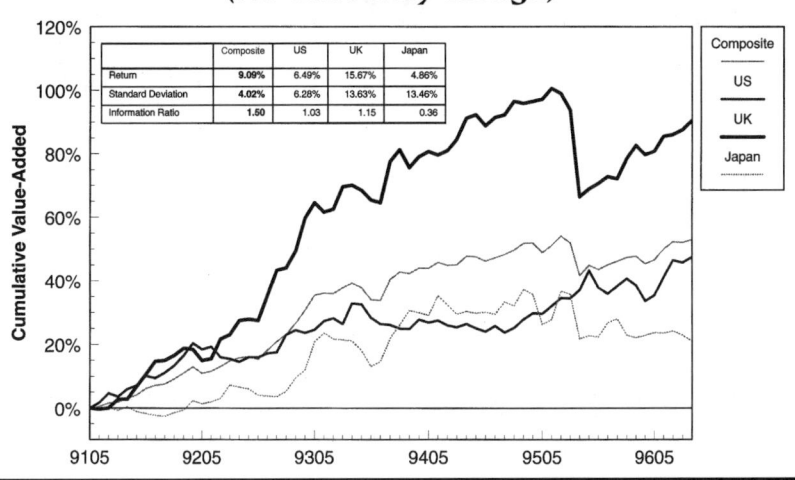

Exhibit 9: Three Country Market Neutral Portfolio (No Currency Hedge)

	Composite	US	UK	Japan
Return	9.09%	6.49%	15.67%	4.86%
Standard Deviation	4.02%	6.28%	13.63%	13.46%
Information Ratio	1.50	1.03	1.15	0.36

EQUITIZATION AND ALPHA TRANSPORT

Market neutral portfolios offer an extremely effective method of producing alpha, but by definition they are inherently market neutral. This market neutrality is imposed by an optimizer constraint to hold equal beta, equal value long and short sides. This very exclusion of the market is not desirable for many investors. Fortunately, it is a simple matter to restore market exposure through the use of stock index futures. This equitization with futures delivers the best of two worlds — equity market returns plus high market neutral alpha.

To illustrate the potential of even straight-forward equitization, we will show the performance of a U.S. market neutral portfolio equitized to the S&P500. We compare this to a long style managed portfolio and the S&P500, as seen in Exhibit 10. Notice that the equitized market neutral has delivered more than twice the value-added of the long portfolio, averaging nearly 7% per year above the S&P500. In 1995, this strategy delivered 6.2% above the S&P500. The same is true in the U.K. and Japan, as seen in Exhibits 11 and 12.

The value-added from market neutral portfolios can be transported on top of an equity benchmark by using futures positions in the market for the country associated with the stocks in the portfolio. There is no reason why this "alpha transport" has to be restricted to the equity market associated with the portfolio. The alpha from a U.S. market neutral portfolio can be transported to any benchmark that can be replicated with futures. This would allow, for example, a U.K. equity benchmark, an EAFE equity benchmark, a bond benchmark, or any combination of equity and bond markets. By using this technique, the market neutral portfolio is an "alpha generator" whose output can be used in nearly any portion of an overall global institutional benchmark.

Exhibit 10: U.S. Equitized Market Neutral versus Alternatives

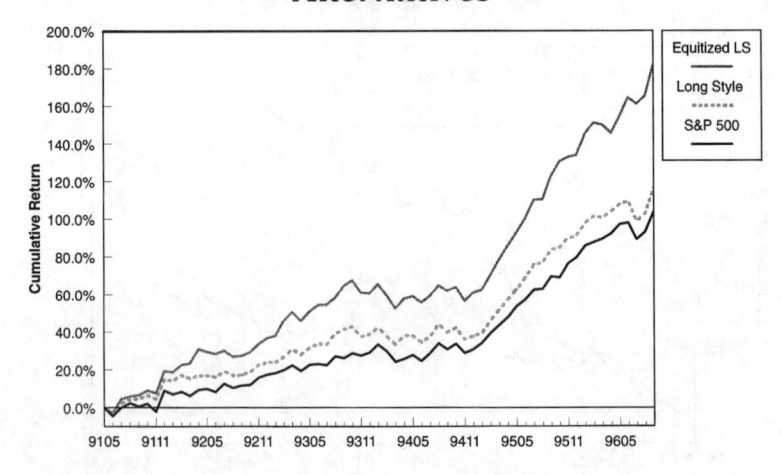

Exhibit 11: U.K. Equitized Market Neutral versus Alternatives

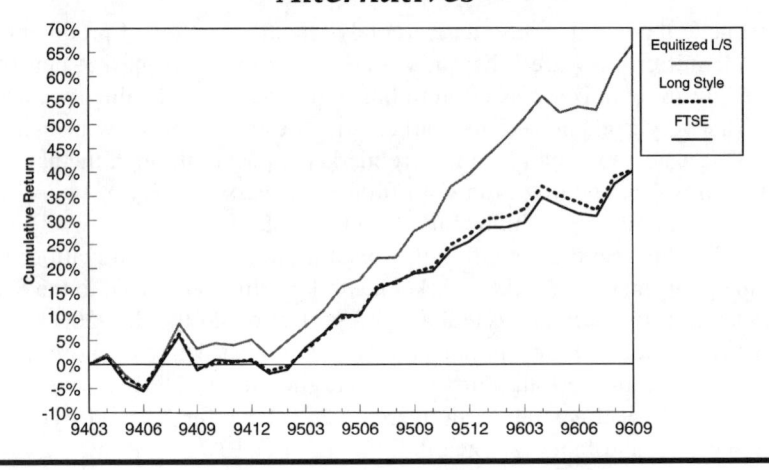

ONE STEP BEYOND PASSIVE EQUITIZATION: GLOBAL TACTICAL ASSET ALLOCATION OVERLAY

We have shown how passive equitization can restore market exposure by using equity market futures. In this section, we use an active global asset allocation overlay strategy applied to the equal weighted market neutral mix. Global tactical asset allocation (GTAA) makes asset allocation decisions which modulate exposure to stocks, bonds, and cash across the U.S., U.K., and Japan.

Exhibit 12: Japanese Equitized Market Neutral versus Alternatives

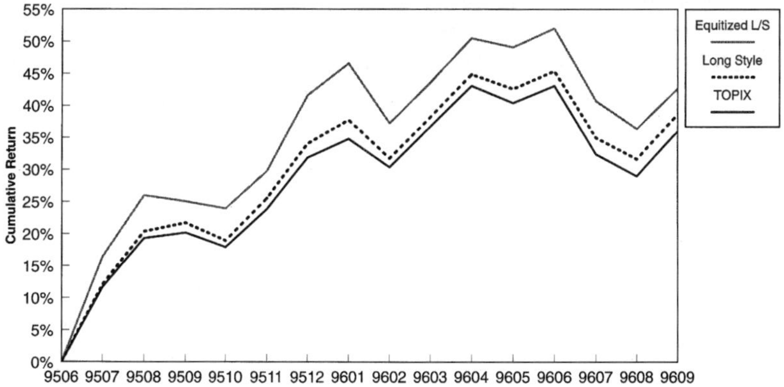

[Chart showing cumulative return from 9506 to 9609 comparing Equitized L/S, Long Style, and TOPIX, with cumulative return ranging from 0% to 55%]

The "default" position for this simulation is 100% local market equity exposure. We have managed live GTAA assets for many years, and have overlaid the historical, real time GTAA signals on the equitized global strategy. We use a longer time period than the prior simulations, from January 1987 to September 1996, to capture a full market cycle. Correspondingly, the simulated periods for the market neutral strategies are also longer.[6]

As seen in Exhibit 13, with the currencies hedged, the GTAA overlay is superior to the passive equitization strategy. Notice, however, that the volatility of the GTAA overlay has been greater than the passive strategy. In Exhibit 14, we see the same is true for the unhedged strategy as well.

To summarize, the market neutral strategy with an active GTAA overlay adds value in two dimensions: (1) "stock picking" in the market neutral portfolios, on both the long and short sides, and by (2) "asset class picking" via GTAA.

TWO STEPS BEYOND PASSIVE EQUITIZATION: TACTICAL CURRENCY OVERLAY

Now, in addition to the GTAA overlay, we add an active currency overlay. Instead of a passive fully hedged or unhedged policy, we make active currency decisions using the tactical currency allocation (TCA) discipline we have applied to live assets.[7] The simulation period is again from June 1991 to September 1996, com-

---

[6] The time period for this analysis is January 1987 - September 1996 (we used a longer time period to look at a full market cycle). We used an overlay with "actual" GTAA and TCA signals on equitized equal-weighted global market neutral strategy. Actual equity performance is used for these periods: U.S. June 1991 - September 1996, U.K. April 1994 - September 1996, and Japan June 1995 - September 1996. Simulated results are used for other periods. Actual GTAA signals are used for the full period.

prising the full live period of the U.S. market neutral strategy. We use the historical, real time TCA currency signals for the U.S. dollar, Japanese yen, and British pound, starting in April 1992.[8] These were used for live assets over this period.

Exhibit 13: Three Country Equitized Market Neutral Returns with GTAA Overlay
(Currency Hedged)

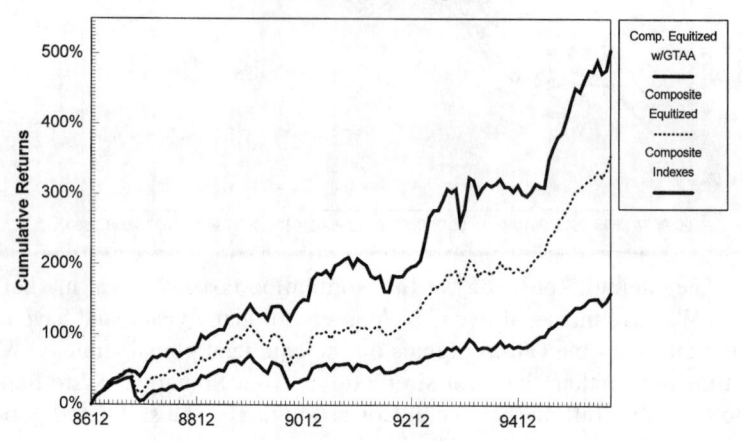

Exhibit 14: Three Country Equitized Market Neutral Returns with GTAA Overlay
(No Currency Hedge)

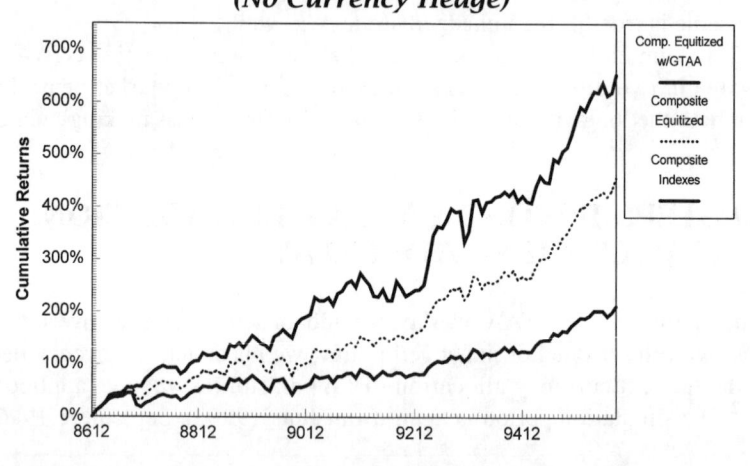

---

[7] R. Arnott and T. Pham, "Tactical Currency Allocation," *Financial Analysts Journal* (July/August 1993). (An October 1995 updated version is available.)

[8] The combination of real and simulated equity returns for this is simulation is the same as was used in the previous examples. TCA signals (dollar, yen and sterling) are real starting in April 1992.

Exhibit 15: Three Country Equitized Market Neutral Returns with GTAA & TCA Overlays
(Currency Hedged Benchmark

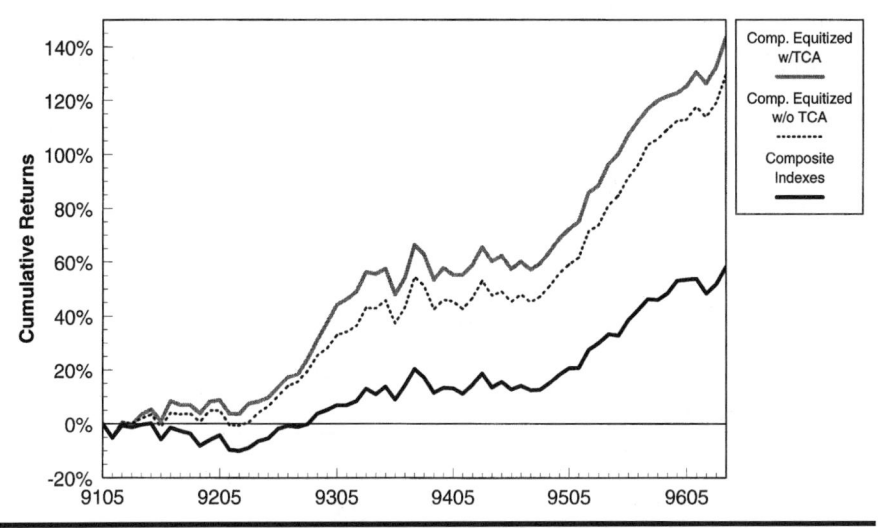

We will look at three scenarios to evaluate performance based on currency hedged, unhedged, and 50% hedged benchmarks. The 50% hedged passive policy may be the most appropriate benchmark for an any active currency strategy, since it provides a means to evaluate active currency exposure decisions in either direction. However, the other alternatives are commonly used, so we have included them as well.

TCA currency signals are driven by fundamental factors, not technical factors. They tend to produce stable longer-term signals, with commensurately low turnover. Exhibits 15, 16, and 17 show the added value of TCA overlays relative to benchmarks corresponding to the three passive currency hedging decisions. We see that the value added is similar and in all cases over 9.0% per year for the hedged, unhedged, and 50% hedged benchmarks.

SUMMARY

Market neutral portfolios lend themselves to a wide variety of institutional needs, from cash enhancement, to multi-level alpha strategies. They are extraordinarily diversifying and are an extremely useful tool for financial engineering of the risk and return profiles for institutional investments. Their alpha can be transported passively to any benchmark that can be replicated with futures. Additional layers of alpha can be added by active asset allocation and currency policies.

Exhibit 16: Three Country Equitized Market Neutral Returns with GTAA & TCA Overlays
(Unhedged Currency Benchmark)

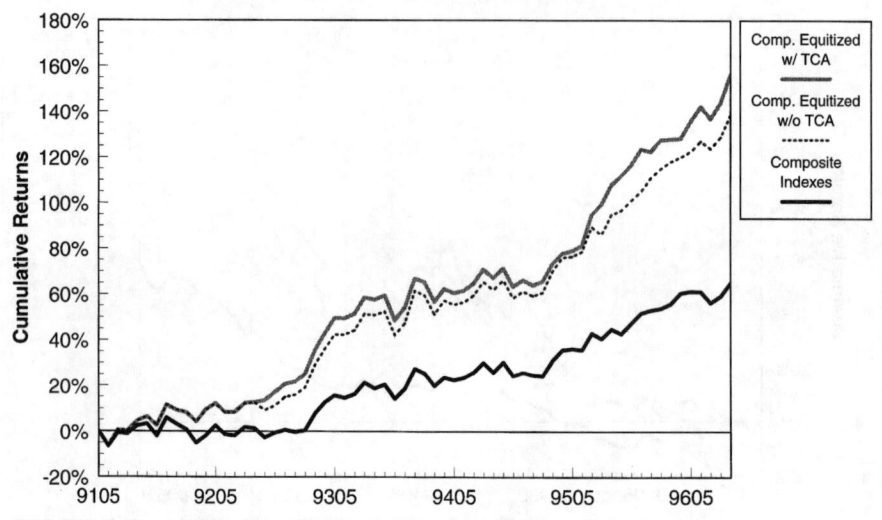

Exhibit 17: Three Country Equitized Market Neutral Returns with GTAA & TCA Overlays
(50% Hedged Currency Benchmark)

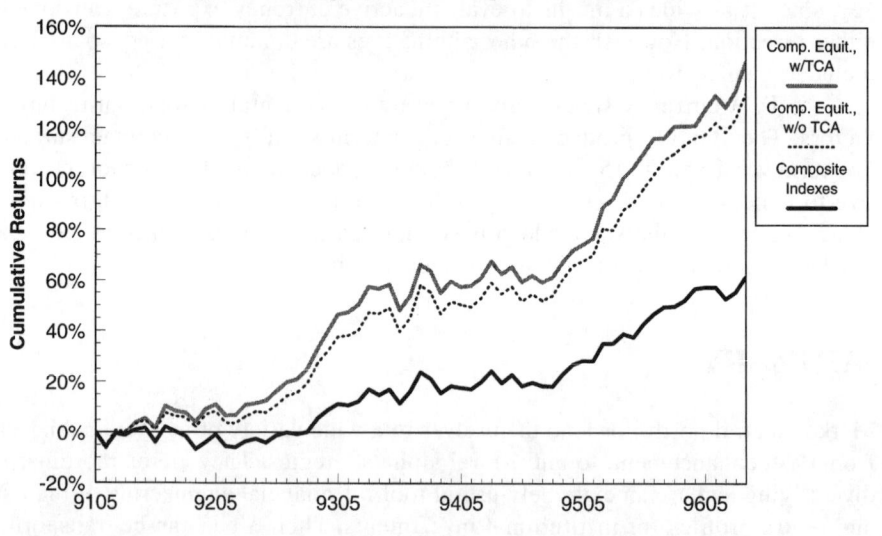

Chapter 13

Comparing International Style Indexes: Independence International Associates versus Parametric Portfolio Associates

David A. Umstead, Ph.D., CFA
Senior Vice President
Independence International Associates, Inc.
A Subsidiary of Independence Investment Associates, Inc.

INTRODUCTION

At a 1996 conference on equity style management, I described the construction methodology for Independence International Associates (IIA) international style indexes and I reported on the performance of these indexes for the Europe/Pacific markets.[1] My conclusions were as follows:

> Twenty years of results in 20 markets make it clear that passive investors in the Europe/Pacific region should focus their portfolios on the value end of these markets. The results are profound. The size, consistency and statistical significance of the value/ growth spread is extraordinary. We have found that country diversification is the key to controlling the volatility of the spread. We have decomposed the spread and found that value-added comes from both sector selection and stock selection

---

[1] Second Annual IMN/Fabozzi Equity Style Management Conference, Boca Raton, FL, January 1996.

within sector. We have looked at different levels of aggressiveness and found a clear, direct relationship between value and return. We have assessed turnover and transaction costs and found them to be modest. Finally, we have surveyed the literature and found a number of solid theoretical reasons for the value/growth spread. In summary, we have identified a tremendous opportunity for astute investors to capture higher returns in the passive portion of their portfolios.

Ken Winston, Managing Director at Richards & Tierney, challenged this conclusion. Ken's talk (which followed mine) entitled, "International Investment Styles: Do They Exist?", warned the audience to "beware of analyses of statistical noise" and concluded that the "value effect hasn't appeared in the past 11 years."

Ken based his conclusion on the style indexes produced by Parametric Portfolio Associates (PPA) in Seattle. Parametric, like IIA, produces style indexes as a by-product of its research process. One of the graphs that Ken used is shown in Exhibit 1. The exhibit does indeed show an 11-year spread in favor of growth. The comparable IIA indexes, shown in Exhibit 2, show the opposite.

WHAT'S GOING ON HERE?

The annualized rates of return are summarized in Exhibit 3. What is going on here? Are the technical differences in the construction of these indexes enough to completely reverse the results?

Exhibit 1: Parametric World Indexes
December 31, 1984 - December 31, 1995

PPA Growth 16.3%/yr — 5.25
PPA Value 15.1%/yr — 4.71

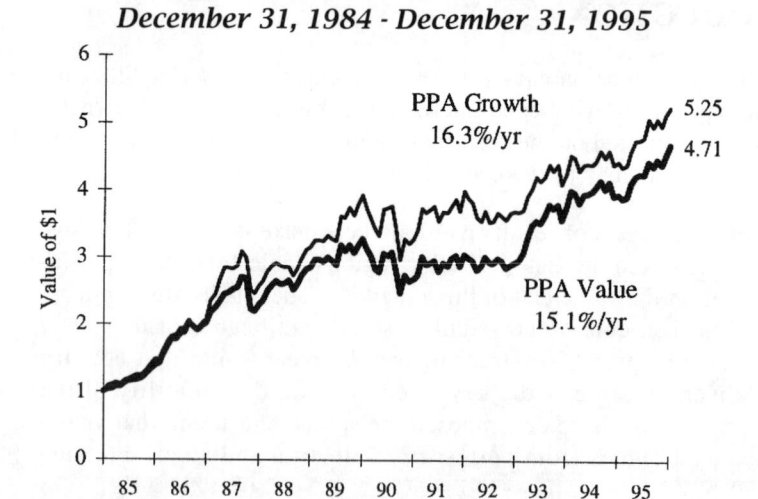

Exhibit 2: Independence World Indexes
December 31, 1984 - December 31, 1995

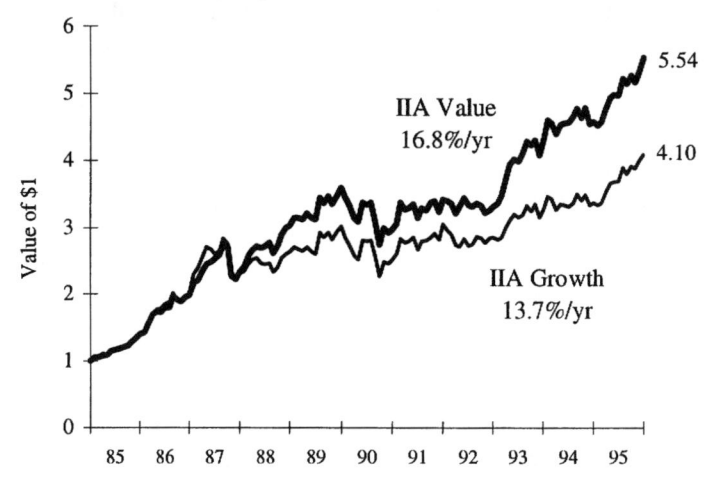

```
                                                              5.54
                          IIA Value
                          16.8%/yr                            4.10

                                              IIA Growth
                                              13.7%/yr
```

Exhibit 3: World Style Indexes — Annualized Returns
December 31, 1984 to December 31, 1995

PPA		IIA	
Value	15.1%	Value	16.8%
Growth	16.3	Growth	13.7
Spread	−1.2%	Spread	3.1%

IIA's value and growth indexes are designed to identify relative cheapness as measured by a stock's current book-to-price ratio relative to other stocks in the same country. The rules for dividing each market by book-to-price are applied consistently at each year end. The index is dynamic, with approximately 20% of the market changing style designation from value to growth (or vice versa) each year. IIA has shown that this definition of cheapness identifies a value index which has consistently out performed its growth counterpart both internationally and globally during the past two decades. IIA uses the Morgan Stanley Capital International database, as published each month in the ubiquitous blue books, as its starting universe in most countries. The IIA style indexes begin on December 31, 1974 and currently cover about 2,000 stocks for EAFE countries and 2,600 stocks globally.

Parametric's value and growth indexes are designed to identify long-term style characteristics rather than short-term cheapness. Parametric's index construction rules have evolved over time, but book-to-price and dividend yield are the major variables currently used for style classification. Book-to-price and dividend yield are normally the sole determinants of style for stocks in the highest or lowest quintile. Style classifications for stocks in the gray area (the middle three quintiles) are made only after examining other variables, including a variety of historical information, on a case-by-case basis. Classification of a stock's style requires committee approval and, in the middle three quintiles, the committee looks for evidence beyond current book-to-price and current dividend yield for clues as to how the stock should be classified. The committee is reluctant to reclassify a stock without considerable long-term evidence that its characteristics have changed. Parametric's turnover from style reclassification averages less than 5% per year. Parametric's universe of stocks has broadened over time and is generally drawn from the Interactive Data Corporation database. Parametric's style indexes begin on December 31, 1984 and currently cover about 4,400 stocks for EAFE countries and 6,800 globally.

Over the most recent six years value out performs growth according to both sets of indexes. Annual rates of return over the six years ending December 31, 1995 are given in Exhibit 4.

Parametric's growth return is 0.4 percentage points lower than IIA's and their value return is 1.4 percentage points lower resulting in a value-growth spread that is in the same direction, but 1.0 percentage points less. Most observers will agree that these are not substantial differences. The differences, such as they are, are mostly due to the differing starting universes. The broader Parametric universe produced lower returns over this period. Since most of the blue-chip, large-cap stocks are in both universes and tend to be classified in the growth half, the value half is where the effect of the broader universe has its greatest impact.

RESOLVING THE DIFFERENCES

The first five years in Ken Winston's 11-year comparison is where the significant performance variances occur. Exhibit 5 shows the annual rates of return for the five years ending December 31, 1989.

IIA shows a large value premium while Parametric shows a large growth premium. Since both sets of indexes were highly concentrated in just two markets during this period, it is useful to look individually at these markets. In the last half of the 80s, the United States represented about 30% of the global equity market and Japan about 40%. Exhibit 6 shows that the two sets of indexes produce similar results in the United States, but very different results in Japan.

Exhibit 4: World Style Indexes — Annualized Returns
December 31, 1989 to December 31, 1995

PPA		IIA	
Value	6.1%	Value	7.5%
Growth	4.9	Growth	5.3
Spread	1.2	Spread	2.2

Exhibit 5: World Style Indexes — Annualized Returns
December 31, 1984 to December 31, 1989

PPA		IIA	
Value	26.9%	Value	29.1%
Growth	31.6	Growth	24.7
Spread	−4.7%	Spread	4.4%

Exhibit 6: Country Style Indexes — Annualized Returns
December 31, 1984 to December 31, 1989

	PPA	IIA
United States		
Value	17.8%	19.5%
Growth	20.1	20.2
Spread	−2.3%	−0.7%
Japan		
Value	39.0%	43.6%
Growth	47.4	34.9
Spread	−8.4%	8.7%

In the United States, the Parametric and IIA growth indexes produce nearly identical returns. Parametric's value index under performs IIA's by 1.7 percentage points and this is mostly due to the differing starting universes. The increased representation of small-cap stocks in Parametric's universe drove down the return of their U.S. value index in this period.

In Japan, Parametric shows value under performing by 8.4 percentage points; IIA shows value out performing by 8.7 percentage points. What is going on here? The Japanese banks provide part of the answer. The banks were emerging from a heavily regulated environment and became one of the key forces behind the great speculative Japanese bubble. These stocks had huge capitalizations and where they were classified — value or growth — had an enormous impact on style index performance in this period.

The banks comprised about 25% of the Japanese market in the last half of the 1980s and as a group they produced an average annual return of 45.2% versus an overall market return of 39.1%. Simple arithmetic reveals that if the classification of the banks were the only difference between the PPA and IIA value and growth indexes for Japan, this would explain about half of the observed differences. Since we know that the market was up 39.1% and the banks at about 25% of the market were up 45.2%, we can easily determine that the remainder of the Japanese market was up about 37%. If PPA classified all the banks in the growth half, banks would comprise about 50% in their growth index and this single decision would move the growth index return up to 41%. With the value index return at 37%, this would provide a spread of 4 percentage points in favor of growth. If

IIA did the opposite and classified all of the banks in the value half, IIA's spread would be 4 percentage points in favor of value.

Parametric's Japanese universe contained 53 banks during most of this period and Parametric did indeed classify all of them in the growth half of the market from beginning to end. IIA's universe covered 17 banks at the beginning of the period and 34 at the end. Exhibit 7 shows how our price-to-book rule split the banks at each rebalance.

Our December 31, 1984 rebalance put five out of 17 banks in our value index. At this point, the banks were 23.8% of our Japanese universe and 3.6% of our value index. Our December 31, 1985 rebalance gave us just one bank in the value index. The banks were still 24% of our universe but less than 1% of our value index. By December 31, 1986 the banks had dropped to 18.5% of the market and seven were cheap enough to get into the value index for 1987 with a combined weight of 6.4%. These banks, with an aggregate price-to-book ratio of 4.0, were not cheap in absolute terms, but relative to the overall market they were. On December 31, 1986, the Japanese market was so expensive that the breakpoint between value and growth occurred at a price-to-book ratio of 5.5.

Our Japan value index, with an average bank weighting of 5.1% versus 22.0% for the overall market, was indeed under weighted in banks in the last half of the 1980s, but unlike Parametric's value index IIA's value index had some exposure to banks and Exhibit 8 makes it clear that the banks that were cheap enough to make it into our value index performed very well.

Exhibit 7: Japanese Banks

	IIA Market Index		IIA Value Index	
	Weight	# Stocks	Weight	# Stocks
12/31/84	23.8	17	3.6	5
12/31/85	24.0	17	0.6	1
12/31/86	18.5	17	6.4	7
12/31/87	22.1	17	6.4	7
12/31/88	21.6	34	8.3	22
Average	22.0		5.1	

Exhibit 8: IIA Japan Style Indexes — Returns (%)

	Market	Value	Growth	All Banks	Value Banks	Growth Banks
1985	44.1	45.0	43.3	51.5	87.4	48.8
1986	95.0	91.6	98.3	82.4	41.4	82.8
1987	39.8	44.2	38.8	78.7	100.2	75.1
1988	30.1	40.8	19.0	30.4	30.1	30.8
1989	1.8	8.4	−4.8	0.2	18.7	−3.5
Annualized	39.1	43.6	34.9	45.2	52.3	43.1

Exhibit 9: Japanese Finance Sector

	IIA Market Index		IIA Value Index	
	Weight	# Stocks	Weight	# Stocks
12/31/84	32.6	36	9.5	15
12/31/85	34.5	36	6.4	10
12/31/86	32.1	39	11.5	20
12/31/87	32.0	40	13.7	23
12/31/88	32.7	65	19.0	42
Average	32.8		12.0	

Exhibit 10: IIA Japan Style Indexes — Returns (%)

	Market	Value	Growth	All Finance	Value Finance	Growth Finance
1985	44.1	45.0	43.3	54.2	70.8	51.4
1986	95.0	91.6	98.3	100.8	150.4	95.8
1987	39.8	44.2	38.8	59.4	65.1	58.2
1988	30.1	40.8	19.0	33.5	38.5	32.4
1989	1.8	8.4	–4.8	–1.2	5.4	–3.9
Annualized	39.1	43.6	34.9	45.5	59.5	42.9

The second column from the right in Exhibit 8 shows that cheap banks averaged 52.3% per year, out performing the overall market by a whopping 13.2 percentage points per year. IIA's value index performance was hurt by the fact that it was under-weighted in the banks, but the under weight was considerably less than PPA's and was partly offset by the superb performance of the few banks that were cheap enough to make it to the value half of the market.

It is interesting to perform the same analysis on the entire financial sector. Exhibit 9 shows that the sector, which includes financial services, insurance and real estate in addition to banks, was consistently about one third of the Japanese market in the last half of the 1980s. Although about half of the stocks in the sector were classified in the value half of the market, the value index was consistently under-weighted at an average weight of 12.0% versus 32.8% for the market.

Exhibit 10 shows that although our value index performance was hurt by being under-weight in the sector, the finance stocks that were cheap enough to make it into the value half of the market performed exceedingly well.

The third column from the right in Exhibit 10 shows that the sector out performed the market by 6.4 percentage points per year, but the next column shows that finance stocks in the value half of the market out performed the market by an average of 20.4 percentage points per year. Finance stocks in the growth half out performed by just 3.8 percentage points per year. Cheap finance stocks out performed expensive finance stocks every single year with an average spread of 16.6 percentage points.

SUMMARY

In summary, IIA has shown that a simple price-to-book definition of short-term cheapness identifies a value index which has consistently out performed its growth counterpart both internationally and globally during the past two decades. Parametric's indexes have an 11-year history and are constructed with rules that have evolved over time. Over the last six years, the Parametric and IIA style indexes have fairly similar construction rules and produce similar results. Both show a value premium in the global equity markets.

Over the first five years of the Parametric indexes, the latter half of the 1980s, we see substantial performance differences between Parametric and IIA. Parametric's classification rules at that time were more eclectic and more judgmental than they are today. Parametric's indexes are live indexes and one can respect the reasons that Parametric had at the time for classifying Japanese banks in the growth half of their market. The banks as a group were selling at a price-to-book ratio of 4.75 on December 31, 1984.

At the same time we have to marvel at the robustness of IIA's simple price-to-book rule as a stock-selection model during this very unusual period in Japan. The rule puts some banks in the value half of the market and this decision, along with similar decisions in the other high-priced industries in the financial sector, produces a value index in Japan that out performs its growth counterpart by an average of 8.7 percentage points per year. IIA's value index in Japan outperforms growth four years out of five in this period.

Chapter 14

The Role of Completion Funds in Equity Style Management

Christopher J. Campisano, CFA
Manager, Trust Investments
Xerox Corporation

Maarten Nederlof
Vice President
Capital Market Risk Advisors, Inc.

INTRODUCTION

Most pension fund sponsors allocate assets to domestic equities through a multi-manager approach that involves attempting to replicate the stock market as a whole by piecing together representative portfolios of differing specialties, such as growth- or value-oriented managers, as well as large- and small-capitalization managers. This mosaic of managers is designed so that its return and risk characteristics match the market that drives the original asset allocation assumptions. If the manager mix is not perfectly balanced, however, a multi-manager structure may have a significant tilt away from the benchmark, exposing the fund to unintended risks.

One way to avoid these risks is to use a *dynamic completion fund*. A completion fund is a portfolio that is adaptive in nature and explicitly changes its risk characteristics to compensate for unintentional tilts caused by the "building block" nature of the manager selection process. In this chapter, we discuss the dynamic completion fund concept and its relationship to equity style investing.

INVESTMENT RISK STRUCTURE

The risk structure of institutional investments can be broken into several sources, or layers, for better understanding. Exhibit 1 is a schematic representation of the steps. The asset allocation decision remains the dominant determinant of return and risk. Large and complex funds, however, often find it necessary to hire several investment managers to represent the assets chosen at the asset allocation level. The type of investment managers, or the approach they use to building asset portfolios, can have a significant impact on fund performance.

The systematic effect of manager style is most profound in domestic equity portfolios, although the effect is similar in fixed-income management. The immunization (or neutralization of sensitivity to interest rate changes) of bond portfolios is commonplace in fixed-income management, eliminating the most important risk to the bond investor. Convexity, credit, and sovereign risk are also commonly managed risks that could be categorized as systematic.

The most prevalent equity risk factors chosen by the institutional community have to do with capitalization (small versus large) and more recently "style," such as growth versus value. The impact of these risk factors on a fund's performance can be enormous as evidenced by the considerable volatility in the returns of BARRA's style indexes that we see in Exhibit 2.

Exhibit 1: Risk Structure Layers

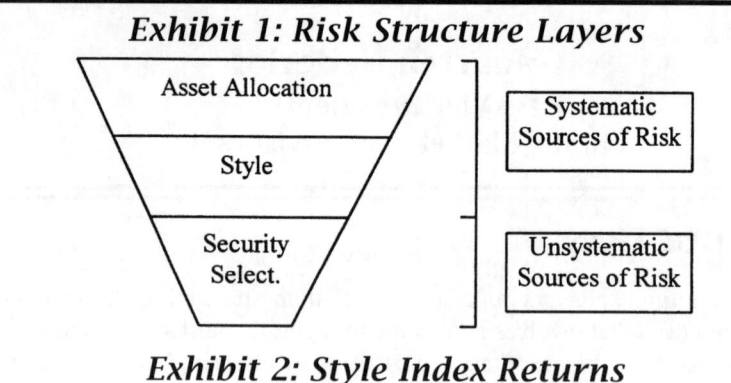

Exhibit 2: Style Index Returns

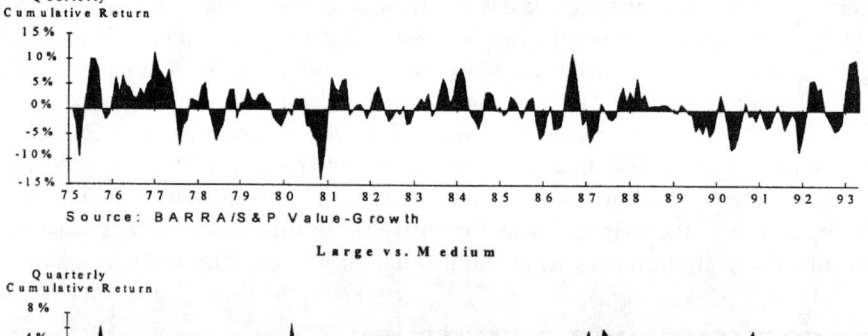

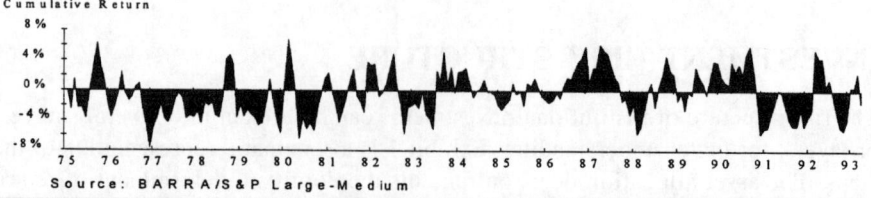

Managers matching these representative style indexes are likely to have the same volatility in performance, thus forming a second layer of return versus risk. The more extreme a manager is on either the capitalization or the growth-value continuum, the greater the return swings attributable to "style" effects. If an institution selects a group of managers who are biased toward a particular systematic style risk, the fund will tend to have volatility in performance due to that bias. This tilt can have a significant impact on return that is often unintended, since managers are usually selected for their ability to generate excess returns (alpha) as opposed to their style of management. The accurate assessment of style bias requires a thorough understanding of the manager's normal style.

The final risk structure layer is the security selection layer. The risk that derives from security selection is called several names, among them the unsystematic, diversifiable "alpha," and stock-specific risk. If a manager passively replicates a benchmark, there is no security selection risk, and no prospect for return enhancement over the benchmark. The selection of superior securities for return enhancement purposes will necessarily lead to deviations in performance from the benchmark (the sponsor hopes these are positive deviations). The volatility of deviations is measured as tracking error, or the standard deviation of the difference in returns between the actively managed portfolio and its benchmark.

METHODS OF STYLE DETERMINATION

To get an accurate assessment of the second risk layer, it is necessary to assess the normal style of each manager by a process known as custom benchmarking. Comparing managers against a custom benchmark or normal portfolio that represents the way they invest allows the separation of performance data into that attributable to manager "style," or asset class exposure of the manager, and manager skill within that particular individual style.

The basic concept behind developing a normal or benchmark portfolio is to capture all of the manager's systematic biases to produce the portfolio that would result from naively implementing the systematic biases in the manager's investment process. In theory, if this is perfectly accomplished, it would be a simple matter to identify manager styles that benefit from manager skill, and manager styles that should be represented through passive investments.

While normal or benchmark portfolios serve the dual role of identifying manager style and evaluating individual manager performance, it is the former that is key in implementing a completion portfolio. Regardless of the particular benchmarking methodology chosen, the first step toward managing aggregate portfolio tracking error versus a target benchmark is to identify the asset class (style) exposure that exists through passively implementing the systematic biases in all of the underlying managers' investment processes.

It is understood that there are three broad approaches to establishing custom benchmarks: index-based, factor-based, and asset-based benchmarking. We describe them only briefly here. Index-based benchmarking was first described by William Sharpe in 1992 in his survey of mutual fund performance, shown in Exhibit 3. This approach regresses the historic returns of a portfolio against a series of common benchmarks. In Exhibit 3, the benchmarks are the BARRA Large Value, Large Growth, Medium Capitalization and Small indexes.

Performance attribution, as it is also known, describes the contribution to performance of a series of benchmarks. Note that in his study of mutual funds Sharpe estimates that 97% of Fidelity's Magellan Fund's performance is attributable to the concurrent return on a passive portfolio constituted as described in Exhibit 3.[1] The choice of benchmarks is arbitrary, but is usually based on metrics like capitalization and style.

Factor-based benchmarking involves the comparison of risk factors common to the manager portfolios and a particular style. This depends on being able to detect certain management styles by their risk factor "fingerprints." We give an example of a style's fingerprint in our analysis of the outperformance of Large Value by Large Growth, and the returns attributable to seven key risk characteristics as defined by BARRA. Exhibit 4 graphs the correlations between the performance value-growth differential and the returns to each risk factor.

Exhibit 3: Sharpe's Analysis of Mutual Funds
Results of Style Analysis of Mutual Funds
(1985 - 1989) As Percentages

Funds	Approximate Exposures to Styles					Average Performance Explained by	
	Value	Growth	Medium	Small	Other	Style	Selection
161 Growth Equity	12	41	15	20	12	90	10
118 Growth and Income	28	29	14	10	19	91	9
4 Utility Funds	44	Negligible	Negligible	Negligible	56	59	41
5 Convertible Bonds	13	14	11	17	45	89	11
Vanguard's Trustees Commingled	70	Negligible	Negligible	30	0	92	8
Fidelity's Magellan	Negligible	45	30	18	7	97	3

Source: Summarized from William Sharpe, "Asset Allocation: Management Style and Performance Measurement," *Journal of Portfolio Management*, Winter 1992, pp. 11-15.

---

[1] William F. Sharpe, "Asset-Allocation: Management Style and Performance Measurement," *Journal of Portfolio Management* (Winter 1992), pp. 12-13.

Exhibit 4: Style Risk Factor "Fingerprint"
Correlation Between BARRA Factor Returns and S&P/BARRA Value versus Growth Index (1975 - 1994)

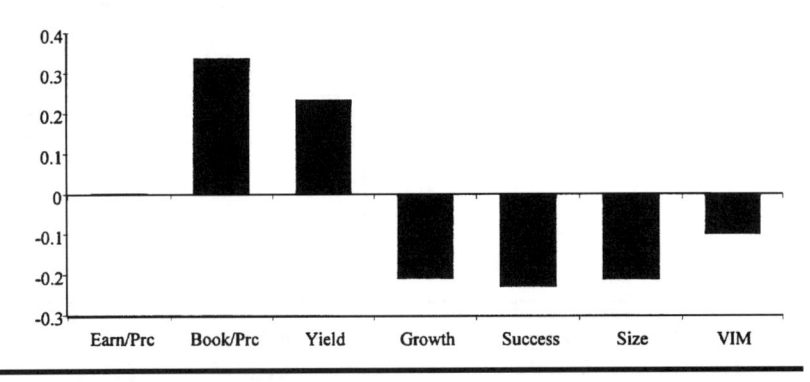

Individual Correlation

Factor	Correlation
Earn/Prc	~0.35
Book/Prc	~0.25
Yield	~0
Growth	~-0.25
Success	~-0.28
Size	~-0.2
VIM	~-0.1

Note that book-to-price (the factor used to differentiate between growth and value in the benchmark construction) and dividend yield are rewarded when value investors are rewarded. Also, earnings growth, success (relative strength), size (capitalization), and variability in markets are all associated with the outperformance of growth versus value. Knowing these characteristics allows any manager's portfolio to be assigned to either growth, value, or some mix between the two. This same analysis can also be performed using macroeconomic, industry-based, or statistically derived factor models, as long as there is a high degree of confidence that the styles can be fingerprinted accurately.

There are several different methods of asset-based benchmarking, but all attempt to get a more accurate benchmark by specifying a "normal" portfolio or benchmark portfolio as opposed to a parametric approach (a "style mix" of indexes, or a series of factor exposures). The benchmark construction process often involves studying the individual holdings of a manager's active portfolio over a sufficient period, drawing conclusions as to which issues are always present (i.e., identifying the systematic biases), and creating a proxy portfolio (benchmark or normal) by naive execution of the manager's selection criteria. This process requires manager interaction feedback, since the manager must approve the benchmark as investable (it must be attainable), and as a good representation of his or her approach.

Quantitative analysis alone cannot differentiate between systematic biases in the manager's investment process and strategic bets that will ultimately mature. For example, assume a quantitative review of a manager's historical portfolio reveals no exposure to utility stocks. If the manager purposely excludes utilities, this should be reflected by excluding utilities from the benchmark. If discussion with the manager reveals that the absence of utilities is a strategic, long-term active bet, utilities should be included in the benchmark so as to evaluate the strategic bet.

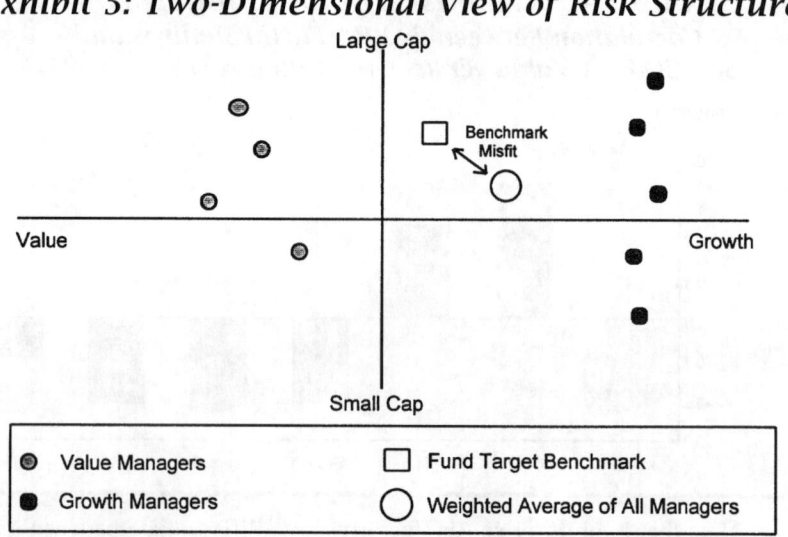

Exhibit 5: Two-Dimensional View of Risk Structure

- Value Managers
- Growth Managers
- Fund Target Benchmark
- Weighted Average of All Managers

A VIEW OF EQUITY FUND RISK STRUCTURE

Once each manager is being compared against an appropriate benchmark, it is possible to view the risk structure of the fund along several dimensions. Exhibit 5 is a two-dimensional plot that shows the location of each manager's benchmark on a scale of growth to value and small- to large-capitalization. The risk factors considered here can be combined linearly, meaning that it is possible to calculate the location on this "map" of the weighted average of the managers represented (the large empty circle). This represents the location of the portfolio that would result from all managers investing in their special benchmark portfolios passively (i.e., an aggregate of all the manager benchmarks).

If this portfolio is not in the same location as the fund's target benchmark (represented by the square), the fund has not accurately represented the desired target, and it is bearing an unintended risk. In this example, if small growth managers underperform other styles of investing, this fund will underperform the target, possibly threatening the incremental returns gained by active management because the aggregate benchmark is smaller and more growth-oriented than the target benchmark.

The distance between the aggregated benchmarks and the fund's target benchmark is called the *misfit*, and is usually quoted in tracking error terms. A misfit risk of 200 basis points refers to the annualized standard deviation of the difference in performance between the aggregated benchmarks and the target benchmark. This can then be translated into crude probability terms. For example, assuming a normal distribution, a tracking error of 200 basis points would imply that the portfolio return should fall within ±400 basis points of the benchmark about 95% of the time.

ANALYZING THE MISFIT

Misfit can have many sources. It is rarely due to a "simple tilt toward growth," for example. We often find that a particular industry (e.g., oil stocks) or type of stock (e.g., high-yield stocks) is purposely avoided by a particular manager. Our approach involves using a factor fingerprint to analyze the misfit. The misfit is generated by differences in both systematic and nonsystematic characteristics of the fund. There are typically differences in the style layer shown in Exhibit 1 as well as in the security selection process that describes each manager's benchmark.

Subtracting the aggregate of the managers' benchmarks from the target benchmark yields a long/short portfolio that, if transacted, would convert the aggregate of the managers' benchmarks to the target benchmark. The long/short approach is the most efficient method of constructing a completion fund. It is the membership in this long/short portfolio that exactly characterizes the misfit risk:

(Target Benchmark − Aggregate of Managers' Benchmarks)
= Misfit Long/Short Portfolio

(shown in Exhibit 6).

Note that the long misfit portfolio includes those stocks that need to be bought, and the short portfolio includes those stocks that need to be sold in order to bring the manager benchmarks in line with the target benchmark. Factor fingerprinting of this long/short portfolio will yield the sources of misfit. It may be necessary to use several different factor models to capture an accurate picture of the sources of risk, since some dimensions may not be visible from a single perspective. While it is convenient to analyze or locate portfolios visually in two-factor space (Small-Large, Value-Growth), this is usually insufficient to fully analyze and manage misfit. BARRA factors, industry composition, and macroeconomic APT models are all useful to give descriptions of the misfit.

Exhibit 6: Derivation of the Misfit Long/Short Portfolio

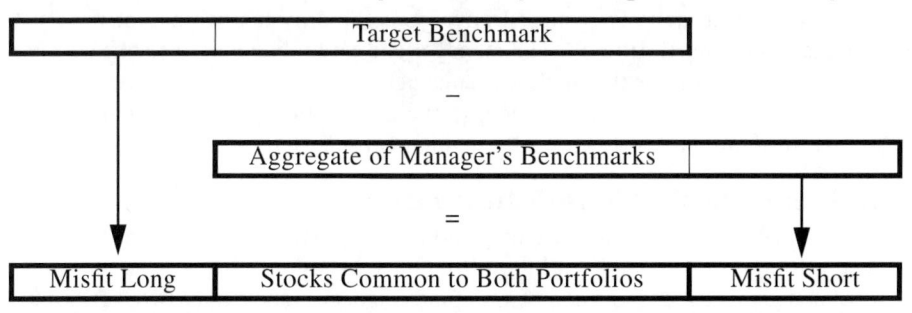

	Target Benchmark	
	−	
	Aggregate of Manager's Benchmarks	
	=	
Misfit Long	Stocks Common to Both Portfolios	Misfit Short

Misfit Long = Stocks in Target Benchmark, not in Aggregate (Need to Buy)
Misfit Short = Stock in Aggregate, not in Benchmark (Need to Sell)

APPROACHES TO PENSION FUND STYLE MANAGEMENT

Once the misfit is understood, a solution can be devised. Simple alternatives range from shifting physical assets between managers (to return the aggregate mix to the target benchmark) to doing nothing and hoping that the misfit risk will go your way. A more deterministic approach would be to build a dynamic completion portfolio that is updated periodically. This is a portfolio that approximates the characteristics of the misfit long/short portfolio. It contains issues that specifically counter the biases detected with the intent of controlling the misfit risk.

The Role of Completion Funds

A completion fund is a portfolio that is specifically designed with the objective of controlling or managing the misfit risk. If the completion portfolio were exactly the misfit long/short portfolio described earlier, all the misfit risk would be eliminated, and the only deviation away from the target benchmark would be from the active bets by the individual managers. That portfolio may not be investable, however, and needs to be represented in an investable manner. Additionally, many funds do not want to short stocks (or cannot), making it difficult to replicate the short portion of the completion portfolio.

The long portfolio is made up of under-represented issues, and is straightforward to replicate. The short portfolio consists of issues that are over-weighted in the fund benchmarks. These are not easily dealt with when shorting is not allowed. The only way to replicate the short position is to throw more assets into all of the other industries, dwarfing the overweighted groups. While it is possible, and in fact done in practice, increasing industry exposures is not as efficient a use of assets as using the long/short approach.

Passive replication of the misfit portfolio, while straightforward, is not as effective, since the periodic rebalancing process and its transactions costs tend to cause a performance drag. Some active stock selection, applied with the restriction that the systematic goal of the completion fund must be maintained, can be used to offset transactions costs. Turnover is created by the passage of time and its impact on the portfolio mix. The manager and target benchmarks shift because of changes in pricing or the method of management. No rebalancing of manager portfolios is required, however, because the completion portfolio adapts to the new risk structure and is dynamically maintained in a risk-reducing position.

Implementing a Completion Fund

Once it is decided whether to use a long/short or long-only fund, and once an investable portfolio is constructed, transition from the existing structure to the new structure of active managers and a completion fund can occur. The choice of securities for a completion fund can be made while taking into account their risk "fingerprint" as well as their potential for positive stock selection return. In order to reduce costs, the portfolio construction process can weigh the benefits of stock appreciation potential versus transaction costs; those stocks already in the portfolio that meet the risk and return requirements are preferable to those that would need to be bought.

Transactions Cost Savings Significant savings in transactions costs are possible if the completion fund acts as the transition portfolio for any major changes in allocations to equity managers. For example, if a growth manager is terminated in a multi-manager structure, the response by the fund as a whole would typically be a tilt to value. The completion fund would then have to become more growth-like to compensate. This shift would make the completion fund the natural buyer of some of the growth stocks that would otherwise need to be traded, assuming the risk characteristics of those stocks satisfy the other requirements for inclusion.

Retention of Best Value-Added Managers The dynamic nature of the completion portfolio obviates the need to shift assets between managers. Should a group of growth managers be performing particularly well (whether because of systematic outperformance of the growth style of management, or skilled stock selection by that subset of managers), that outperformance would require rebalancing periodically. A completion fund can compensate for the tilt to growth, preventing the need to take assets away from the most successful managers.

Providing the Ability to Add Value The completion portfolio does not have to be passively implemented. Periodic rebalancing costs can be offset by application of some active security selection within the completion portfolio, which at a minimum should recover the costs of running the fund. The trade-off that should be considered is the amount of tracking error between the invested portfolio and the completion benchmark. A long-only completion portfolio with about 150 basis points of tracking error should be able to recover all transactions costs in the long run. A more aggressive active management mandate can also be applied in order to provide more opportunity to add value to a greater portion of the overall fund's assets.

Managing the Misfit Risk

We believe the most significant issue in the management of a multi-manager equity fund is the explicit management of the misfit risk. Misfit risk is the difference in performance between the fund's target benchmark and the collection of managers' benchmarks chosen to represent it. Unless the fund's target is replicated passively, there will be some misfit. Periodic physical rebalancing of managers can keep the misfit low, but this is a costly and unpopular strategy (taking assets from the best-performing managers). The completion fund can centralize the misfit management process and approach it in a more cost-effective manner.

The dynamic completion fund can also be a valuable tool in the process of changing allocations to equity managers (through restructuring or termination) in a multi-manager structure. As a result, some plan sponsors find the completion fund concept an effective way to manage misfit risk in multi-manager portfolios. For an example, see Chapter 15.

Chapter 15
Equity Style Benchmarks for Fund Analysis

Mary Ida Compton
Senior Associate
Alan D. Biller & Associates

INTRODUCTION

The investment community has become more articulate in describing investments. What was once referred to as a domestic equity may now be called a value stock or a small-cap growth stock. The securities in the universe of stocks have not changed; our categorization of those securities has merely become more technical. We slice the market primarily in two ways: by market cap, and by some measure of relative value (such as price-to-earnings, price-to-book, or price-to-cash flow) to indicate a value or growth classification.

As the classification of securities has become more precise, so has the classification of equity managers. The manager once referred to as a domestic equity manager is now more precisely described as a mid-cap growth manager, or a small-cap value manager, or possibly a style rotator. The plan sponsor community, in an attempt to diversify its portfolios, selects managers from each style group.

Evaluating manager performance requires consideration of the manager's investment style. "Good" managers outperform their benchmarks. When small-cap value stocks outperform the broad market, a small-cap value manager should also outperform the broad market. Style indexes, such as the Russell 1000 Growth Index or the S&P/BARRA Value Index, have been developed as style benchmarks for these more precisely defined markets. Consulting firms take this precision to the extreme to develop a distinct benchmark for each manager, known as a normal portfolio.

This chapter illustrates the various uses of style benchmarks for a plan sponsor. We describe different types of style benchmarks, including style indexes

---

The author gratefully acknowledges H. Russell Fogler for attentive editing.

and normal portfolios, and discuss their appropriateness for a particular equity manager. We illustrate the way an organization develops normal portfolios for its managers and explain a low-tech alternative style analysis used as an internal check. The chapter should provide some insight into the process of developing style benchmarks as it highlights some of the issues that can surface.

PERFORMANCE ANALYSIS USING STYLE BENCHMARKS

There are two fundamental uses for style benchmarks in the context of performance measurement. The first is to measure manager performance. Style benchmarks "take the market out of" manager returns. They are intended to reveal the manager's ability to add value over the market, and provide a more appropriate hurdle for calculating performance-based fees. The manager's performance is decomposed as follows:

| Manager Alpha |
| Market Risk Premium |
| Risk-Free Rate |

The objective of using style benchmarks is to measure a manager's ability to outperform some nonmanaged alternative, such as an index fund or normal portfolio run by consultants or banks. The appropriate style benchmark for a manager may be as broad as the Russell 3000 index or as precise as a list of specific securities. Performance comparisons of manager returns relative to the style benchmark are sometimes used to calculate compensation when a plan sponsor pays the manager. In some cases, as is true with one of the large-cap managers in this study, the manager "owns" the normal portfolio and compensates individual portfolio managers on the basis of their performance relative to this normal.

The second use of style benchmarks is to measure the plan sponsor's performance. This is achieved by compiling the style benchmarks for all the sponsor's managers. Comparison of this aggregate style benchmark to the target benchmark of the fund exposes any "misfit" between the group of managers and the policy established by the directors. This is most easily accomplished by translating each manager's benchmark into a portfolio of securities, or "normal portfolio," and analyzing the characteristics of both the aggregate of all the managers' normal portfolios and the target policy benchmark for the fund.

The benchmark for this particular Growth Fund, for example, is the Russell Growth Index. This index is the target portfolio for the aggregate of the managers' normal portfolios, weighted appropriately. The misfit, or difference in risk as measured in standard deviations, between the aggregate normal and the index is 4%, which is moderate. (In terms of variance, this is 16%.) This is illustrated in Exhibit 1 for December 31, 1993.

Each bar in the graph indicates how much risk is associated with the portfolio's exposure to systematic or market risk, to common factor or "portfolio characteristic" risk, and to specific or individual security risk. The active bar represents the portfolio's actual risk exposures in excess of its normal exposures. The misfit bar represents the normal risk exposures relative to the target benchmark. The bias is the sum of the first two bars. The systematic risk is essentially zero for each bar, since market risk is roughly equal for the managed, normal, and benchmark portfolios.

The misfit of the Growth Fund comes primarily from the managers' aggressiveness in the growth area and their small-cap emphasis, as illustrated in Exhibit 2. This growth emphasis is seen in the large exposure relative to the index in successful stocks (SCS) that have strong momentum, and in stocks with high growth characteristics (GRO). The "variability in markets" (VIM) factor is highly correlated with smaller-cap stocks, and is therefore higher for the fund than it is for the index.

Conversations with our managers have led us to accept this deviation from the target as managers' attempts to add value to the benchmark by choosing stocks opportunistically from this group of high growth stocks. We can compare the performance of the aggregate normal to the benchmark to determine whether this has been a good decision.

Since the inception of this aggregate on July 1, 1993, the aggregate normal has outperformed the Russell Growth index by 3.4%. To test managers' attention to growth stocks regardless of cap size, we analyzed the portfolio relative to a target that includes a percentage of the Russell 2000 Growth Index. At 50/50 to 60/40 weightings of the 1000 and 2000 growth indexes, respectively, we reduce the misfit risk to between 1% and 2%, an excellent fit.

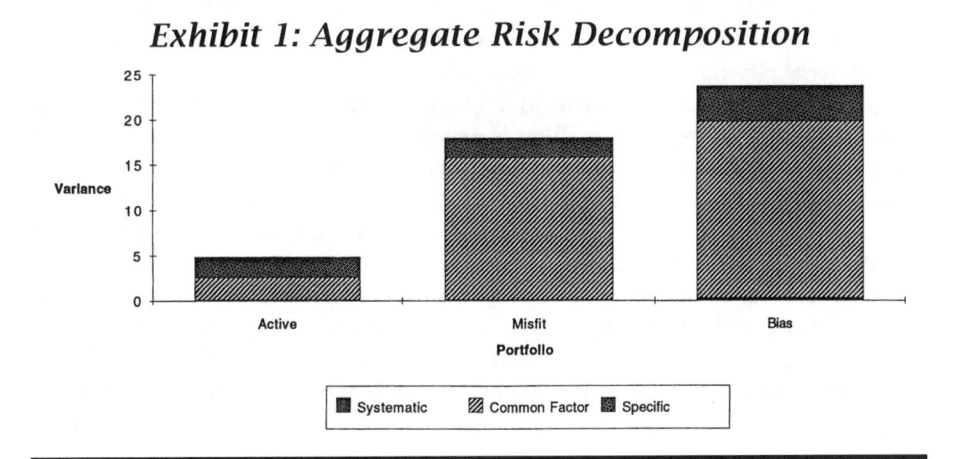

Exhibit 1: Aggregate Risk Decomposition

Exhibit 2: Aggregate Risk Index Exposures

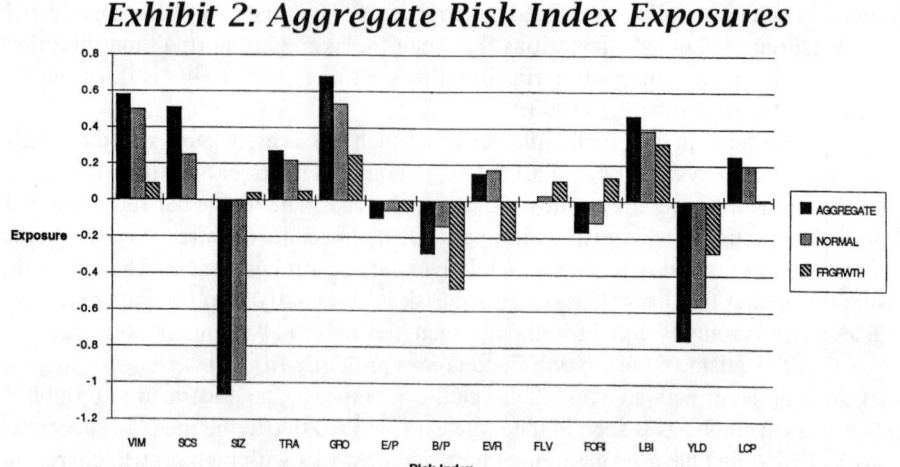

[Bar chart showing Aggregate, Normal, and FRGRWTH exposures across risk indexes: VIM, SCS, SZ, TRA, GRO, E/P, B/P, EVR, FLV, FOR, LBI, YLD, LCP]

To eliminate the misfit between managers and the target index of the fund, several managers offer completeness funds. (Completeness funds are discussed in Chapter 14.) The premise behind using a completeness fund is that it allows the plan sponsor to benefit from the alpha of each of the managers and reduce the tracking error to the target benchmark. Even if each manager is adding value to his or her normal portfolio, the group in aggregate may not precisely match the index against which the fund is measured. This divergence from the target is undesirable, and the plan sponsor should bring the fund in line with its benchmark. The two alternatives are to hire a group of new managers to fill these gaps or to use a completeness fund.

The completeness fund has the mandate to invest in areas the managers are avoiding, thus exposing the fund to all areas of the market and reducing the possibility of unintended bets. It is generally felt that closely matching all other important risk factors sufficiently reduces the tracking error of the portfolio. The risk exposures of the aggregate portfolio including the completeness fund will thus be very close to those of the target index.

The misfit of the normals to the target index in terms of market cap is the most difficult to correct, as the fund is usually considerably lower in market cap than a cap-weighted index because managers are equal weighting the securities in a portfolio. To correct this would require a large overexposure in the largest market cap securities at the expense of closely matching several other important risk factors. Thus, any misfit not eradicated through the use of a completeness fund manager is a deliberate bet by the sponsor, and this performance can be measured.

The logistics of using a completeness fund are straightforward. The plan sponsor (or consultant) provides the manager of the completeness fund with the normal portfolios of the managers in the fund. This information is updated semiannually, as the normal portfolios are rebalanced. This manager creates a "difference portfolio" of securities and possibly derivatives that aligns the risk exposures of the entire fund with the target index. This is typically done using 10% of the assets of the fund.

TYPES OF STYLE BENCHMARKS

Style benchmarks come in various forms. Different types are appropriate for different types of managers. The process of developing normal portfolios is tedious and time consuming, and requires regular attention. For some plan sponsors, this is reason enough to employ another form of style benchmark. Style benchmarks have a variety of applications beyond performance measurement.

Three basic types of style benchmark are commonly used. The first is a basket of stocks, or normal portfolio, which represents the universe of securities a particular manager would consider reasonable for inclusion in the portfolio. These securities are weighted in some appropriate way to reflect the manager's style, resulting in a portfolio whose traditional characteristics match those of the manager's invested portfolio. The screens used to determine the securities in this basket should fairly closely imitate the manager's investment process, with no significant sector bets in the normal that the manager would not consider making. The normal should include more names than the actual portfolio, usually more than 300 stocks, and the overlap with the manager's stocks should be high, at least 80%. Normals with less than 70% coverage of the active portfolio are considered inadequate. Normals are typically rebalanced semiannually.

The second type of style benchmark is a style index or weighted average of a selection of style indexes. These style benchmarks are easy to create, maintain, and understand. For example, a value manager who concentrates in small-cap value stocks but occasionally strays into larger-cap stocks may have a style benchmark composed of 75% Russell 2000 Value and 25% Russell 1000 Value indexes. A special case of a style index could be an industry index, a reasonable choice for the manager who focuses his investments in one industry or sector, such as technology.

Using an index as a portfolio benchmark is also useful for the "farm team" of managers. In some multiple-manager domestic equity funds, a constantly changing group of small managers is used, as selected by a consultant. These managers individually may not have the history or the assets to warrant being weighted in the fund to the magnitude of the other managers. The investment style of this group of managers is relatively consistent over time, and that style is best captured as a weighted average of indexes.

A third type of style benchmark is a style universe mean or median. The Frank Russell Company and other consultants track enough managers to categorize them by investment style, such as growth managers, or market-oriented managers with a value tilt. Relative performance of a sponsor's manager is clear and quantifiable using risk/return scatters and quartile charts, as seen in Exhibits 3 and 4. The rationale for using such a style benchmark is to compare managers to their peers.

244 Equity Style Benchmarks for Fund Analysis

Exhibit 3: Universe of Equity Funds (US$)
10 Years Ending March 31, 1994

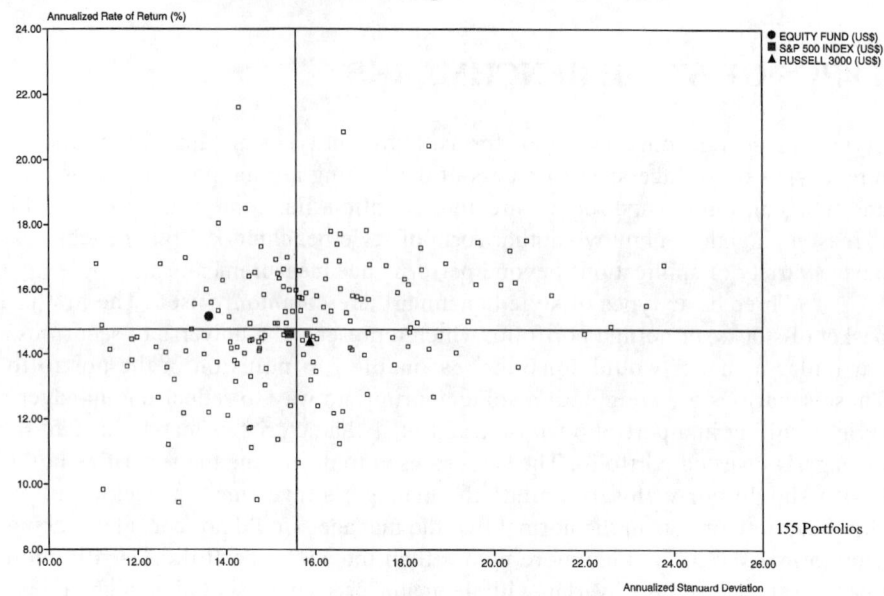

155 Portfolios

Source: Frank Russell Company

Exhibit 4: Universe of Equity Funds (US$)
Ending March 31, 1994

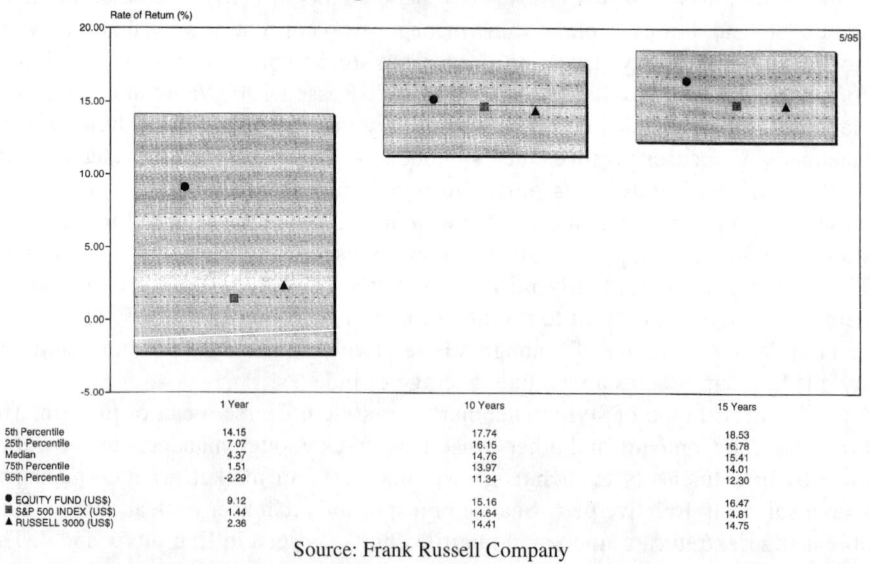

	1 Year	10 Years	15 Years
5th Percentile	14.15	17.74	18.53
25th Percentile	7.07	16.15	16.78
Median	4.37	14.76	15.41
75th Percentile	1.51	13.97	14.01
95th Percentile	-2.29	11.34	12.30
● EQUITY FUND (US$)	9.12	15.16	16.47
■ S&P 500 INDEX (US$)	1.44	14.64	14.81
▲ RUSSELL 3000 (US$)	2.36	14.41	14.75

Source: Frank Russell Company

One aspect to keep in mind, which the manager may point out, is the strong survivorship bias that exists when universe results are created. The analyst is looking back in time to see how a manager performed relative to a peer group. The median manager from this universe is actually above the median of the group of managers in existence on day one, X years ago, because some of those managers have gone out of business during the X years. The plan sponsor may argue that it would not have chosen one of the since-vanished managers X years ago, so such a universe is indeed valid for comparative purposes.

THE APPROPRIATE STYLE BENCHMARK

In a diversified fund, no single type of analysis will give equally precise information about each manager. To gain the most information on each manager, the plan sponsor must realize that different types of benchmarks are required for different managers. The objective is to imitate the manager's portfolio over time as closely as possible in terms of performance pattern without using a subjective stock selection process.

The easiest managers to measure using style benchmarks are likely to be both the quantitative managers who use linear models and the traditional stock-pickers who use a rigorous selection process based only on security characteristics. These managers often begin the selection process using a computer-generated stock screening model, which is easy to replicate given the appropriate database and software. For these managers, the most accurate style benchmark is the normal portfolio of securities selected through successive screens of the universe of stocks. This is not simply a mechanical process, however, because some of the managers' screens may use custom statistics, such as free cash flow calculated from individual companies' financial statements.

The portfolios of opportunistic managers are more difficult to model using normal portfolios. This difficulty stems from the changing style of these managers. As different styles (growth or value), industries, or market cap ranges appear to be attractive, these managers attempt to take advantage of their potential profits. Thus, the basket of securities an opportunistic manager would consider for investment purposes is the entire universe of securities. These managers require a broader benchmark, such as the Russell 3000.

Some managers are asked to outperform the better of two indexes. I have seen this in practice only in the international area, where a manager is asked to outperform the international market, as well as the domestic alternative (in order to justify investing internationally). For contrarian growth/value managers who sway with opportunity, the analogous request would be to outperform the greater of the Russell Growth and Value indexes. In practice, however, these managers prefer to be measured against the broad market, generally the S&P 500.

The most difficult manager to model may be the hedge manager. Some hedge managers hold a high percentage of derivative and international securities, which are not captured well by either a basket of securities or an index. Yet most equity managers can be compared to some universe of managers, and the hedge fund manager is no exception.

Universes exist for large- or small-cap growth or value managers, yield-driven managers, broad market managers with or without style tilt, and more recently for hedge fund, risk arbitrage, and market-neutral managers. Using universe percentiles is less labor-intensive than creating custom normal portfolios for the managers, but it has its drawbacks as well. In some cases, the data are available only quarterly. To see how well a manager is tracking a benchmark, more frequent data are desirable.

Another possible drawback is that some of the participants of these universes do not belong in their universe. This is a serious problem and common in the industry. Many data compilers take managers literally when they claim to be "value" managers, but who would claim to buy overpriced stocks? Thus, the participants in a particular universe should be reviewed before using it for comparative purposes. Also, as discussed above, there is the problem of survivorship bias.

We use universe comparisons internally with some caution. Universe data are most helpful when looking at risk/return scatter diagrams. We do not currently use universe medians for individual manager benchmarks, as we prefer normal portfolios where appropriate, and for our other managers, the universe comparisons lack sufficient history.

DEVELOPING NORMAL PORTFOLIOS

Sponsors generally work with a consultant to create, update, and maintain manager normal portfolios. In some cases, the manager already has a working relationship with some consultant, and has previously constructed and is maintaining his or her normal portfolio. Through this relationship, the manager truly understands a particular investment style as well as the implications of any performance attribution results that are produced by these systems. This interest in and attention to normal portfolios tells us (and a plan sponsor) something about the manager's sophistication.

Creating a normal portfolio for a manager is a time-consuming process that requires attention at least annually, preferably semiannually. It also requires extensive computer resources and databases, which are becoming easier to obtain. At least three years of monthly portfolios are needed for construction of a meaningful normal. Unless the plan sponsor has the human resources necessary, which is unlikely, the best route is to hire a consultant for the initial task and ongoing maintenance. This creates a three-party arrangement, which can sometimes result in circular arguments.

Managers have a variety of reactions to having a normal portfolio created. Some managers are eager to find a benchmark that closely mirrors their style and performance results. These managers become actively involved in communications with the consultant, and in some cases, also engage their own consultant to verify or argue the nuances of the normal construction.

In the reevaluation process, we have seen a variety of responses to the normals presented to the managers. One of the value managers, for example, argued that the industry weights that fell out of the screening process were inappropriate. Usually, industry adjustments are not made in the normal portfolio unless it is a defined element of the manager's stock selection process, which it was in this case. The normal was altered to reflect this investment restriction.

A high-yield equity managers argued that the primary screen employed in his normal (yield > market) was not strong enough to capture his style. His yield was consistently higher than the yield of the normal portfolio, but the yield of the normal was much closer to the yield of his portfolio than to that of the market. The problem with using a more restrictive universe is that not enough names appear to result in a diversified normal. The normal needs to be large enough that its performance is not impacted by the performance of any single stock in it.

A third manager provided normal portfolios for two of his strategies that the consultant found unacceptable. One normal had several risk exposure values that were significantly different from his managed portfolio. The most extreme difference was in the exposure to the size factor, where the normal differed from the actual portfolio by 0.77 standard deviations. Size is the most easily captured variable, and 0.10 standard deviations is the maximum difference this consultant would tolerate.

The other normal portfolio had a problem with coverage of the actual investments. The normal contained 746 securities, the active portfolio held 53 names, and the overlap in names was 17, or 32% of the managed portfolio. The consultant considers a coverage of 70% to be the minimum tolerated for a meaningful normal.

Some managers feel their investment process is proprietary, and should not be revealed for construction of a normal portfolio. Others feel it is impossible to imitate their investment process with a black box. Rather than specify an exact process, a manager may decide to let the historical portfolio speak for itself. These managers may not want compensation to be based on their performance relative to a normal that they had no part in constructing. Sponsors should note that it is still important to maintain a normal on such managers for internal measurement purposes.

Once normal portfolios or weighted index benchmarks have been established for each manager, it is important to run the entire analysis through a single consultant for consistency. The resulting information should be shared with the managers. To avoid any misinterpretation because of different calculations of portfolio characteristics by different software or databases, the listing of securities in the normal should be shared with managers. Managers can then perform any analysis on this portfolio that they would perform on their own databases of stocks used in everyday security selection, and see the similarity between their invested and normal portfolios.

The ultimate decision to use some type of style benchmark rests with the plan sponsor. Some plan sponsors have refused to hire a manager who was not willing both to participate in the construction of a normal portfolio and to be compensated on the basis of performance relative to this normal. Other sponsors may analyze managers using some form of style analysis without the manager's awareness.

The concept of normal portfolios is becoming more widely accepted among equity managers, however, and many of them have BARRA'S PC product in-house. They construct their own normal portfolio, and adjust their portfolios using this system. It is optimal for a manager to own, or at least take ownership in, a benchmark. The best scenario is one in which the manager works with the sponsor or consultant to create a normal portfolio to be used for several clients, and one upon which manager compensation is based.

INTERNAL USE OF STYLE BENCHMARKS

We use style benchmarks primarily in three ways. First, we analyze the manager's past performance relative to their normal portfolios. Second, we consider the current risk exposures of the portfolios and the aggregate relative to those of our performance target. Third, we look for changes in a manager's or a fund's style by considering changes in the risk profile.

Comparison of manager performance to the performance of a normal portfolio is more precise than a similar comparison to an index. The characteristics of an index vary considerably from those of a manager's portfolio. For instance, as of December 1993, financial service and utility stocks constituted 24% and 23% of the Russell Value index, respectively. These weightings were significantly higher than the universe of value managers, and considerably higher than either the Equity-Income fund or Value Equity fund, as seen in Exhibit 5. This means that the market's love or hate of the financial sector could cause our fund to under- or overperform. A normal portfolio will not have these extreme biases relative to the managed portfolio. We also note that we believe that significant outperformance of a normal portfolio is rare.[1]

To understand the potential for tracking error in the future, current risk exposures of the managed portfolios are compared to the risk profile of the performance target. In the Growth Equity fund, as seen above, there is a bias toward smaller-cap securities in the growth area. This is a deliberate exposure, as the sponsor has confidence in the managers and has not chosen to neutralize this bias with a completeness fund. Understanding this bias helps us understand the strong outperformance of the fund during periods when small-cap stocks were the big winners in the market.

---

[1] Measuring outperformance is a complex issue, and requires a chapter of its own. Two primary issues must be addressed. The first is that the alpha/noise ratio is usually too small to establish a statistically significant relationship. This is almost always true unless a manager's returns have an R2 above 0.95 with the style benchmark, which is rare. (For the mathematics, see H. Russell Fogler, "A Modern Theory of Security Analysis," *Journal of Portfolio Management* (Spring 1993), p. 11.) The second issue is that the returns from the style benchmark should be adjusted to reflect rebalancing costs, which should reflect true transactions costs. These costs are subject to estimation error, particularly for less liquid stocks.

Exhibit 5: Universe Economic Sectors
Price Driven Universe
December 31, 1993

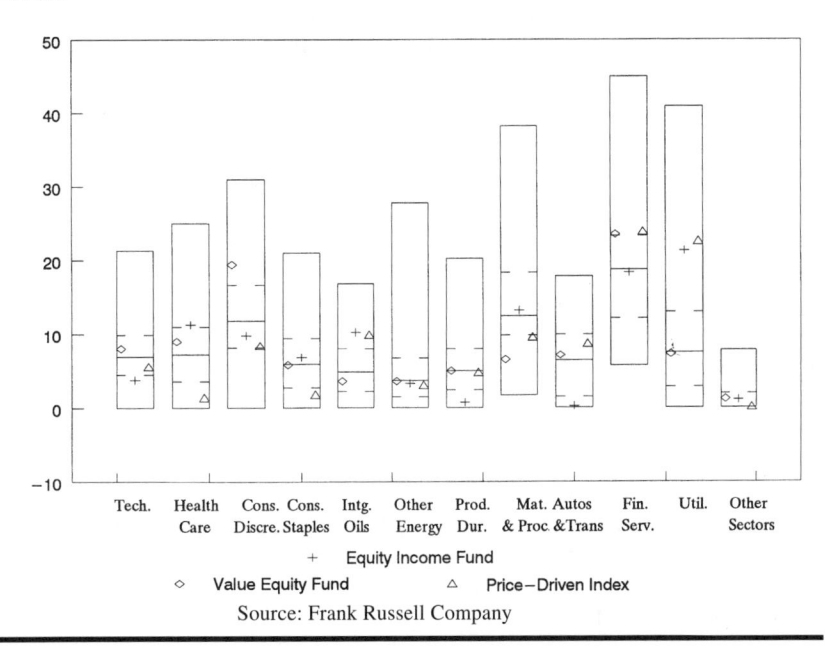

Percent of Portfolio

[Chart showing bar ranges for economic sectors: Tech., Health Care, Cons. Discre., Cons. Staples, Intg. Oils, Other Energy, Prod. Dur., Mat. & Proc., Autos & Trans, Fin. Serv., Util., Other Sectors]

+ Equity Income Fund
◊ Value Equity Fund
△ Price-Driven Index

Source: Frank Russell Company

While we have not seen significant changes in any manager's style, an analysis of the risk characteristics of an aggregate normal has exposed a drift in style of a fund over time. As new managers were introduced and the weighting of existing managers in the fund changed, the market cap of the fund dropped, and "variability in markets" increased. The misfit of the fund was increasing, so a new manager was added employing a large-cap style to correct this misfit. As a result, the fund is much closer in risk profile to its target benchmark, and the sponsor is confident that the tracking error has been reduced.

ALTERNATIVE FORMS OF STYLE ANALYSIS

Not all plan sponsors have the resources necessary to develop manager style analysis using normal portfolios. And while there is no substitute for sophisticated style analysis, there is a more user-friendly approach that we use as a check on our system and as a backup. This method is a combination of two types of analysis.

The first analysis examines the traditional portfolio characteristics of the managers, the fund, and the target index over time. These are readily available from the custodian in most cases. The plan sponsor can look at these characteristics (such as market cap, P/E, P/B, earnings growth) to determine the deviation and growth in deviation of the managers and the fund from the index. This gives insight into the current risk exposure of the fund, the change in this exposure over time, and the potential for tracking error in the future.

The second type of analysis is based on historical performance of the fund, and is commonly referred to as "style analysis." Several consultants provide this software, which may be installed in the plan sponsor's computer or network. The program produces a two-dimensional map with a range of large- to small-cap on one axis, and a range of value to growth emphasis on the other. The market cap and value/growth dimensions are defined by the user according to a selection of indexes, such as the Russell 1000 and 2000 Growth and Value indexes. Then, the fund, the target index, and individual manager's return histories are plotted according to optimal fit along these dimensions.

This analysis gives insight into performance similarity of managers and funds to the indexes over time, and rolling time periods may be used to see the migration of style over time. The style of a fund in its current composition can be seen by creating a composite of the managers currently in use at their current weights, indicating any adjustments made by the plan sponsor to better track the target of the fund.

These two analyses introduce the sponsor to equity style analysis, and may spark an interest in using normal portfolios at some future time.

CONCLUSION

We believe it is important to remember that most managers have an expertise in some niche of the market, and their performance should be analyzed relative to that niche. While the performance of each manager is important, it is vital that performance of an entire fund meet target expectations with very few negative surprises. The most rigorous approach to date involves the use of normal portfolios created for each manager and aggregated for each fund. The setup costs are high, but the detail of the resulting analysis makes it well worth the effort.

Chapter 16

Style Management: The Greatest Opportunity in Investments

Garry M. Allen, CFA
President and Chief Investment Officer
Virtus Capital Management, Inc.

INTRODUCTION

This chapter is written from the point-of-view of the plan sponsor, the consultant, and the investment advisor because all three are driven by style impacts. One of the overall themes of this chapter is that the greatest risk the plan sponsor, consultant, and investment advisor jointly face is the risk of the money manager being *out-of-favor* in the equity markets.

There are many traditional ways that risk is measured in the success or failure of a money manager — the variability or variance of returns, upside-downside capture, semi-standard deviations, and negative returns. However, the risk that overshadows and supersedes all of these — and is actually a composite of all these forms of risk — is the risk of being out-of-favor. This will ultimately cost the pension fund more real dollars than anything else. Style management is of critical importance to plan sponsors, consultants, and money managers because it confronts this out-of-favor risk directly. For the plan sponsor, style management represents an opportunity for both excess returns and risk control. For the consultant, style management is a mechanism by which below-median and out-of-favor managers can best be identified and controlled. For the money manager, style management represents a significant path to excess returns.

There are over 22,000 registered investment advisory firms in America — the last thing the investment world needs is "just another" growth manager, or "just another" value manager. Beating the S&P 500 has become such an effort that three out of every four money managers have failed going back across the last fifteen years. The number of mutual funds is now three times the number of stocks on the New York Stock Exchange. All of this leads to greater efficiency in the market and makes pure stock selection much more difficult — which is why so few money managers are in fact beating the S&P 500 over the last fifteen years. Clearly, the investment world is operating in reverse when the vast majority of investment advisors principally attempt stock selection to beat the highly efficient benchmark indexes. It has been demonstrated by a Nobel Laureate (William F. Sharpe) that style and size explain 80% to 90% of money management returns, while stock selection accounts for only the residual 10% to 20%.

The success of individual money managers operating within a single style investment philosophy is circular in nature because of the "style cyclicality" in the markets. Peer group comparisons are weak because they can compare an out-of-favor manager within an out-of-favor peer group style, without addressing its out-of-favor cause — style cyclicality. In reality, anything below median for a period of one to three years is a drag on the fund regardless of its peer group comparison and ranking. And more and more agitated plan sponsors are saying — "If you knew you were going out-of-favor, why didn't you tell me or change your style." The answer to this dilemma is pure style management.

STYLE EMPOWERS THE PLAN SPONSOR

The most powerful information any plan sponsor can know over a 1- to 3-year period (market cycle divided by style) is what style will be in favor. Armed with this, the plan sponsor can enhance, tilt, or move more aggressively to position the "aggregate" plan sponsor portfolio. Style knowledge and action would guard against the plan sponsors hiring a value or growth manager at the peak of their respective style cycles; it would lead to the proper tilt in the overall fund aggregate; and provide the greatest opportunity for consistent, above-median performance results.

Clearly, the most successful plan sponsors, manage the structure and the style focus of the fund; produce an excess return alpha from manager selection; and possess the ability to mix these components (especially manager selection) in such a way that the sum of the parts is greater than the whole. In fact, the value of these plan sponsors probably exceeds the value of the individual money managers.

In managing the structure and the aggregate portfolio of the pension fund, the plan sponsor becomes the ultimate asset manager in the form of selecting and mixing styles and managers. In fact, many investment experts believe it is harder to select a value-added money manager than it is to select a stock. With a stock you can evaluate the 10K, 10Q, annual reports, talk to company management, and look at competitive position. In selecting a money manager, even with the most exhaustive of due diligence, the propriety of the investment process is usually held back in some form for competitive reasons. Therefore, the tasks of plan sponsors are truly more difficult than that of money managers. This "veil of propriety" is another reason a large portion of the investment world is passively indexed. Money managers must provide the degree of confidence that plan sponsors need for the risk of hiring the investment firm. Unfortunately, if a plan sponsor avoids style management, it puts all the burden of excess returns on outstanding manager selection, which is extremely difficult to do in the aggregate. Over time, lack of success in this area can push the plan sponsor toward passive management. The plan sponsor needs a way to systematically get at the largest set of returns in the capital markets while paying the highest level of attention to the structure and aggregate risk control of the pension fund.

STYLE MANAGEMENT VERSUS STYLE NEUTRALITY

The systematic forces that move excess returns in the capital markets are style (as defined by value and growth) and size (as defined by large and small capitalization stocks). These are the giant forces that drive stock returns. Style management forms the basis for the strongest form of tilt and enhancement to the S&P 500, as well as the widest active path to the most significant of excess returns in the capital markets. Above all else, expertise in style management is the rarest of investment skills.

Style neutrality is not style management in its active form. It is neither pure style management nor style rotation when style forces are neutralized. Style neutrality is designed to offset the impacts of active style management. Style neutrality arises because of the plan sponsor's strong desire for risk control. However, risk control by itself is a very lonely objective. The skill of combining risk control and style management, with the complement of manager selection, is the highest form of skill for plan sponsors. Plan sponsors who neutralize the most powerful value-added style forces place the full weight of excess return of the pension fund on manager selection. Ironically, because of style cyclicality, picking a significant number of exceptional money managers on a very consistent value-added basis has proved to be the greatest challenge for plan sponsors and consultants. Style neutrality is a strategy by which the plan sponsor and/or consultant can add value at the manager selection level. In other words, style neutrality implies the question, "Can the plan sponsor and consultant produce a manager selection alpha determined by a manager's stock selection skill?" Without a manager selection alpha, style neutrality becomes a very expensive form of risk control, existing without the proper balance created from the excess return side of successful pension fund management.

Plan sponsors need more insights from their consultants. No manager search is complete without the inclusion of a style manager because style management represents the best combination of both value and growth. Style management offers a tremendous opportunistic core alternative. Style management goes back to the creation of value and growth as separate investment philosophies. However, style management now combines the rewards of both value and growth into an opportunistic investment philosophy.

The history of consulting has been to diversify each of the four corners of style — large value, large growth, small value, and small growth. However, the best constructed style portfolios already have diversification of sub-styles built into their investment process. In fact, the best decision a plan sponsor can make when a single style manager goes out-of-favor is to replace that manager with a full style manager, in order to bring back to the fund the diversification effect of stocks spread across all styles. Because style management represents so many different sub-styles, it takes the benefit of diversification to the highest level. This is a powerful risk control feature. Consultants need a way to avoid making individual manager recommendations that immediately go out-of-style. The consultant's due diligence process is one that looks at the money manager as a going investment concern. The consultant's due diligence process does not evaluate whether the individual money manager is about to move in-style or out-of-favor when recommendations are made to plan sponsors. This is the missing link between the plan sponsor and the consultant. Fortunately, it is the investment domain of the active style manager to fill this challenge in the pension fund. This is why style management aligns the critical needs of its three vested partners — the plan sponsor, the consultant, and the money manager — more than any other investment process or philosophy. No pension fund is complete without style management.

RISK CONTROL FOR STYLE MANAGEMENT

The following is a risk control checklist for plan sponsors and consultants as it relates to style management:

1. Captures turning points in style.
2. Reduces out-of-favor style risk.
3. Avoids below-median performance.
4. Diversification across sub-styles.
5. Improves style alignment and sponsor's management structure.

REASONS WHY PLAN SPONSORS SHOULD BE INVESTED WITH A STYLE MANAGER

Here are six reasons why plan sponsors should be invested with a style manager:

1. The efficiency of the markets with respect to individual stock selection.
2. Style drives the largest of systematic excess returns in the capital markets.
3. The capacity of style management to manage large amounts of money.
4. The ability of style management in a very low-risk way to add returns to the S&P 500 as an index while remaining principally passive.

5. Style drives the structure of the pension fund.
6. Style managers are more consistently in-favor than any other "single" style of manager.

REASONS WHY CONSULTANTS SHOULD BE INTERESTED IN STYLE MANAGEMENT

Following are four reasons why style management should be of interest to consultants:

1. Style management creates the opportunity for consultants to discover unique and differentiating solutions for plan sponsors.
2. Consultants have a high level of vested interest in style at the point in time where a manager recommendation occurs.
3. Style management creates the opportunity to better manage below-median results for the plan sponsor.
4. The opportunity for consultants to provide value-added recommendations to plan sponsors.

REASONS WHY PLAN SPONSORS MUST UNDERSTAND EQUITY STYLE MANAGEMENT

It is important for plan sponsors to achieve a high level of understanding of equity style management. The reasons are summarized below:

1. Style (value and growth) and size (large and small) represent two of the major components of systematic risk and return in the equity market.
2. Style dominates even the most skillful manager's returns.
3. Style movements are driven by the business cycle.
4. The lack of sponsor implementation of style management leads to excessive manager turnover because reasons for termination are miss-identified.
5. The exclusion of style in decision making minimizes the impact of manager hire/terminate/retain decisions.
6. Manager fees may be ineffectively and unproductively spent when manager returns are not related to style by plan sponsors.
7. Many skillful managers are terminated because style and skill are not separated. Conversely, managers in a timely style may be retained because style bias is not accounted for.

8. Avoiding style management ignores the plan sponsor's highest responsibility for strategic management of the structure of the total equity fund.
9. In the absence of style management, huge amounts of added value can be lost through faults in the structure of the pension fund.
10. The true level of active risk is identified when style risk and active risk are separated and accounted for.
11. Style management leads to a more sensible allocation of assets among a fund's top managers.
12. Style management positions the plan sponsor for a stronger management fee negotiation position.
13. Style management reduces the level of uncompensated risk in the plan, and thus improves the risk-reward trade off.
14. Style management identifies and captures greater rewards from truly active management.
15. Style management is among the richest sources of excess return in the marketplace.

STYLE MEGATRENDS FOR THE 21ST CENTURY

To this author, style management is truly the greatest opportunity in investments. Here are the reasons why I believe this is so:

1. Plan sponsors with the ability to pro-actively manage style within a pension fund surpass the value-added input of the most successful money management firms.
2. Style management begins to take assets away from Tactical Asset Allocation strategy for plan sponsors, who want an all equity-driven allocation strategy.
3. Style management provides the most successful tilt and enhancement strategy for index funds seeking an alternative to fully passive management.
4. Style cycles, rather than market cycles, provide the greatest information and insights into the style success of active management.
5. The strategic level of the pension fund is viewed as the area of greatest impact due to the contributions of style management in its purest form. No pension fund is complete without addressing style management.

Chapter 17

The Persistence of Equity Style Performance: Evidence from Mutual Fund Data

Ronald N. Kahn, Ph.D.
Director of Research
BARRA, Inc.

Andrew Rudd, Ph.D.
CEO
BARRA, Inc.

INTRODUCTION

The question of whether historical performance predicts future performance is central to investing. We recently published the results of a comprehensive study of this question in the *Financial Analysts Journal*.[1] Using style analysis, we analyzed the persistence of performance for equity and fixed income mutual funds. We explicitly accounted for survivorship bias, fees and expenses, and used multiple databases to minimize the incidence of data errors. We found no evidence for persistence of equity fund performance. We found some evidence of persistence of fixed income mutual fund performance; however, this persistence did not provide investors with a sufficient edge to overcome the average underperformance of these mutual funds.

Here we will update and extend the previous study for equity mutual funds along five lines of investigation. We will study a new time period. We will explicitly look at the issue of survivorship bias using this new time period. We will sharpen a

---

[1] Ronald N. Kahn and Andrew Rudd. "Does Historical Performance Predict Future Performance?" *Financial Analysts Journal* (November/December 1995), pp. 43-52.

blunt methodological tool, which tested whether above median funds remained above median, and now test whether top quartile funds persist. We will distinguish between fund persistence and manager persistence. And, to minimize reliance on style analysis, we will explicitly focus on just one type of fund, in this case, equity growth funds.

PREVIOUS RESEARCH

Many academics have investigated the persistence of performance, and their studies fall into two camps. Several studies have shown, based on different asset classes and different time periods, that performance does not persist. Jensen looked at the performance of 115 mutual funds over the period 1945-1964 and found no evidence for persistence.[2] Kritzman reached the same conclusion examining the 32 fixed income managers retained by AT&T for at least 10 years.[3] Dunn and Theisen found no evidence of persistence in 201 institutional portfolios from 1973 to 1982.[4] And Elton, Gruber, and Rentzler showed that performance did not persist for 51 publicly offered commodity funds from 1980 to 1988.[5]

Several other diverse studies, however, have found that performance does persist. Grinblatt and Titman found evidence of persistence in 157 mutual funds over the period 1975 to 1984.[6] Lehman and Modest report similar results looking at 130 mutual funds from 1968 to 1982.[7] In the U.K., Brown and Draper demonstrated evidence for persistence using data on 550 pension managers from 1981 to 1990.[8] Hendricks, Patel, and Zeckhauser documented persistence of performance in 165 equity mutual funds from 1974 to 1988.[9] Recently Goetzmann and Ibbotson showed evidence for persistence using 728 mutual funds over the period 1976 to 1988.[10]

In our previous study, after accounting for several effects which may have biased other studies, we found no evidence for persistence of performance

---

[2] M. Jensen, "The Performance of Mutual Funds in the Period 1945–1964," *Journal of Finance*, 23 (1968) pp. 389–416.
[3] M. Kritzman, "Can Bond Managers Perform Consistently?" *Journal of Portfolio Management*, 9 (1983), pp. 54–56.
[4] P. Dunn and R. Theisen, "How Consistently Do Active Managers Win?" *Journal of Portfolio Management*, 9 (1983), pp. 47–50.
[5] E. Elton, M. Gruber, and J. Rentzler, "The Performance of Publicly Offered Commodity Funds," *Financial Analysts Journal*, 46 (1990), pp. 23–30.
[6] M. Grinblatt and S. Titman, "The Evaluation of Mutual Fund Performance: An Analysis of Monthly Returns," Working Paper 13-86, *John E. Anderson Graduate School of Management*, University of California at Los Angeles (1988).
[7] B. Lehmann and D. Modest, "Mutual Fund Performance Evaluation: A Comparison of Benchmarks and Benchmark Comparisons," *Journal of Finance*, 21 (1987), pp. 233–265.
[8] G. Brown and P. Draper, "Consistency of U.K. Pension Fund Investment Performance," *University of Strath Clyde Department of Accounting and Finance*, Working Paper (1992).
[9] D. Hendricks, J. Patel, and R. Zeckhauser, "Hot Hands in Mutual Funds: Short-Run Persistence of Performance in Relative Performance, 1974–1988," *Journal of Finance* (March 1993), pp. 93–130.
[10] W. N. Goetzmann and R. Ibbotson, "Do Winners Repeat?" *Journal of Portfolio Management* (Winter 1994), pp. 9–18 .

for 300 equity funds from October 1988 through September 1994. We did however find evidence for persistence of performance for 195 bond funds from October 1991 through September 1994. Unfortunately, the persistence we found in bond fund returns was insufficient for an outperforming investment strategy: it could not overcome the average underperformance of bond mutual funds.

Further studies of this topic continue to generate mixed results. Looking at equity funds, Malkiel found evidence for persistence of performance in the 1970s disappearing in the 1980s.[11] However, Gruber, also looking at equity mutual funds from 1985-1994, found persistence so strong, he argued, as to explain the growth in active mutual funds. [12]

Now we will describe our methodology, summarize our previous results, and then present the new results.

PERFORMANCE MEASURES

We can measure mutual fund performance in several possible ways, including total or excess returns, risk-adjusted returns (alphas or selection returns), and information ratios (ratios of return to risk). We can extract alphas from excess returns through the following regression:

$$r_n(t) = \alpha_n + \beta_n \times r_B(t) + \varepsilon_n(t) \tag{1}$$

where $r_n(t)$ is the monthly excess return to the fund in month t, $r_B(t)$ is the monthly excess return to the benchmark, and α_n is the fund's estimated alpha. The information ratio is the annualized ratio of residual return to residual risk. In equation (1), it is the ratio of alpha to the standard deviation of $\varepsilon_n(t)$, annualized.

The past studies of performance persistence have mainly defined performance using total returns or alphas. Lehman and Modest have shown that the choice of benchmark can critically impact the resulting estimated alpha. Although the benchmark has a severe impact on individual fund alphas, it has somewhat less influence on fund performance rankings. In the context of arbitrage pricing theory models, Lehman and Modest emphasized the importance of knowing the appropriate risk and return benchmark.

STYLE ANALYSIS

We will look at performance using style analysis (as developed by Sharpe[13]) to extract both selection returns and information ratios. Selection (or style-adjusted)

---

[11] Malkiel, Burton G., "Returns from Investing in Equity Mutual Funds 1971-1991," *Journal of Finance* (June 1995), pp. 549-572.
[12] Gruber, Martin J., "Another Puzzle: The Growth in Actively Managed Mutual Funds," *Journal of Finance* (July 1996), pp. 783-810.
[13] William F. Sharpe, "Asset Allocation: Management Style and Performance Measurement," *Journal of Portfolio Management* (Winter 1992), pp. 7-19.

returns credit manager performance relative to a "style" benchmark. Generalizing on equation (1), we estimate selection returns using only the portfolio's returns, plus the returns to a set of style indices; formally,

$$r(t) = \sum w_j \cdot f_j(t) + \psi(t) \qquad (2)$$

where w_j is the portfolio's weight in style j. These weights define the style benchmark, and $\psi(t)$ is the return in excess of that benchmark. We estimate these weights and the selection returns, $\psi(t)$ using a quadratic program to minimize $Var[\psi(t)]$ subject to the constraints that the weights are positive and sum to 1.

For equity funds, the style indices include the S&P500/BARRA value and growth indexes, the S&P midcap 400/BARRA value and growth indexes, and the S&P small-cap 600 index, plus a Treasury bill index.

In contrast to alphas estimated via the unconstrained regression (equation (1)), which are uncorrelated (by mathematical construction) with the benchmark, selection returns estimated with constraints on style weights can contain remaining market exposures. The beta of the equity style benchmark is bound by the betas of the lowest and highest index betas.

The style weights define the style benchmark as a weighted average of the style indexes. For performance analysis, we estimate this style benchmark at time t, using returns in a 36- to 60-month trailing window (based on data availability), with a one month lag. Thus the style benchmark at time t is based on returns from

$$\{(t-2) \text{ to } (t-1), (t-3) \text{ to } (t-2), ..., (t-61) \text{ to } (t-60)\}$$

The selection return over the period from t to $(t+1)$ is then the portfolio return over that period minus the style benchmark return. This method for estimating the style benchmark insures an out-of-sample selection return, and the one-month lag, in principle, allows the manager to know the relevant benchmark before time t.

We believe selection returns as estimated above to be the best estimate currently available (using only returns data) of a "level playing field" on which to compare manager performance. This formulation is an embellishment of Jensen's original idea of controlling for market exposure before analyzing performance. Style analysis controls for several investment styles. Looking forward, the investor chooses an appropriate style benchmark for investment and then selects managers to exceed that benchmark.

In the context of style analysis, the information ratio is the ratio of selection return mean to standard deviation, annualized. If investors wish to maximize the risk adjusted selection returns defined in the standard mean/variance framework, $\alpha - \lambda \omega^2$, then they will always prefer the highest information ratio managers.[14] Looking forward, after choosing the style benchmark, investors will wish to select the managers with the highest information ratios.

Exhibit 1: Contingency Table

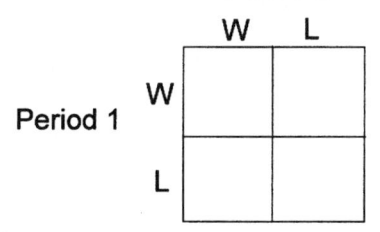

	Period 2	
	W	L
Period 1 W		
L		

METHODOLOGY

Our first test of persistence will use regression analysis, regressing period T performance against period $T-1$ performance.

$$\text{Performance }(T) = a + b \times \text{Performance }(T-1) + \varepsilon \qquad (3)$$

where "performance" can be cumulative total returns, cumulative selection returns, or information ratios. Positive estimates of the coefficient b with significant t-statistics are evidence of persistence: Period 1 performance contains useful information for predicting Period 2 performance.

We will also use contingency tables to analyze performance persistence. For contingency analysis, we sort the funds into winners and losers in period $T-1$, and winners and losers in period T. We distinguish winners from losers by ranking fund performance according to the performance measure of interest and defining the top half of the list as winners and the bottom half of the list as losers. Statistical evidence showing that winners in period 1 remain winners in period 2, helps prove the case for persistence of performance. The contingency tables show the numbers of funds that were winners in both periods, losers in both periods, winners then losers, and losers then winners. Exhibit 1 is an example of such a 2×2 contingency table. Later we will also use 4×4 contingency tables, with performance each period ranked into quartiles.

Because half the funds are winners and half are losers in each period by definition, if performance does not persist, the numbers in each bin should be equal. Evidence for persistence will be (statistically significantly) higher numbers in the diagonal bins (winners remaining winners and losers remaining losers). To analyze statistical significance we calculate:

$$\chi^2 = \sum \frac{(O_i - E_i)^2}{E_i} \qquad (4)$$

---

[14] For further justification of this point, see Richard C. Grinold and Ronald N. Kahn, *Active Portfolio Management* (Chicago: Probus Publishing, 1995).

where O_i is the observed number in each bin, and E_i is the expected number in each bin, and χ^2 follows a chi-square distribution with 1 degree of freedom in the case of a two-by-two table, and $(R-1)\times(C-1)$ degrees of freedom in an R by C contingency matrix.

In our original study, we looked at whether equity fund performance from October 1988 through September 1991 (Period 1 or "P1") persisted in the period from October 1991 through September 1994 ("P2"). Exhibit 2 displays all our results for equity mutual funds. The exhibit displays several test results for our three performance measures, for several particular studies. Each displayed test result includes a raw measure, a related statistic, and an estimate of statistical significance, with results highlighted if the statistical significance for persistence exceeds 95%.

For the contingency tables, the raw measure was the probability of winners remaining winners or top quartile performers remaining winners, the statistic was the χ^2 statistic, and the statistical significance was the probability that random data would generate a χ^2 statistic that large. For the regression analysis, the raw measure was the estimated slope (b coefficient), the statistic was the t-statistic, and the statistical significance was the probability that random data would generate a t-statistic that large in magnitude.

Our *Financial Analysts Journal* study looked just at persistence from Period 1 to Period 2 (the "FAJ study" in the exhibit), using two tests (the winners/losers contingency tables, or "W→W" in the exhibit; and the slope and t-statistic from the regression analysis). The results (but not the conclusions) in Exhibit 2 differ slightly from previously published numbers, due to some error corrections in the raw returns data.

Exhibit 2 shows that we found no statistically significant evidence (at the 95% confidence level) for the persistence of total returns, selection returns, or information ratios, using regression analysis and contingency tables. We do see significant contingency tables for total returns, but these identify mean reversion, not persistence. Period 1 winners had only a 41.3% chance of remaining winners in Period 2. Top quartile funds in Period 1 had only a 46.7% chance of being Period 2 winners.

THE NEW STUDY

We will now describe the results of several extensions to the previous study. We have extended our study to a third period from October 1994 through November 1995 (labeled "P3"). We have looked at evidence for persistence of performance from Period 2 of our previous study through Period 3 of the new study. Let's focus on tests based on regression analysis and two way (winner/loser) contingency tables.

Exhibit 2 includes these results in the study labeled "P2→P3 regular." Based on these tests, we see no evidence of persistence of performance from Period 2 to Period 3 for total returns, selection returns, or information ratios.

Exhibit 2: Equity Fund Results

Study		N	W→W χ^2 (p)	T→W χ^2 (p)	Slope t-stat (p)
Total Returns					
P1→P2	FAJ study	300	41.3% 9.01 (0.003)	46.7% 26.1 (0.002)	−0.037 −0.80 (0.427)
P2→P3	regular	291	53.1% 1.24 (0.265)	45.8% 23.89 (0.004)	0.074 1.55 (0.121)
P2→P3	inc. deceased funds	300	53.3% 1.33 (0.248)		
P1→P2	managers not funds	160	42.5% 3.60 (0.058)	50.0% 10.40 (0.319)	0.010 0.171 (0.865)
P1→P2	long tenure managers	95	42.6% 1.78 (0.182)	52.2% 10.64 (0.302)	0.054 0.68 (0.498)
P1→P2	equity growth funds	116	41.4% 3.45 (0.063)	41.4% 11.72 (0.229)	0.001 0.02 (0.984)
Selection Returns					
P1→P2	FAJ study	300	52.7% 0.85 (0.356)	52.0 13.81 (0.129)	0.068 1.07 (0.284)
P2→P3	regular	291	54.5% 2.50 (0.114)	50.0% 41.46 (0.001)	0.078 1.85 (0.066)
P2→P3	inc. deceased funds	300	54.0% 1.92 (0.166)		
P1→P2	managers	160	46.2% 0.90 (0.343)	50.0% 10.20 (0.335)	0.202 2.46 (0.015)
P1→P2	long tenure managers	95	55.3% 1.27 (0.259)	56.5% 11.13 (0.267)	0.299 2.87 (0.005)
P1→P2	growth funds	116	53.4% 0.55 (0.458)	51.7% 6.21 (0.719)	0.138 1.76 (0.080)

Exhibit 2 (Continued)

Study		N	W→W χ^2 (p)	T→W χ^2 (p)	Slope t-stat (p)
Information Ratios					
P1→P2	FAJ study	300	52.0% 0.48 (0.488)	50.7% 4.32 (0.889)	0.14 1.83 (0.069)
P2→P3	regular	291	51.0% 0.17 (0.682)	59.7% 18.12 (0.034)	0.010 0.08 (0.938)
P2→P3	inc. deceased funds	300	52.7 0.85 (0.356)		
P1→P2	managers not funds	160	48.8% 0.10 (0.752)	47.5% 3.00 (0.964)	0.107 1.30 (0.195)
P1→P2	long tenure managers	95	57.4% 2.37 (0.124)	56.5% 6.18 (0.722)	0.197 2.07 (0.041)
P1→P2	growth funds	116	51.7% 0.14 (0.710)	51.7% 5.10 (0.825)	0.142 1.44 (0.154)

Of the 300 equity funds previously studied, 291 survived through Period 3. When we looked at persistence of winner and losers from Period 2 to Period 3, we used data only from the surviving funds. To understand some of the implications of survivorship bias, we went back and redefined all deceased funds as losers in Period 3. Exhibit 2 labels these results as the "P2→P3 including deceased funds" study. Exhibit 2 shows that the equity contingency tables were all insignificant before and after this change.

Quartile Analysis

One criticism of our previous study was that it focused only on winners and losers — those in the top half of funds and those in the bottom half of funds. Since investors often focus on top quartile performers, we've extended our study to look at performance of different quartiles, and persistence of performance in quartiles, to see whether this more detailed analysis can find evidence of persistence.

To summarize our results, Exhibit 2 shows the probability of top quartile funds in one period being above median funds in the next period (labeled "T→W" in the tables), along with χ^2 statistics and probabilities of observing them with random data. Unfortunately the χ^2 test just looks for any deviations from random, whether the deviation implies persistence, mean reversion, or some other perverse pattern (e.g. second quartile moving to fourth quartile). To detect persistence, we will look for probabilities well above 50%, combined with significant χ^2 statistics.

Exhibit 3: Equity IR: Period 2-Period 3

		Period 3			
		Top	2	3	Bottom
Period 2	Top	23 / 31.9	20 / 27.8	12 / 16.7	17 / 23.6
	2	18 / 24.7	13 / 17.8	29 / 39.7	13 / 17.8
	3	12 / 16.4	22 / 30.1	18 / 24.7	21 / 28.8
	Bottom	19 / 26.0	18 / 24.7	14 / 19.2	22 / 30.1

Winner → Winner: 51%

Exhibit 4: Investment Implications: Equity IR

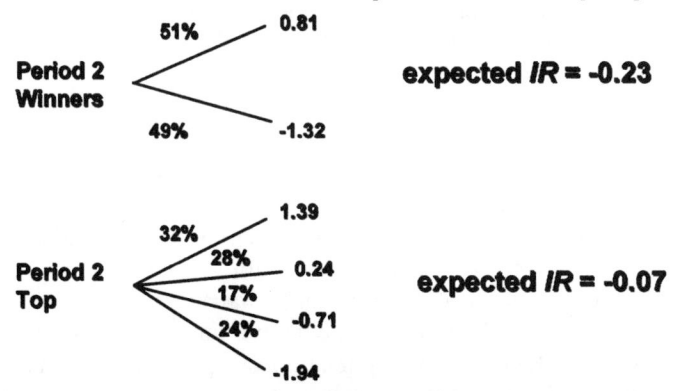

Period 2 Winners:
- 51% → 0.81
- 49% → -1.32

expected IR = -0.23

Period 2 Top:
- 32% → 1.39
- 28% → 0.24
- 17% → -0.71
- 24% → -1.94

expected IR = -0.07

There appears to be evidence of persistence in the quartile analysis for equity selection returns and information ratios from Period 2 to Period 3. The persistence among the equity funds was somewhat surprising. Exhibit 3 shows the results. For equity information ratios from Period 2 to Period 3, the probability of a winner remaining a winner, i.e. remaining in the top half of all funds, was 51%. However, the probability of that top quartile fund remaining in the top half in period two was 59.7%, an enhanced result.

We then looked at the investment implications, focusing on information ratios. We display the relevant data in Exhibit 4. Using quartile rankings improves investment performance, but not enough to rise above water. The investment strategy of betting on winners achieves an information ratio of –0.23. The investment strategy of betting on top quartile funds achieves an information ratio of –0.07.

Given the probability of a top quartile performer shifting into each of the four quartiles in the next period and the average information ratio in each of those quartiles, even this edge can't overcome the average underperformance.

Fund Persistence versus Manager Persistence

In our previous study, we looked effectively at fund persistence, not manager persistence. We did not screen funds based on whether they maintained the same manager over the entire time period. And, we didn't compile statistics on manager performance if they moved from one fund to another. To extend our study to look at manager persistence, we focused on Period 1 and Period 2 again and deleted all funds that changed managers over these periods. Since our analysis requires an extensive in-sample period to determine initial fund styles, we also studied the effect of requiring the same manager over Periods 1 and 2, and the in-sample period. For both studies, we used the Morningstar Database of manager tenure at the end of Period 2 to delete funds where the tenure didn't extend back at least to the beginning of Period 1 or the beginning of the in-sample period.

Exhibit 2 presents these results. The studies labeled "P1→P2, managers not funds" require the same manager over the two out-of-sample periods. The studies labeled "P1→P2, long tenure managers" require the same manager over the two out-of-sample periods as well as the in-sample period. For the equity funds the first restriction reduced us from 300 funds to 160 managers, and the second restriction reduced us further to 95 managers.

For the equity funds, we found only slight differences when looking at managers not funds. Focusing on the equity fund managers, we found only one significant result: the t-statistic from analyzing selection returns became significant. At the same time, the χ^2 statistic was insignificant.

Focusing on the long tenure equity managers, we see another increase in significance. We now see significant t-statistics for selection returns and information ratios. We still do not see any significant χ^2 statistics for the long tenure managers. Once again, part of the problem may be the small sample size. At the same time, our approach to focusing on long tenure managers may exacerbate survivorship bias problems. So we do not interpret these results as strong evidence for persistence.

EQUITY GROWTH FUNDS

Another criticism of our previous study was that we lumped together different types of equity funds, and, for example, compared value managers outperforming value benchmarks to growth managers outperforming growth benchmarks. Of course, this is one important use of style analysis. Still, to investigate such criticisms, we have extended the study to focus on just one particular fund group to minimize this effect. We looked at equity growth funds, choosing a large group of funds to help with the statistical analysis of the results. Once again, we looked at Period 1 to Period 2 persistence, and we deleted all equity funds, unless their objective according to Morningstar was growth. This left us with 116 funds. Exhibit 2 displays the results in the study labeled "P1→P2, growth funds."

We see no significant persistence anywhere for these growth funds. One could argue that growth funds focus on a relatively efficient part of the market, and we should look at small cap funds instead. However, there we may not have enough fund data for a statistically valid analysis.

PERSPECTIVE

How can we put all these results in perspective? These studies have focused on past performance and effectively looked at means and at aggregate performance of different groups. They show that historical analysis of returns alone cannot pick out the persistent winners. This is distinct from saying that there are no persistent winners. We have simply shown that a variety of quantitative screens of past returns cannot consistently separate the persistent winners from the lucky.

Here is another way to think about this. Imagine that there are two different populations in the world. There are persistent winners who consistently flip heads. And, then there are coin tossers who flip heads or tails at random, though with tails slightly more likely so that the probability of heads and tails is equal over the sum of these two populations.

We can then analyze persistence of coin toss ability on the total population. The persistent winners will always show persistence. Some of the coin tossers will show persistence and some won't. From the observed amount of persistence though, we can back out what fraction of our population are the persistent winners, even if no statistical screen can identify them precisely.

This isn't quite a perfect model of skillful active managers. Even the best managers can't outperform every single quarter. Still, we've applied this idea to the persistence results for equity information ratios. It appears that roughly 3% of all funds might be persistent winners. We're just not sure which funds those are.

CONCLUSION

We've extended our 1995 *Financial Analysts Journal* study of persistence of mutual fund performance. Focusing only on equity funds, our new results are consistent with those of the previous study. The past return history isn't enough to predict the future. There may be skillful and persistent managers out there, but it's hard to find them.

Chapter 18

Global Performance Evaluation and Equity Style: Introducing Portfolio Opportunity Distributions

Ron Surz
Managing Director
Roxbury Capital Management

INTRODUCTION

In this chapter, we bring together performance evaluation and international styles, two topics discussed by other authors in this book, to describe a breakthrough in the evaluation of global investment performance. By global investments, we mean both U.S. and non-U.S. markets. U.S. investors usually refer to the latter as international markets.

Because it determines the acceptability of past investment decisions, performance evaluation forms the cornerstone for change. Substantial sums of money are routinely re-allocated based on both "good" and "bad" performance evaluations. The ebb and flow of funds to investment management institutions can be traced primarily to performance evaluations, despite cautions by experts against relying strictly on the numbers. Aside from the costs involved in these moves from one manager to another, substantial evidence indicates that re-allocations frequently hurt performance. Too often assets are shifted in pursuit of the "hot dot" — last year's winner — without regard to the manager's style and the relevant opportunities available within the style.

So how do you really know if your investment manager is doing a good job? The answer to this question relies upon the answer to another question: "Relative to what?" The usual method of evaluating performance is to compare it with the performance of a stock market index such as the S&P 500 or the Europe, Australia, Far East (EAFE) index. For reasons described in this chapter, these indexes are not appropriate benchmarks and cannot be relied upon for evaluating investment performance. Similarly, comparisons with other portfolios can be highly misleading due to significant biases inherent in such "peer groups."

Proper performance evaluation requires an accurate and unbiased standard. Such a standard did not exist until recently. A new breakthrough called *Portfolio Opportunity Distributions* provides the proper way to evaluate management of any given portfolio, especially international portfolios. A Portfolio Opportunity Distribution combines the desirable aspects of peer groups with those of benchmarks while eliminating their undesirable properties. In this chapter we explain the problems with current performance evaluation approaches and examine how this innovative new approach overcomes these problems.

THE PROBLEMS WITH BENCHMARKS

Despite their common usage, market indexes are generally poor performance yardsticks. This is due to the fact that most managers adhere to a specific investment style, such as value or growth. These styles go in and out of favor, even over long time periods, as shown in Exhibit 1.

A given performance result can easily be judged as good or bad compared with the broad market merely because of a manager's style orientation. For example, a specialist in managing portfolios of small U.S. companies is at a distinct disadvantage over the time period shown in Exhibit 1, so a comparison with the broad market provides an unfair evaluation. The U.S. small company market segment, identified as small cap in the top panel of Exhibit 1, earned a mere 6.1% return per year, lagging the total market return of 14.1% by a significant margin; this underperformance occurred over a fairly long period of 10.5 years. However, this history of underperformance by a given segment of the market does not mean that this segment should be abandoned by investors. Quite the contrary, periods of underperformance are frequently followed by periods of outperformance. Also, enhanced diversification is achieved by combining uncorrelated asset groups such as those shown in Exhibit 2.

As can be seen in Exhibit 2, the small cap segments of the market are generally uncorrelated with their larger cap counterparts. Accordingly, they make good diversification partners for these counterparts. For example, the residual correlation of -0.393 between small growth and mid value says that returns on these two sectors tend to move in opposite directions relative to the market.

Exhibit 1: Style Return Summary
U.S. Style Results for January 1986 to June 1996 (10.5 Years)

	Return	Standard Deviation	Capitalization	P/E	Yield
Large					
Value	15.7	12.8	23.0	12.5	4.6
Core	13.6	14.3	25.5	17.9	2.8
Growth	13.9	16.6	19.3	25.4	1.8
Middle					
Value	15.3	15.3	1.8	12.0	4.1
Core	13.1	16.1	1.7	19.5	1.9
Growth	12.7	18.6	1.5	25.2	1.0
Small					
Value	12.6	18.7	0.1	13.2	2.6
Core	8.1	22.6	0.1	38.7	0.5
Growth	−3.6	24.0	0.1	−12.3	0.3
MARKET	14.1	14.8	14.1	19.0	2.9
Large Cap	14.6	14.0	22.3	17.1	3.2
Middle Cap	14.0	16.3	1.7	17.3	2.5
Small Cap	6.1	20.9	0.1	38.6	1.4
Value	15.4	13.4	14.9	12.3	4.3
Core	13.2	14.7	16.6	19.0	2.4
Growth	12.7	17.1	12.9	26.6	1.5

Non-U.S. Style Results for January 1992 to June 1996 (4.5 Years)

	$US Return	Local Return	Standard Deviation	Capitalization	P/E	Yield
Large						
Value	13.0	15.5	10.7	14.8	18.8	4.9
Core	9.0	7.8	10.7	18.3	36.5	1.8
Growth	4.3	2.4	20.2	29.0	128.9	0.8
Middle						
Value	14.4	16.8	11.3	1.9	17.9	4.1
Core	8.6	8.3	9.7	1.9	31.0	1.7
Growth	2.4	1.3	17.0	1.9	74.2	0.8
Small						
Value	14.2	17.3	12.6	0.2	13.7	5.5
Core	13.5	15.8	11.2	0.2	26.6	2.3
Growth	10.6	12.4	13.1	0.2	59.7	0.9
MARKET	8.8	8.8	10.3	14.0	61.2	2.4

Notes:
(1) See footnote 1 of text for style definitions.
(2) All results are based on quarterly data.
(3) Capitalization, P/E, and yield are calculated at the beginning of each quarter as the capitalization-weighted average across all stocks. Then cumulative measures are calculated as equal-weighted averages across time.
(4) Capitalization is price times shares outstanding in $billions. P/E is current price divided by trailing 12-month earnings. Yield is indicated dividend divided by current price.
(5) Cumulative periods shown are for the full history of the indexes.

Source: PPCA

Exhibit 2: Correlations of Market-Adjusted (Residual) Returns

U.S. Style Correlations for January 1986 to June 1996 (10.5 Years)

	Large			Middle			Small	
	Value	Core	Growth	Value	Core	Growth	Value	Core
Small								
Growth	–0.118	–0.106	0.196	–0.393	–0.182	0.484	–0.817	–0.077
Core	–0.444	–0.001	0.496	–0.579	0.064	0.579	–0.489	
Value	0.351	0.078	–0.444	0.673	0.116	–0.750		
Middle								
Growth	–0.519	–0.060	0.616	–0.922	–0.099			
Core	–0.315	0.386	0.126	–0.293				
Value	0.618	–0.092	–0.638					
Large								
Growth	–0.863	–0.081						
Core	–0.425							

Non-U.S. Correlations for January 1992 to June 1996 (4.5 Years)

	Large			Middle			Small	
	Value	Core	Growth	Value	Core	Growth	Value	Core
Small								
Growth	0.061	–0.455	–0.372	0.381	0.689	0.155	0.591	0.575
Core	0.730	–0.091	–0.886	0.904	0.659	–0.654	0.893	
Value	0.635	–0.155	–0.841	0.878	0.491	–0.552		
Middle								
Growth	–0.923	–0.131	0.788	–0.822	–0.065			
Core	0.181	–0.128	–0.454	0.433				
Value	0.895	–0.153	–0.967					
Large								
Growth	–0.920	0.090						
Core	–0.065							

Notes:
(1) See Footnote 1 of text for style definitions.
(2) All results are based on quarterly data.
(3) Cumulative periods shown are for the full history of the indexes.

Source: PPCA

A fairer and more accurate evaluation can be achieved by using custom benchmarks, designed to capture the essence of the investment approach. A practice that is gaining in popularity combines style benchmarks in proportion to the manager's history of effective style mix. As discussed elsewhere in this book, this practice is being applied globally. This results in a better benchmark, but still leaves the evaluator with the job of interpreting the difference between the benchmark and actual performance. The issue becomes one of significance: how much outperformance constitutes meaningful success? Several studies have shown that it takes a relatively long period of time, generally more than 10 years, to draw valid inferences of success or failure versus custom benchmarks. Of course, in many cases the management team has changed enough during this time to render the inferences invalid.

THE PROBLEMS WITH PEER GROUPS

Peer groups solve this waiting-time problem, but have a whole set of other problems. Comparing your portfolio's performance with that of other managed portfolios, such as a mutual fund database, is called a "peer group" comparison. Professional performance evaluators have used this approach for the past three decades. The idea is to give the manager a report card based on his or her ranking among competitors with the same style of management.

Critics of the peer group approach have documented various biases that render such evaluations meaningless. Three of these biases are classification, clientele, and survivorship. *Classification bias* results from the practice of forcing every manager into some pre-specified pigeonhole, such as growth or value. It is now commonly understood that many managers employ a blend of styles, so that pigeonhole classification can misrepresent the manager's actual style as well as that of peers.

Clientele biases result both from concentrations of certain fund types in databases, such as bank commingled funds, and from small sample size. International managers and socially responsible managers cannot be properly evaluated because there are no databases of adequate size. For example, one of the larger non-U.S. databases, the WM Universe, covers only $21 billion, which is less than 0.2% of the non-U.S. market. Also, manager search databases suffer from clientele biases because poorly performing managers withhold their data, and composites are often slanted toward better performance. Despite their valiant efforts to police data submissions, providers of manager-supplied databases ultimately must settle for the input they receive.

Survivorship bias causes performance results to be overstated because accounts that have been terminated are no longer in the database. This is the most documented and best understood source of peer group bias.

All these biases cause performance yardsticks based on peer groups to be unpredictably too long or too short, so that managers are frequently fired or retained for the wrong reasons.

PORTFOLIO OPPORTUNITY DISTRIBUTIONS

A new approach known as Portfolio Opportunity Distributions (PODs) eliminates these biases and, in so doing, creates a superior backdrop for performance evaluations. PODs harness together today's computing power with classical statistics to create all the possible portfolios a manager could conceivably hold following the manager's own unique decision processes.

The theory behind this innovation is based on the fact that, in common practice, the statistician constantly compares his or her results with those expected purely by chance. By applying this concept to performance evaluation, POD generates thousands of simulated, unmanaged portfolios at random, drawn from the manager's normal universe of stocks, using the manager's portfolio construction rules. This assures that the resulting opportunity distribution fairly reflects the manager's decision processes. For example, the average commitment to a stock, across all simulated portfolios, is the stock's weighting in the manager's normal universe.

The resulting distribution provides a grading system that shows the full range of results (or opportunities) that could have been achieved by the manager while eliminating the biases inherent to peer group universes. These PODs have a custom benchmark as their median, with fractiles around the median representing degrees of success or failure. A ranking in the top decile of a POD universe gives the statistician 90% confidence that the return was not merely random, but a significant indication of success. Similarly, a ranking in the bottom decile is a significant indicator of failure.

Evaluation against a POD universe tells the investor whether the observed performance result was good or bad relative to the unique opportunities available. As discussed earlier, no index, benchmark, or peer group universe can provide this insight. Further investigations into the reasons for success or failure — such as attribution analyses and manager interviews — can reveal the manager's level of skill.

POD universes can replace the need for peer groups and custom benchmarks. Valid inferences of success or failure can be made immediately, without bias — providing fairness, accuracy, and timeliness far superior to current approaches. Furthermore, the methodology has now been extended beyond U.S. borders so that superior evaluations can be achieved for international investment programs. This is particularly important because international investing is on the rise, creating a growing need for accurate performance evaluations that cannot be met by current approaches.

THE RESULTS

PODs are available through several service providers, including Effron, Ibbotson, Mobïus, Thomson, and Zephyr. Generally, POD universes are very similar to large managed universes when such universes exist. Because of survivorship biases, this similarity diminishes over longer time periods, with managed medians tending to exceed POD medians. When managed universes are small, as is the case with non-U.S. markets, PODs are materially different and substantially more accurate. This is especially true for international specialties such as Pacific Basin ex-Japan and Large Value. Also, after-tax PODs can be tailored to fit an investor's unique situation.

Ideally, PODs are constructed by carefully defining the manager's investment universe, decision rules, and portfolio construction processes. These are then used to computer-generate all possible portfolios. As a practical matter, these inputs are seldom available, so certain building blocks have been established to facilitate POD construction. Manager styles are defined as a mix of more than 200 market segments spanning the globe, as shown in Exhibit 3. Market segments are first defined by geography, such as U.S., Europe, or Japan. Then within each geographic region, nine style groups are based on size and orientation, such as large growth, small value, etc.[1] Industry groups are also created within regions, as shown in the bottom panel of Exhibit 3. Once a manager's style is defined in terms of these building blocks, a corresponding POD universe is generated. For example, we can create a universe unique to all of the opportunities available to a manager with the following style: 26% mid cap/value/U.S., 36% large cap/growth/Japan, and 38% World ex-Japan and U.S.

The middle, or median, of a POD universe is the manager's custom benchmark; it captures the manager's essence. The difference between the actual return and this median is the value added or subtracted by security selection and style rotation. The ranking within a POD universe is the significance of this value added or subtracted.

A real-life example is presented in Exhibit 4, which shows a POD-based evaluation for a real manager with a mandate of Pacific Basin ex-Japan who employs a small growth style. The exhibit shows EAFE as the risk/reward origin, along with all the opportunities available given the manager's mandate over the four and one half years ending June 30, 1996. The manager's performance exceeds EAFE by more than 25% per year, which is extraordinary. Exhibit 4 puts this outperformance into perspective by contrasting it with the opportunities available to the manager's mandate. As can be seen in the exhibit, the manager has delivered returns that are on the high side of both risk and reward. In other words, the manager has taken above-average risk within the mandate, and this risk has been rewarded. It can also be seen from the mandate's outperformance of EAFE and the upward slope of the POD opportunities that this has been a high risk/high reward mandate during the period evaluated. The manager ranks in the top third in terms of both risk and return; an acceptable result, but not the "home run" suggested by the comparison with the EAFE index.

---

[1] Style groupings are based on data provided by Compustat. Two security databases are used. The U.S. database covers more than 7,500 firms, with total capitalization exceeding $7 trillion. The non-U.S. database coverage exceeds 5,500 firms, 20 countries, and $9 trillion — substantially broader than EAFE. To construct style groupings, we first break the Compustat database for the region into size groups based on market capitalization, calculated by multiplying shares outstanding by price per share. Beginning with the largest capitalization company, we add companies until 60% of the entire capitalization of the region is covered. This group of stocks is then categorized as "large cap" (capitalization). For the U.S. region, this group currently comprises 240 stocks, all with capitalizations in excess of $6 billion. The second size group represents the next 35% of market capitalization and is called "mid-cap." Finally, the bottom 5% is called "small cap," or "mini cap." Then, within each size group, a further breakout is made on the basis of orientation. Value, core, and growth stock groupings within each size category are defined by establishing an aggressiveness measure. Aggressiveness is a proprietary measure that combines dividend yield and price/earnings ratio. The top 40% (by count) of stocks in aggressiveness are designated as "growth," while the bottom 40% are called "value," with the 20% in the middle falling into "core."

Exhibit 3: Regional Style and Industry Returns for the Year Ending 6/30/96

	Large			Middle			Small			
	Value	Core	Growth	Value	Core	Growth	Value	Core	Growth	TOTAL
Global	27.55	15.63	8.94	19.07	13.19	12.10	14.30	16.93	18.31	16.53
GLOxJPN	27.99	21.84	11.51	21.13	16.23	12.15	13.70	15.99	8.56	18.27
GLOexUK	29.82	15.13	8.19	18.87	12.23	12.00	14.47	12.86	17.41	16.53
GLOexUS	16.18	10.46	5.52	16.04	14.47	13.59	13.02	16.01	19.37	11.93
GxUS&JP	20.02	10.55	5.22	17.67	12.60	10.91	13.21	14.69	9.92	12.23
NorAmer	32.96	32.93	17.31	28.50	25.04	18.00	15.84	19.33	12.01	25.37
FarEast	14.18	6.22	8.60	14.19	9.87	18.23	21.08	24.16	34.03	12.46
EASxJPN	28.33	14.82	9.89	25.39	15.41	8.16	23.90	16.87	17.71	16.78
Europe	19.91	7.06	14.41	16.09	16.28	11.91	8.70	16.17	7.33	14.67
EURexUK	21.53	21.16	9.40	14.55	10.99	8.61	5.36	7.62	−1.73	13.67
EmrgMkt	15.61	16.48	−16.00	18.40	1.23	7.60	7.50	3.40	6.95	2.09
U S A	32.00	29.98	19.73	23.59	20.08	24.43	26.81	32.03	28.12	25.36
Japan	10.02	11.31	6.48	9.69	10.22	20.23	25.35	20.87	43.43	11.35
U K	7.88	23.92	15.65	16.13	27.88	20.52	13.69	22.43	24.90	16.51
Canada	19.78	12.93	17.67	14.87	17.50	12.05	12.77	6.55	21.22	16.05
Ireland	4.56	7.48	61.80	31.37	30.55	41.76	25.90	84.68	50.65	28.00
Austral	35.32	27.87	21.38	34.28	40.11	33.63	49.19	34.32	62.55	30.75
Germany	28.65	4.37	7.35	−3.76	4.37	0.81	−11.89	−9.78	−20.70	7.94
France	10.93	2.47	21.26	6.83	5.47	10.92	9.82	8.24	7.75	10.88
Switzld	24.35	33.31	23.25	7.88	9.82	18.39	1.60	2.88	−1.00	20.67
Nethrld	27.64	41.66	10.63	10.66	18.10	35.21	16.15	13.30	13.75	24.73
OthCtry	20.86	−18.77	−3.73	20.63	10.29	5.39	8.49	5.08	6.44	5.04

	Non-Dur	Durables	Mat&Ser	CapGds	Tech	Energy	Transpo	Utility	Finance	Total
Global	17.77	22.24	10.24	9.74	23.06	25.80	16.37	6.55	10.71	16.53
GLOxJPN	17.35	22.92	8.01	2.82	25.43	26.88	19.97	15.77	14.92	18.27
GLOexUK	18.14	22.37	9.85	9.35	24.03	25.85	15.83	6.49	9.55	16.53
GLOexUS	14.11	18.79	9.04	8.29	17.94	21.49	11.14	5.31	6.98	11.93
GxUS&JP	12.00	16.61	5.69	−1.20	22.53	23.48	11.36	18.17	9.75	12.23
NorAmer	22.94	31.20	14.02	23.33	26.51	28.96	30.75	11.38	29.41	25.37
FarEast	19.52	20.68	16.53	17.64	6.49	13.30	11.13	−10.40	7.67	12.46
EASxJPN	18.35	20.52	13.30	6.45	4.51	20.56	12.15	1.39	23.67	16.78
Europe	13.79	16.50	16.38	−1.15	21.67	23.55	11.65	14.11	12.05	14.67
EURexUK	12.99	15.08	18.14	−4.71	28.33	22.04	3.12	19.55	7.41	13.67
EmrgMkt	1.30	19.67	−22.99	−4.79	21.05	24.79	8.76	25.34	2.56	2.09
U S A	25.02	26.43	16.44	17.51	26.35	29.62	29.22	19.01	29.35	25.36
Japan	19.76	20.67	17.43	18.68	6.67	7.93	10.89	−12.88	3.36	11.35
U K	15.17	21.93	12.73	15.84	10.60	25.76	22.12	3.53	22.10	16.51
Canada	10.66	3.36	8.29	5.40	32.75	18.97	23.30	16.19	21.30	16.05
Ireland	30.12	47.41	18.34	82.32	80.76	57.60	0.00	0.00	20.63	28.00
Austral	28.06	30.44	30.46	39.95	60.82	25.94	18.83	41.26	34.70	30.75
Germany	−1.47	17.15	23.25	−5.00	16.18	−15.16	−10.95	7.56	−4.66	7.94
France	20.33	18.78	9.03	−6.54	24.97	14.84	11.67	5.33	−8.42	10.88
Switzld	11.56	19.17	36.56	−2.07	32.30	0.00	34.36	10.89	7.83	20.67
Nethrld	27.45	5.54	6.18	14.45	16.02	33.29	−3.17	0.00	26.80	24.73
OthCtry	3.45	12.70	−13.33	−4.47	23.07	11.46	6.56	28.54	5.41	5.04

Source: PPCA

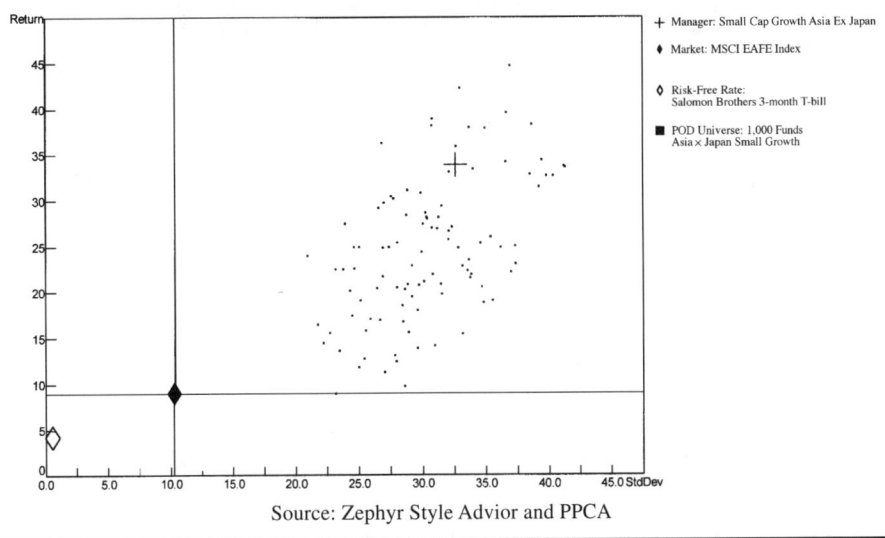

Exhibit 4: Risk-Return Analysis
March 1992-June 1996, 18-Quarter Window

+ Manager: Small Cap Growth Asia Ex Japan
♦ Market: MSCI EAFE Index
◊ Risk-Free Rate: Salomon Brothers 3-month T-bill
■ POD Universe: 1,000 Funds Asia × Japan Small Growth

Source: Zephyr Style Advior and PPCA

U.S. and international POD universes for the year ending June 30, 1996 are shown in Exhibit 5. Using the data presented here, you can rank your own performance within the appropriate universe. For example, let's say your international return is 12%. This puts you near the median for the total opportunity set available outside the United States (middle panel). But did your manager succeed or fail during the year? Inspection of the table shows that with a return of 12%, large growth managers would be considered a success, whereas large value managers would have failed. The bottom panel of Exhibit 5 can be used to further evaluate the currency component of your international return.

THE FUTURE

Performance evaluations can now be customized to capture the opportunities available with any blend of style management around the world. Accordingly, investors can know with confidence whether their managers have succeeded. This should result in superior global investment programs.

Exhibit 5: POD Universes for the Year Ending 6/30/96
U. S. Returns

	5th Percentile	Top Quartile	Median	Bottom Quartile	95th Percentile
Large					
Value	48.3	38.7	32.0	27.0	21.4
Core	41.2	33.7	30.0	26.1	17.7
Growth	30.8	25.1	19.7	15.8	7.7
Middle					
Value	38.1	28.6	23.6	19.0	11.3
Core	40.8	26.7	20.1	13.4	4.4
Growth	46.6	34.0	24.4	15.1	2.3
Small					
Value	57.1	36.4	26.8	20.8	10.0
Core	70.2	44.9	32.0	18.0	3.1
Growth	76.1	43.2	28.1	15.2	−0.3
TOTAL	42.1	30.6	25.4	19.8	8.2

Non-U.S. Returns in $U.S.

	5th Percentile	Top Quartile	Median	Bottom Quartile	95th Percentile
Large					
Value	24.8	20.3	16.2	13.1	8.0
Core	22.2	14.8	10.5	6.0	−2.6
Growth	16.2	9.9	5.5	1.1	−3.4
Middle					
Value	25.5	20.8	16.0	9.1	1.9
Core	26.4	18.0	14.5	10.4	6.3
Growth	26.1	16.7	13.6	7.2	1.7
Small					
Value	27.4	18.2	13.0	7.2	−1.0
Core	29.0	22.1	16.0	10.8	4.5
Growth	36.0	26.3	19.4	13.9	5.1
TOTAL	23.0	16.6	11.9	8.0	1.5

Non-U.S. Currency Returns (Exchange to $U.S.)

	5th Percentile	Top Quartile	Median	Bottom Quartile	95th Percentile
Large					
Value	−2.9	−4.0	−5.2	−5.9	−7.7
Core	−11.2	−13.2	−15.1	−16.7	−20.4
Growth	−20.6	−22.8	−26.5	−30.0	−34.6
Middle					
Value	−2.9	−4.2	−5.2	−6.5	−11.7
Core	−11.6	−13.9	−15.2	−17.1	−19.9
Growth	−18.6	−21.4	−23.8	−26.3	−30.2
Small					
Value	−1.0	−2.8	−3.7	−4.6	−7.6
Core	−4.1	−6.3	−7.8	−9.4	−11.5
Growth	−11.5	−14.8	−16.7	−18.7	−22.6
TOTAL	−11.1	−13.9	−15.8	−18.2	−22.3

Source: PPCA

Chapter 19

Value and Growth Index Derivatives

Joanne M. Hill, Ph.D.
Vice President
Goldman, Sachs & Co.

Maria E. Tsu
Research Associate
Goldman, Sachs & Co.

INTRODUCTION

On November 6, 1995 the Chicago Mercantile Exchange (CME) and Chicago Board Options Exchange (CBOE) began trading futures, futures options, and index options based on the *S&P 500/BARRA Value and Growth*[TM/SM] indexes. These indexes represent a division of the stocks in the S&P 500 index into two *equal* capitalization pieces, each representing a different "style." We expect the most significant benefit of these derivatives will arise from the ability to mesh them (in different weights) with each other, as well as with other index futures currently available, to obtain a more "finely-tuned" hedge or replication of actively managed portfolios.

Over the last few years many investors have categorized their investment management style into *value* or *growth*. These styles, along with size, are the primary dimensions used in determining the performance characteristics of U.S. equity portfolios. Indexes that categorize stocks by style have been used as performance benchmarks for active managers and mutual funds. They also serve as the basis for passive investment approaches.

© Copyright 1995 by Goldman Sachs.
Rochelle Sokol made a significant contribution to this chapter as editor and assisting in compiling the information herein. The authors would also like to thank Mark Zurack, Barbara Dunn, Mark Eisner, Kevin Foote, Rebecca Cheong, and Nish Shah of Equity Derivatives Research; and Ravi Singh and Kevin Boullianne of Goldman Sachs U.S. Portfolio Trading.

In May 1992, Standard & Poor's and BARRA introduced two style indexes: S&P 500/BARRA Value and S&P 500/BARRA Growth. The 500 stocks in the S&P 500 index were divided into two mutually exclusive groups, each representing 50% of the total market capitalization of the S&P 500. The composition of the style indexes is rebalanced semiannually on the last business day of December and June, with the changes pre-announced several weeks prior to the rebalance. As of the end of December 1995, the S&P 500/BARRA Value index (the *Value* index) contained 337 stocks, while the S&P 500/BARRA Growth index (the *Growth* index) had fewer companies (163) but about the same market value.

Several competing benchmarks exist in the style category, with each differing in the methodology used for dividing stocks according to style and in breadth of coverage. Value and Growth style indexes have been constructed on a few other indexes, including: Russell 1000 Value and Growth®, and Wilshire Top 750 Value and Growth.$^{TM/SM}$ These indexes are widely used by fund managers as benchmarks and for passive indexing, and also serve as benchmarks for investment management products.

While the underlying S&P 500/BARRA indexes have competition as benchmarks for style-based investing, they have the *best* characteristics for launching potentially successful derivatives products for two reasons. First, the S&P 500/BARRA style indexes are based on some of the most actively traded stocks in the U.S. market, to which a substantial amount of arbitrage capital has already been committed through the S&P 500 futures contract. Second, the sum of the dollar amount of the value and growth futures has been designed to be close to that of the S&P 500 futures. This means that dealers and market-makers can quickly facilitate demand for long or short style exposure via arbitrage trades or spread trades to S&P 500 futures.

The S&P 500/BARRA Value and Growth indexes have sufficient correlation with other style benchmarks and actively managed portfolios in order to provide incremental value as products for facilitating portfolio trades, hedging equity benchmark risk, or replicating benchmark exposure. Some combination of the value or growth futures with S&P 500 and S&P MidCap futures often provides a lower tracking error (higher correlation) to equity portfolios than can currently be achieved with the current mix of available futures contracts. There is also the possibility that the cost of trading for active managers with style "habitats" who use portfolio trading could be positively impacted by the availability of these instruments to dealers hedging their portfolio books.

This chapter reviews the characteristics of the indexes and their derivatives — including their performance, contract specifications, and factors affecting valuation. We also examine potential applications of futures and options. Case studies are provided based on widely held mutual funds and portfolios tilted toward growth and value fundamentals.

Performance Analysis

Even though the Value and Growth indexes are both market-cap, broad-based indexes like the S&P 500, they have had differences in performance from one another and from the S&P 500 that at times have been substantial. This contrasts with their volatility characteristics which, as we see later in this section, are very similar to those of the S&P 500.

Exhibit 1 shows a moving 12-month cumulative total return for the style indexes relative to the S&P 500 index. Note that the relative performance has moved in cycles at times lasting several years. There has been a tendency for the Value index to have the widest performance spread to the Growth index in poor equity markets, and the Growth index to perform better in sharply rising markets. Except for 1975 and 1976, the Growth index has gained more than the Value index in years when the indexes were up more than 20%. The annual return differentials relative to the S&P 500 have been primarily within a + or − 10% band. Relative to one another, the largest return differential between the Value and Growth indexes was over 20% in early 1977, and over 15% in mid-1990 and 1993.

On a calendar year basis, we see that the Value index has outperformed the Growth index in about half of the 21 years. Exhibit 2 shows performances for the S&P 500 and the Value and Growth components for individual years back to 1991. The best performing style index for each period is presented in italics. Most recently, the Growth index has been dominant, in part, due to its larger weight in technology and drug stocks.

Exhibit 1: S&P 500/BARRA Value and Growth Indexes - S&P 500: Monthly Rolling Annual Total Returns

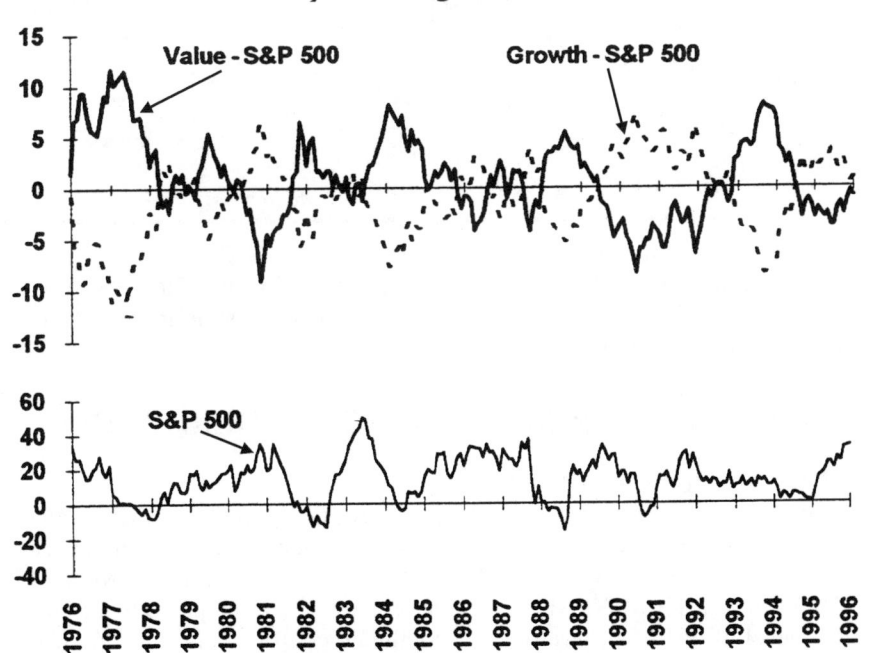

Exhibit 2: Total Returns by Year: Monthly Compounding

Period	S&P 500	S&P 500/BARRA Value	S&P 500/BARRA Growth
1995	37.58	37.00	*38.13*
1994	1.32	–0.64	*3.13*
1993	10.08	*18.60*	1.68
1992	7.64	*10.53*	5.09
1991	30.47	22.56	*38.37*

Exhibit 3: S&P 500/BARRA Value and Growth Indexes: Monthly Cumulative Returns

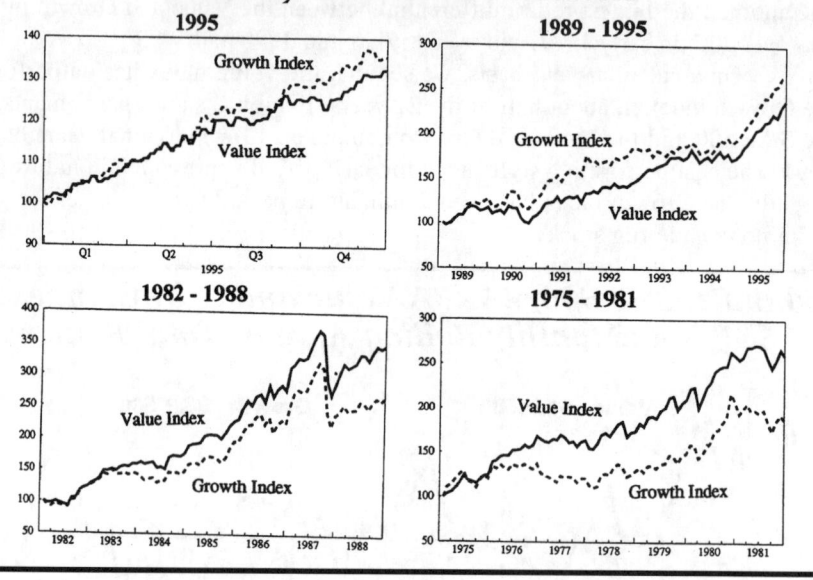

Exhibit 3 shows cumulative performance for 1995 and three 7-year periods. Where the Value index has clearly outperformed in the 1975-1988 period, the last seven years have seen a smaller spread between the style index returns with the Growth index a slight favorite.

FEATURES AND PRICING OF STYLE DERIVATIVES

Contract Specifications

As the contract specifications in Exhibit 4 show, the S&P 500/BARRA Value and Growth futures and options contracts have been constructed with similar features to those based on the S&P 500. The index values as of 2/12/96 were 345.84 (SVX) and 327.47 (SGX) which together equal 673.31 compared to an S&P 500 index level of 661.45. Therefore, the combined contract values of the two style indexes are close to that of the S&P 500.

Exhibit 4: Contract Specifications for S&P 500/BARRA Value and Growth Products

	Futures	Futures Options	Index Options
Exchange	CME	CME	CBOE
Ticker	SG (Growth) SU (Value)	SG (Growth) SU (Value)	SGX (Growth) SVX (Value)
Trading Hours (Chicago time)	8:30 A.M. - 3:15 P.M.	8:30 A.M. - 3:15 P.M.	8:30 A.M. - 3:15 P.M.
Contract Size/ Multiplier	$500 × Index	One Futures Contract	$100
Tick Size	0.05 index points (equiv. to $25)	0.05 index points (equiv. to $25)	$3 or less: 1/16 greater than $3: 1/8
Expiration Cycle	Four months in the March quarterly cycle	Four months in quarterly cycle and two nearest serial contract months	Up to three near-term plus (up to) three cycle months.

Price Limits*	Normal: O I IN M
	         3 6 10 15 Points
	 Expanded: O I IN1 IN2 M
	            3 6 10 15 25
		n/a	

GLOBEX	Available, Limit 6		
Expiration Day	Third Friday of the contract month at open.	Quarterly: same as futures Serial: Close of third Friday of contract month.	Third Friday of the month.
Exercise	n/a	American style	European
Regular Strike Intervals (Index Pts)	n/a	1st and 2nd mos. = 2.5 3rd and 4th mos. = 5	Will bracket the index in 2.5 point intervals.

* O: Open; I: Initial; IN: Intermediate; M: Maximum; Normal = Day of Initial Move; Expanded = Day After Limits Reached in First Day.

The way in which these indexes are constructed, reset to equal capitalization pieces every six months, produces a situation in which the index values *cannot* be made to sum *perfectly* to equal the S&P 500 index level. Therefore, traders arbitraging both pieces against the S&P 500 will have to use the ratio of the (Value + Growth indexes)/S&P 500 index to determine appropriate transactions sizes for each. Note that the futures and futures options position limits have been set based on combined net positions across *all* contracts derived from the S&P 500 index, including Value, Growth, and S&P 500 futures and futures options.

Price limits for Value and Growth futures are one-half of those for the S&P 500 futures, except for the opening price limit which is 3 points. This is designed to insure these contracts hit limits close to the time S&P 500 futures begin trading limit up or down. An intricate set of related price limit rules have been designed to coordinate price limits across S&P 500 and the associated Value and Growth index futures contracts. The goal is to insure the Value and Growth futures (1) do not trade with tighter or looser price limits than the S&P 500 futures, or (2) do not come off their limits while the S&P 500 futures are in a price limit period.

Options on the S&P 500/BARRA Value & Growth indexes will be traded as American futures options on the CME and European options on the CBOE. In both cases, the nearest four months and two subsequent end-of-quarter months will have options trading. The availability of the futures will help provide liquidity to the options market (and vice versa) because the futures can be used as a hedge by option market makers.

Futures Pricing and Activity

Average daily volume of style index futures may not serve as a good indicator of interest in these style index contracts, or of their potential liquidity. These futures may not have as natural a fit to "trading-oriented" accounts as do S&P 500 futures. Potential applications of style index futures are more conducive to sporadic trades of medium/large size than to a steady order flow as we see with S&P 500 futures. Open interest in these contracts is expected to be quite large relative to volume as is common in contracts whose activity is dominated by institutional interest in exposure management.

The key to understanding the pricing of S&P 500/BARRA style index futures is that the ease of arbitrage given the liquidity of the underlying stocks and opportunity to do spread trades with other S&P futures should enable large trading interests to be "digested" when they arise. Since the combination of these futures is roughly equivalent to the S&P 500 futures, there are two routes to take for arbitraging perceived deviations from fair value. This is shown in Exhibit 5.

The choice of "A" or "B" for a given misvaluation of S&P 500/BARRA Growth futures depends on the following factors:

1. The cost of trading the stocks (commission, market impact).
2. For dealers or market makers, the financing costs of carrying the stocks.
3. The cost of trading all three futures (commission and market impact).
4. The richness/cheapness of all three futures.

Exhibit 5: Two Arbitrage Strategies

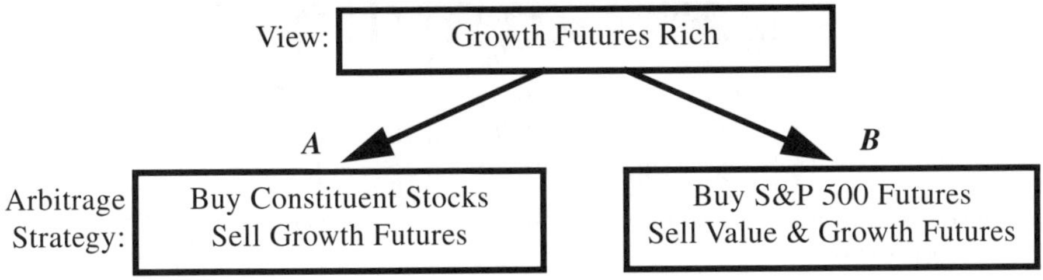

View: **Growth Futures Rich**

A — Arbitrage Strategy: Buy Constituent Stocks / Sell Growth Futures

B — Buy S&P 500 Futures / Sell Value & Growth Futures

We expect that arbitrageurs will monitor these factors on an ongoing basis to exploit trading opportunities. Financing costs and capital requirements can become important because dealers and upstairs market-makers engaged in arbitrage have a choice of buying stocks on margin or buying S&P 500 futures with an "embedded" financing cost.

In most circumstances the futures arbitrage (choice "B") should be the "cheaper" route from the standpoint of trading costs, use of capital, and trading efficiency since all pieces of the trade can be done on the CME floor. However, there will be circumstances where stock/futures arbitrage (choice "A") is more attractive. For example, if an investor is shifting a large amount of funds from a Growth to Value style via these futures, buying and selling pressure may cause the richness of the Growth future to be offset by cheapness in the Value future. Alternatively, richness of S&P 500 futures in a broad market rally may also make the pure futures arbitrage less economical.

Options Pricing and Volatility Patterns

Initially, we expect that there will be more interest in the style index futures than in the options; however, for option-based hedging or overwriting applications for actively managed portfolios, we should typically find a role for the Value and Growth indexes in the best mix of options contracts. In contrast to sector index options, these style options should be priced closer to broad-based index options because their volatilities are closer to those of S&P 500 options than to sector index options.

The pattern of historical volatility of the Growth and Value indexes has generally followed that of the S&P 500, with the Growth index moving at times to a 2-3% positive spread to the S&P 500 and the Value index volatility. Exhibit 6 shows recent volatility statistics based on daily data. Exhibit 7 shows moving 12-month volatility based on monthly total return data back to 1976.

With the Value index volatility closely tracking that of the S&P 500 index, we would expect the Value index options to trade at premiums close to those of S&P 500 options (as a percentage of index levels). Options on the Growth index should be a bit more expensive, even when historical volatilities are the same because of the potential for higher volatility in this index. Toward the end of 1995, the spread of Growth/Value volatility had dipped below 0 to around –0.5%.

Exhibit 6: Historical Volatility by Period* (Annualized)

Period	S&P 500	Value	Growth
1995	7.92	8.12	8.88
1994	10.01	10.28	10.35
1993	8.74	8.78	10.46
1991 - 1995	10.10	10.02	11.25

* One-year volatility for 1993-1995 is based on daily returns of cash index; 5-year volatility is based on monthly total returns.

Exhibit 7: S&P 500/BARRA Value, Growth, and S&P 500:12-Month Rolling Historical Volatility

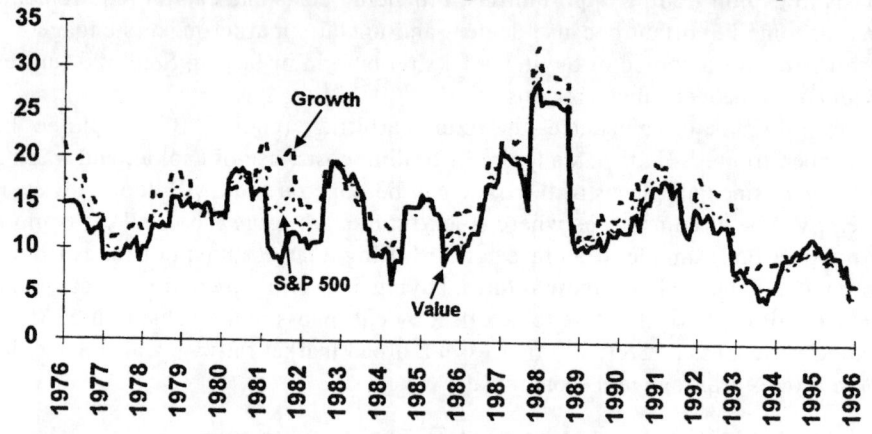

INDEX REBALANCING AND PLACEMENT OF S&P 500 ADDITIONS

The S&P 500/BARRA Value and Growth indexes are rebalanced semiannually to restore the indexes to a near 50/50 split of the S&P 500 market capitalization. The rebalancings are based on a sort of the *May 31* and the *November 30* BARRA Book-to-Price (B/P) exposure factors for each asset in the S&P 500. The changes are preannounced but are not implemented until *June 30* (using the May 31 sort) and *December 31* (using the November 30 sort).[1]

The BARRA B/P factors are normalized values of each stock's actual book-to-price ratio.[2] Once the factors are determined, the S&P 500 stocks are sorted by this factor in descending order. Starting at the top of the list, stocks are

---

[1] Specific dates for preannouncement of rebalancing have not yet been determined, but is expected to be early in June and December.

[2] Each stock's book-to-price ratio is first adjusted, if necessary, for FASB's Statement of Financial Accounting Standard #106 (SFAS106) and then normalized by subtracting the mean and dividing by the standard deviation of the book-to-price values for the BARRA universe of approximately 1,300 U.S. equities.

then selected to be in the Value index until its weight is just below 50% of the capitalization of the S&P 500 index. The remaining stocks are placed in the Growth index. The BARRA Book-to-Price factor for the last stock included in the Value index becomes the "cut-off" B/P factor. This cut-off value is important for the Value or Growth designation of any subsequent additions to the S&P 500.[3]

Another consequence of the semiannual rebalancing is that the dividend points and divisor for each index will change to reflect the new constituents and their aggregate capitalizations. However, even before each rebalancing occurs, all futures contracts with expirations beyond the effective date will have as their underlying instrument the "rebalanced" Value or Growth index. Thus, the futures may be a valuable way for S&P 500/BARRA Value or Growth fund managers to moderate the transaction/trading effects of the semiannual rebalancing.

PROFILE OF THE STYLE INDEXES

Exhibit 8 compares the capitalization, fundamental, and liquidity characteristics of the S&P 500/BARRA Value & Growth indexes to one another, to the S&P 500, and to the Russell 1000 Value and Growth indexes. We chose the Russell 1000 style indexes as a basis of comparison because of their wide use as benchmarks for passive and active money managers. The Russell 1000 style indexes differ from the S&P 500 style indexes in several respects, the most important of which are:

1. The Russell 1000 style indexes are divisions of an index of the *1,000* largest U.S.-domiciled stocks and therefore contain more medium-cap issues.
2. Their division of market capitalization into two style indexes is based on both book/price as in the S&P indexes, as well as prospective earnings growth.
3. The capitalization of several stocks are split between the Value and Growth indexes because they do not clearly fall in one category or another; therefore, the number of stocks across both Russell style indexes sums to more than 1000.

Capitalization Comparison

The S&P 500/BARRA style indexes differ in terms of the median and average size companies. The stocks in the Growth index are considerably larger in market-cap than those in the Value index (the average size Growth company is $14 billion versus about $7 billion for the average Value company). This large of a capitalization spread does not prevail in the Russell style indexes because there are a large number of growth companies among the smaller stocks in the Russell 1000 index

---

[3] For example, suppose a stock is added to the S&P 500 index in August. If its most recent B/P factor is *greater* than the May 31 cut-off factor, the stock is placed in the Value index, otherwise it would go into the Growth index.

which serve to balance the market-cap bias of growth stocks at the top end of the capitalization range. Both Russell style indexes have an average market-cap of around $5.5 billion. The impact of these size differences on return profiles is not as material because of the capitalization-weighting of both S&P 500 and Russell 1000 indexes.

Fundamentals

Since the objective of creating style indexes is to produce portfolios that differ in their fundamental orientation, it is significant to see how this is reflected in each index. We see clear differences in dividend yields and P/E ratios between the S&P 500/BARRA style indexes, in addition to the expected differences in Price/Book ratios. Note that the cap-weighted fundamental statistics for the Russell 1000 style indexes are very similar to those for the S&P 500 style indexes despite their differences in the size of the average stock. This helps to explain the close correlation (greater than 0.98) of their return patterns.

Exhibit 8: Style Index Characteristics

	S&P 500	S&P 500/BARRA		Russell 1000*	
		Value	Growth	Value	Growth
Number of Stocks	500	317	183	641	628
Market Capitalization *($Bil)*					
Total	4,309	2,115	2,194	2,366	2,425
Average Size Company	8.62	6.67	11.99	5.00	5.35
Median Size Company	4.50	3.95	5.64	2.31	2.19
% of Combined Mkt Cap	100	49.1	50.9	49.4	50.6
Dividend Yield (%)	2.40	3.04	1.80	3.16	1.49
P/E *(including neg. earnings)*	17.0	13.7	21.0	13.9	21.9
Price/Book	3.34	1.99	4.65	2.13	4.81
Average Share Price	47.62	44.97	50.49	42.87	45.17
Bid/Ask Spread *(basis pts)*	35	38	32	41	42
% Stocks Traded OTC	7.8	6.0	10.9	24.2	11.9
NYSE	91.0	92.4	88.5	71.9	87.7
% Mkt.Cap Traded OTC	6.4	2.8	9.9	4.7	15.9
NYSE	93.0	96.7	89.3	94.2	83.5
% Day's Vol to Trade $50m**	1.26	1.28	1.24	1.07	0.86

* Russell index capitalization and fundamental statistics from the Frank Russell Company; liquidity statistics calculated by Goldman Sachs & Co.
**$100 million for the S&P 500 basket; source: BARRA 9/30/95

Liquidity Measures
Both style components of the S&P 500 are quite liquid with bid/ask spreads under 40 basis points. The Growth index is a bit more liquid than the Value index, primarily due to its inclusion of a larger-cap group of S&P 500 stocks. Only a small percentage of the S&P 500/BARRA index stocks and market-cap trade in the OTC market; the Growth index includes larger percentages, but among these are several liquid technology issues including Microsoft and Intel. The Russell 1000 style indexes are somewhat less liquid with average bid/ask spreads just over 40 basis points and a larger percent of names and capitalization trading in the OTC market. The percent of a typical day's trading volume to trade a $50 million basket of each of the four style indexes is low at around 1%. (The higher percent for the S&P 500 style components is reflective of their smaller number of names.)

Overlap of Style Benchmarks
There is considerable overlap between the S&P 500/BARRA style indexes and those based on the Russell 1000 index, both in terms of market-cap and stocks represented. As of the end of September, some 74% of the Russell 1000 Value index market-cap was contained in the S&P 500/BARRA Value index with 11% in the Growth index; similarly 71% of the Russell 1000 Growth index market-cap was contained in the S&P 500/BARRA Growth index with 8% in the S&P Value counterpart. Exhibit 9 shows the overlap in number of stocks and market-cap between from the standpoint of the S&P 500 style indexes.

Note that for S&P 500 stocks where the full market-cap is carried in Russell Value or Growth, there is little difference in classification between the two indexes: only a handful of S&P Value names (0.49% of the S&P Value market-cap) are considered Growth names by Russell; and only five S&P Growth stocks (less than 1.4% of the market-cap) are classified as Value stocks by Russell. There is, however, a large portion (25%) of the S&P 500 index capitalization that ends up being split between the two Russell 1000 style indexes.

Exhibit 9: Overlap of Stocks and Market-Cap: S&P 500/BARRA vs. Russell 1000 Style Indexes

S&P 500/ BARRA	Total	Number of S&P Names in R1000				Percent of S&P Cap. in R1000			
		Value (only)	Growth (only)	In Both	Not In R1000	Value (only)	Growth (only)	In Both	Not In R1000
Value	317	184	4	92	37	67.8	0.4	23.8	8.0
Growth	183	5	113	55	10	1.4	62.2	27.0	9.4
S&P 500	500	189	117	147	47	34.6	31.3	25.4	8.7

In terms of number of names, 92 of the 317 S&P 500/BARRA Value stocks (24% of the market cap) have a split treatment according to Russell, and 55 of the 183 growth stocks or 27% of the market cap. Also, there are some 47 S&P 500 names (37 in the Value index and 10 in the Growth index) which are not represented at all in the Russell indexes; these represent approximately 8.0% and 9.4% of the respective S&P 500/BARRA style index capitalizations. This occurs because of different index inclusion criteria between the two indexes. Most of the divergence in coverage comes because of some large stocks in the S&P 500 index that are foreign-domiciled such as Royal Dutch, Unilever and Inco.

Industry Weightings and Largest Stocks

The sector/industry differences are illustrated in Exhibit 10. Again, the S&P 500/BARRA Growth index is dominated by the 53% weighting in Consumer Nondurables and 25% weighting in the Capital Goods sector which includes the technology-related industries. The Value index has a large weight in Financials (23%), Utilities (16%) and Energy (16%) stocks.

Exhibit 10: Breakdown on Sector Weights
S&P 500/BARRA Value Index

Sector	Percent
Financials	23
Utilities	16
Energy	16
Capital Goods	15
Consumer Non-durables	13
Basic	9
Consumer Durables	6
Transports	2

S&P 500/BARRA Growth Index

Sector	Percent
Consumer Non-durables	53
Capital Goods	25
Utilities	10
Basic	5
Financials	5
Consumer Durables	2

The following are the key industry differences among the S&P 500, S&P 500/BARRA style, and the Russell 1000 style indexes:

- The *largest* industries in the S&P 500/BARRA Value index include banks (11.75%), local telephone (7.26%), international oil (8.76%) and electric utilities (7.11%).
- The *largest* industries in the S&P 500/BARRA Growth index include pharmaceutical/drugs (13.59%), electronics (5.74%), computer software/services (7.49%) and long-distance telephone (9.15%).
- Compared to the S&P 500/BARRA Value index, the Russell 1000 Value index has *higher* weightings in telephone (+4.3%) and electric utilities (+2.4%) but *lower* weightings in international oil (−1.5%) and oil refining/distribution (−2.2%)
- The S&P 500/BARRA Value index draws its largest constituents from oil, telephone, and some cyclical stocks. The largest stocks in the S&P 500/BARRA Growth index are mostly consumer nondurables or technology-related companies.

Tracking Analysis

The potential usefulness of the S&P/BARRA style index futures and options will hinge, in part, on the ability of these indexes to better match the movements of portfolios that have either a value or growth orientation. One way to quantify the degree of co-movement between an index and a portfolio is to measure the "tracking error" between the two. Tracking error is the annualized standard deviation of the difference in weekly or monthly returns between the portfolio and the benchmark index. For example, a portfolio with a tracking error of 3.0% to the S&P 500 index, will have an annual return within + or − 3.0% of the S&P 500 annual return approximately two-thirds of the time.

Exhibit 11 provides the tracking errors and correlations between the S&P/BARRA Value and Growth Indexes and the S&P 500 index and the Russell 1000 style indexes. Both the BARRA model and the statistical results using weekly capital or monthly total returns are shown.

As shown, the tracking error between the S&P/BARRA Value Index and a S&P 500 portfolio ranges from 2.8-3.2%, depending on whether it is determined from the BARRA Risk Factors approach or a statistical analysis; the S&P/BARRA Growth Index tracks the S&P 500 portfolio by 2.7-3.0%. Tracking between the S&P/BARRA Value and Russell 1000 Value indexes is fairly tight, about 1.5%. The S&P/BARRA Growth index has a slightly higher tracking error to the Russell 1000 Growth index, ranging from 1.5-2.0%.[4]

---

[4] Note that the statistical results are based on the original Russell 1000 style indexes which were not recalculated to reflect the new methodology implemented as of the 6/30/95 rebalancing.

Exhibit 11: Tracking and Correlation Using S&P500/ BARRA Style Index Futures

S&P 500 Index	Value vs. S&P 500			Growth vs. S&P 500		
	BARRA	1-Year*	3-Year**	BARRA	1-Year*	3-Year**
Beta	1.01	0.88	0.88	0.91	0.89	0.83
Correlation	0.97	0.94	0.92	0.98	0.94	0.93
Tracking Error (%)	3.2	2.8	3.2	2.8	2.7	3.0

R1000 Style Index	Value vs. R1000 Value		Growth vs. R1000 Growth	
	BARRA	3-Year**	BARRA	3-Year**
Beta	0.97	0.96	1.02	1.0
Correlation	0.99	0.98	0.99	0.99
Tracking Error (%):	1.5	1.5	2.1	1.5

* Estimated statistically from one-year of weekly capital returns.
** Three years of monthly total returns.
Source: Frank Russell Co. and Standard & Poor's

Since the Russell 1000 Growth index covers many medium-cap stocks which are absent from the S&P 500/BARRA Growth indexes, we would expect a greater degree of cross-index trading risk. The Russell 1000 Growth index tracking error can be reduced by almost a full percentage to 1.11%, by constructing an optimal mix of S&P 500/BARRA Value index futures and S&P MidCap futures.

OVERVIEW OF INDEX APPLICATIONS

The basic applications of futures and options contracts on style indexes should be very similar to those of S&P 500 contracts except that they will deliver long or short returns on the portion of the index representing value- or growth-oriented stocks. Some of these applications include:

1. equitizing cash from dividend flows or other additions;
2. hedging equity exposure;
3. overlay asset mix management;
4. transitions from cash into portfolios via synthetic index funds;
5. overwriting equity holdings;
6. capturing upside exposure;
7. managing the risk of dealer portfolio and volatility books.

These applications can also be viewed in the context of different types of investors who might find them more flexible with style index futures included in their tool kit. These investors are:

- *passive managers* who have developed specific products designed to deliver the returns of style benchmarks;
- *asset allocators* interested in choosing a particular style tilt within an equity market based on an analysis of corporate and economic variables relative to market prices;
- *active managers* who will have more powerful and flexible tools to manage their risk and cash flows via these derivatives; *long/short* equity managers can use these futures to offset style mismatches between their long and short equity holdings;
- *pension funds and foundations* who can more easily manage their style exposure independent of the selection of external equity managers; they can maintain a style mix while transitions or cash flows are occurring that would otherwise disrupt the equity asset strategy mix and "fine-tune" hedging strategies to their mix of stock managers and their respective holdings;
- *portfolio traders* can better hedge their positions and thus may pass some of the benefits of risk reduction to investment managers in the form of trading cost savings; and
- *relative value or sector investors* who now have expanded choices for futures spread trades based on technical or fundamental views. Each index has its mix of industry tilts so that traders will be able to indirectly capitalize on outperformance of one industry versus another, e.g. technology or banks, via style futures.

We expect most applications of style index futures and options will be for style index funds, style "overlay" management, or for active managers as a component of a hedge or cash equivalent that includes S&P 500 and perhaps S&P MidCap derivatives as well. Much of the potential of these new tools comes from being able to select weighting schemes and thereby construct customized combinations that track an investor's target portfolio better than S&P 500 futures alone.

Customizing Mixes of Derivatives for Active and Passive Portfolios

To illustrate some applications of these index futures and options, we show below a general example and then some case studies in the next section. First, consider the limited range of choices, with only derivatives based on S&P 500 and S&P MidCap indexes for broad-based portfolio risk management applications. The columns in Exhibit 12 are drawn to scale to represent these tools in proportion to their relative market capitalization. As an example, we show how they can be combined to form a synthetic portfolio that tracks the returns of the Russell 1000 benchmark with a mix of 86% S&P 500 futures options and 15% S&P MidCap futures options.

Exhibit 12: Tool Kit without S&P 500/BARRA Style Derivatives

RUS 1000
- MidCap 14.8%
- S&P500 86.0%
- S&PMidCap

Exhibit 13: Tool Kit with S&P 500/BARRA Style Derivatives

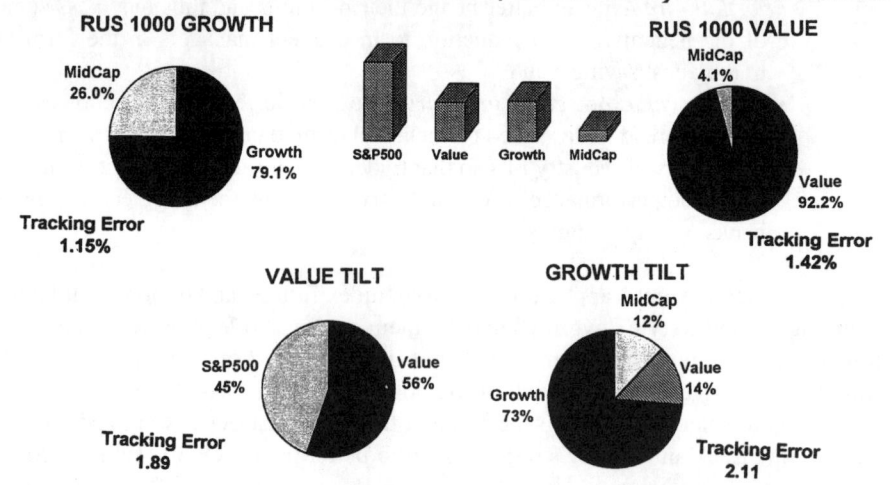

RUS 1000 GROWTH
- MidCap 26.0%
- Growth 79.1%
- Tracking Error 1.15%

RUS 1000 VALUE
- MidCap 4.1%
- Value 92.2%
- Tracking Error 1.42%

S&P500, Value, Growth, MidCap

VALUE TILT
- S&P500 45%
- Value 56%
- Tracking Error 1.89

GROWTH TILT
- MidCap 12%
- Value 14%
- Growth 73%
- Tracking Error 2.11

* Based on 100-stock portfolio with S&P 500 tracking errors of 2.58% (value tilt) to S&P 500 and 2.76% (growth tilt) to S&P 500; see Exhibit 14 for more details.

When we add S&P 500/BARRA Value and Growth derivatives to our tool kit, we now have four indexes to choose from for designing synthetic positions to track or hedge a particular investment portfolio. Similar to the diagram in Exhibit 12, each index shown in Exhibit 13 is represented by a column drawn in proportion to its market capitalization. We now use these indexes proportionally to replicate four different investment strategies:

1. A Russell 1000 Value index fund;
2. A hypothetical portfolio favoring value stocks;
3. A hypothetical portfolio favoring growth stocks;
4. A Russell 1000 Growth index fund.

Note how important the S&P 500/BARRA Value and Growth indexes are to the passive Russell 1000 style funds. Because the Russell indexes go more deeply into the capitalization range, it is not surprising that some S&P MidCap futures would be used as well in replicating the Russell style indexes with futures. These are more important in the Russell 1000 Growth fund where there are more growth-oriented companies represented in the medium-capitalization range.

We would expect actively managed portfolios with a value or growth style bias to track mixes of futures or options similar to those shown in the diagram as value and growth "tilt" funds. S&P 500 futures can typically be used as a component of the best mix of derivatives because it would be unusual to see large-cap managers restrict themselves only to the universe of stocks represented within each of the style indexes. Usually two mixes have similar tracking error — one with S&P 500 and a style future, and another with both style index futures. At times S&P MidCap futures also come into the potential mix. The choice between the two alternatives will depend on liquidity and futures pricing of the mix containing S&P 500 futures versus the one containing the two style indexes only.

The key here is that the balance of Value and Growth can be modestly shifted away from the "forced" 50/50 balance embedded in S&P 500 futures, or moved more aggressively to a style posture. This is illustrated in the value and growth tilt portfolios in Exhibit 13.

The value tilt mix would be typical for most value managers who define themselves as having a greater *preference* for value-oriented companies than the S&P 500 index (which by definition has a 50/50 split here between value and growth). Similarly, so-called "growth" managers may find a mix that looks something like the one shown for the growth-tilt portfolio, with some S&P MidCap futures or options included, but the highest weight accorded to the Growth index futures.

Applications in Derivative Strategies, Portfolio Trading, and Pension Funds

Many managers offer investment strategies in which S&P 500 futures are a key component. These include overlay asset allocators, enhanced index funds, and long/short managers. Pension funds and mutual funds also use S&P 500 futures to equitize cash to maintain target equity exposure levels. Often temporary positions in futures are moved into stocks via an exchange-for-physical (EFP) transaction. These enhancement or overlay style asset allocation strategies can be implemented with these futures, assuming the fund manager has a strategic or tactical view on target weights for the value and growth components of the funds. A few money managers have products in place for tactical style allocation which can now be managed more efficiently with futures (and options) to execute or facilitate style shifts.

Some pension funds think of their U.S. equity exposure in "style" terms and target specific amounts of money to each component. From time-to-time they may switch from one to another, or may be in the process of replacing a manager in one category. These are occasions when the opportunity to shift funds or maintain temporary positions via the style futures will be handy. Alternatively new fund contributions are allocated to a style category and a multi-manager portfolio trade is the means to fund the managers with stock; to facilitate such trades, portfolio traders at dealers would also use style index futures to hedge their risk. By paying a lower cost to acquire the desired stocks, the pension fund should benefit from the fact that the portfolio trader can maintain a lower risk profile by using some component of style futures.

Options on the S&P 500 style indexes can help in customizing hedging or overwriting strategies to the stock portfolios of value or growth managers. Similar to S&P 500 index options, style index options can aid in designing payoff patterns that best conform to a market view or relative preferences for upside versus downside performance. Also, if a pension plan wishes to engage in overwriting or hedging across their aggregate equity exposure, the mix of options can reflect any value or growth manager bias the fund may have in these aggregate U.S. equity holdings.

CASE STUDIES: STYLE TILT PORTFOLIO AND MUTUAL FUNDS

The most significant aspect of the introduction of the S&P 500/BARRA Value and Growth futures and options is the potential these indexes have to provide a better fit to portfolios with either a value or growth orientation.

Optimal Hedge for Value and Growth Tilt Portfolios

To further illustrate how a *quantitative equity manager* might use these derivatives, we built two 100 stock portfolios using the BARRA optimizer, designed to track the S&P 500 with tracking error of less than 3%. These portfolios are shown in Exhibit 14. For each of these portfolios, we assigned an alpha to several BARRA factors that we commonly find overweighted in portfolios of managers identified as fitting into value and growth categories. We then found the best hedge for these portfolios from S&P 500, MidCap, Value and Growth index futures that trade at the CME.

Note that in each case a combination that included a heavy component of Value and Growth futures reduced tracking error to the S&P 500 substantially, suggesting these would be better alternatives for equitizing cash or facilitating portfolio trades for these particular portfolios.

In both cases tracking error is reduced by approximately 25% by allocating some portion of the position to Value or Growth futures. The size of the portfolio and liquidity of the futures will determine how large a role they can play in all of the above applications. However, since these futures can be easily arbitraged, hidden liquidity should appear when trading interest emerges.

Exhibit 14: Tracking Error of Style-Tilt Portfolios

	TrkErr S&P 500	Trk Err to Mix	S&P 500 Wgt	Value Wgt	Growth Wgt	MidCap Wgt
Value Tilt Portfolio	2.58%		98%			
Mix 1		1.89%	45%	56%		
Mix 2		1.86%		75%	21%	5%
Growth Tilt Portfolio	2.76%		102%			
Mix 1		2.21%	44%		55%	
Mix 2		2.11%		14%	73%	12%

Source: BARRA 9/29/95

Exhibit 15: Correlation Coefficients*
Value (Income & Growth) Oriented Mutual Funds

Mutual Fund	S&P 500 Index	Value	Growth
Income Fund of America	0.80	0.81	0.71
Fidelity Equity & Income	0.93	0.96	0.81
Fidelity Equity & Income II	0.81	0.81	0.73
Capital Income Builder	0.82	0.82	0.73
T. Rowe Price Equity-Income	0.92	0.94	0.82
Invesco Industrial Income	0.88	0.83	0.84

Growth Oriented Mutual Funds

Mutual Fund	S&P 500 Index	Value	Growth
Fidelity Magellan	0.90	0.87	0.82
Fidelity Contrafund	0.85	0.82	0.80
Growth Fund of America	0.90	0.82	0.88
Fidelity Blue Chip Growth	0.87	0.78	0.86
AIM Weingarten A	0.88	0.73	0.91
IDS New Dimensions A	0.91	0.81	0.90

* Based on monthly returns 1/91 to 8/95; Source: Strategic Insight.

Mutual Fund Applications

Exhibit 15 provides an illustration of how these tools may be used by mutual fund managers for equitizing cash or hedging applications. To select candidates for a more detailed case study, we first examined the correlation of several U.S. equity mutual funds. These funds have either "Growth" or "Income & Growth" as their stated investment objective with indexes on which futures are based. The correlations are based on monthly total returns for each fund from 1/91 to 8/95 versus the total returns for the S&P 500 and S&P 500/BARRA Value and Growth indexes.

For the value-type funds, the S&P 500/BARRA Value index provides the highest correlation for all funds in the sample except two, the Fidelity Equity & Income II fund and Invesco Industrial Income fund which had return patterns related closer to the S&P 500 index. Most of the growth-oriented funds, however, were more highly correlated to the S&P 500 index. However, the AIM Weingarten A fund did show a higher correlation to the S&P 500/BARRA Growth fund. Although the Fidelity Blue Chip Growth and the IDS New Dimensions fund showed comparable correlation to the Growth index and to the S&P 500 index.

Correlations against a single index, however, do not demonstrate the potential advantage of using the S&P 500/BARRA Value and Growth indexes with different weights in combination with each other, or with the S&P 500 index. Thus, a more detailed analysis is provided for one of the value funds (the Fidelity Equity Income fund) and one of the growth funds (the IDS New Dimensions A fund).

Value-Type Fund

Exhibit 16 provides the tracking error analysis for the Fidelity Equity Income fund versus the S&P 500, Value, Growth, MidCap and various combinations of these indexes. Tracking error results are shown from the BARRA U.S. Equity Model analysis of the fund's U.S. common equity holdings as of the 7/31/95 semiannual report. The BARRA analysis is based on a single snapshot of the fund's holdings; we also show statistical tracking error based on the best mix estimated from the fund's historical total return pattern.

Exhibit 16: Example Best Hedge Analysis: Fidelity Equity Income Fund

Index Combinations	BARRA Index Weight %				BARRA Tr Err (%)*	Statistical Tr Err (%)**
	S&P 500	Value	Growth	MidCap		
S&P500 only	100				2.72	3.35
S&P500 and MidCap	85			14	2.62	3.22
Value only	102				2.83	2.50
S&P500 and Value	48	53			2.27	2.38
Value and Growth		75	27		2.27	2.38
Value and MidCap		83		19	2.61	2.00
S&P500, Value, MidCap	47	46		9	2.22	1.96
Value, Growth, MidCap		69	24	9	2.22	1.96

* Based on BARRA U.S. Equity Model (as of 1/31/96) analysis of the U.S. equity holdings of FEI as of 7/31/95.
** Based on monthly total returns, 1/91 - 8/95. Source: Strategic Insight.

The best index combination using only S&P 500 and S&P Midcap futures would be an 85% S&P 500/14% MidCap mix with a tracking error of 2.62%. Alternatively, using Value index futures alone provides comparable tracking error of 2.83%. An even lower tracking error of 2.27% is achieved by combining 48% S&P 500 with 53% Value index futures or combining 75% Value with 27% Growth. Finally, a mix of three indexes gives a tracking error of 2.22%.

Based on these results and considering the low liquidity in the S&P MidCap futures, using a 48%/53% mix of S&P 500 and Value index futures would provide a reduction in tracking error but with the liquidity advantage of the S&P 500 futures.

Growth-Type Fund

Exhibit 17 provides the tracking error analysis for the IDS New Dimensions Fund versus the S&P 500, Value, Growth, MidCap and various combinations of these indexes. The tracking error results are shown from the BARRA U.S. Equity Model analysis of the fund's U.S. common equity holdings as of the 3/31/95 semiannual report. Statistical tracking error is also provided based on the fund's historical monthly total returns since 1991.

The best index combination using only S&P 500 and S&P Midcap futures is an 81% S&P 500/32% Midcap mix with a tracking error of 4.13%. Alternatively, using Growth index futures *alone* provides a somewhat higher tracking error of 4.63%. Combining S&P 500 with Growth index futures or Value and Growth Index futures reduces tracking error to 4.26%. Finally, a mix of three indexes reduces tracking error to 3.74%. The statistical results show a comparable degree of tracking error reduction.

Exhibit 17: Example Best Hedge Analysis: IDS New Dimensions Fund

Index Combinations	BARRA Index Weight %				BARRA Tr Err (%)*	Statistical Tr Err (%)**
	S&P 500	Value	Growth	MidCap		
S&P500 only	114				4.49	5.29
MidCap only				104	5.84	3.61
S&P500 and MidCap	81			32	4.13	3.28
Growth Index only			105		4.63	5.35
S&P500 and Growth	64		47		4.26	5.02
Value and Growth		32	79		4.26	5.02
Growth and MidCap			68	42	3.75	3.16
S&P500, Growth, MidCap	13		59	38	3.74	3.15
Value, Growth, MidCap		7	65	38	3.74	3.15

* Based on BARRA U.S. Equity Model (as of 1/31/96) analysis of the U.S. equity holdings of IDS NDF as of 3/31/95.
** Based on monthly total returns, 1/91 - 8/95. Source: Strategic Insight.

Chapter 20

Is Equity Style Management Worth the Effort?: Some Critical Issues for Plan Sponsors

Charles Trzcinka, Ph.D.
Professor of Finance
State University of New York at Buffalo

INTRODUCTION

As the previous chapters document, the use of equity style management is now well established in the money management business. Pension fund sponsors demand that managers identify their "investment style" and consultants are designing ever more sophisticated methods of determining the "true" investment style of managers. The source of these efforts is a belief that measuring and monitoring style improves the portfolios of sponsors. In Chapter 5, Richard Roll shows that there seems to be an extra return per unit of risk for paying attention to style, if risk measures meet certain technical requirements. But is it worth the cost trying to find this extra return? Forcing money managers into investment styles or allocating money based on investment style can have significant costs in terms of total performance. A manager who is forced into a style will not invest in certain securities and any constraint on the selection of securities can result in sub-optimal performance, that is, lower returns or higher risk. Furthermore, even if style manager earns extra returns on average, not all money managers will achieve the style's excess returns. This means that a sponsor must spend resources on monitoring the style of managers. Thus, before style investing is adopted the costs and benefits must be carefully weighed.

The purpose of this chapter is to use the data and analyses developed in previous chapters to help sponsors decide whether style management is worth the effort. We outline the questions that a pension fund sponsor needs to answer in order to determine the costs and benefits of managing a large fund by using style management. We choose the perspective of a sponsor because the demand by sponsors for style management appears to be the major change in money management over the past five years. We argue that sponsors must first decide what style management is intended to achieve. Once sponsors have a clear idea of the purpose of style management, then they can estimate (i.e., guess) the costs and benefits using the management and measurement tools discussed in this book. In short, the answer to the question in the title of this chapter, "Is equity style management worth the effort?" depends on how a sponsor answers the questions detailed below.

A CONSENSUS DEFINITION OF "STYLE MANAGEMENT"

While the authors in the previous chapters have given a variety of definitions of "style management," there is considerable consensus among these definitions. Generically, "style management" is defined as making investments in two phases. In the first phase, either the money manager or the sponsor identifies the set of securities that the manager intends to consider and the general approach to buying the securities in this set. When a money manger chooses an approach and identifies a set of securities, he is said to adopt an "investment style." For example, a "small growth" money manager considers only growth companies with a comparatively low equity capitalization. The second phase of "style management" occurs when a sponsor allocates most or all of the available money based primarily on investment styles offered by managers.

THE PURPOSES OF STYLE MANAGEMENT

There are multiple motives for adopting style management but sponsors must believe that each purpose ultimately increases the return of the total portfolio. On a basic level the sponsor may simply want to enhance communication with the money manager. In more advanced uses style management may facilitate performance measurement, allow better risk control and diversification, and allow the sponsor to share the control — and responsibility — of active management. We discuss each of these in turn.

Communication
By identifying the investment style of a money manager the sponsor is obtaining information about the money manager's expertise, organization and possibly the manager's likely success. For example, a value manager who carefully analyzes the financial statements of low price-to-book stocks that have recently been depressed by negative press coverage will look very different than a growth manager who is

evaluating the market potential of a new software firm with a promising product line. The growth manager specializes in finding small companies with good ideas. This manager will have very different contacts and expertise than the value manager who invests in large, stable, but temporarily depressed, companies producing comparatively constant earnings. By identifying the investment style the sponsor is more informed about the subset of stocks that the manager will consider and the sponsor can judge whether the money manager's organization — contacts, administration, coordination of efforts — is effective for the investment style. In short, style management provides a basis for the on-going discussions between the sponsor and manager. It is an efficient way of classifying and summarizing portfolio selection and a tool used by the sponsor to evaluate the manager's "culture" and organization.

Performance Benchmark

The second purpose of style management is to measure the manager's performance. A manager with an objectively identifiable style may earn a higher return than other managers with the same style but the style may do poorly. If measured against broad market benchmarks the manager will be a poor performer. However, knowing that the manager did well relative to other managers in the style may help in predicting the future of performance of the manager. The overall performance may improve as the returns to the style increase and a good manager in a "hot" style may be quite valuable.

Even if a style earns only an average risk-adjusted return, the sponsor may have an objective of investing in particular styles because of portfolio constraints. For example, political objectives (i.e., non-investment management related) may give a sponsor an incentive to allocate money to managers who specialize in small firms. This constraint makes it clearly important to determine the best small firm manager. Some portfolio constraints may not be as obvious, however. For example a sponsor may need to justify the selection of stocks using easily understood concepts. Investing by style and measuring performance by style may serve this purpose.

Measuring performance relative to a style benchmark may also provide information about the future performance of the manager. A style benchmark is simply a portfolio of stocks constructed from the subset of securities defined by the style. It represents a passive investment strategy. If the manager can consistently beat this passive strategy then either the passive strategy itself is a consistent poor performer or the manager has valuable information or abilities. The style benchmark can be constructed so that the sponsor can determine the likelihood that the benchmark itself is poor performer. If a manager consistently beats such a benchmark it may imply that the manager will do well in the future. Of course, there is still the possibility that the style will do poorly but at least the sponsor has more information about the quality of the manager.

Finally, style benchmarks are always "conditional" on the style. The sponsor selects the manager with a particular style and then measures him against the style. Recent research has shown that benchmarks that are "conditional" on economic factors are much better measures of performance than benchmarks that are "unconditional" such as the SP500.[1] Using a style benchmark is equivalent to using a "conditional" benchmark that is conditional on those factors that determine the style.

Diversification and Risk Control by Sponsor

Diversification consists of choosing securities for a portfolio that have low correlations. If the securities are perfectly, negatively (i.e., inversely) correlated, then only two securities need to be selected. Typically, however, securities are positively correlated so that portfolio managers need many stocks to fully diversify. The key problem in diversifying is to be able to predict the *future* correlation of the securities. The correlation between two securities is very unstable over any time period and models of correlation do not predict correlations very well.[2] Style management can be a useful tool in diversifying a portfolio because the correlation among investment styles is much more stable than the correlation among securities. For example, Exhibit 1 in Chapter 1 and Exhibits 2-5 in Chapter 5 show that there is significant correlation over time in variables that are typically used to represent style. The relatively stable correlation over time, enables a sponsor to diversify the whole portfolio by selecting managers with a large number of stocks in each style. This may provide better diversification than simply trying to diversify using the characteristics of stocks.

The correlation is not the only statistic that is more stable for investment styles than securities. A consistent research finding is that standard measures of risk and return are more stable for groups of assets than for individual assets.[3] This means that a sponsor can use an objectively identifiable style for risk control. Risky styles can be eliminated or added to determine the total risk of the overall portfolio. The sponsor is more assured of the future risk of the portfolio than if only a few managers with broad market investments had selected.

Finally, if a sponsor is allocating money to a group of managers based on some criteria other than investment style and is not paying attention to the balance of styles of a fund, the fund may be over-invested in some styles and under-represented in other styles. Measuring the styles of the manager selected and allocating money to a fund that "completes" the balance of the fund with respect to styles is another way to diversify the fund. These funds are called "completeness funds" and are described in Chapter 14.

---

[1] Wayne Ferson and Rudi Schadt, "Measuring Fund Strategy and Performance in Changing Economic Conditions," *Journal of Finance* (June 1996).

[2] See Campbell Harvey, "Time-Varying Conditional Covariances in Tests of Asset-Pricing Models," *Journal of Financial Economics*, 24 (1989), pp. 289-317, for extensive tests of the time-variation of covariances.

[3] For a recent discussion of this point see Eugene Fama and Kenneth French, "The Cross Section of Expected Stock Returns," *Journal of Finance* (June 1992).

Sharing Control

The fourth use of style management occurs when a sponsors wishes to share some of the control over the portfolio allocation. Sponsors may believe they have an ability to predict which style will earn the higher return or sponsors may decide that some styles are simply not worthy of attention. The sponsor allocates money to those managers who are in the styles that are expected to do well. The strategy is similar to market timing where a portfolio manager tries to predict the future performance of risky securities versus cash. There is little evidence that market timing is better than being fully invested in risky securities but market timing is common among money management.[4] To the best of our knowledge, there have been no studies of whether trying to predict a style is a successful strategy. It is worth noting, style betting does not have the same costs as market timing. The most significant cost of market timing is that the investor will be in cash when prices of risky assets are increasing. In contrast, if a sponsor tries to bet on styles and the bet is wrong, the portfolio can still be invested in risky assets and can be well-diversified.

THE REQUIREMENTS OF STYLE MANAGEMENT

A critical element in the decision of whether to adopt style management is the effectiveness of the tools used in style management. Since the requirements of style management depend on the purpose, the definition of an effective tool will vary. This section will discuss each purpose's requirements after first elaborating style management's basic elements. The next section will discuss how effective the tools of style management are likely to be in meeting these requirements.

Basic Requirements

Style management begins with the ability to define some criteria that clearly identify the set of assets that the money manager intends to buy. The criteria most often used are firm-specific characteristics that classify stocks into a "growth" or "value" category or a size category. While there are other criteria currently in use, the key feature of each is that there is some relationship with the expected return, risk or potential for diversification. The criteria must also be objectively identifiable by an observer who is independent of the manager. This is important, and controversial, because the next step in the process is to determine which criteria describe a manager. If the criteria that define a style are to be believed, they must be relatively easy to verify. The controversy, which we will discuss later, occurs in the means of verifying the criteria.

---

[4] For a review of over 200 studies of performance measurement see Ravi Shukla and Charles Trzcinka, "Performance Measurement of Managed Portfolios," *Financial Markets, Institutions and Instruments Series*, Volume 1, Number 4, Basil Blackwell Publishers, 1992.

Communication

If the purpose of style management is to communicate the investment strategy of the money manager then effective criteria will place a manager into some unique subset, such as a "growth" or "value" manager. If the manager is classified into more than one subset the criteria lose their ability to effectively communicate. It makes no sense, for example, to classify a manager as a "value-growth" manager because it reveals little about the type of stocks that the manager will buy.

There are, however, a number of "value-growth" managers. The *Mobius Group* surveys institutional money managers every quarter. In the June 1996 survey there were 252 active, domestic equity money managers (out of 1,526) who thought that *both* value and growth were "accurate" or "very accurate" descriptions of their portfolio. Most (if not all) of these portfolios fall into the hybrid "growth at a reasonable price" category. These managers had $143.7 billion under management in 26,649 accounts. Clearly the "value" and "growth" classification for these managers is less useful than for the 503 managers who were unambiguously in the growth category and the 460 managers who were unambiguously in the value category.[5]

A second requirement of effective criteria is that it must reveal useful characteristics about the manager. The criteria are usually related to the securities purchased but not always. For example, a small capitalization manager buys firms with a capitalization below some level but what type of firms does a "quantitative" manager buy? The quantitative style classification is useful because it describes the approach the manager uses in selecting securities but it reveals little about the securities themselves.

Finally, to communicate what the manager is doing the manager must have a stable style. This means that the manager must stay in the set of securities or use the approach for some time. If most managers are stable and a few managers wander between styles, perhaps in some predictable manner, then the instability itself will still communicate information about the manager. However, this only works if most managers are stable. If all managers wander then there will be less information revealed about their investment choices.

Performance Measurement

When style management is used for performance measurement the manager is measured against a benchmark that represents a passive manager in the style. Therefore to be useful for this purpose it must be possible to construct such a benchmark from the securities and different styles must have different performance over time. It need not be the case that one style has a consistently higher

---

[5] The 503 growth managers are managers who believed that growth was an "accurate" or a "very accurate" description of their portfolio *and* that it "wrong to apply" value. These managers had $509 billion in 49,487 accounts. The 460 value managers believed that value was an "accurate" or "very accurate" description of their portfolio *and* that it "wrong to apply" growth. These managers had about $610 billion in 32,047 accounts.

return or risk than another but each style must have a different return. Each style must have clear enough criteria so that a benchmark can be constructed that is widely believed to represent the style. This means that the performance of the style must be observable independently of observing a manager. It defeats the purpose of the style to simply compute the average of all managers who claim to use the style because they all could underperform a simple, passive strategy that captures the style.[6] Finally, the manager must have a stable style. If the manager's style wanders unpredictably then the benchmark will not represent the performance of the manager. As Steve Hardy argues in Chapter 3, if the manager's style is a predictable from a set of weights on appropriate indices, then style management is useful to measure performance.

Diversification and Risk Control

When style management is used to diversify a fund and control risks the manager's style must be objectively identifiable and a manager must have a unique and stable style. The style must be clearly related to systematic risk if style management is used to measure and control risk which means that the criteria should be related to either betas of securities or the responses of securities to factors. The stability of the manager's style is critical because it is impossible to control risk if manager's styles are constantly changing.

If style management use criteria that are broad enough then selecting managers from each style can well-diversify the portfolio. If the criteria are narrow, such as "small-growth" or "large-value," then the fund may have to use a "completeness" fund to more fully diversify the portfolio (see Chapter 14). In contrast to risk control, if the style management is used to diversify a fund the manager's style need not be very stable if the tendency to change style is uncorrelated across managers. If managers change style randomly then simply choosing a relatively large number of managers will diversify the fund. If managers are perfectly stable then choosing a large number of styles will diversify the fund. Only if managers tend to move toward the same securities, for example, widely-publicized stocks, will the change in styles reduce the ability of style management to diversify.

Sharing of Control

Allocating money to those styles expected to perform well in the future requires that the manager have an objectively identifiable style. The style must define a segment of the market where the prices of the assets are determined by supply and demand within the segment. This means that there must be some reasons why the supply and demand from other market segments are restricted from eliminating the differences in prices.

---

[6] See Jeffery Bailey, "Are Manager Universes Acceptable Performance Benchmarks?" *Journal of Portfolio Management* (Spring 1992). Bailey uses conceptual arguments and presents empirical evidence to show that manager universes are *not* acceptable.

Using style management to bet on future performance of a sector of the market typically requires careful construction of the style benchmarks that are used to measure the performance of the manager. The sponsor who is betting on style usually wants to determine whether the manager is a top performer within the style because of chance or because of effective management. This is not logically a requirement of style betting because the sponsor will make money with a below average performer for the style if the sponsor guesses the style correctly. If sponsors have information about style performance however, they do not want to use this information on poor managers and will typically demand well-constructed style benchmarks.

THE TOOLS OF STYLE MANAGEMENT

The tools of style management are the ways that a manager can be objectively classified into a style. There are two general approaches, portfolio-based and returns-based. We discuss each in turn.

Portfolio-Based Approach

A portfolio-based approach is (or is claimed to be) an intensive examination of the manager's portfolio and security-selection procedures. The categorization of a manager can use objective criteria or subjective criteria or both. For example, the Frank Russell Company has developed an objective probability model that is based on the weights of various securities in the portfolio.

The strength of this approach is that it carefully examines the individual manager organization and assets selected. This may lead to much better predictions of the manager's *future* style and can help refine the definition of "style" itself. Several authors in this book argue that style should be a characteristic of the securities selected. Examining how managers fit securities together can lead to various subcategories of a particular style. For example, managers have recently offered "midcap" portfolios of stocks that are neither large nor small, but "in between."

This tool is very good for communication and evaluation of the manager's selection process and it is good for determining the diversification of the portfolio. The strength of the portfolio approach is based on the basic principle that more information in the evaluation process will, on average, produce a more accurate guess of the manager's style if the evaluation is unbiased and complete. The portfolio weights and selection process reveal much more about how the portfolio will be managed in the future than examining the returns of the portfolio. This approach may also be good at judging the diversification of the portfolio since each security can be individually evaluated.

The potential weakness of this approach is that it is not easy to determine whether the evaluation has been complete and unbiased. The evaluator may have biases that cause certain information not to be evaluated or to be systematically miss-evaluated. To determine the biases of this approach, sponsors often use the next tool — the returns based analysis.

Returns-Based Approach

This tool uses a statistical relationship between the returns of the managed portfolio and some benchmark portfolio or portfolios to define the style of the managed portfolio. In Chapter 3, Steve Hardy shows that there are several important decisions in a returns-based analysis. First, an appropriate benchmark (or benchmarks) must be selected. Second, the analyst must decide the time period over which the managed portfolio will be judged. Third, the analyst must determine the type of statistical model. We briefly discuss each.

The indices chosen to represent styles is probably the most critical choice. The analyst can select some basic portfolios representing broad style categories, such as small-large and value-growth. An alternative strategy is to select indices that represent important factors in stock prices. William Sharpe suggests a model using twelve indices representing both domestic and international factors affecting stock prices.[7] The Sharpe factors are based on the type of securities. The BARRA corporation uses 68 stock-specific factors.[8] As Richard Roll discusses in Chapter 5, published research suggests no more than five factors are relevant for representing security returns.

The choice of a time period and model are less important than the choice of indices but can significantly influence the results. In selecting a time-period, the shorter the time period the more likely that the manager will have a stable style. But short time periods may not capture the ability of the manager to earn high returns and can be statistically unreliable. Three years is a commonly used but for volatile styles this may be too short. In selecting a model, usually the choice is among models that constrain the coefficients of the indices to sum to one or leave the coefficients unconstrained. If the coefficients are unconstrained the model can better represent the manager's style — the statistical jargon is that it has more "degrees of freedom." If the coefficients are constrained, they can be interpreted as portfolio weights on the indices. Constrained models must be estimated with some "optimization" technique while unconstrained models can be estimated with statistical techniques that have well-developed properties. Whether the choice of a model or a time-period is important depends on the nature of the managers returns and any returns-based approach needs to be tested for reliability.

---

[7] William F. Sharpe, "Asset Allocation, Management Style and Performance Measurement," *Journal of Portfolio Management* (Winter 1992). The indices he uses are: the Salomon Brothers 90-day Treasury bill index, the Lehman Brothers Intermediate-Term Government Bond Index, the Lehman Brothers Long-Term Government Bond Index, the Lehman Brothers corporate bond index, the Lehman Brothers Mortgage Backed Securities Index, the Sharpe/BARRA Value Stock index, the Sharpe BARRA Growth Stock Index, the Sharpe/BARRA medium cap index, the Sharpe/BARRA small cap index, the Salomon Brothers Non-US Government Bond Index, the FTA Euro_Pacific Ex-Japan Index, the FTA Japan Index.

[8] See the BARRA Newsletter, Spring 1994 for a description of the factor returns and their use in performance attribution.

The strength of this tool is that it is objective — once the indices, the time-period and the model are selected. The returns of the managed portfolio are used in a statistical model that relates them to the indices or the factors. If another investigator has the data, the results can be replicated. Generally, sponsors will be much more confident in results that can be replicated than in results that cannot. Replication also has the advantage of making the style easily understood.

The weakness of this tool is that the statistical models are notoriously unstable.[9] Stock return data have a very low "signal-to-noise" ratio and using such data to estimate statistical models does not produce very reliable estimates. Moreover, managers can change styles intentionally and unintentionally. The portfolio based approach is, at least in principle, much more able to capture changing styles.

In summary, the returns-based approach is better for performance evaluation where the results need to be objective. It may also be better for style betting since it is very easy to examine the manager's performance against a broad array of sectors and style-indices. It may be less useful for communication and diversification than the portfolio-based approach because it examines less information than the portfolio-based approach.

WHAT DO WE KNOW EMPIRICALLY ABOUT STYLE MANAGEMENT?

I believe the answer to this question is unfortunately "not much." Generally, in a securities market where the price of securities capture all relevant information, style management will not be more profitable than investing in any arbitrary subset of stocks. Further, if the sponsor does not diversify across styles then style management will cause the sponsor's portfolio to be mean-variance *inefficient* and will earn a less return per unit of risk than an efficient portfolio. Thus, evidence that style management earns a higher than expected risk-adjusted return is evidence that the security market is inefficient or that the risk-adjustment model is wrong.

There has been considerable work on whether the variables that are commonly used to define styles, such as book to price, have some predictable relationship to expected returns. In a 1996 paper, Eugene Fama and Kenneth French argue that a simple three factor model explains most if not all the excess return normally attributed to investment "style."[10] In direct contrast to the Fama and French study is another 1996 study by Robert Hugen and Nardin Baker who argue that combi-

---

[9] William Schwert in "Why Does Stock Volatility Change Over Time?" *Journal of Finance*, 19 (1989), pp. 1115-1151 argues that very long time series such as 50 years or more are needed to estimate statistically reliable relationships. If models are estimated with 16 or 20 quarters of data they may have very unstable parameters.

[10] Eugene Fama and Kenneth French, "Multifactor Explanations of Asset Pricing Anomalies," *Journal of Finance* (March 1996). The simple three factor model is the excess return of the market, the difference in return between a small stocks and large and the difference in return between high book to price and low.

nations of styles produce "super" stocks with high returns and low risk.[11] The differences in the studies involves a set of statistical and data questions that are too complex to discuss here. However, neither study deals with the question of whether style *management* adds value.

Even in an efficient market where there are no excess returns to a style, style management may be valuable as a communication device and a diversification tool. Managers may specialize in subsets of assets simply to minimize transactions costs and the specialization can be useful for building the total portfolio. However, the belief persists that style managers can earn excess risk-adjusted returns. Mary Compton in Chapter 15 writes "We believe it is important to remember that most managers have an expertise in some niche of the market."

Jon Christopherson and C. Nola Williams in Chapter 1 and Richard Roll in Chapter 5 provide direct evidence of the returns to style management. Christopherson and Williams show style returns relative to the Russell indices. Roll shows that three variables that are commonly used to define equity style, (size, earnings/price and book/market), are statistically significant determinants of risk-adjusted returns. Both of these chapters conclude that there can be substantial returns to managing a portfolio by equity style. However, Roll observes that a subtle technical problem may make style management seem more profitable than it actually is. If the indices used to adjust for risk or to measure style are not themselves efficient portfolios then the extra return earned by a style manager could actually be the return earned by an efficient portfolio. In short, the extra return may have nothing do with style.

Other than the work in this book, there has been little direct evidence on investment styles as used by practitioners. Equity style management is not new but its popularity has grown substantially over the past decade and the performance of style managers has been available for only a few years. It is likely that more direct evidence will be published soon.

There is indirect evidence on two aspects of style management. First, as discussed above, there have been numerous studies of the risk-return relationship. Roll summarizes this evidence in Chapter 5 and uses it effectively to show the potential for style management. Second, any evidence of market inefficiency is evidence that style management can potentially earn greater than a risk-adjusted return. On this question, Fama provides a comprehensive review of the hundreds of studies on the question.[12] They can be quite useful for specific approaches by money managers. Market efficiency studies often provide careful descriptions of security prices vary and how information changes the price. As Fama observes "Academics large agree on the facts that emerge from the tests, even when they disagree about their implications for efficiency." However, he notes that logically any test of market efficiency is a test of the asset pricing model and efficiency, He

---

[11] Robert Haugen and Nardin Baker, "Commonality in the Determinants of Expected Stock Returns," *Journal of Financial Economics* (July 1996).
[12] Eugene Fama, "Efficient Capital Markets II," *Journal of Finance*, 46 (1991), pp. 1575-1618.

concludes that "It is a disappointing fact that, because of the joint-hypothesis problem, precise inferences about the degree of market efficiency are likely to remain impossible."

SUMMARY: CHOICES AND QUESTIONS ABOUT EQUITY STYLE MANAGEMENT

What should a sponsor do about equity style management? There are two possible answers. First, a sponsor can ignore it. Sponsors can look at the available evidence and the returns earned by style managers and decide that the costs of being potentially undiversified and of having to monitor all the styles is not worth the benefit. The fact that there was $143 billion being managed in June 1996 by managers who were *both* growth and value can be viewed as evidence that not all sponsors think that style management is worth the cost.

Second, a sponsor can adopt it. If so, the immediate question is how? As we discussed above the requirements of style management and how style management is implemented is dependent on how it is used. If the sponsor uses style management to focus on the manager then style management can be used primarily for communication and measuring performance. It can provide a description of how the manager selects securities and it can help to distinguish the manager's performance from passive strategies. We argued that if the sponsor focuses primarily on the total portfolio then style management can be used for diversification of the portfolio and for making bets on styles.

In either case it seems clear that, in principle, the best measurement approach is to use *both* returns-based analysis and a portfolio-based approach to determining the style of a manager and how the style fits into the total portfolio. In practice the tools used depends on their cost and the vendors always have the obligation to justify the cost.

CONCLUSION

In conclusion, borrowing a concept from engineering, it is worth remembering that the securities markets all have a very low "signal-to-noise" ratio. This means that the information in stock prices is very hard to extract. It is difficult to determine if securities are overpriced or underpriced, it is difficult to judge the actual risk of a portfolio, and it is difficult to determine whether a manager is adding value or is lucky. Style management is an attempt by market participants — that is, people confronted with real choices — to make sensible decisions in a noisy, capricious market. Whether it continues to be popular depends entirely on whether it helps people make better decisions for a reasonable cost.

INDEX

A

Abnormal profit, 172, 173, 175, 178
Absolute returns, 137, 139
Active asset allocation, 210, 219
Active currency management, 210
Active equity strategies, 189
Active management. See Factor returns
    factors usage, 202-207
Active manager, 78, 293
Active mutual funds, 259
Active risk, 256
Active style management, 180, 192
    strategies, 208
Actual portfolios
    comparison. See Hypothetical portfolios
    derivatives mixes customization, 293-295
Adaptive expectations hypothesis, test, 157-166
ADRs, 24
Alpha/alphas, 124, 125, 130, 168-170, 231, 252, 259, 296
Alpha generator, 215
Alpha strategies, 210. See also Multi-level alpha strategies
Alpha transport, 215-216
AMEX, 40, 96, 158
Annual reports, 252
APT. See Arbitrage Pricing Theory
Arbitrage Pricing Theory (APT), 94-96, 105, 116, 127. See also Macroeconomic APT models; Multi-factor APT
    factors, 106, 113, 118
    risk, 109
        factors, 111
Arbitrageurs, 285
Arnott, R., 189, 199, 218
Artificial neural networks, 200
Asset allocation, 121
    assumptions, 229
    overlay. See Global tactical asset allocation overlay
Asset allocators, 293
Asset class picking, 217

Asset groups, 270
Asset-based benchmarking, 233
Autoregressive properties, 198

B

Bailey, Jeffery, 307
Baker, Nardin, 176, 311
Banz, Rolf W., 116
BARRA, 23, 26, 43, 44, 122, 192, 193, 230, 232, 309. See also Standard & Poor's 500
    book-to-price (B/P) factors, 286
    PC product, 248
    U.S. Equity Model analysis, 298
BARRA factors, 235
BARRA models, 190, 191
BARRA multifactor model, 189
Bauman, W. Scott, 152, 158
Benchmark exposure, 280
Benchmark portfolio, 168, 170, 231, 233, 234, 241
Benchmark risk, 280
Benchmarking managers, 122
Benchmarks, 44, 83, 86, 121, 171-178, 193, 207, 232, 259, 260, 272, 303, 304. See also Customized benchmarks; Equity benchmark; Passive benchmark; Style benchmarks; T-bill benchmark; Value benchmark
    problems, 270-273
Best-revision stocks, 138
Betas, 153, 157. See also Growth-value betas; Large-small betas; Style betas
BIA. See Boston International Advisors
Bias, 174-176. See also Growth managers abilities; Value managers abilities
Bid/ask spread, 289
Bienstock, S., 183
Black, Fischer, 94
Blake, Christopher R., 170
B/M. See Book equity/market equity; Book-to-market equity
B/M portfolio, 104, 119
B/M stocks, 110, 118
Bond benchmark, 215

313

314   Index

Bond markets, 189
Book equity, value, 24
Book equity/market equity (B/M), 96, 97, 102, 105, 106, 108, 109, 111, 116
Book equity-to-market price, 171
Bond portfolios, 230
Book value, 80
Book/market ratio, 94
Book/price (B/P), 79, 80
  companies, 130
  factors. See BARRA methodology, 123
Book-to-market equity (B/M), 95
Book-to-price ratio (B/P), 85, 87, 89, 122, 123, 181, 182, 223
Boston International Advisors (BIA), 66
B/P. See Book/price, Book-to-price ratio
Breakpoints, 84
Breush, T.S., 113
Broad-based benchmark, 61
Broad-based generic benchmark, 62
Brown, G., 258
Brown, Stephen J., 94, 170
Brush, John S., 193

C

Cap stocks, 165
Capaul, C., 186
Capital Asset Pricing Model (CAPM), 95, 105, 106, 191, 192
  risk, 109
Capitalization comparison, 287-288
Capitalization weighting, 83
CAPM. See Capital Asset Pricing Model
Cap-weighted index, 242
Cap-weighted table, 23
Cash flow/price (CF/P), 79
Cash flow-to-price indicator, 172
CBOE. See Chicago Board Options Exchange
CF/P. See Cash flow/price
Chan, K.C., 95
Cheapness, 172, 174, 284. See also Short-term cheapness
Chen, Nai-fu, 95
Chicago Board Options Exchange (CBOE), 279, 284

Chicago Mercantile Exchange (CME), 279, 284, 285, 296
CK. See Connor/Korajczyk
Classification bias, 273
Clientele biases, 273
CME. See Chicago Mercantile Exchange
Coggin, Daniel T., 96, 167, 168, 170, 172, 176
Combined market neutral portfolios, 213-215
Commodity funds, 258
Commodity prices, 198
Communication, 302-303, 306
Company evolution, 128-129
Completeness fund, 242, 304
Completion funds
  implementation, 236-237
  role. See Equity style management
Completion portfolio, 231, 236
COMPUSTAT, 94, 158
Connor, Gregory, 108
Connor/Korajczyk (CK)
  factor method, 110
  factors, 108
  method, 108
Consistent growth managers, 5
Consultants, 255
Contingency analysis, 261
Contract specifications, 282-284
Contrarian managers, 4
Control, sharing, 305, 307-308
Copeland, W., 189
Core long equity strategies, 202
Core long portfolios, 205
Core portfolios, quantitative management, 179-208
  introduction, 179-180
  summary, 207-208
Core strategies, 206
Cross-border influences, 200
Cross-correlation problem, 125
Cross-correlations, 213
Cross-sectional dependence, correction, 111-115
CRSP, 158
  database, 96
Custom core portfolio, 64

Customized benchmarks, building style indexes usage, 59-62
Cut-off value, 287
Cyclicality, 198

D

Das, Sanjin, 169
Data, 22-23. See also Fundamental data
 descriptive characteristics, 22
 errors, 257
 fundamental characteristics, 23
Debt-free companies, 191
Debt-to-capital, 23
 ratios, 25, 40, 46
Deceased funds, 264
Derivatives strategies, applications, 295-296
Dhrymes, Phoebus J., 96
Difference portfolio, 242
Discriminant analysis, 87
Discriminant model, 89
Diversification, 302, 304, 305, 307, 308. See also International diversification; Sponsor; Style diversification
 effect, 254
 lack, 24
Diversified portfolios, nondiversified portfolios comparison, 147-149
Dividend Discount Model, 79, 200
Dividend payouts, 25
Dividend yields, 35, 183, 198, 223, 288
Draper, P., 258
Dunn, P., 258
Dynamic completion fund, 229

E

EAFE, 55, 56, 66, 275. See also Morgan Stanley EAFE Index
 countries, 223, 224
 equity benchmark, 215
 Index, 270, 275
Earnings momentum managers, 5
Earnings per share (EPS), 46, 49, 157-160
 forecast bias, persistence, 164-165
 growth rates, 161-163
Earnings per share/price (E/P), 96, 97, 102, 106, 108-110, 118
 dimension, 105, 107, 116

portfolio, 119
ratios, 105
stocks, 116
style dimension, 104
Earnings surprises, price/earnings ratio criterion, 159-160
Earnings variables, 183
Earnings-estimate revisions, 133
Earnings/price (E/P), 79-81, 85, 87, 88, 95
Earnings-to-price indicators, 172
Economic cycles, 152
Efficient market hypothesis, 168
Efficient Market Line, 173-177
Effron, 274
EGDH. See Elton-Gruber-Das-Hlavka model
Elton, Edwin J., 169, 258
Elton-Gruber-Das-Hlavka (EGDH) model, 169
E/P. See Earnings per share/price; Earnings/price
EPS. See Earnings per share
Equal-weighted diversified portfolios, 134
Equitization, 215-216. See also Passive equitization
Equity benchmark, 190
Equity exposure, 292, 296
Equity fund risk structure, 234
Equity funds, 264
Equity growth funds, 258, 266-267
Equity holdings, 292
Equity information ratios, 265
Equity managers, 75, 266
Equity managers, performance analysis, 167-170
 data, 168-170
 introduction, 167-168
 methodology, 168-170
 results, 170
Equity market, 205
 futures, 216
Equity portfolio, 18
Equity returns, 197. See also Target equity returns
Equity risk factors, 230
Equity style, 1-19, 179-208, 269-278, 311
 definition, 1-3
 introduction, 1, 179-180, 269-270
 model, 169

summary, 19, 207-208
types, 3-6
Equity style benchmarks, 21, 260. See also Fund analysis
Equity style classification, fundamental factors, 73-92
  introduction, 73-74
  summary, 92
Equity style indexes, difference/similarities, 21-53
  conclusion, 22
  introduction, 21-22
Equity style management, 197, 209, 255-256, 312
  completion funds role, 229-237
    introduction, 229
    conclusion, 312
  introduction, 301-302
  summary, 312
Equity style performance, persistence, 257-267
  conclusion, 267
  introduction, 257-258
  methodology, 261-262
  perspective, 267
  research, 258-259
  study, 262-267
Equity-based assets, 213
Estimate revisions. See Portfolio returns
Estimate-revision stocks, 146
Europe/Pacific markets, 221
Excess return, 130
Exchange-for-physical (EFP) transaction, 295

F

Fabozzi, Frank J., 167, 168, 170, 189
Factor approach, 233. See also Style
Factor based classification models, 86
Factor models, style management, 191-192
Factor return forecasters, character/performance, 200-202
Factor returns
  active management, 192-193
  forecasting, 197-200
  perfect foresight tests, 194-196
  variability, 196-197
Factor-based style, 91

Factors. See Active management
Fama, Eugene R., 85, 95, 174, 304, 310, 311
FAS. See Financial Accounting Statement
Ferson, Wayne, 304
Financial Accounting Statement (FAS), 24, 25, 181
Financial leverage, 200
Firms, size, 163-164
Fixed income mutual funds, 257
Fixed-income management, 230
Fogler, H. Russell, 239, 248
Forecast bias. See Earnings per share
Forecasting, 193
Frank Russell Company, 3, 23, 167, 243
French, Kenneth R., 85, 95, 174, 304, 310
Friend, Irwin, 96
FTA, 211
Fund analysis, equity style benchmarks, 239-250
  conclusion, 250
  introduction, 239-240
Fund persistence, manager persistence comparison, 266
Fundamental analysis, 133
Fundamental characteristics. See Data
  critical points, calculation, 53
  methodology, 52-53
Fundamental data, 53
Fundamental factor models, 190
Fundamentals, 128, 137, 288
Futures pricing/activity, 284-285

G

GA. See Genetic algorithm
GARCH, 200
GARP. See Growth at a Reasonable Price
Gastineau, Gary L., 214
General redemption prices, 12
Generalized style, 183-184
Genetic algorithm (GA), 199
Germeten, J. Von, 189
Gibbons, Michael R., 114
Global equity market, 224
Global institutional benchmark, 215
Global investment programs, 277
Global market neutral strategies, returns structuring, 209-220

introduction, 209-210
summary, 219-220
Global performance evaluation, 269-278
  introduction, 269-270
Global tactical asset allocation (GTAA) overlay, 216-217
Goetzmann, William N., 94, 170, 258
Griffiths, William E., 104
Grinblatt, M., 258
Grinold, Richard C., 261
GRO. See Growth characteristics
Gross of fees, 170
Growth, 76-78. See also Small growth
  defining, 75-87
  expectations, 75-76
  historical returns, 184-186
  value comparison, 29, 35, 167-170
Growth at a price managers, 6
Growth benchmarks, 266
Growth characteristics (GRO), 241
Growth funds. See Equity growth funds
Growth index derivatives, 279-299
  introduction, 279-282
Growth index return, 225
Growth indexes, 26-28, 89
Growth investor, 2
Growth managers, 84, 170, 176, 184, 237, 239, 246, 251, 295
Growth managers abilities, imprecision/bias effects, 171-178
  introduction, 171-172
  summary, 178
Growth orientation, 74
Growth portfolios, 44-46, 179-208
  introduction, 179-180
  summary, 207-208
Growth rate. See Earnings per share
Growth at a Reasonable Price (GARP), 176
Growth stock manager, 75, 85
Growth stock portfolios, 76, 151
Growth stocks, 25, 77, 81-82, 90, 109, 122, 127, 180, 184, 205
  market-cap bias, 288
Growth stocks/managers, 170
Growth style
  category, 5
  value style, comparison, 157
Growth tilt portfolios, 296-297

Growth-biased managers, 5
Growth-oriented managers, 229
Growth-tilt portfolio, 295
Growth-type fund, 299
Growth-value betas, 130
Growth-value continuum, 231
Growth-value sensitivity, 125
Growth/value style investing, 96
Gruber, Martin J., 169, 170, 258, 259
GTAA. See Global tactical asset allocation
Gultekin, N. Bulent, 96

H

Hagin, Robert, 133
Hardy, Steve, 307
Harvey, Campbell, 304
Haugen, Robert, 174, 176, 311
Haugen/Baker (HB), 176, 177
HB. See Haugen/Baker
Hendricks, D., 258
High-yield equity managers, 247
High-yield stocks, 235
Hill, R. Carter, 104
Hlavka, Matthew, 169
Holland, J., 199
Hsieh, David A., 95
Hunter, John E., 96
Hypothetical portfolios, actual portfolio comparison, 165-166

I

Ibbotson, Roger G., 94, 170, 274, 258
I/B/E/S, 23, 53
  forecast growth rate, 25
IBES Growth, 182
IBES long-term growth forecast, 181
IC. See Information coefficient
IIA. See Independence International Associates
Imprecision, 172-174. See also Growth managers abilities; Value managers abilities
Independence International Associates (IIA), Parametric Portfolio Associates comparison, 221-228
  differences, resolving, 224-227
  introduction, 221-222
  summary, 228

Index applications, overview, 292-296
Index rebalancing, 286-287
Index returns, 198
Indexes, description, 24-26
Industrial production, 199
Industry weightings, 290-291
Inflation measures, 199
Information coefficient (IC), 201
Information ratio, 214, 259, 262, 265. See also Equity information ratios
In-sample period, 266
Institutional pension plan sponsors, 62
Institutional portfolios, 258
International diversification, 210-213
International equity investments, 210
International managers, return-based analysis, 66-71
International markets, 195
International style returns, 186-188
  comparison, 221-228
    introduction, 221-222
    summary, 228
Investable Universe, 207
Investment managers, 230
  database, 167
Investment opportunities, 93-119, 251-256
  summary, 118-119
Investment portfolio, 294
Investment risk structure, 229-231
Investment style returns, explanations, 93-96
Investment styles, 94, 151-166, 302, 311
  introduction, 151-152
  summary, 166
Investor expectations, 151-166
  introduction, 151-152
  summary, 166
Investor psychological behavior, 151

J

Japanese bubble, 225
Jensen, M., 258
Judge, George G., 104

K

Kahn, Ronald N., 257, 261
Kalman filters, 200
Kernel estimation, 200

Korajczyk, Robert A., 108
Kothari, S.P., 94
Kritzman, M., 258

L

Large-cap stocks, 110, 113, 114
Large-cap style benchmarks, 26-35
Large-cap styles, 6
Large-capitalization
  growth, 56
  value, 56
Large-small betas, 127, 130
Large-small sensitivity, 125
Large-small spread, 127
Lehman, B., 258
Lehman Brothers Government and Corporate Bond Index, 55
Leinweber, D., 199
Leverage, 95
Lintner, John, 95
Liquidity measures, 289
Long-only fund, 236
Long-only portfolios, 194
Long-short portfolios, 193-194, 209
Long/short portfolio, 236
Long-term style forecasts, 188-190
Low P/E managers, 4
Lutkepohl, Helmut, 104

M

Macroeconomic APT models, 235
Macroeconomic data, 199
Macroeconomic sector distribution, 23
  points, 27
Malkiel, Burton G., 259
Managed portfolios, 241, 248
Management fees, 60
Manager holdings, 184
Manager persistence, comparison. See Fund persistence
Manager style, determining, 184-186
Market benchmark, 64
Market cap, 250
Market capitalization, 23, 25, 74, 94, 97, 116, 171, 192, 197, 286, 294
  stocks, 110
Market cycle, 153, 154, 156, 256

Market illiquidity, 151
Market investments, 304
Market makers, 284
Market neutral portfolios, 193-194, 202, 209, 212, 213, 215, 217. See also Combined market neutral portfolios; Perfect foresight market neutral portfolios
Market neutral strategies, 202-205, 213, 218. See also Global market neutral strategies
Market neutral style portfolios, 210
Market prices, 173
Market risk, 106, 107
Market timing measure, 168
Market values, 105
Market-cap bias. See Growth stocks
Market-cap statistics, 23
Market-normal managers, 6
Market-oriented managers, 5
Market-oriented style category, 5-6
Market-relative returns, 135, 137, 139
MFMs. See Multifactor Models
Mid-cap growth
   mid-cap value comparison, 43-44
   variations, 36-40
Mid-cap indexes, 51
Mid-cap style benchmarks, 36-44
Mid-cap value
   comparison. See Mid-cap growth
   consistency, 40-43
Miller, Paul, 133, 134
Miller, Robert E., 152, 158
Misclassification, 127-128
Misfit, 234, 240, 241, 249
   analysis, 235
   risk, 236, 237
Mobius, 66, 274
Modest, D., 258
Money management, 301, 302, 305
Money managers, 252, 254, 287, 306
Morgan Stanley Capital International database, 223
Morgan Stanley EAFE Index, 55
Morningstar, 66, 76
Multifactor approach, 84-85
Multi-factor APT, 119
Multifactor Models (MFMs), 87, 183-184, 191, 192

Multifactor probabilistic, 183
Multifactor style models, 183-184
Multi-factor theory, 95
Multi-level alpha strategies, 219
Multi-manager portfolio, 296
Multi-manager structure, 229
Multiple-manager domestic equity funds, 243
Multivariate regression, 113
Multi-year periods, 186
Mutual exclusivity, 24
Mutual fund applications, 297-298
Mutual fund data, 257-267
   conclusion, 267
   introduction, 257-258
   methodology, 261-262
   perspective, 267
   research, 258-259
   study, 262-266
Mutual fund database, 273
Mutual fund managers, 168, 297
Mutual fund portfolios, 152
Mutual funds, 66, 151, 257, 259, 295
   case studies, 296-299

N

NASDAQ, 49
Near-term business dynamics, 138
New York Stock Exchange (NYSE), 26, 29, 40, 46, 49, 96, 158, 252
Nondiversified portfolios, comparison. See Diversified portfolios
Non-stationarity. See Extra-risk return
Normal portfolios, 233, 239-243
   development, 246-248
Normalization factor, 160
NYSE. See New York Stock Exchange

O

OLS. See Ordinary least squares
Optimal hedge. See Value
Optimizer, 193
Options pricing, 285-286
Ordinary least squares (OLS), 113
OTC. See Over-the-counter
Out-of-favor cause, 252
Out-of-favor risk, 251

Out-of-favor style risk, 254
Out-of-sample, 60, 62
  period, 266
  return, 260
Over-the-counter (OTC) market, 289
Over-the-counter (OTC) stocks, 96, 118

P

Pairs identification, 130
Pairs trading, 130
Pagan, A.R., 113
Paper portfolio, 82
Parametric Portfolio Associates (PPA), comparison. See Independence International Associates
Passive benchmark, 184
Passive currency hedging, 219
Passive equitization, 216-219
  strategy, 217
Passive indexing, 280
Passive managers, 293
Passive portfolios, 60, 232
  derivatives mixes customization, 293-295
Passive strategy, 303
Patel, J., 258
Payout ratios, 77
P/B. See Price-to-book ratio
P/E. See Portfolio returns; Price/earnings ratio
  managers. See Low p/e managers
Peer groups, 270
  comparisons, 252
  problems, 273
Pension fund management, 253
Pension fund managers, 168
Pension fund portfolios, 152
Pension fund sponsors, 301
Pension fund style management, 236-237
Pension funds, 151, 293
  applications, 295-296
PER. See Price/earnings ratio
Perfect foresight market neutral portfolios, 202
Perfect foresight style switching, 186
Perfect foresight tests. See Factor returns
Performance analysis, 280-282. See also Equity managers
  style benchmarks usage, 240-243

Performance attribution, 232
Performance based incentive fees, 83
Performance benchmark, 279, 303-304
Performance evaluations, 274
Performance measurement, 75, 306-307
Performance measures, 259
Performance pattern, 244
Performance profile, 85-87
Performance statistics, 23
Performance-based fees, 240
Pham, T., 218
Plan sponsors, 63, 237, 243, 247, 252-256
  critical issues, 301-312
  conclusion, 312
  introduction, 301-302
  summary, 312
  style empowerment, 252-253
Plaxco, Lisa, 179
PODs. See Portfolio opportunity distributions
Political objectives, 303
Pooled time series/cross-section regression, 104
Portfolio allocation, 305
Portfolio analysis, 127
Portfolio benchmark, 243
Portfolio characteristics, 6-16
Portfolio construction, 84
  tool, 91
Portfolio investment performance. See Style portfolio investment performance
Portfolio management, 83
Portfolio managers, 150
Portfolio mix, 236
Portfolio opportunity distributions (PODs), 269-278
  future, 277-278
  introduction, 269-270
  results, 274-277
Portfolio optimization, 193
Portfolio performance, 151-166
  introduction, 151-152
  style group ranking, 154-156
  style ranking, 152-154
  summary, 166
Portfolio policy constraints, 151
Portfolio returns
  estimate revisions usage, 136-138

P/E ratio usage, 134-136
  value scores, 138-142
Portfolio risk, 150
Portfolio traders, 293
Portfolio tradings, applications, 295-296
Portfolio weights, 309
Portfolio-based approach, 308-310, 312
Portfolios. See Diversified portfolios; Normal portfolios
  comparison. See Style metric
Portfolio-weighted average sensitivity, 127
PPA. See Independence International Associates; Parametric Portfolio Associates
Priced abnormal profit, 172, 173
Price/earnings portfolio, 135, 136, 139, 148
Price/earnings (P/E) ratio (PER), 2, 4, 23, 27, 40, 43, 48, 133-136, 139, 142, 148, 150, 157, 164, 183, 25. See also Portfolio returns
  criterion, 158-159. See also Earnings surprises
  portfolios, 163
  stocks, 160
Price/earnings (P/E) securities, 134
Price/earnings (P/E) stocks, 136, 146
Price momentum, 95
Price/earnings ratio, 94
Price-earnings ratio, 198
Price/sales ratios, 4
Price-to-book, 23, 26, 40, 46, 239
  cutoff, 25
  definition, 228
  equity ratios, 24
  rule split, 226
  sort-based indexes, 36
  split, 181
  value, 4, 29
Price-to-book (P/B) ratio, 25, 180, 183, 226, 250
  style definitions, 190
  style split, 184
Price-to-cash flow, 239
Price-to-earnings, 239
Price-to-sales, 23, 40, 44, 46
Pricing efficiency, 118
Proxy portfolio, 233
Prudential Securities (PSI), 24, 26, 35, 36, 40, 43, 44, 46, 48, 51, 52

growth index, 27
index, 29
PSI. See Prudential Securities
Pure value, 176, 182

Q

Quantitative analysis, 233
Quantitative management. See Core portfolios; Growth portfolios; Value portfolios
Quantitative managers, 244
Quartile analysis, 264-265

R

Rahman, Shafiqur, 168, 170
Random walk, 163
Rebalancing frequency, 82
Reevaluation process, 247
REITs, 24, 48
Relative value investors, 293
Rentzler, J., 258
Residual reversal effect, 130
Return on assets (ROA), 23, 29, 44, 49
Return differentials, 93, 94
Return on equity (ROE), 23, 26, 29, 44, 49, 77
Return-based analysis. See International managers
Return-based style analysis, 55-71
  conclusion, 71
  theory, 55-59
Returns. See Excess return; Extra-risk return; Portfolio returns; Raw returns; Value
Refined style techniques, value adding usage, 190-191
Returns-based analysis, 312
Returns-based approach, 309-310
Return-to-risk ratio, 158, 161
Reward-to-risk performance ratios, 157
Reward-to-risk ratios, 154
Re-weighting, 82-83
Richness, 284
Risk, 301
Risk adjusted selection returns, 26
Risk adjustment, 19, 118
Risk coefficients, 111
Risk control, 193, 253, 254, 302, 307. See also Sponsor; Style management

Risk exposures, 243
Risk factors, 113, 232, 234
Risk measures, 301
Risk premiums, 93-119
  summary, 118-119
Risk profile, 248
Risk sources, 110
Risk variables, 104
Risk-adjusted basis, 158
Risk-adjusted excess return, 169
Risk-adjusted portfolio returns, 163
Risk-adjusted present value, 172
Risk-adjusted returns, 259, 303
Risk-free interest rate, 192, 209
Risk/return model, 95, 96
Risk/return profiles. See Style profiles
Risk/return scatter diagrams, 246
ROA. See Return on assets
Robust regressions, 200
Roll, Richard, 118, 301
Ross, Stephen A., 94, 118, 170
Rowley, I., 186
Rudd, Andrew, 257
Russell. See Frank Russell Company
Russell 1000, 181, 182, 207
  Growth fund, 295
  Growth Index, 239, 241, 250, 280, 287, 292
    fund, 294
    index, 287
    style funds, 295
    style index, 288, 291
  Value Index, 19, 56, 243, 250, 280, 287
    fund, 294
Russell 2000, 25, 44, 169, 182
  Growth Index, 241, 250
  Value Index, 243, 250
Russell 3000, 27, 61, 63, 240, 245
Russell Growth Index, 25, 171, 172, 240
Russell Growth Stock Index, 172
Russell Style Indexes, 60
Russell Value Index, 25, 171, 172

S

Sales growth, 95
Sales-to-price indicators, 172
Schadt, Rudi, 304
Schwert, William, 310
Seasonals, 95
Sector investors, 293
Sector representation, 83-84
Sector/industry differences, 290
Sector-neutral portfolios, 138, 139
Security analysts, 166
Selection returns, 259-260, 262
Selection strategies, sector-by-sector comparison, 142-147
Sell-side analysts, 164
Setup costs, 250
Shanken, Jay, 94
Sharpe, William F., 55, 71, 95, 180, 184, 186, 232, 259, 309
Sherred, Jay, 133, 134
Short-term cheapness, 223
Short-term performance, 130, 165
Short-term price fluctuation, 82
Shukla, Ravi, 305
Signal-to-noise ratio, 310, 312
Single-factor market return, 106
Single-factor market risk, 107, 111
Size dimension, 74-75
Size distribution, 22-23
Sloan, Richard G., 94
Small growth, 78
Small-cap growth, value comparison, 49-52
Small-cap growth managers, 6, 65
Small-cap growth portfolios, 46
Small-cap market-oriented managers, 6
Small-cap stocks, 105, 225, 248
Small-cap style benchmarks, 44-52
Small-cap value managers, 6
Small-cap value stocks, 243
Small-capitalization growth, 56
Small-capitalization managers, 6
Small-capitalization style category, 6
Small-capitalization value, 56
Sorensen, E., 183
Sponsor
  diversification, 304
  risk control, 304
Sponsor/consultant, 84
Standard & Poor's Corporation, 75
Standard & Poor's (S&P) Indexes, 28, 29, 285

S&P/BARRA Growth and Value Indexes, 25, 27, 29, 35, 36, 44, 46, 48, 49, 123, 124, 279, 280, 284, 286, 289
S&P/BARRA style indices, 180
S&P/BARRA Value Index, 239
Standard & Poor's 400 MidCap, 43
Standard & Poor's 500 (S&P500), 25, 61-63, 65, 71, 102, 104, 118, 121, 122, 169, 180, 185, 195, 202, 205, 210, 211, 215, 244, 251, 254, 270, 280-282, 293, 297
  additions placement, 286-287
  contracts, 292
  fund managers, 287
  futures, 295, 299
  futures options, 293
  Growth/Value return spreads, 189
  Index, 55, 107, 152, 291
  index options, 296
  options, 285
  S&P500/BARRA index stocks, 289
  S&P500/BARRA style index capitalizations, 290
  S&P500/BARRA Value and Growth derivatives, 294
  S&P500/BARRA Value and Growth indexes, 295, 297, 298
  S&P500/BARRA Value index, 298
  S&P500/BARRA Value index futures, 292
  S&P500/BARRA Value stocks, 290, 291
  style indexes, 288, 296
  Total Return Index, 59
Starting up expenses, 163
Stock market cycles, 151-166
  introduction, 151-152
  summary, 166
Stock performance, 138
Stock picking, 217
Stock portfolios, 151
Stock price, 134
Stock returns, 136
Stock-specific factors, 309
Stock-specific risk, 231
Straight-forward equitization, 215
Style. See Equity style; Generalized style classes, 205-207
  conclusions, 156-157
  definition, 122, 180-184, 205-207
  evidence, 6-18
  factor approach, advantages, 91-92
  reasons, 121-122
Style analysis, 259-261. See also Total equity fund
  alternative forms, 249-250
  controls, 260
Style benchmarks, 239, 245-246, 308
  internal use, 248-249
  overlap, 289-290
  testing, 62-63
  types, 243-245
  usage. See Performance analysis
Style betas, 121-131
  conclusion, 130-131
  introduction, 121
  mathematics, 123-127
  research, 130
  uses, 127-130
Style cycles, 256
Style cyclicality, 252, 253
Style derivatives, features/pricing, 282-286
Style determination, methods, 231-234
Style dimensions, 119
Style diversification, 18-19
Style empowerment. See Plan sponsor
Style forecasts, 188. See also Long-term style forecasts
Style index portfolio, 183
Style index returns, 282
Style indexes/indices, 88, 122, 189. See also Customized benchmarks
  defining, 23-24
  profile, 287-292
Style management, 83, 184-207, 255, 301. See also Equity style management; Factor models
  consensus definition, 302
  introduction, 251-252
  knowledge, 310-312
  purposes, 302-305
  requirements, 305-308
  risk control, 254
  style neutrality comparison, 253-254
  tools, 308-310
Style managers, investment, 254-255

Style map, 90
Style megatrends, 256
Style metric, 82, 84, 87-91
   portfolios, comparison, 90-91
Style mix, 233, 272
Style neutrality, 253
   comparison. See Style management
Style performance, 122
   significance, 104-105
Style portfolio investment
   performance, 102-118
   returns, 104
Style portfolios, 113
   returns, 108
   risk/return profiles, 110-111
Style proxy, 1
Style ranking. See Portfolio performance
Style return differentials, 93-119
   experimental design, 96-102
   summary, 118-119
Style returns. See International style returns; Investment style returns
Style shift, 128
Style switching, 186-188. See also Perfect foresight style switching
   strategy, 188, 196
Style techniques. See Refined style techniques
Style tilt portfolio, case study, 296-299
Style tilts, 208
   implementation, 188
   motivation, 184-186
Style-segregated portfolios, 207
Sub-styles, 254
Successful stocks (SCS), 241
Super stocks, 176-177, 311
Survivorship bias, 257, 264, 273
Switching strategies, 188

T

Tactical currency allocation (TCA), 217-219
Tactical currency overlay, 217-219
Target benchmark, 234, 235, 237
Target equity returns, 16-18
Target index, 249
Target portfolio, 240
TCA. See Tactical currency allocation

T-bill benchmark, 205
Theisen, R., 258
Thomson, 274
Three-party arrangement, 246
Time period, 257, 270
Titman, S., 258
Top-down style forecasting, 188
TOPIX, 211, 212
Total equity fund, style analysis, 63-65
Tracking analysis, 291-292
Tracking error, 234, 237, 242, 249, 296, 298, 299
Trading costs, 285
Trading-oriented accounts, 284
Transaction costs, 188, 194, 237
Transactions cost savings, 237
True abnormal profit, 172, 174, 176
Trzcinka, Charles, 96, 108, 172, 176, 305
Tsoung-Chao, Lee, 104
Turnover ratio, 141, 142

V

Value. See Book equity; Mid-cap value comparison. See Growth; Small-cap growth
   defining, 75-87
   examination, 29
   expectations, 75-76
   historical returns, 184-186
   optimal hedge, 296-297
Value benchmark, 207, 266
Value index derivatives, 279-299
   introduction, 279-282
Value index performance, 227
Value indexes, 89
   differences, 46-49
Value investor, 2
Value managers, 84, 176, 246, 251
Value managers abilities, imprecision/bias effects, 171-178
   introduction, 171-172
   summary, 178
Value portfolio, 80, 85
Value portfolios, quantitative management, 179-208
   introduction, 179-180
   summary, 207-208

Value scores, 181, 182. See also Portfolio returns
Value stock, 173, 180, 184
  portfolios, 151, 158
Value stocks, 25, 78-80, 81-82, 90, 109, 127, 175, 196, 205
Value stocks/managers, 170
Value style
  category, 3-4
  comparison. See Growth style
Value-added managers, retention, 237
Value-based equity strategies, 133-150
  conclusion, 150
  introduction, 133-134
Value-based portfolios, 136
Value-biased managers, 5
Value-growth managers, 306
Value/growth spread, 222
Value-oriented managers, 229
Value-score approach, 140-142
Value-score portfolios, 148
Value-type fund, 298-299
Variability in markets (VIM), 241, 249
Variance, analysis, 104
VIM. See Variability in markets
Volatility, 214
  patterns, 285-286

W

Weighted index benchmarks, 247
Weighting, 82-83, 291
Wilshire 5000 Index, 74, 77, 86
Wilshire Asset Management, 44, 76
Wilshire Growth Indexes, 26, 86
Wilshire Small Value Index, 83
Wilshire Style Indexes, 86, 92
Wilshire Value Indexes, 26, 40
Working list, 78
Worst-revision stocks, 138
Writeoffs, 163, 181

Y

Yield curve information, 198
Yield managers, 4

Z

Zeckhauser, R., 258
Zellner, Arnold, 113
Zephyr, 274
Zone of profitability, 201